MW00850978

Right Brain Psychotherapy

The Norton Series on Interpersonal Neurobiology

Louis Cozolino, PhD, Series Editor
Allan N. Schore, PhD, Series Editor, 2007–2014
Daniel J. Siegel, MD, Founding Editor

The field of mental health is in a tremendously exciting period of growth and conceptual reorganization. Independent findings from a variety of scientific endeavors are converging in an interdisciplinary view of the mind and mental well-being. An interpersonal neurobiology of human development enables us to understand that the structure and function of the mind and brain are shaped by experiences, especially those involving emotional relationships.

The Norton Series on Interpersonal Neurobiology provides cutting-edge, multidisciplinary views that further our understanding of the complex neurobiology of the human mind. By drawing on a wide range of traditionally independent fields of research—such as neurobiology, genetics, memory, attachment, complex systems, anthropology, and evolutionary psychology—these texts offer mental health professionals a review and synthesis of scientific findings often inaccessible to clinicians. The books advance our understanding of human experience by finding the unity of knowledge, or consilience, that emerges with the translation of findings from numerous domains of study into a common language and conceptual framework. The series integrates the best of modern science with the healing art of psychotherapy.

A NORTON PROFESSIONAL BOOK

Right Brain
Psychotherapy

ALLAN N. SCHORE

W. W. Norton & Company
Independent Publishers Since 1923
New York · London

Note to Readers: Standards of clinical practice and protocol change over time, and no technique or recommendation is guaranteed to be safe or effective in all circumstances. This volume is intended as a general information resource for professionals practicing in the field of psychotherapy and mental health; it is not a substitute for appropriate training, peer review, and/or clinical supervision. Neither the publisher nor the author(s) can guarantee the complete accuracy, efficacy, or appropriateness of any particular recommendation in every respect.

Copyright © 2019 by Allan N. Schore

All rights reserved
Printed in the United States of America
First Edition

For information about permission to reproduce selections from this book, write to Permissions, W. W. Norton & Company, Inc., 500 Fifth Avenue, New York, NY 10110

For information about special discounts for bulk purchases, please contact W. W. Norton Special Sales at specialsales@wwnorton.com or 800-233-4830

Manufacturing by Lake Book Manufacturing, Inc.
Production manager: Katelyn MacKenzie

Library of Congress Cataloging-in-Publication Data

Names: Schore, Allan N., 1943- author.
Title: Right brain psychotherapy / Allan N. Schore.
Other titles: Norton series on interpersonal neurobiology.
Description: First edition. | New York : W. W. Norton & Company, [2019] |
Series: The norton series on interpersonal neurobiology | "A Norton
  Professional Book." | Includes bibliographical references and index.
Identifiers: LCCN 2018049776 | ISBN 9780393712858 (hardcover)
Subjects: | MESH: Psychotherapy--methods | Brain | Dominance, Cerebral |
  Emotions | Communication
Classification: LCC RC480 | NLM WM 420 | DDC 616.89/14—dc23
LC record available at https://lccn.loc.gov/2018049776

W. W. Norton & Company, Inc., 500 Fifth Avenue, New York, N.Y. 10110
www.wwnorton.com

W. W. Norton & Company Ltd., 15 Carlisle Street, London W1D 3BS

1 2 3 4 5 6 7 8 9 0

The important thing is not to stop questioning. Curiosity has its own reason for existing. One cannot help but be in awe when he contemplates the mysteries of eternity, of life, of the marvelous structure of reality. It is enough if one tries merely to comprehend a little of this mystery every day. Never lose a holy curiosity.

—Albert Einstein

To diligent practitioners of the science of the art of psychotherapy

Contents

Acknowledgments

IN 1994, I overviewed twentieth century developmental science to offer my first book *Affect Regulation and the Origin of the Self.* In the opening sentence of that volume, now published as a Classic Edition, I boldly asserted "The understanding of early development is one of the fundamental objectives of science. The beginnings of living systems set the stage for every aspect of an organism's internal and external functioning throughout the life span." In that inaugural volume of regulation theory as well as three that followed, I articulated and elaborated the interpersonal neurobiological thesis that runs throughout my work: that events occurring during human infancy, especially transactions with the social environment, are indelibly imprinted into the brain structures that are maturing in the first years of life. This book and its companion *The Development of the Unconscious Mind* further expand regulation theory, and continue to delve, deeply and widely, into a number of essential brain/mind/body functions that are central to the human condition.

Since my last 2012 volume *The Science of the Art of Psychotherapy* I continue to write, research, lecture, and share my work with audiences around the world. I take great pride in the fact that my publications over a variety of disciplines have increased to now well over 20,000 citations in Google Scholar. In my global travels over the past decade I have also been very interested in finding new authors for the rapidly expanding field of interpersonal neurobiology. More times than not these individuals have sought me out, and many have actively participated in my Study Groups, which have spanned from Los Angeles and Vancouver to Boulder and Melbourne. Even more so than before I spend time mentoring individuals in a number of disciplines, especially mental health professionals who are adept at integrating science and clinical work, describing the coupling between biological and psychological processes, and combining an objective perspective with one steeped in bodily-based, emotional subjectivity. Indeed, these mentoring efforts are in part reflected in the forewords I've written for a number of Norton authors.

I would like to express my gratefulness to a group of remarkable conference organizers who have sponsored a number of important national and international personal appearances, including Marion Solomon, Jane Ryan, Joe Tucci, Ravi Kumar, Alessandro Carmelita, and Dan Hill. I also greatly value the contributions of my research partners, Ruth Lanius in Canada, and Jennifer Mcintosh and Craig Olsson in Australia. I'd like to thank the Norton staff, especially Mariah Eppes and Sara McBride for the work they've done on this book. Most notably, I express deep appreciation to my publisher and valued colleague Deborah Malmud for not only two decades of a productive and gratifying business and personal relationship, but for her continual advocacy of not only my work but the Norton Series.

Once again, I offer my love and gratitude to family: to David, for his professional computer skills; to Beth, for her talents in computer graphics and the design for the cover and a number of illustrations within this book; and to Judy, for providing so many forms of essential support for my life's work.

Right Brain Psychotherapy

Implications of Recent Advances in Neuroscience for an Interpersonal Neurobiological Paradigm of Psychotherapy

T HIS BOOK, like all books in the Norton Series on Interpersonal Neuro- biology, begins with a mission statement opposite the title page: "An interpersonal neurobiology of human development enables us to under- stand that the structure and function of the mind and brain are shaped by experiences, especially those involving emotional relationships." Note the explicit reference to affective processes. I suggest that the series, for which I have served as editor, has contributed to the current intense inter- est in affect and affect regulation in psychotherapy among clinicians and researchers. The definition also describes the primacy of emotional well- being in all developmental periods, including infancy. My own ongoing work on the adaptive functions of the emotional right brain describes not only affect and affect regulation *within* minds and brains via a one- person psychology, but also the communication and interactive regulation of affects *between* minds and brains and the perspective of a two-person psychology. As applied to the Norton organizing principle, social interac- tions *between* brains shape emotional circuits *within* brains, especially in early critical periods when brain circuits are maturing. More specifically, I continue to offer evidence in this book, *Right Brain Psychotherapy*, and the companion volume, *The Development of the Unconscious Mind*, that emotional interactions reflect right brain-to-right brain affective commu- nication in early development, where the mother shapes limbic-autonomic circuits in the infant's early developing right hemisphere. The essential right brain functions of communication and interactive regulation thus refer to two-person psychobiological interaction, as expressed in dynamic interpersonal and intersubjective contexts.

That said, I propose that the series definition is incomplete in describing the fundamental focus of the field: the exploration of the neurobiological mechanisms that are central factors in development, in psychopathology, and in psychotherapy. These *interpersonal* mechanisms are expressed in brain-to-brain *social* interactions and thereby are activated in *relational* contexts, especially those in which two emotionally communicating right brains are aligned and synchronized. Thus I will argue that there are two basic principles of interpersonal neurobiology, and that the series description needs an update: *An interpersonal neurobiology of human development enables us to understand that the structure and function of the mind and brain are shaped by experiences, especially those involving emotional relationships, and to understand the relational mechanisms by which communicating brains align and synchronize their neural activities with other brains.* Actually, the latter principle of interbrain synchronization is more fundamental—it acts as an underlying reciprocal psychoneurobiological mechanism by which minds and brains are shaped by other minds and brains. Thus, "the self organization of the developing brain occurs in the context of a relationship with another brain, another self" (Schore, 1996, p. 60). The operations of this moment-to-moment social synchronization mechanism, central to human bonding and to all later emotional communications including those in the psychotherapeutic relationship, cannot be described in a one-person psychology but can in a dynamic two-person psychology.

At the beginning of my past volume, *The Science of the Art of Psychotherapy*, I integrated then current neuroscience research and updated clinical data in an opening chapter, "Toward a New Paradigm of Psychotherapy" (Schore, 2012). Since that time, all forms of psychotherapy have become even more emotionally focused and more relational. Furthermore, neuroscience itself has been undergoing a paradigm shift. This paradigm shift is expressed in advances in brain research from previous studies of a single brain to recent technologies that allow for simultaneous measurement of two brains interacting with each other in real time. I will suggest that the current shift from a one-person to a two-person theoretical perspective can generate an overarching integrated model of the interactive relationships of the dual brain hemispheres and of the unconscious and conscious minds. This current technological leap forward is as important as the 1990s and the emergence of "the decade of the brain," the onset of neuroimaging research into emotional, social, and implicit (unconscious) functions, and the appearance of modern developmental, psychological, and psychiatric models grounded in current neuroscience.

Indeed, over the past three decades, my 1994, 2003, and 2012 books have described the progression of the field of interpersonal neurobiology and the generation of heuristic, clinically relevant two-person models of development, psychopathogenesis, and psychotherapy. My 1994 publication *Affect Regulation and the Origin of the Self: The Neurobiology of Emotional Development* overviewed and synthesized research and clinical data of the past century to generate the first explication of the field of interpersonal neurobiology. This inceptive volume appeared just before the decade of the brain in the mid-1990s, and it offered a two-person psychological description of how the early developing right brain is shaped by early emotional experiences and how this synchronized, spontaneous interpersonal mechanism is expressed in both the attachment and psychotherapeutic relationships. In my subsequent 2003 volume, *Affect Regulation and the Repair of the Self*, I overviewed the shift from 20th-century neuroscience to 21st-century neuroscience, partly induced by the advent of more complex neuroimaging techniques, especially those exploring the problem of emotion. Looking backward I offered thoughts on the progression of the field by the beginning of this century, and looking forward I suggested where the field needed to go as the technology continued to rapidly change. In the following, I offer a synopsis of the problem of "The isolated brain and a one-person psychology, the interacting brain and a two-person psychology," which first appeared in Chapter 7 of my 2003 volume, *Affect Regulation and the Repair of the Self*:

> In 1997 the neuroscientist Leslie Brothers asserted, "The brain has been implicitly seen as a 'knower' of the world, as a socially isolated organ whose purpose is to grasp the inanimate world outside

it." This paradigm, with its almost restrictive focus on cognition, the action or faculty of knowing, has been automatically applied as the major, if not exclusive experimental methodology for studying affective phenomena. . . . It is no coincidence that this "objective" "intra-brain" neurological perspective is paralleled by psychoanalytic models that emphasize an almost exclusive "intrapsychic" perspective. . . . "Consciousness," a mental state of "cold cognition" is thus seen as the critical manifestation of the human experience, and autonomy and autoregulation the desired end-state. Since intense negative affect interferes with this state of consciousness, it must be autoregulated and controlled.

As opposed to this intra-brain focus, now extensively used in cognitive neuroscience, the newer fields of affective neuroscience and especially social neuroscience are exploring inter-brain interactions. . . . A primary focus of this perspective is on not only subjective affective phenomena but also on the reception and expression of affective communications and "hot cognitions" between the brains of different individuals. . . . Trevarthen's (1993) classic studies of the two-person psychology of the early mother-infant relationship asserted that "The emotions constitute a time-space field of intrinsic brain states of mental and behavioral vitality that are signaled for communication to other subjects and that are open to immediate influence from the signals of these others" (p. 155).

An inter-brain paradigm thus supports current "relational" models that operate under the principles of a "two-person psychology." Relational psychoanalytic models thus emphasize the potent intersubjective influences that flow between two affectively communicating minds. These communications are occurring on both conscious, and more importantly, unconscious levels. . . . This model of brain-brain interactions is strongly supported by studies of the critical role of the right hemisphere in the processing of social and emotional information and by research that highlights the role of right brain-to-right brain affective communications, at levels beneath awareness in both mother-infant and therapist-patient dyads.

These ideas lead to the suggestion that *the next generation of brain research should simultaneously measure the different activation patterns of two brains as they are interacting with each other during different classes of affectively-charged interpersonal interactions.* The stress-inducing and stress-regulating transactions of mother-infant and therapist-patient dyads are obvious candidates for such research. Such studies could offer us more detailed information about the subtle socioaffective signals that trigger changes in different patterns of psychobiological state in both brains. These transitions may represent switch points between right brain interactive and autoregulatory modes. Ultimately, the most powerful theoretical and clinical models of both psychoanalysis and neuroscience must incorporate both aspects of the one-person psychology of an autoregulating isolated brain, and the two-person psychology of an interactively regulating brain. (Schore, 2003, pp. 212–216, italics added)

Turning now to the subsequent decade, in 2012 I published *The Science of the Art of Psychotherapy*, wherein again I looked both backward and forward in time in order to describe ongoing changes in basic theory and practice from the perspective of interpersonal neurobiology. Echoing my 2003 book, I wrote:

With respect to the paradigm shift toward relationally oriented psychotherapy, clinical interpersonal neurobiological models of therapeutic change are now moving from left brain to right brain, from the mind to the body, and from the central to the autonomic nervous system. This shift in paradigm into relational models of psychotherapy is being paralleled in social neuroscience studies of the essential role of the right brain in social interaction. Indeed, there is now a call to "move from a classical one-brain neuroscience toward a novel two-body approach" (Dumas, 2011, p. 349). (Schore, 2012, pp. 7–8)

In the years after my 2012 volume, where has the technology now moved, especially evolving neuroimaging techniques that can assess dynamic, real-time, spontaneous social interactions between two communicating brains? Dumas's (2011) paradigm shift parallels the ongoing theoretical and clinical transformation from a one-person psychology of an autoregulating isolated brain to a two-person psychology of an interactively regulating brain. Indeed in this current decade, hyperscanning methodologies utilizing simultaneous electroencephalography (EEG), functional magnetic resonance imaging (fMRI), near-infrared spectroscopy (NIRS), and magnetoencephalography (MEG) measurements have been created. This technological advance now allows the study of two brains in real-time social interactions with each other, including during rapid emotional communications. Dumas and his colleagues reported simultaneous measurement of brain activities of each member of a dyad during interpersonal communications, where "both participants are continuously active, each modifying their own actions in response to the continuously changing actions of their partner" (2010, p. 1).

Inspired by studies of nonverbal communication and coordination between a mother and her infant and by research on spontaneous imitation in preverbal infants, these authors offered a dual EEG study of interbrain synchronization during a spontaneous social interaction characterized by reciprocal communication and turn taking. In this relational context, both share attention and compare cues of self and other's actions. They reported specific changes in both brains during nonverbal imitation, a central foundation of socialization and communication, specifically an interbrain synchronization of the right centroparietal regions on a milliseconds timescale in both interacting partners. Furthermore, these researchers documented that the right temporoparietal cortex in one partner is synchronized with the right temporoparietal cortex of the other (Dumas et al., 2010). They pointed out that the right temporoparietal (TPO) junction is known to be activated in social interactions and is centrally involved in states of attention processing, perceptual awareness, face and voice processing, and empathic understanding. The right TPO junction integrates input from visual, auditory, somesthetic, and limbic areas and is thus a pivotal neural locus for self-functions. This right-lateralized system also allows for "making sense of another mind" (Saxe & Wexler, 2005). Figure

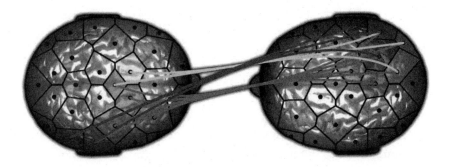

FIGURE 1.1 Right-lateralized interbrain synchronization of a spontaneous nonverbal communication. Adapted from "Toward a Two-Body Neuroscience" by Dumas (2011). Copyright 2011 by Landes Bioscience. Adapted with permission. See insert for color.

1.1 shows this interbrain synchronization, lateralized to the right hemispheres of each member of a communicating dyad. Note that the figure also represents what I have called "right brain-to-right brain" interaction between one subjective self and another that creates a co-constructed intersubjective field.

The right brain-to-right brain synchronized communication model is also supported in a hyperscanning study by Stolk and his colleagues (2014). These authors reported simultaneous fMRI brain images on each participant of a communicating dyad, where "both partners mutually learned to adjust to each other" (a fundamental mechanism of secure attachment communications). Simultaneously measuring cerebral activities in pairs of communicators, these researchers reported that establishing mutual understanding of *novel signals* synchronizes cerebral dynamics across both communicators' right temporal lobes. Importantly, *interpersonal synchronization occurred only in pairs with shared communicative history.* These authors documented that in this nonverbal intersubjective communication, the processing of novelty and meaning is generated in the right (and not left) hemisphere. In a previous work using magnetoencephalography, this laboratory documented neural activity in the right temporal lobe and right ventromedial cortex (both limbic structures) when two individuals generate and understand *novel shared symbols during live communicative interactions* (Stolk et al., 2013). Note that the data of these studies are directly relevant to right brain-to-right brain clinician-patient communications in an ongoing therapeutic relationship.

In another study, "Brain Mechanisms Underlying Human Communication," Noordzij and colleagues (2009) offered research demonstrating that planning new communicative actions (by a sender) and recognizing the communicative intention of the same actions (by a receiver) relied on spatially overlapping portions of their brains, specifically the right posterior superior temporal sulcus (pSTS). The response of this region was lateralized to the right hemisphere, modulated by the ambiguity in meaning of the communicative acts. Via this right-lateralized system, the sender of a communicative signal uses his own intention recognition system to make a prediction of the intention recognition performed by the receiver. The authors concluded that these data confirm the crucial role of the right pSTS for processing pragmatic aspects of linguistic material (Jung-Beeman et al., 2004; Mashal et al., 2007), an instance of the right-hemispheric dominance for inferring the communicative intentions of a conversational partner (Sabbagh, 1999).

In further support of this model of right-lateralized interbrain synchronization, functional neuroimaging research is now exploring the critical role of the right hemisphere in adult social interactions (Semrud-Clikeman, Fine, & Zhu, 2011). Indeed, live face-to-face interaction during fMRI shows "greater activation in brain regions involved in social cognition and reward, including the right temporoparietal junction, anterior cingulate cortex, right superior temporal sulcus, ventral striatum, and amygdala" (Redcay et al., 2010, p. 1639). Other imaging studies now demonstrate that a flow of affective information exists between communicating brains (Anders et al., 2011), and that emotions promote social interactions by synchronizing brain activity across individuals (Nummenmaa et al., 2012). These studies clearly describe events within the face-to-face context of psychotherapy.

In a recent issue of *Frontiers in Psychology*, Ray and his colleagues (2017) offered a forward-looking "hypothesis and theory" article, "Neural

Substrate of Group Mental Health: Insights from Multi-brain Reference Frame in Functional Neuroimaging," in which they argued that all mental disorders unfold in an *interpersonal* context, and that a great deal of relevant information regarding mental health is contained in the interpersonal interactions that cannot be fully captured by limiting our search to markers of individual brains. In contrast, they discussed a recently developed approach in functional neuroimaging that calls for a shift from a focus on neural information contained *within* brain space to a multi-brain framework exploring degrees of similarity/dissimilarity of neural signals *between* multiple interacting brains.

These authors documented paradigm shifts in neuroimaging from the late 20th century to the present. The primary research strategy for the period of the first appearance of neuroimaging technology was the localization of a specific brain function in particular brain regions, and the *intrabrain* focus of these studies was on brain activity during sensory, motor, or cognitive tasks (Figure 1.2A). Over the past two decades, there has been a shift of the reference frame from brain regions to the whole brain, accompanied by use of functional connectivity analysis (Figure 1.2B). They note that at present, functional neuroimaging is on the brink of another paradigm shift, *quantifying the brain interactions between individuals transcending the boundary of the skull.* Thus, a more complex understanding of brain activity requires framing it in an interpersonal context, as can now be done in *interbrain* connectivity analyses in functional neuroimaging (see Figure 1.2C, which repeats the Dumas image of right-lateralized interbrain synchronization of Figure 1.1).

Ray and his colleagues (2017) asserted that among all forms of interbrain communications, the communication of emotion is the most important process to mental health. They then offered clinical applications of this new and state-of-the-art "multi-brain" functional neuroimaging methodology. With respect to psychopathology, they argued that the interpersonal perspective of between-brain functional connectivity can allow for a deeper understanding of the relational deficits of depression, autism spectrum disorders, schizophrenia, personality disorders, social anxiety disorder, somatic symptom disorder, eating disorders, sexual dysfunctions, and suicide. Most

A.

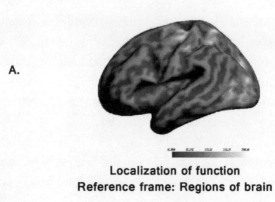

Localization of function
Reference frame: Regions of brain

B.

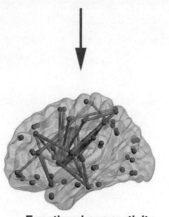

Functional connectivity
Reference frame: Individual brains

C.

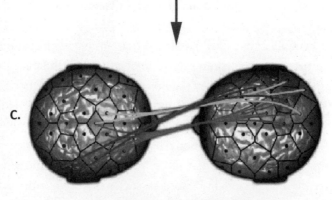

Between-brain connectivity
Reference frame: Mutiple brains

intriguingly, they see the direct application of this paradigm shift in inter-brain neuroimaging to the therapeutic alliance, which is defined as the collaborative bond between patient and therapist and now considered as "the quintessential integrative variable" (Wolfe & Goldfried, 1988). Furthermore, they stressed the need for interbrain connectivity between the patient and the therapist, especially for early detection and repair of rupture of the therapeutic alliance.

Over the past three decades, a major focus of my own work in interpersonal neurobiology has been on the synchronized, right-lateralized interbrain communication of emotions within the co-constructed attachment relationship embedded in the therapeutic alliance. In my first volume, I offered discussions of both face-to-face nonverbal communications between the mother's right hemisphere and the infant's right hemisphere and of "right hemisphere-to-right hemisphere" affective communications in psychotherapeutic transference-countertransference transactions between the patient and the therapist that occur in ruptures of the therapeutic alliance (Schore, 1994). In a 2001 article, first presented in London as the Seventh Annual John Bowlby Memorial Lecture, I applied my right brain-to-right brain model to the co-construction of a synchronized emotional communication system in the therapeutic relationship:

FIGURE 1.2 (*opposite*) © 2017 Ray D, Roy D, Sindhu B, Sharan P and Banerjee A l
Front. Psychol., 28 September 2017 | https://doi.org/10.3389/fpsyg.2017.01627
  Functional neuroimaging: evolution of reference frame. (**A**) In its early years, the sole focus of functional neuroimaging techniques (e.g., fMRI) was to localize brain functions to discrete regions. (**B**) The first paradigm shift took place with experimental validation of functional integration over distinct brain areas using measures of functional connectivity and shifting of the reference frame to the whole of the brain. Adapted from "Decreased Functional Brain Connectivity in Adolescents with Internet Addiction" by Hong et al. (2013). Copyright 2013 by Hong et al. Used under Creative Commons Attribution license. (**C**) The emerging techniques to assess between-brain functional connectivity calls for a second paradigm shift from a single brain to a multi-brain reference frame. Copyright 2011 by Landes Bioscience. Adapted with permission. Adapted from Guillaume Dumas, Communicative & Integrative Biology Vol 4:3 pp. 349-352 (2011). See insert for color.

> The attuned, intuitive clinician, from the first point of contact, is learning the nonverbal moment-to-moment rhythmic structures of the patient's internal states, and is relatively flexibly and fluidly modifying her own behavior to *synchronize* with that structure, thereby creating a context for the organization of the therapeutic alliance. (Schore, 2001)

In addition, note the commonality with my characterization of *synchronized right brain-to-right brain "state sharing"* in psychotherapy:

> Dynamically fluctuating moment-to-moment state-sharing represents an organized dialogue occurring within milliseconds, and acts as an interactive matrix in which both partners match states and then simultaneously adjust their social attention, stimulation, and accelerating arousal in response to their partner's signals. (Schore, 2003)

Note the similarity of this description of reciprocal right brain-to-right brain psychotherapeutic state sharing and Dumas and colleagues' reciprocal, right-lateralized interbrain synchronization in which "both participants are continuously active, each modifying their own actions in response to the continuously changing actions of their partner" (2010, p. 1). It is this two-person, synchronized, right brain-to-right brain implicit emotional communication and affect regulation that lies at the core of the right brain change mechanisms of psychotherapy, underscoring their fundamental role in the psychotherapeutic repair of the self (Schore, 1994, 2003, 2012). The centrality of these interpersonal neurobiological mechanisms is reflected in the large body of research—now stretching over decades—that indicates the therapeutic alliance is the best predictor of outcome across a wide range of psychotherapeutic modalities (e.g., Castonguay, Constantno, & Holtforth, 2006; Horvath & Symonds, 1991; Martin, Garske, & Davis, 2000).

Echoing the above shift in neuroimaging research from a one-person, within-brain to a two-person, between-brain perspective, Meares observed, "Self, as a form of consciousness, cannot exist in isolation. It arises from a brain state. But a brain, seen as a system isolated from the world, is . . . an abstraction. It is always interacting with the environment, of which, when speaking of self, the social environment is the most important part" (2017, p. 139). Indeed, he now describes the prime therapeutic aim to be right hemisphere integration and, citing my work, suggests that the "therapeutic conversation" can be conceived as "a dynamic interplay between two right hemispheres."

In a research study, "Toward a Neural Basis of Interactive Alignment in Conversation," Menenti, Pickering, and Garrod (2012) pointed out that language alone is not sufficient to have a proper conversation and that alignment of nonlinguistic processes and turn taking is necessary to keep a conversation going. They concluded that "body posture, prosody, and gesture are vital aspects of conversation and are taken into account effortlessly when trying to infer what a speaker intends" (p. 6). According to Jasmin and colleagues (2016), both participants in a conversation tend to change their postures and fixate their gazes at around the same time, and this alignment aids mutual understanding. These data are consonant with my studies of synchronized right brain, nonverbal, bodily-based attachment communications embedded in the therapeutic alliance.

With this introduction in mind, the following chapters in this volume represent further expansions of the ongoing paradigm shift from a one-person to a two-person perspective across scientific and clinical fields. The theme of synchronized right brain-to-right brain communications appears at the core of each chapter and interview, where I describe the clinical interpersonal neurobiological mechanisms that underlie therapeutic relational psychodynamics, reciprocal nonverbal affective communications, patient-therapist transference-countertransference transactions, clinical empathic synchronization within an emotionally energetic intersubjective field, and interactive affect regulation, as well as clinical work with synchronized mutual regressions, mutual defenses, and mutual creativity. Psychotherapeutic synchronized and interactively regulated right-lateralized interbrain communications facilitate neuroplastic right-lateralized intrabrain structural changes in the patient's regulatory systems, which in turn allow for optimal treatment outcomes in both symptom-reducing and especially growth-promoting psychotherapy.

In the next chapter, "The Right Brain Is Dominant in Psychotherapy," I discuss how recent studies of the right brain, which is dominant for the implicit, nonverbal, intuitive, holistic processing of emotional information and social interactions, can elucidate the neurobiological mechanisms that underlie the relational foundations of psychotherapy. Utilizing the interpersonal neurobiological perspective of regulation theory, I present interdisciplinary evidence documenting right brain functions in early attachment processes, in emotional communications within the therapeutic alliance, in mutual therapeutic re-enactments of early "relational trauma," a construct I introduced in 2001, and in therapeutic change processes. This work highlights the fact that the current emphasis on two-person relational processes is shared by, cross-fertilizing, and indeed transforming both psychology and neuroscience, with important consequences for clinical psychological models of psychotherapeutic change.

In the third and fourth chapters, "The Growth-Promoting Role of Mutual Regressions in Deep Psychotherapy, Parts One and Two," I describe the importance of synchronized shifts in hemispheric dominance between the left and right hemispheres, the unconscious and conscious minds, and the creation of a theoretical perspective that integrates both a one-person and a two-person psychology. In this centerpiece chapter of the book, I discuss the critical role of synchronized transient clinical regressions—defined as the process of returning to an earlier stage of development—in deep psychotherapy. In heightened affective moments of the session when the patient is experiencing a right brain emotional state, the psychobiologically-attuned therapist implicitly instantiates a regression, a "reversible dominance of the left over the right hemisphere." Over time the creative clinician, sensitive to even low levels of the patient's shifts into and out of affective states, learns how to fluidly synchronize this shift in hemispheric dominance with the patient shifts. This right-lateralized interbrain synchronization allows for the communication and regulation of not just conscious but unconscious affects.

In this further expansion of regulation theory, I present neuropsychoanalytic models and clinical case examples in order to differentiate the roles of the character defenses of dissociation and repression in working with regressions in growth promoting psychotherapy, on both sides of the therapeutic dyad. Towards that end, I offer a clinical model for working with the defensive coping strategies embedded in clinical regressions, especially those involving unconscious dissociated affect in spontaneous mutual regressions, and unconscious repressed affect in voluntary mutual regressions. I will suggest that although the paradoxical process of regression may reflect a clinical deterioration, it may also represent a creative return to fundamentals and origins that can facilitate a potential reorganization leading to better integration, healthy individuation, and increases in the adaptive capacities of play and intimacy.

The chapter also describes the importance of the clinician's and patient's creativity in the therapeutic action, a theme further elaborated in the fourth chapter with my coauthor, Terry Marks-Tarlow, on the role of the right brain in the early origins of love and creativity. The fifth chapter presents my keynote address to the American Psychological Association Division of Psychoanalysis, "Moving Forward: New Findings on the Right Brain and Their Implications for Psychoanalysis," where utilizing an interpersonal neurobiological perspective, I offer thoughts on the future of the field within and beyond the consulting room. In the sixth and seventh chapters, I present a series of more personal interviews that delineate the origins and implication of synchronized right brain-to-right brain communication models for psychotherapy. Finally, the eighth chapter presents my 2014 keynote address at UCLA, "Looking Back and Looking Forward: Our Professional and Personal Journey."

As the reader will see, each upcoming chapter on the psychotherapy relationship will support the earlier proposal that the operational definition of field needs to be re-framed: An interpersonal neurobiology of human development enables us to understand that the *structure and function of the mind and brain are shaped by experiences,* especially those involving emotional relationships, and to understand *the relational mechanisms by which communicating brains align and synchronize their neural activities with other brains.*

CHAPTER 2

The Right Brain Is Dominant in Psychotherapy

In 2009, the American Psychological Association (APA) invited me to present a plenary address, and so I offered "The Paradigm Shift: The Right Brain and the Relational Unconscious." In fact, that was the first time an APA plenary address was given by a member in private practice who was also a psychoanalytically informed clinician. Citing 15 years of my interdisciplinary research, I argued that a paradigm shift was occurring not only within psychology but also across disciplines, and that psychology now needed to enter into a more intense dialogue with its neighboring biological sciences. I emphasized the relevance of developmental and affective neuroscience (more so than cognitive neuroscience) for clinical and abnormal psychology. And so I reported that both clinicians and researchers were now shifting focus from left brain conscious cognition to right brain unconscious emotional and relational functions (Schore, 2009a). Only a few years before the APA had explicitly articulated its new-found emphasis on the relational foundations of psychotherapy, where the APA Presidential Task Force on Evidence-Based Practice (2006) boldly stated,

> Central to clinical expertise is interpersonal skill, which is manifested in forming a therapeutic relationship, encoding and decoding verbal and nonverbal responses, creating realistic but positive expectations, and responding empathically to the patient's explicit and implicit experiences and concerns. (p. 277)

The relational trend in psychotherapy, of course, had evolved because of the contributions of earlier psychoanalytic theoreticians, including Ferenczi (1926/1980), Fairbairn (1952), Sullivan (1953), Kohut (1971), Mitchell (1988), and most recently Bromberg (2011).

Over this same time, in parallel to psychotherapy, the relational perspective had also progressed within both developmental psychology and developmental neuroscience, especially in the recently created transdisciplinary field of interpersonal neurobiology (Schore, 1994, 2003a, 2003b, 2012). In my own contributions, I have utilized this perspective to model the attachment mechanisms of early development and the problem of how relational experiences, for better or worse, impact the early development of psychic structure and the emergent subjective self. The organizing principle of this developmental relational conception dictates that "the self-organization of the developing brain occurs in the context of a relationship with another self, another brain" (Schore, 1996, p. 60). For two decades I have elaborated and expanded regulation theory to model the development, psychopathogenesis, and treatment of the right brain implicit self. Thus in 1994 and 2001, I outlined the relational origins of secure attachment (Schore, 1994, 2001a) and created the construct of "relational trauma" (Schore, 2001b), which induces dissociation, an emotional disconnection from self and other. In 2003, continuing to build on earlier work, I applied regulation theory to offer a psychoneurobiological model of right brain attachment communications within the therapeutic alliance (Schore, 2003b). In my most recent book, *The Science of the Art of Psychotherapy* (2012), I have argued that more so than the interpretation and cognitive insight, relational-affective processes between patient and therapist are at the core of the change mechanism.

A major purpose of regulation theory is to construct more complex theoretical models that can generate both heuristic experimental research and clinically relevant conceptions of human development, including progressions of development in growth-promoting psychotherapy. My studies on the interpersonal neurobiology of the relational construct of the therapeutic alliance, the collaborative bond between therapist and patient, indicate that therapist-patient relational communications operate rapidly, beneath levels of conscious awareness, while my research in developmental neuropsychoanalysis describes the early evolution of a "relational unconscious" and a right lateralized "social brain" that represents the biological substrate of the human unconscious. A large body of brain laterality studies now confirms the principle that "The left side is involved with conscious response and the right with the unconscious mind" (Mlot, 1998, p. 1006). Regulation theory thus strongly supports currently evolving psychodynamic models of psychotherapy, especially in the treatment of early forming attachment trauma.

In the following, I briefly summarize the relational perspective of regulation theory, offering interpersonal neurobiological models of attachment in early development, in the therapeutic alliance, and in therapeutic change processes. This ongoing work indicates that the current transdisciplinary emphasis on relational processes is shared by, cross-fertilizing, and indeed transforming both psychology and neuroscience, with important consequences for clinical psychological models of psychotherapeutic change. (Throughout, the term "psychodynamic" can be equated with "psychoanalytic," and "psychotherapist" can be equated with "analyst".)

INTERPERSONAL NEUROBIOLOGY OF ATTACHMENT: INTERACTIVE
REGULATION AND THE MATURATION OF THE RIGHT BRAIN

A major contributor to the current relational trend derives from recent advances in attachment theory, now the most influential theory of early socioemotional development available to science. Across four volumes and numerous articles and chapters, I have utilized an interdisciplinary relational perspective to describe and integrate the developmental psychological, biological, and neurochemical processes that underlie the formation of an attachment bond of emotional communication between the infant and primary caregiver (Schore, 1994, 2003a, 2003b, 2012). Throughout my work I have offered a large body of research and clinical data that underscore the centrality of the evolutionary mechanism of early attachment bonding for all later aspects of human development, especially adaptive socioemotional functions essential for survival. Building upon and expanding John Bowlby's (1969) pioneering studies that integrated psychology, biology, and psychoanalysis, modern attachment theory incorporates current advances in developmental and affective neuroscience in order to offer an overarching theoretical model of interpersonal psychoneurobiological attachment dynamics (J. Schore & A. Schore, 2008). At the core of the model is the relational, interactive regulation of affects, which in turn impacts and shapes the maturation of the early developing right brain. On the other hand, early interactive dysregulation represents a central source of the psychopathology that brings the patient into psychotherapy. Clinicians across all forms of psychotherapy are now utilizing updated attachment models in the treatment of right brain relational-emotional dysfunctions of every psychiatric disorder, a theme I will expand in the second section of this chapter. I now present a succinct summary of my work in the neurobiology of attachment, first proposed in 1994 and subsequently expanded over the past two decades.

A central principle of regulation theory dictates that attachment is the relational unfolding of an evolutionary mechanism, and that the essential developmental task of the first 2 years of human infancy is the co-creation of an attachment bond of emotional communication and regulation between the infant and the primary caregiver. Building upon prenatal communications between mother and fetus, in ensuing perinatal and postnatal periods affective transactions are rapidly transmitted within the dyad, using more and more complex nonverbal sensoriaffective communications. In order to facilitate this relational-emotional mechanism, the mother must be psychobiologically attuned to the dynamic shifts in the infant's bodily-based internal states of central and autonomic arousal. Although initially these communications are expressed in olfactory, gustatory, and tactile modalities, by the end of the second month the dyad utilizes more integrated visual and auditory channels of communications in mutual gaze episodes.

During dyadic synchronized, reciprocal attachment transactions, the sensitive primary caregiver, at levels beneath conscious awareness, perceives (recognizes), appraises, and regulates nonverbal expressions of the infant's more and more intense states of positive and negative affective arousal. Via these communications, the mother regulates the infant's postnatally developing central (CNS) and autonomic (ANS) nervous systems. The attachment relationship thus mediates the dyadic regulation of bodily-based emotional states. In this ongoing co-created dialogue, the "good enough" mother and her infant co-construct multiple cycles of both "affect synchrony" that up-regulates positive affect (e.g., joy-elation, interest-excitement) and "rupture and repair" that down-regulates negative affect (e.g., fear-terror, sadness-depression, shame, disgust). These cycles of inter-subjective and intrasubjective attunement/misattunement/re-attunement represent a preverbal psychobiological relational matrix that forms the core of the infant's emerging implicit corporeal self.

There is now agreement that emotion is initially regulated by others, but over the course of infancy it increasingly becomes self-regulated as a result of neurophysiological development and actual lived experience. These adaptive capacities are central to the emergence of self-regulation, the ability to flexibly regulate an expanding array of positive and negative affectively charged psychobiological states in various dynamic relational contexts, thereby allowing for the assimilation of various adaptive emotional-motivational states into a coherent and integrated self-system. Optimal attachment experiences that engender a secure attachment with the primary caregiver thus facilitate both types of self-regulation: interactive regulation of emotions accessed while subjectively engaged with other humans in interconnected contexts, and autoregulation of emotions activated while subjectively disengaged from other humans in autonomous contexts. Modern attachment theory defines emotional well-being as nonconscious yet efficient and resilient, switching between these two modes (interconnectedness and autonomy), depending on the relational context. Internal working models of attachment encode both of these modes of coping strategies of affect regulation. At the most fundamental level, modern attachment theory is a regulation theory (J. Schore & A. Schore, 2008).

Synchronized, affectively charged relational attachment dynamics represent the biopsychosocial mechanism by which we are sociophysiologically connected to others in order to co-regulate our internal homeostatic affective states. The evolutionary mechanism of attachment, the interactive regulation of emotion, thus represents the regulation of biological synchronicity between and within organisms (Bradshaw & Schore, 2007; Schore, 1994). At all points of the life span, interactive psychobiological regulation supports the survival functions of the right-lateralized human implicit self-system (Schore, 2000, 2003a, 2003b). This principle is echoed in developmental brain research, where Ovtscharoff and Braun (2001) reported,

> The dyadic interaction between the newborn and the mother . . .
> serves as a regulator of the developing individual's internal homeo-
> stasis. The regulatory function of the newborn-mother interaction
> may be an essential promoter to ensure the normal development
> and maintenance of synaptic connections during the establishment
> of functional brain circuits. (p. 33)

In this manner, dyadic attachment regulatory transactions impact the
development of psychic structure; that is, they generate brain development
(Schore, 1994).

In a number of contributions, I have elucidated how the maturation of
the emotion-processing limbic circuits of specifically the infant's developing right brain are influenced by implicit intersubjective affective transactions embedded in the attachment relationship with the primary caregiver
(Schore, 1994, 2003b, 2009a, 2012, 2013). More and more complex right-
lateralized visual-facial, auditory-prosodic, and tactile-gestural nonverbal,
implicit affective communications lie at the psychobiological core of the
emotional attachment bond between the infant and primary caregiver.
Implicit processing underlies the quick and automatic handling of nonverbal affective cues in infancy and is "repetitive, automatic, provides quick
categorization and decision-making, and operates *outside the realm of
focal attention and verbalized experience*" (Lyons-Ruth, 1999, p. 576, italics
added). The synchronization of the mother's responses to the infant's signals is a key aspect of the mother's embodied and *pre-reflective sensitivity*,
expressed in the promptness of her response to immediate moment-to-
moment changes in the child's emotional states (Guedeney et al., 2011;
Manini et al., 2013). Neurobiologically, the *nonconscious* joint processing of
these attachment communications is thus the product of the synchronized
operations of the infant's right brain interacting with the mother's right
brain. Internal representations of attachment experiences are imprinted in
right-lateralized implicit-procedural memory as an internal working model
that encodes nonconscious strategies of affect regulation. The regulatory
functions of mother-infant socioemotional interactions thereby impact the
wiring of right brain circuits in critical periods of infancy (Ammaniti &

Trentini, 2009; Cozolino, 2002; Henry, 1993; Schore, 1994, 2003a, 2012; Siegel, 1999).

In support of this model, neuroscientists now document that the right hemisphere shows an earlier maturation than the left in prenatal and post-natal stages of human development (Gupta et al., 2005; Sun et al., 2005), that the strong and consistent predominance for the right hemisphere emerges postnatally (Allman et al., 2005), and that the mother's right hemi-sphere is more involved than the left in emotional processing and moth-ering (Lenzi et al., 2009). Studying structural connectivity asymmetry of the neonatal brain in the first month of life, Meaney and his colleagues concluded,

> In early life the right cerebral hemisphere could be better able to process . . . emotion (Schore, 2000; Wada & Davis, 1977). This idea appears consistent with our findings of rightward asymmetry in . . . limbic structures. . . . These neural substrates function as hubs in the right hemisphere for emotion processes and mother and child interaction. (Ratnarajah et al., 2013, p. 193)

Tronick's group has shown that 6- to 12-month-old infants use left-sided gestures generated by the right hemisphere in order to cope with the stress-ful face-to-face still-face paradigm. They interpreted these data as being "consistent with Schore's (2005) hypotheses of hemispheric right-sided acti-vation of emotions and their regulation during infant–mother interactions and his argument that the left side of the brain is less developed than the right side" (Montirosso et al., 2012, p. 826). In a near-infrared spectroscopy study of infant-mother attachment at 12 months, Minagawa-Kawai and col-leagues observed, "Our results are in agreement with that of Schore (2000) who addressed the importance of the right hemisphere in the attachment system" (2009, p. 289).

Relational attachment transactions thus shape the experience-dependent maturation of right subcortical-cortical systems, and in this manner they impact later personality development and functions, especially of survival functions that act at ultrafast time frames, beneath conscious awareness. In all stages of human development, the nonconscious relational attachment mechanism is a major regulator of the right brain. My work in developmental neuropsychoanalysis further indicates that the implicit self-system of the right brain that evolves in preverbal stages of development represents the biological substrate of Freud's dynamic unconscious (Schore, 1997a, 2002a). Indeed, the relational attachment mechanism represents nonverbal communications between the mother's unconscious and the infant's unconscious (Schore, 2012, 2013). This right brain-to-right brain mechanism mediates the intergenerational transmission of unconscious structures and functions between the generations.

Consonant with this proposal, the neuropsychologist Don Tucker has asserted, "The right hemisphere's specialization for emotional communication through nonverbal channels seems to suggest a domain of the mind that is close to the motivationally charged psychoanalytic unconscious" (Tucker & Moller, 2007, p. 91). Indeed, a growing body of studies documents that unconscious processing of emotional information is mainly subsumed by a right hemisphere subcortical route (Gainotti, 2012), that unconscious emotional memories are stored in the right hemisphere (Gainotti, 2006), and that this hemisphere is centrally involved in maintaining a coherent, continuous, and unified sense of self (Devinsky, 2000; McGilchrist, 2009). From infancy throughout all later stages of the life span, this right-lateralized system's rapidly acting emotional processes are centrally involved in the control of vital functions supporting survival, in enabling the organism to cope with stresses and challenges, and thus in emotional resilience and well-being. Indeed, a body of research now indicates that right (and not left) lateralized prefrontal systems are responsible for the highest-level regulation of affect and stress in the brain (Cerqueira, Almeida, & Sousa, 2008; Perez-Cruz et al., 2009; Schore, 1994; Stevenson et al., 2008; Sullivan & Gratton, 2002; Wang et al., 2005).

RIGHT BRAIN ATTACHMENT COMMUNICATIONS WITHIN THE THERAPEUTIC ALLIANCE

A central tenet of regulation theory dictates that early socioemotional experiences may be either predominantly regulated or dysregulated, imprinting secure or insecure attachments. Developmental neuroscience now clearly demonstrates that all children are not "resilient" but "malleable," for better or worse (Leckman & March, 2011). In marked contrast to the earlier described optimal attachment scenario, in a relational growth-inhibiting early environment of abuse or neglect the primary caregiver of an insecure disorganized-disoriented infant induces traumatic states of enduring negative affect in the child (Schore, 2001b, 2002b). This caregiver is too frequently emotionally inaccessible and reacts to her infant's expressions of stressful affects inconsistently and inappropriately (massive intrusiveness or massive disengagement) and therefore shows minimal or unpredictable participation in the various types of relational arousal regulating processes. Instead of modulating, she induces extreme levels of stressful stimulation and arousal, very high in abuse or very low in neglect. Due to the fact that too frequently she provides no interactive repair, the infant's intense negative affective states last for long periods of time.

A large body of research in the field of developmental psychopathology now highlights the central role of insecure attachments in the psychoneuropathogenesis of all psychiatric disorders (Schore, 1996, 1997b, 2003a, 2012, 2013). Watt observed, "If children grow up with dominant experiences of separation, distress, fear and rage, then they will go down a bad pathogenic developmental pathway, and it's not just a bad psychological pathway but a bad neurological pathway" (2003, p. 109). More specifically, during early critical periods, frequent dysregulated and unrepaired organized and disorganized-disoriented insecure attachment histories are "affectively burnt in" the infant's early developing right brain (Schore, 1994, 2003a). Less than optimal early experiences, including the "relational trauma" of abuse and neglect (Schore, 2001b), are imprinted into right cortical-subcortical systems, encoding disorganized-disoriented insecure internal working models that are nonconsciously accessed at later points of interpersonal emotional stress. Not only traumatic experiences but also the defense against overwhelming trauma, dissociation, is stored in implicit-procedural memory.

Regulation theory suggests that these right-lateralized insecure working models are a central focus of affectively focused psychotherapy of early forming self-pathologies and personality disorders. Such right brain relational deficits are described by Feinberg and Keenan (2005):

> The right hemisphere, particularly the right frontal region, under
> normal circumstances plays a crucial role in establishing the appro-
> priate relationship between the self and the world . . . dysfunction
> results in a two-way disturbance of personal relatedness between the
> self and the environment that can lead to disorders of both under
> and over relatedness between the self and the world. (p. 15)

There is now consensus that deficits in these right brain relational processes and resulting affect dysregulation are fundamental elements of the
treatment. All models of therapeutic intervention across a span of psychopathologies share a common goal of improving the effectiveness of emotional
self-regulatory processes (Schore, 1994, 2003a, 2003b, 2012). At every stage
of the life span, relational, affectively focused infant, child, adolescent, and
adult psychotherapy can facilitate the intrinsic plasticity of the right brain.

Bowlby (1988), a psychoanalyst, asserted that the reassessment of *nonconscious* internal working models of attachment is a primary goal of any
psychotherapeutic encounter. These interactive representations of early
attachment experiences encode strategies of affect regulation and contain
coping mechanisms for maintaining basic regulation and positive affect
in the face of stressful environmental challenge. Acting at levels beneath
conscious awareness, this internal working model is accessed to perceive,
appraise, and regulate socioemotional information and guide action in
familiar and especially novel interpersonal environments. Following Bowlby's interdisciplinary perspective, my work indicates that in "heightened
affective moments" the patient's unconscious internal working model of
attachment, whether secure or insecure, is reactivated in right-lateralized
implicit-procedural memory and reenacted in the psychotherapeutic
relationship.

As in early development, right brain-to-right brain attachment communications are expressed within the therapeutic alliance, between the
patient's and therapist's "right minds" (Ornstein, 1997). Neuroscientists
contend that the right hemisphere processes unconscious emotional material, while the left is involved in the conscious processing of emotional
stimuli (Wexler et al., 1992). Thus, in my writings on the central role of
attachment dynamics in psychotherapy, I have focused not on the verbal

narratives expressed between the left brain conscious minds of the patient and the therapist, but on the moment-to-moment nonverbal dialogues between the right brain unconscious minds of the members of the therapeutic dyad. Relationally oriented therapeutic contexts that optimize right brain intersubjective communication and interactive regulation attempt to explore and alter inefficient nonconscious insecure internal working models of the self and the world.

In light of the commonality of nonverbal, intersubjective, implicit right brain-to-right brain emotion transacting and regulating mechanisms in the caregiver-infant relationship and the therapist-patient relationship, developmental attachment studies have direct relevance to the treatment process. As the right hemisphere is dominant for nonverbal communication (Benowitz et al., 1983), subjective emotional experiences (Wittling & Roschmann, 1993), and implicit learning (Hugdahl, 1995), the implicit communication of affective states between the right brains of the members of the patient-therapist dyad (as in the infant-mother dyad) is thus best described as "intersubjectivity." The clinician acts as a "participant observer" (Sullivan, 1953) of not only the patient's external behavior but also the patient's internal subjective states.

In accord with a relational model of psychotherapy, right brain processes that are reciprocally activated on both sides of the therapeutic alliance lie at the core of the psychotherapeutic change process. These implicit clinical dialogues convey much more essential organismic information than left brain explicit, verbal information. Rather, right brain interactions "beneath the words" nonverbally communicate essential, nonconscious, bodily-based affective relational information about the inner world of the patient (and therapist). Decety and Chaminade's (2003) assertion "mental states that are in essence private to the self may be shared between individuals" clearly describes the intimate context of psychotherapy. Rapid communications between the right-lateralized "emotional brain" ("right mind") of each member of the therapeutic alliance allow for moment-to-moment, right brain-to-right brain "self-state sharing," a co-created, organized, dynamically changing dialogue of mutual influence. According to Bromberg (2011):

Self-states are highly individualized modules *of being*, each config-
ured by its own organization of cognitions, beliefs, dominant affect,
and mood, access to memory, skills, behaviors, values, action, and
regulatory physiology. (p. 73)

In this interactive relational matrix, both partners match the dynamic con-
tours of different emotional-motivational self-states and simultaneously synchronize and adjust their social attention, stimulation, and accelerating/
decelerating arousal in response to the partner's signals.

Regulation theory offers a deeper understanding of the mutual psychobiological mechanisms that underlie any clinical encounter, whatever the
verbal content. It is now accepted that the "nonverbal, pre-rational stream
of expression that binds the infant to its parent continues throughout life to
be a primary medium of intuitively felt affective-relational communication
between persons" (Orlinksy & Howard, 1986, p. 343). Lyons-Ruth (2000)
characterized the affective exchanges that communicate implicit relational
knowledge within the therapeutic alliance. She observed that most relational transactions rely on a substrate of affective cues that give an evaluative valence or direction to each relational communication. These occur at
an implicit level of cueing and response that occurs too rapidly for verbal
transaction and conscious reflection. Neuroscience now characterizes the
fundamental role of the right brain in these face-to-face communications. At
all stages of the life span, "The neural substrates of the perception of voices,
faces, gestures, smells and pheromones, as evidenced by modern neuroimaging techniques, are characterized by a general pattern of right-hemispheric
functional asymmetry" (Brancucci et al., 2009, p. 895). van Lancker Sidtis
concluded, "Pattern recognition and comprehension of several types of stimuli, such as faces, chords, complex pitch, graphic images, and voices, has
been described as superior in the normal right hemisphere" (2006, p. 233).

In the clinical literature, Scaer (2005) described essential implicit communication patterns embedded within the therapist-client relationship:

Many features of social interaction are nonverbal, consisting of subtle variations of facial expression that set the tone for the content of

the interaction. Body postures and movement patterns of the therapist . . . also may reflect emotions such as disapproval, support, humor, and fear. Tone and volume of voice, patterns and speed of verbal communication, and eye contact also contain elements of subliminal communication and contribute to the unconscious establishment of a safe, healing environment. (pp. 167–168)

These implicit nonconscious right brain/mind/body nonverbal communications are bidirectional and intersubjective, and thereby potentially valuable to the clinician. Meares (2005) observed,

Not only is the therapist being unconsciously influenced by a series of slight and, in some cases, subliminal signals, so also is the patient. Details of the therapist's posture, gaze, tone of voice, even respiration, are recorded and processed. A sophisticated therapist may use this processing in a beneficial way, potentiating a change in the patient's state without, or in addition to, the use of words. (p. 124)

More so than conscious left brain verbalizations, these right brain-to-right brain visual-facial, auditory-prosodic, and tactile-gestural communications reveal the deeper aspects of the personality of the patient, as well as the personality of the therapist (see Schore, 2003b, for a right brain-to-right brain model of projective identification, a fundamental process of implicit communication between the relational unconscious systems of patient and therapist within the therapeutic alliance).

In order to receive and monitor the patient's nonverbal bodily-based attachment communications, the affectively attuned clinician must shift from constricted left-hemispheric attention that focuses on local detail to more widely expanded right-hemispheric attention that focuses on global detail (Derryberry & Tucker, 1994), a characterization that fits with Freud's (1912/1957) description of the importance of the clinician's "evenly suspended attention." In the session, the empathic therapist is consciously, explicitly attending to the patient's verbalizations in order to objectively diagnose and rationalize the patient's dysregulating symptomatology. However, the therapist is also listening and interacting at another level, an experience-near subjective level, one that implicitly processes moment-to-moment attachment communications and socioemotional information at levels beneath awareness. An essential relational element of any treatment encounter is how we work with what is being communicated but not symbolized with words. How we understand and relate to an unexpressed unconscious emotion depends on our capacity to receive and express nonverbal communications. In discussing "presymbolic processing," Bucci observed, "We recognize changes in emotional states of others based on perception of subtle shifts in their facial expression or posture, and recognize changes in our own states based on somatic or kinesthetic experience" (2002, p. 194). These implicit communications are expressed within the therapeutic alliance between the client's and therapist's right brain systems.

Writing on therapeutic "nonverbal implicit communications," Chused asserted, "It is not that the information they contain cannot be verbalized, only that sometimes only a nonverbal approach can deliver the information in a way it can be used, particularly when there is no conscious awareness of the underlying concerns involved" (2007, p. 879). These ideas were echoed by Hutterer and Liss (2006), who stated that nonverbal variables such as tone, tempo, rhythm, timbre, prosody, and amplitude of speech, as well as body language signals may need to be reexamined as essential aspects of therapeutic technique. The right hemisphere is dominant for nonverbal (Benowitz et al., 1983), spontaneous (Blonder et al., 1995), emotional (Blonder, Bowers, & Heilman, 1991), and prosodic (George et al., 1996; Ross & Monnot, 2008) communication, as well as for the holistic processing of musical patterns (Nicholson et al., 2003) and the emotional experience of listening to music (Satoh et al., 2011). The right hemisphere is thus important in the processing of the "music behind the words."

Indeed, neurobiological data suggest, "While the left hemisphere mediates most linguistic behaviors, the right hemisphere is important for broader aspects of communication" (van Lancker & Cummings, 1999, p. 95). Furthermore, reciprocal attachment communications within the therapeutic alliance are examples of "primary process communication." According to Dorpat, "The primary process system analyzes, regulates, and communicates an individual's relations with the environment" (2001, p. 449). He observed, "Affective and object-relational information is transmitted predominantly by primary process communication. Nonverbal communication includes body movements (kinesics), posture, gesture, facial expression, voice inflection, and the sequence, rhythm, and pitch of the spoken words" (2001, p. 451).

The organizing principle of working with unconscious primary process communications dictates just as the left brain communicates its states to other left brains via conscious linguistic behaviors, so the right nonverbally communicates its unconscious states to other right brains that are tuned to receive these communications. In his recent book, Bromberg (2011) concluded,

> Allan Schore writes about a right brain-to-right brain channel of affective communication—a channel that he sees as "an organized dialogue" comprised of "dynamically fluctuating moment-to-moment state sharing." I believe it to be this process of state sharing that . . . allows . . . "a good psychoanalytic match." (p. 169)

Writing in the psychiatry literature, Meares (2012, p. 315) suggested that "an important component of this approach is a form of therapeutic conversation that can be conceived . . . as a dynamic interplay between two right hemispheres" (for recent clinical examples of right brain-to-right brain tracking, see Bromberg, 2011; Chapman, 2014; Gant & Badenoch, 2013; Marks-Tarlow, 2012, Meares, 2012; Montgomery, 2013; Schore, 2012).

Regulation theory thus describes how beneath the exchanges of language, the implicit affects of the patient are communicated to and regulated by implicit systems of the therapist. From the first point of intersubjective contact, the psychobiologically attuned intuitive clinician tracks the nonverbal moment-to-moment rhythmic structures of the patient's internal states and is flexibly and fluidly modifying his or her own behavior to synchronize with that structure, thereby co-creating with the client a growth-facilitating context for the organization of the therapeutic alliance. The attachment between therapist and client is established over time, allowing for the expression of unconscious socioemotional experiences that resonate with the original infant-mother (and later toddler-father) attachment history. Over the ensuing stages of the treatment, the sensitive, empathic clinician's monitoring of unconscious psychobiological process, rather than conscious verbal content, calls for right brain attention in order to match the patient's implicit affective-arousal self-states. The intuitive therapist also resonates with the client's simultaneous implicit nonverbal expressions of engagement and disengagement within the co-constructed therapeutic alliance.

On the matter of the verbal content, the words in psychotherapy, it has long been assumed in the psychotherapeutic literature that all forms of language reflect left-hemispheric functioning. Current neuroscience now indicates this is incorrect. Indeed, in an overarching review Ross and Monnot concluded, "Thus, the traditional concept that language is a dominant and lateralized function of the left hemisphere is no longer tenable" (2008, p. 51). They reported,

> Over the last three decades, there has been growing realization that the right hemisphere is essential for language and communication competency and psychological well-being through its ability to modulate affective prosody and gestural behavior, decode connotative (non-standard) word meanings, make thematic inferences, and process metaphor, complex linguistic relationships and non-literal (idiomatic) types of expressions. (p. 51)

Intersubjectivity is more than a communication or match of explicit verbal cognitions. Regulated and dysregulated bodily-based affects are communicated within the intersubjective field co-constructed by two individuals, an energy-transmitting field that includes not just two minds but two bodies (Schore, 1994, 2003a, 2003b, 2012). At the psychobiological core of the co-constructed intersubjective field is the attachment bond of emotional communication and interactive regulation. Implicit intersubjective communications within the therapeutic alliance are expressed in psychobiologically dysregulated and regulated, unconscious, bodily-based emotional self-states, not just conscious cognitive "mental" states. The essential biological function of attachment communications in all human interactions, including those embedded in the psychobiological core of the therapeutic alliance, is the regulation of right brain/mind/body states.

Intersubjective, relational affect-focused psychotherapy is not the "talking cure" but the "affect communicating cure."

TRANSFERENCE-COUNTERTRANSFERENCE
COMMUNICATIONS WITHIN MUTUAL ENACTMENTS

Regulation theory's relational perspective of the treatment process allows for a deeper understanding of the critical intersubjective brain/mind/body mechanisms that operate at implicit levels of the therapeutic alliance, beneath the exchanges of language and explicit cognitions. One such essential mechanism is the transference-countertransference relationship. There is now a growing consensus that despite the existence of a number of distinct theoretical perspectives in clinical work, the concepts of transference and countertransference have now been (re-) incorporated into all forms of psychotherapy. Transference-countertransference affective transactions are currently seen as an essential relational element in the treatment of all patients, but especially the severe psychopathologies.

In such cases, implicit right brain-to-right brain nonverbal communications (facial expressions, prosody-tone of voice, gesture) convey unconscious transference-countertransference affective transactions, which revive earlier attachment memories, especially of intensely dysregulated affective states. Gainotti observed that "the right hemisphere may be crucially involved in those emotional memories which must be reactivated and reworked during the psychoanalytical treatment" (2006, p. 167). In discussing the role of the right hemisphere as "the seat of implicit memory," Mancia noted: "The discovery of the implicit memory has extended the concept of the unconscious and supports the hypothesis that this is where the emotional and affective— sometimes traumatic—presymbolic and preverbal experiences of the primary mother-infant relations are stored" (2006, p. 83). Right-lateralized implicit memory also encodes the dissociative defense against reexperiencing relational trauma (Schore, 2009b). Transference has been described as "an expression of the patient's implicit memories" (Bornstein, 1999, p. 170). These memories are expressed in "heightened affective moments" as transferential right brain-to-right brain nonverbal communications of fast acting, automatic, dysregulated bodily-based states of stressful emotional arousal.

Recent psychodynamic models of transference now contend, "no appreciation of transference can do without emotion" (Pincus, Freeman, & Modell, 2007, p. 634). Clinical theoreticians describe transference as "an established pattern of relating and emotional responding that is cued by something in the present, but oftentimes calls up both an affective state and thoughts that may have more to do with past experience than present ones" (Maroda, 2005, p. 134). This conception is echoed in neuroscience, where Shuren and Grafman (2002) asserted:

> The right hemisphere holds representations of the emotional states associated with events experienced by the individual. When that individual encounters a familiar scenario, representations of past emotional experiences are retrieved by the right hemisphere and are incorporated into the reasoning process. (p. 918)

A body of research has now established that the right hemisphere is fundamentally involved in the unconscious processing of emotional stimuli (Mlot, 1998) and in autobiographical memory (Markowitsch et al., 2000).

Recall Racker's (1968) classic dictum, "Every transference situation provokes a countertransference situation." Translating this into modern neuropsychoanalytic terms, transference-countertransference transactions are expressions of bidirectional, nonconscious, nonverbal, right brain/mind/body stressful communications between patient and therapist. These reciprocal psychoneurobiological exchanges reflect activities of both the central and autonomic nervous systems. Behaviorally, the patient's transferential communications are expressed in nonverbal, visual and auditory affective cues that are spontaneously and quickly expressed from the face, voice, and body of the patient. Countertransference is similarly defined in nonverbal implicit terms as the therapist's "autonomic responses that are reactions on an unconscious level to nonverbal messages" (Jacobs, 1994, p. 749). In my first book I stated,

> Countertransferential processes are currently understood to be manifest in the capacity to recognize and utilize the sensory (visual, auditory, tactile, kinesthetic, and olfactory) and affective qualities

of imagery which the patient generates in the psychotherapist . . . countertransference dynamics are appraised by the therapist's observations of his own visceral reactions to the patient's material. (Schore, 1994, p. 451)

As the empathic clinician monitors the patient's nonverbal communications, her psychobiologically attuned right brain tracks, at a preconscious level, not only the patterns of arousal rhythms and flows of the patient's affective states, but also her own somatic countertransferential, interoceptive, bodily-based affective responses to the patient's right brain implicit facial, prosodic, and gestural transferential communications. In convergent writings, theoreticians are now asserting "transference is distinctive in that it depends on early patterns of emotional attachment with caregivers" (Pincus et al., 2007, p. 636), while clinicians are describing the clinical importance of "making conscious the organizing patterns of affect" (Mohaupt et al., 2006). Neuroscientists now assert, "Simply stated, the left hemisphere specializes in analyzing sequences, while the right hemisphere gives evidence of superiority in processing patterns" (van Lancker & Cummings, 1999, p. 95).

Via these right brain mechanisms the intuitive, psychobiologically attuned therapist, on a moment-to-moment basis, nonconsciously focuses her right brain countertransferential broad attentional processes (Derryberry & Tucker, 1994) upon patterns of rhythmic crescendos/decrescendos of the patient's regulated and dysregulated states of affective autonomic arousal. Freud's (1915/1957) dictum, "It is a very remarkable thing that the *Ucs* of one human being can react upon that of another, without passing through the *Cs*" (p. 194), is thus neuropsychoanalytically understood as a right brain-to-right brain communication from one relational unconscious to another. In this manner, "The right hemisphere, in fact, truly interprets the mental state not only of its own brain, but the brains (and minds) of others" (Keenan et al., 2005, p. 702).

Right brain-to-right brain, nonverbal, transferential-countertransferential unconscious communications between the patient's and therapist's internal worlds represent an essential relational matrix for the therapeutic expression of unconscious negative emotion (Sato & Aoki, 2006; Yang et al., 2011) and dissociated affects (Schore, 2012). These affective communications were neither intersubjectively shared nor interactively regulated by the original attachment object in the historical context, but now the patient has the possibility of a reparative relational experience. According to Borgogno and Vigna-Taglianti (2008),

> In patients whose psychic suffering originates in . . . preverbal trauma . . . transference occurs mostly at a more primitive level of expression that involves in an unconscious way . . . not only the patient but also the analyst. . . . . These more archaic forms of the transference-countertransference issue—which frequently set aside verbal contents—take shape in the analytical setting through actual mutual enactments (p. 314).

Right brain bodily-based dialogues between the relational unconscious of the patient and the relational unconscious of the affectively sensitive therapist are thus activated and enhanced in the "heightened affective moments" of reenactments of early relational trauma (see Schore, 2012, for an extensive interpersonal neurobiological model of working in clinical enactments). Ginot (2007) noted, "Increasingly, enactments are understood as powerful manifestations of the intersubjective process and as inevitable expressions of complex, though largely unconscious self-states and relational patterns" (p. 317).

The relational mechanism of mutual enactments represents an interaction between the patient's emotional vulnerability and the clinician's emotional availability (the ability to "take" the transference). It is most fully operational during ruptures of the therapeutic alliance, described by Aspland and colleagues (2008) as "points of emotional disconnections between client and therapist that create a negative shift in the quality of the alliance" (p. 699), which act as "episodes of covert or overt behavior that trap both participants in negative complementary interactions" (p. 700). Although such ruptures of the alliance are the most stressful moments of the treatment, these (defensive) "collisions" of the therapist's and patient's subjectivities also represent an intersubjective context of potential "collaboration" between their subjectivities, and thereby a context of interactive repair, a fundamental mechanism of therapeutic change. This co-created new relational structure within the therapeutic alliance contains a more efficient feedback system of not only right brain communications but also right brain interactive regulations of intensely dysregulated affective states associated with early relational trauma.

The essential biological homeostatic functions of affective, bodily-based attachment communications in all human interactions, including those embedded in the psychobiological core of the therapeutic alliance, are involved in the regulation of right brain/mind/body states. Aron observed,

> Patient and analyst mutually regulate each other's behaviors, enactments, and states of consciousness such that each gets under the other's skin, each reaches into the other's guts, each is breathed in and absorbed by the other . . . the analyst must be attuned to the nonverbal, the affective . . . to his or her bodily responses. (1998, p. 26)

The importance of this intersubjective right limbic-autonomic connection is stressed by Whitehead:

> Every time we make therapeutic contact with our patients we are engaging profound processes that tap into essential life forces in our selves and in those we work with. . . . *Emotions are deepened in intensity and sustained in time when they are intersubjectively shared.* This occurs at moments of deep contact. (2006, p. 624, italics in original)

At moments of deep contact, intersubjective psychobiological resonance between the patient's relational unconscious and the clinician's relational unconscious generates an interactively regulated amplification of arousal and affect, and so unconscious affects are deepened in intensity and sustained in time. This dyadic increase of emotional intensity (energetic arousal) allows dissociated affects beneath levels of awareness to emerge into consciousness in both members of the therapeutic dyad (Schore, 2012).

"Heightened affective moments" of the treatment thus afford an opportunity for interactive affect regulation, the core of the attachment process. Neuroscientists now assert, "The ability to modulate emotions is at the heart of the human experience . . . emotional self-regulatory processes constitutes the core of several modern psychotherapeutic approaches" (Beauregard, Levesque, & Bourgouin, 2001, p. R165). Echoing this principle in the clinical literature, Ogden and her colleagues concluded,

> Interactive psychobiological regulation . . . provides the relational context under which the client can safely contact, describe and eventually regulate inner experience. . . . It is the patient's experience of empowering action in the context of safety provided by a background of the empathic clinician's psychobiologically attuned interactive affect regulation that helps effect . . . change. (2005, p. 22)

In a seminal article in the clinical psychology literature, Leslie Greenberg described a "self-control" form of emotion regulation involving higher levels of cognitive executive function that allows individuals "to change the way they feel by consciously changing the way they think" (2007, p. 415). He proposed that this explicit form of affect regulation is performed by the verbal left hemisphere, and unconscious bodily-based emotion is usually not addressed. This regulatory mechanism is at the core of verbal-analytic understanding and controlled reasoning and is heavily emphasized in models of cognitive behavioral therapy. In contrast to this conscious emotion regulation system, Greenberg described a second, more fundamental, implicit affect regulatory process performed by the right hemisphere. This system rapidly and automatically processes facial expression, vocal quality, and eye contact in a relational context. This type of therapy attempts not control but the "acceptance or facilitation of particular emotions," including "previously avoided emotion," in order to allow the patient to tolerate and transform them into "adaptive emotions." Citing my work, he asserted that "it is the building of implicit or automatic emotion regulation capacities that is important for enduring change, especially for highly fragile personality-disordered clients" (2007, p. 416).

RIGHT BRAIN RELATIONAL MECHANISMS OF THERAPEUTIC CHANGE

In cases of early attachment maturational failures, especially histories of relational trauma, deep emotional contact and implicit interactive affect regulation are central mechanisms of right brain psychotherapy change processes. Recall, the hallmark of trauma is damage to the relational life (Herman, 1992). The repair and resolution of relational trauma therefore must occur in a therapeutic relational context. In this challenging work, more so than cognitive understanding, relational factors lie at the core of the change mechanism. Therapeutic contexts that optimize changes in traumatic reenactments involve a profound commitment by both participants in the therapeutic dyad and a deep emotional involvement on the part of the therapist (Tutte, 2004). These types of cases, difficult as they may be, represent valuable learning experiences for the therapist, as they provide for the learning and mastery of expert skills (Schore, 2012). Ultimately, effective psychotherapeutic treatment of early evolving self-pathologies (including personality disorders) can facilitate neuroplastic changes in the right brain, which is dominant for attachment functions throughout the life span. This interpersonal neurobiological mechanism allows optimal long-term treatment to potentially transform disorganized-disoriented attachments into "earned secure" attachments.

That said, the developing right brain system ("right mind") is relationally impacted in all attachment histories, including insecure organized and secure attachments. Regulation theory's transtheoretical clinical perspective that describes the basic psychoneurobiological processes of therapeutic action applies to all patients, insecure and secure, and to all forms of psychotherapy. In 1994, I offered thoughts on "the neurobiological characterization of psychotherapeutically induced psychic structural change," specifically alterations in the patient's right-lateralized cortical-subcortical circuits (Schore, 1994). In 2005, the Nobel Prize–winning psychiatrist Eric Kandel concluded there is no longer any doubt that psychotherapy can result in detectable changes in the brain (Etkin et al., 2005). By 2008, Glass summarized the commonly accepted view: "Recent research in brain imaging, molecular biology, and neurogenetics has shown that psychotherapy changes brain function and structure. Such studies have shown that psychotherapy affects regional cerebral blood, neurotransmitter metabolism, gene expression, and persistent modifications in synaptic plasticity" (2008, p. 1589).

For two decades, I have utilized a rapidly expanding body of neurobiological research in order to construct a theory that models more precisely how psychotherapy facilitates changes in the patient's brain, mind, and body (see Schore, 1994, 2003b, 2012). In a recent neuroimaging study, Tschacher, Schildt, and Sander contended that "psychotherapy research is no longer concerned with efficacy but rather with how effective change occurs" (2010, p. 578). Changes mediated by affectively focused, relationally oriented psychotherapy are imprinted into the right brain, which is dominant for the nonverbal, holistic processing of emotional information and social interactions (Decety & Lamm, 2007; Schore, 2012; Semrud-Clikeman, Fine, & Zhu, 2011). The right brain is centrally involved in implicit (vs. explicit) affectivity, defined as "individual differences in the *automatic* activation of cognitive representations of emotions *that do not result from self-reflection*" (Quirin et al., 2009, p. 4012, italics added). It also predominates over the left for coping with and assimilating novel situations (Podell, Lovell, & Goldberg, 2001) and ensuring the formation of a new program of interactions with a new environment (Ezhov & Krivoschekov, 2004). These adaptive functions are mobilized in the change process of psychotherapy.

Relational contexts of long-term treatment allow for the evolution of more complex psychic structure, which in turn can process more complex right brain functions (e.g., intersubjectivity, empathy, affect tolerance, and stress regulation). The growth-facilitating relational environment of a deeper therapeutic exploration can induce plasticity in both the cortical and subcortical systems of the right brain. This increased connectivity in turn generates more complex development of the right-lateralized biological substrate of the human unconscious (Joseph, 1992; Schore, 1994), including alterations of the patient's nonconscious internal working model that encodes more effective coping strategies of implicit affect regulation and thereby expanded resilience and flexibility of the implicit self. I suggest that this interpersonal neurobiological mechanism underlies Jordan's assertion that "people grow through and toward relationship throughout the life span" (2000, p. 1007).

The intrinsically relational aspect of regulation theory also models the reciprocal changes in the clinician's right brain that result from working repeatedly with therapeutic processes (Schore, 2012). Recall the APA's characterization of clinical expertise as "interpersonal skill," expressed in "encoding and decoding verbal and nonverbal responses" and "responding empathically to the patient's explicit and implicit experiences." With clinical experience (the proverbial "10,000 hours"), psychotherapists of all schools can become expert in nonverbal intersubjective processes and *"implicit relational knowledge,"* which enhance therapeutic effectiveness. The professional growth of the clinician reflects progressions in right brain relational processes that underlie clinical skills, including affective empathy (Decety & Chaminade, 2003; Schore, 1994), the ability to tolerate and interactively regulate a broader array of negative and positive affective self-states (Schore, 2003b, 2012), implicit openness to experience (DeYoung, Grazioplene, & Peterson, 2012), clinical intuition (Marks-Tarlow, 2012; Schore, 2012), and creativity (Asari et al., 2008; Mihov, Denzler, & Forster, 2010). Furthermore, in a very recent comprehensive overview of laterality research, Hecht (2014) stated,

> Mounting evidence suggests that the right hemisphere has a relative advantage over the left hemisphere in mediating social intelligence—identifying social stimuli, understanding the intentions of other people, awareness of the dynamics in social relationships, and successful handling of social interactions. (p. 1)

I would argue that clinical experience enhances the therapist's right brain "social intelligence."

Regulation theory proposes that the core clinical skills of any effective psychotherapy are right brain implicit capacities, including the ability to empathically receive and express bodily-based nonverbal communications, the ability to sensitively register very slight changes in another's expression and emotion, an immediate awareness of one's own subjective and intersubjective experience, and the regulation of one's own and the patient's affect. All techniques sit atop this relational substratum. As Valentine and Gabbard have eloquently stated, "Technique, in general, should be invisible. The therapist should be viewed by the patient as engaging in a natural conversational dialog growing out of the patient's concerns; the therapist should not be perceived as applying a stilted, formal technique" (2014, p. 60). Over the course of the treatment, in an array of emotionally charged clinical exchanges, the empathic therapist is flexibly accessing a storehouse of affective experiences gained over the course of his or her career. A relational perspective of professional development dictates that the continually evolving psychotherapist frequently reflects upon the subjective experiences of *being with* patients, including not only *the patients'* unique personalities, but also *their own* conscious and especially unconscious intersubjective co-participation in the therapeutic process.

To be optimally effective in treating the regulatory and relational deficits of both psychiatric and personality disorders, the expert clinician learns how to fluidly access not only the patient's left-lateralized conscious mind and explicit self, but even more important the patient's right-lateralized unconscious mind and implicit, bodily-based self. This principle applies to clinical psychology's models of both assessment and treatment. Notably, as opposed to verbal questionnaires that measure explicit functions, projective tests, such as the Rorschach and the Thematic Apperception Test, directly tap into right brain implicit functions (Asari et al., 2008; Hiraishi et al., 2012. Indeed, Finn (2012) is now applying regulation theory to Rorschach assessments of right brain attachment failures (see also use of the Adult Attachment Projective Picture System by Finn, 2011, and use of the Operant Motive Test by Quirin et al., 2013).

In addition, the *explicit knowledge* the psychologist acquires from studying the rapidly expanding amount of clinically relevant interdisciplinary research is essential to professional growth. My ongoing studies indicate that the current explosion of information on early socioemotional development, attachment, relational trauma, unconscious processes, and developing brain functions is directly relevant to clinical models of psychotherapeutic change. The expanding knowledge of the biological and medical disciplines that border psychology needs to be incorporated into and thereby update our professional curriculum, training, and internship programs, where it can promote more effective relational and therapeutic skills.

The practice of psychotherapy is not just explicitly teaching the patient coping skills. Rather, it is fundamentally relational: The therapeutic alliance, the major vector of change, is in essence a two-person system for (implicit) self-exploration and relational healing. At all points in the life span, this emotional growth of the self that supports emotional well-being is facilitated in relational contexts, as described above. The importance of "context" is currently highlighted by all scientific and clinical disciplines. For most of the past century, science equated context with the organism's physical surround; this has now shifted to the social, relational environment. All human interactions, including those between therapist and patient as well as researcher and experimental subject, occur within a relational context, in which essential nonverbal communications are transmitted at levels beneath conscious awareness, thereby activating/deactivating basic homeostatic processes in both members of an intersubjective dyad. This reciprocal communication between the relational unconscious of both members of the therapeutic alliance is described by Casement: "It is usual for therapists to see themselves as trying to understand the unconscious of the patient. What is not always acknowledged is that the patient also reads the unconscious of the therapist, knowingly or unknowingly" (1985, p. 3). The ubiquitous expression of the relational unconscious in the therapeutic alliance strongly supports psychodynamic, interpersonal models of psychotherapy and amplifies Sigmund Freud's call for paradigm-shifting scientific explorations of the unconscious in everyday life.

At the beginning of this work, I suggested that a paradigm shift is now occurring across a number of disciplines, from left brain conscious cognition to right brain unconscious, relational, emotional functions. Writing in the neuropsychoanalytic literature on "Emotions, Unconscious Processes, and the Right Hemisphere," Gainotti (2005) concluded,

> The right hemispheres may subserve the lower "schematic" level (where emotions are automatically generated and experienced as "true emotions") and the left hemisphere the higher "conceptual" level (where emotions are consciously analysed and submitted to intentional control). (p. 71)

In his masterly review of brain laterality research, Iain McGilchrist (2009) asserted,

> If what one means by consciousness is the part of the mind that brings the world into focus, makes it explicit, allows it to be formulated in language, and is aware of its own awareness, it is reasonable to link the conscious mind to activity almost all of which lies ultimately in the left hemisphere. (p. 188)

On the other hand,

> The right hemisphere, by contrast, yields a world of individual, changing, evolving, interconnected, implicit, incarnate, living beings within the context of the lived world, but in the nature of things never fully graspable, always imperfectly known—and to this world it exists in a relationship of care. (p. 174)

Psychotherapy, "a relationship of care," can alter more than the left-lateralized conscious mind; it also can influence the growth and development of the unconscious "right mind." It is undoubtedly true that both brain hemispheres contribute to effective therapeutic treatment, but in light of the current relational trend that emphasizes "the primacy of affect," the right brain, the "social," "emotional" brain, is dominant in all forms of psychotherapy.

CHAPTER 3

The Growth-Promoting Role of Mutual Regressions in Deep Psychotherapy: Part One

A CENTRAL THEME OF both my ongoing clinical and developmental studies dictates that the human brain and mind are in actuality a dual system. Toward that end, across all my writings I have been offering a continuous stream of clinical data and experimental research to show that the conscious mind resides in the left hemisphere, while the unconscious mind operating at levels beneath awareness resides in the right hemisphere (Schore, 1994, 2003a, 2003b, 2012). This hierarchical model traces back to the foundations of brain laterality research in the 19th century and to the origins of psychoanalysis in the early 20th century. It not only emphasizes the functional differences between the hemispheres but also models the relationships between the cerebral hemispheres, as well as the relationships between the conscious and unconscious minds.

Echoing the classic top-down and bottom-up conceptions of hemispheric dominance, the neurologist Guido Gainotti offered current empirical data showing that "the right hemisphere may subserve the lower 'schematic' level (where emotions are automatically generated and experienced as 'true emotions') and the left hemisphere the higher 'conceptual' level (where emotions are consciously analyzed and submitted to intentional control)" (2005, p. 71). However, more recent models emphasize the bottom-up and top-down roles of the "nondominant" right hemisphere. The neuropsychiatrist Iain McGilchrist cited a large body of studies indicating that "The right hemisphere both grounds our experience of the world at the bottom end, so to speak, and makes sense of it, at the top end," that this hemisphere is more in touch with both affect and the body, and that "neurological evidence supports what is called the primacy of affect and the primacy of unconscious over conscious will" (2015, p. 1591).

In my own work on socioemotional development, I have expanded this hierarchical model of hemispheric dominance, focusing on the central role of the early developing right brain in the unconscious generation of emotions and its enduring impact on unconscious and conscious functions in all later stages of human development. It is now well established that the emotional right hemisphere is dominant in human infancy, that unconscious processing of emotional information is mainly subsumed by a right hemisphere subcortical route, and that unconscious emotional memories are stored in the right hemisphere. Over the course of three decades, I have offered research and clinical evidence to demonstrate that the right hemisphere is the psychobiological substrate of the human unconscious mind. Applying laterality principles to models of psychopathogenesis and psychotherapeutic change, I continue to elaborate specifically how the right hemisphere stores implicit-procedural autobiographical memory of attachment trauma that occurred in the earliest stages of development (Schore, 2013, 2017a, 2017b).

In 2012, I described Krystal's (2002) seminal psychiatric work on "traumatic memories," where he points out that because the registration of the traumatic state is on a preverbal, sensorimotor level, no language is available for the presentation of the memory:

> Traumatic memories are not repressed in the ordinary sense of the word. Something worse happens to them. They are repudiated. . . . Some traumatic perceptions are not compatible with the survival of the self and are never registered consciously or in a form that is recoverable by any normal means; and these are the memories that cannot be remembered or forgotten. It is not just because the past involved enforced passivity, submission, and surrender, but because the *emotional regression to certain infantile forms of relatedness causes an evocation of the infantile and childhood trauma* encapsulated within their memories of the major trauma. (Krystal, 2002, p. 217, italics added)

This raises the clinical problem of regression, a shift of dominance from the later developing conscious left mind to the early developing right unconscious mind that stores strong and even overwhelming emotional memories. The traumatic memory is thus not remembered but relived and reenacted. In my past book, *The Science of the Art of Psychotherapy*, I offered a chapter titled "Therapeutic Enactments: Working in Right Brain Windows Affect Tolerance" in which I suggested that Krystal's "emotional regression" and "evocation" of infantile and childhood trauma occur not within a spoken objective verbal narrative between the patient and the therapist but within an intersubjective, nonverbal, bodily-based communication of an intense negatively charged affect and a sudden rupture of therapeutic alliance (Schore, 2012). In other words, an emotional regression occurs within a dysregulating reliving and reenactment of early relational attachment trauma. Yet in the same book, I discussed the classical psychoanalytic work of Reik (1948) and Kris (1952) on an adaptive creative "regression in the service of the ego," in order to propose that the therapist's interpersonal creativity within the mutual regression of a regulated reenactment of early developing attachment experiences can promote corrective emotional experiences. Note that regression can be maladaptive or adaptive.

In classic psychoanalytic writings, Arlow and Brenner asserted, "Regression is the re-emergence of modes of mental functioning which were characteristic of the psychic activity of the individual during earlier periods of development. It stresses the importance of maturational and developmental processes in shaping the form and function of the psychic apparatus" (1964, p. 71). These authors described the essential clinical characteristics of regression:

1. Regression is a universal tendency of mental functioning. To demonstrate this, they looked to Freud's description of the development of the mind: "Every earlier stage of development persists alongside the later stage which has arisen from it . . . the primitive stages can always be *re-established*; the primitive mind is, in the fullest meaning of the word, imperishable" (1915a/1957, p. 285, italics added). Indeed, regression is a characteristic of normal development of psychic structure (A. Freud, 1963), and accompanies each

advance toward a new level of mental functioning, and in this manner the past is always a potentially active element in mental life.

2. In regression, primitive forms of mental activity are persistent and exist "side-by-side" in the "background" with more "mature" later mental acquisitions that are "more dominant" and in the "foreground" of psychic life. (Note this description also applies to the relationship of the two cerebral hemispheres.) In fact, under appropriate conditions this regression is expressed in daydreaming (and dreaming) and may dominate the mental apparatus.

3. Most regressions are transient and reversible, as opposed to permanent, such as in adaptive regressions in the service of the ego. This ability to initiate regression of its own functions is in the furtherance of its interests. It implies a flexibility, an ability to employ more primitive modes of functioning in the service of its development. Thus, evidence of "controlled" regressive activity is seen in every individual at certain times, including humor, play, sexual relations, imagination, and creative activity in general, moments that "revive earlier forms of ego function" (Arlow & Brenner, 1964, p. 78).

4. Regressions are specific and unique, rather than global and total. They usually affect particular aspects of the personality, rather than the whole, and what functions they do affect are affected to different degrees.

According to the Oxford Dictionary, the term *primitive* is defined as pertaining to an early period or stage.

At the beginning of this century, Tuttman (2002) cited the *Oxford English Dictionary* definition of regression as the act of going back; a return to the place of origin; a previous state or condition. He proposed,

One implication of this definition concerns the undoing of progress, sometimes reflecting a possible deterioration. Yet there is a second possibility: *the return to fundamentals and origins that might facilitate a potential reorganization leading to better integration.* It seems paradoxical that we are dealing with a process often considered to be a central factor in the most serious psychopathology, and yet many acknowledge regression to be a most potent therapeutic possibility. (p. 468, italics added)

Expanding Tuttman's concept, I propose that this "going back" includes a return to functions and structures generated in early socioemotional development and the interpersonal origins of the right brain subjective self. The more current *New Shorter Oxford English Dictionary* defines regression as "The process of returning or a tendency to return to an earlier stage of development."

Furthermore, according to Giovacchini, "Regression implies that there are various levels and layers that are contained within the psychic apparatus. The regressive movements proceed from higher or later psychic levels, to earlier . . . more primitive ones" (1990, p. 228). A long tradition in neuroscience indicates that regression from "higher" to "lower" levels represents a "taking off of the higher" and "at the very same time a letting go, or expression of the lower." In 1994, I suggested that this "temporal regression," a "downward state shift," renews access to older memory stores of previous developmental stages (Schore, 1994). *In terms of developmental neuroscience, this specifically refers to a regression and release of "lower" right brain structures that first evolve in the prenatal and postnatal stages of early brain development—infancy-toddlerhood, the critical period for attachment formation—before later maturing "higher" left brain functions.* These transient regressions to psychic activities of earlier "preoedipal" periods of development are clinically manifest in moments of the reemergence of attachment and early forming transference-countertransference dynamics.

Thus, functional regressions reflect neurobiological structural regressions shifts in dominance between and within the two cerebral hemispheres:

- Regression temporally from the later developing, explicit left hemispheric, secondary process verbal cognitive functions of the conscious mind to the early developing, implicit right hemispheric, primary process nonverbal emotional-imagistic functions of the unconscious mind.
- Regression from conscious cognition to unconscious bodily-based affect; from later forming cortical to early maturing subcortical

systems; from the central nervous system (CNS) to the autonomic nervous system (ANS).

- Regression from a left brain mild/moderate surface emotion (anxiety, pleasure, anger) to a right brain strong deep emotion (e.g., terror, elation, intense love, rage, grief, and utter despair).
- Regression from later forming left brain-to-left brain conscious verbal communication to early forming right brain-to-right brain unconscious nonverbal emotional communication.
- Regression from the left brain conscious analytical mind to the right brain intuitive unconscious mind and bodily-based emotions: a shift in hemispheric dominance of the right hemisphere from the background into the foreground of psychic life.

To give some brief clinical applications, this adaptive transient regression allows empathic psychobiologically attuned psychotherapists to use their right hemisphere to intuitively listen to the patient's nonverbal bodily-based emotional communications (face, voice prosody, gesture) that appear in the first 2 years of life, before the verbal left hemisphere. As opposed to the classical psychodynamic approach of working with later metaphoric and symbolic functions of fully developed object relations and the repressed unconscious, we are now seeing a shift to a form of listening and interacting with the preverbal physiological expressions of the earliest unconscious levels of the personality. This type of deep listening to the early bodily-based unconscious requires a regression from the therapist's left mind to right mind. The clinician's adaptive regression from left brain-to-left brain verbal communication to right brain-to-right brain communication lies at the core of my therapeutic models of how a shift from analytical left to intuitive right brain allows for listening and responding to the psychophysiology of the unconscious.

In addition, a regressive shift from left brain rational to right brain intuitive cognition allows the clinician to perceptually receive what is outside conscious awareness, "beneath the words." In this state of mind, the therapist listens with the right brain reverie and intuition directly to the patient's right brain. This regression is familiar to clinicians, who access the state in order to generate clinical hunches and gists of the patient's communications. Hammer (1990) described a therapeutic mutual regression:

My mental posture, like my physical posture, is not one of leaning forward to catch the clues, but of leaning back to let the mood, the atmosphere, come to me—to hear the meaning between the lines, to listen for the music behind the words. As one *gives oneself to being carried along* by the affective cadence of the patient's session, one may sense its tone and subtleties. By being more *open* in this manner, to resonating to the patient, I find pictures forming in my creative zones; an image crystallizes, reflecting the patient's experience. I have had the sense, at such times, that at the moments when I would pick up some image of the patient's experience, *he was particularly ripe for receiving my perceptions, just as I was for receiving his.* An empathic channel appeared to be established which carried his state or emotion my way via a kind of affective "wireless." This channel, in turn, carried my image back to him, as he stood *open in a special kind of receptivity.* (pp. 99–100, italics added)

Note that right brain activity is expressed in affects, tone, and images, and that both therapist and patient are sharing a communication of an implicit creative state of "openness to experience" (McCrae & Costa, 1997), which is associated with creative ability (Carson, Peterson, & Higgins, 2005; King, Walker, & Broyles, 1996; Miller & Tal, 2007; Wolfradt & Pretz, 2001).

In the Jungian literature, Fordham (1993) characterized the open receptive state the therapist enters to process novel aspects of the patient's subjectivity and to spontaneously generate a clinical response to it:

You must look and listen to your patient as though you have never seen him before so you will not have any knowledge of him. In that way you will be open to him and be in the best position to experience his state of mind today. As you listen you will begin to experience [the patient's] mood and then have some thoughts or feelings, etc. about him. It is out of this that an intervention will arise. (pp. 637–638)

Poincaré (1908) underscored the efficiency of this unconscious process:

A first hypothesis presents itself: the subliminal self is in no way inferior to the conscious self; it is not purely automatic; it is capable of discernment; it has tact, delicacy; it knows how to choose, to divine. . . . It knows better how to divine than the conscious self, since it succeeds where that has failed. (qtd. in Hadamard, 1948, p. 23)

In classic writings, Carl Rogers (1957) proposed therapeutic change occurs when therapist and patient are in a special condition of receptivity to each other, outside of conscious awareness, when both are in "psychological contact":

The two people are to some degree in contact, that each makes some perceived difference in the experiential field of the other. Probably it is sufficient if each makes some "subceived" difference, even though the individual may not be consciously aware of this impact . . . but it is almost certain that at some organic level he does sense this difference. (p. 96)

In this regressed subconscious implicit open-receptive state, the empathic therapist accesses right brain wide-ranging "evenly suspended" attention (Schore, 2003b). The therapist can now receive and send emotional communications between the patient's and the therapist's right brains. Importantly, in order to co-create this intersubjective system with the patient, the therapist must implicitly *synchronize* their right hemispheres. As I will soon discuss, this right-lateralized interbrain synchronization of a spontaneous nonverbal communication is an essential mechanism of mutual regressions (see Figure 1.1 in Chapter 1, in which the right temporoparietal cortex in one partner is synchronized with the right temporoparietal cortex of the other). The right temporoparietal junction is known to be activated in social interactions and self-functions (Decety & Lamm, 2007) and is centrally involved in states of attention processing, perceptual awareness, face and voice processing, and empathy (Schore, 2003a, 2003b, 2012). It also allows for "making sense of another mind" (Saxe & Wexler, 2005).

With this introduction in mind, in this and the next chapter I will present an interpersonal neurobiological model of the growth-promoting role of
mutual regressions in long-term psychotherapy, not only in the patient's but
also in the clinician's own deeper psychotherapeutic explorations. These
transient mutual regressions allow for right-lateralized interbrain synchronizations between the empathic therapist and the patient and thereby a co-
constructed therapeutic right brain-to-right brain implicit communication
system. Over time, these transient mutual regressions from a conscious
regulated state into a reenacted unconscious dysregulated state (pathological regression) allow for an interactively regulated regression in the service
of the ego that can potentially promote a novel corrective emotional experience and repair of the right brain subjective self (adaptive regression).
In long-term psychotherapy, these neuroplastic changes in the patient's
right brain underlie the structural psychotherapeutic transformation of the
patient's unconscious attachment internal working model.

In addition, I will offer psychoanalytic descriptions of the subjectivity
of adaptive regressions from conscious secondary to unconscious primary
process and of the neuropsychoanalytic mechanisms that allow for interhemispheric left-right shifts in dominance into deeper levels of the right
brain unconscious. In heightened affective moments of the session when the
patient is experiencing a right brain emotional state, the psychobiologically
attuned therapist implicitly instantiates a regression, a "reversible dominance
of the left over the right hemisphere," and this "giving oneself to be carried
along" thereby lessens her own resistance to the left-to-right regression. Over
time the creative clinician, sensitive to even low levels of the patient's shifts
into and out of affective states, learns how to fluidly synchronize this shift in
hemispheric dominance with the patient shifts. This allows for the communication and regulation of not just conscious but also unconscious affects.

Another major goal of this expansion of regulation theory (Hill, 2015;
Rass, 2018; Schore, 1994, 2003a, 2003b, 2012) is to explicate the differential
roles of the character defenses of dissociation and repression in working
with regressions in growth-promoting psychotherapy. Integrating a large
body of astute clinical observations from a long-standing tradition of long-
term depth psychotherapy with current advances in interpersonal neurobiology and psychotherapy research, I will offer an evidence-based model for

working with the defensive coping strategies embedded in clinical regressions, especially those involving unconscious dissociated affect in spontaneous mutual regressions and unconscious repressed affect in voluntary mutual regressions. In parallel, I will also elaborate the unconscious neuropsychoanalytic processes that are expressed in these regressions. Toward that end, I will focus on the critical role of regressions in two classical psychoanalytic literatures, object relations theory and ego psychology. With respect to the latter, I will discuss the neurobiological mechanisms that underlie the ego psychological construct of regression in the service of the ego, a primal generator of creativity, defined as the production of an idea that is both novel and useful in a particular social setting (Schore, 2012, 2017c). Indeed, a large body of research indicates that right brain processes are essential to creativity (e.g., Aberg, Doell, & Schwartz, 2017; Asari et al., 2008; Chavez-Eakle et al., 2007; Mihov, Denzler, & Forster, 2010; Wan, Cruts, & Jensen, 2014).

In the middle of the past century, Guilford (1957) posited that when coupled with originality, flexibility of thought allows a creative individual to *respond efficiently and effectively to a constantly changing and regularly challenging environment.* In later groundbreaking neuropsychological split-brain research, J. Bogen and G. Bogen concluded that the right brain is the seat of creativity, and that "*creativity* has not only made the human experience unique in Nature . . . it *gives value and purpose to human experience*" (1969). Consonant with this, in the clinical literature of the same period, Carl Rogers defined creativity as "the emergence in action of a novel relational product, growing out of the uniqueness of the individual on the one hand, and the materials, events, people or circumstances of his life on the other" (1954, p. 251). He gives examples such as painting a picture, composing a symphony, developing a scientific theory, or "*discovering new forms of human relationship.*" These three outcomes of creativity are, of course, major goals of growth-promoting psychotherapy.

More recently, Horner observed that "in the best of treatment situations, the creative minds of both the patient and the therapist may join to enhance the process" (2006, p. 468). In line with the current two-person, relational trend in psychotherapy, this clearly implies moving the construct from an intrapsychic to an interpersonal construct, "interpersonal creativity." Note the relational construct of *interpersonal creativity* refers to the adaptive use of creativity in synchronized interpersonal relationships, and therefore in relatively effective emotional communication and efficient interactive affect regulation. Along with Giovacchini, I agree that "many personalities, particularly writers and artists, have been known to have suffered from severe psychopathologies, but it is unlikely that those parts of their personalities are involved in creative endeavor" (1991, p. 175). Thus a well-integrated personality is fundamental to interpersonal creativity. "Interpersonal creativity" will thus be a subtheme of this study of *mutual synchronized regressions, growth-promoting therapeutic mechanisms that can lead to progressions in the structural and functional complexity of emotional and social development.* These regressions that facilitate progressions in the therapy underlie the well-established clinical principle that the trajectory of the therapy is not a straight line, but nonlinear—movements both forward and backward, which not infrequently feels like "stumbling along together."

Here, as in all my work, I continue to use the term "regulation theory" in order to denote explicitly that what I am offering is a theory, a systematic exposition of the general principles of a science. The power, coherence, and scope of the theory is expressed in its ability to formulate testable hypotheses and generate research and to create explanatory mechanisms that apply to various aspects and levels of human functioning, including in the clinical context. In my writings, I continue to propose that the neuroscience of the right brain and the neuropsychoanalysis of the unconscious mind is an integrating force across different domains of psychoanalysis. Toward that end, the following discussions of the right-lateralized unconscious mind and its relationship to the left-lateralized conscious mind offer both a neurobiologically informed model of psychodynamic psychotherapy and a psychodynamic model of neuropsychoanalysis. I continue to use the device of frequently citing verbatim the current and past voices of master clinicians studying the mind and neuroscientists studying the brain in order to demonstrate their agreement on the centrality of bodily-based affective phenomena and to generate a common language that addresses the subjective emotional realm. That said, my intention here is to specifically describe the changes in the patient's and therapist's unconscious right minds over the course of the treatment, beneath and beyond the verbal narratives. This chapter thus reflects my ongoing efforts to provide a general, unified theory of Freud's psychoanalysis, "the science of the unconscious mind."

PSYCHOANALYTIC CONCEPTUALIZATIONS
OF ADAPTIVE AND PATHOLOGICAL REGRESSIONS

In classic studies in psychoanalytic ego psychology, Kris (1952) proposed that regression in the service of the ego underpinned not only artistic and therapeutic creativity but also other essential adaptive human functions, including fantasy, imagination, and the appreciation of wit and humor. He postulated that the creative person is adept at regression in the service of the ego, in shifting from secondary process (rational, ordered, reality-oriented, purposeful, conscious) thinking to primary process (free-associated, disordered, reverie-like, unconscious) thinking. Primary process cognition and primitive modes of thought act to increase the probability of novel ideas, which are subsequently elaborated at secondary process levels. Kris defined regression in the service of the ego as "a partial, temporary, controlled lowering of the level of psychic functioning" in which the ego permits relatively free play to the primary process in order to accomplish its adaptive tasks. Another pioneer in ego psychology, Hartmann (1958) called it "adaptive regression," and along with Kris conceptualized the regression as a *step going backward*—from secondary process to primary thinking—*in order to be able to go two steps forward*. Furthermore, Kris elaborated two phases of this regression: an inceptive *inspirational phase* in which the unconscious and preconscious primary-process ideation surge into attention and goal-directed thinking is at a minimum, and a subsequent *elaborational* phase in which the inspirational processes are subjected to critical scrutiny and revised into secondary process ideation. He further suggested that in the psychotherapeutic context of this regression, the barriers separating unconscious from preconscious or conscious processes have been loosened.

In parallel contemporary psychoanalytic studies, Reik (1948) emphasized the preconscious-unconscious primary process functions of the creative therapist. His book *Listening with the Third Ear* (1953) posited an unconscious process by which the analyst detects and deciphers clues to the patient's unconscious dynamics: the so-called "third ear." This material is of a nonverbal, melodic character that expresses the affective nuances of unconscious mentation. Reik viewed this primary process as a level of mentation in which "sounds, fleeting images, organic sensations, and emotional currents are not yet differentiated" (1956, p. 9). He also postulated that creative individuals are more capable of shifting between secondary and primary modes of thinking, or to "regress" to primary process cognition, which is necessary for producing novel, original ideas. Although secondary processes are abstract and analytical, primary process cognition refers to states such as dreaming or reverie, but also to abnormal states observed in individuals suffering from mental disorders.

Applying his model clinically, he suggested: "If the analyst surrenders to the regression required to access an uncanny insight, a conscious intuition into the patient's dynamics emerges" (Reik, 1949, p. 329). Thus, since insight originates in the unconscious, then the only way to reach it is through some degree of regression to the primary process. That said, Reik observed: "As rational consciousness gives way to the primary process, it may feel as if 'the ground' is threatening 'to slip away'" (1956, p. 492). Yet it is essential that transient regressions be tolerated, as a rigidly rational consciousness will stifle nonrational hunches. As Reik puts it, "you have to mistrust sweet reason and to abandon yourself to the promptings and suggestions emerging from the unconscious. You will even let the seemingly fanciful and irrational enter your thoughts" (1956, p. 481). Indeed, Reik warned that in therapy, creative insight can be displaced by technical machinations.

Thus both Kris and Reik defined regression in terms of a shift from secondary to primary process cognition. Recall in *The Interpretation of Dreams*, Freud (1900/1953) stated that primary process functions that are highly visual, tactile, and auditory develop in an early stage before secondary processes, which "only take shape gradually during the course of life, inhibiting and overlaying the primary [processes]." In my first book, I cited psychoanalytic and split-brain research showing that primary process is associated with functions of early developing right hemisphere, secondary process with later developing left hemisphere (Schore, 1994).

In a modern reexamination of the ego psychological concept of regression in the service of the ego, Knafo (2002) cited Kris's contrast between "an ego overwhelmed by regression" and a "regression in the service of the ego." The latter form, according to Kris, is only a special case of the more general capacity of a well-integrated ego to regulate and control some of the primary processes. Kris stated that in the moments of a regression in the service of the ego, a well-integrated individual who regresses has the capacity to regulate and utilize some of the primary process creatively. Knafo thus concluded, "There exists a difference between pathological and healthy, or adaptive, regression. . . . If the move backward can open doors, why should it be viewed in pejorative terms? Yes, it is risky; but new and original ideas are not born without risk" (2002, p. 40).

At present, there is currently a paradigm shift in the construct of regression, just as with the related concepts of trauma and clinical reenactments (Schore, 2012). Over most of the past century, the classical psychoanalytic position viewed regression in pejorative terms: "pathological regression." In mid-century, Winnicott (1958a) dealt with this issue head-on:

> It is commonly thought that there is some danger in the regression of a patient during psychoanalysis. The danger does not lie in the regression but in the analyst's unreadiness to meet the regression and the dependence which belongs to it. *When an analyst has had experience that makes him confident in his management of regression,* then it is probably true to say that the more quickly the analyst accepts the regression and meets it fully the less likely is it that the patient will need to enter into an illness with regressive qualities. (p. 261, italics added)

Articulating the idea of coupling regressive and progressive forces in these clinical processes, Winnicott observed "there is an expectation that favourable conditions may arise justifying regression and offering a new chance for forward development, that which was rendered impossible or difficult initially by environmental failure" (1955, p. 18).

In his 1968 classic *The Basic Fault,* Michael Balint pointed out that Freud and Ferenczi agreed that "regression during analytic treatment was considered a dangerous symptom and its value therapeutically completely, or almost completely repressed . . . it was a mechanism of defence difficult to tackle, it was an important factor in pathogenesis, and it was a formidable form of resistance" (1968, p. 153). In addition to studying the dangers of malignant regressions that "overwhelm the ego," Balint (1968) also emphasized the value of benign regressions, suggesting these are beneficial when the clinician provides an accepting atmosphere in which the patient feels safe enough to regress "for the sake of recognition" and "understanding and shared experiencing." This regression work involves encounters with emotional pain that triggers primitive psychological defenses that expose "a basic fault" or (dissociative) "gaps." Thus almost 50 years ago, Balint, with remarkable foresight, was exploring clinical regression in terms of a therapeutic regressive process occurring in a two-person therapeutic relationship. Based on his extensive clinical work, he described the "benign" form of regression as a therapeutic context of "a new beginning."

At the beginning of this century, Tuttman asserted:

> The skillful acceptance of regression to the traumatic developmental phases where something needed for growth was missing, and then facilitating understanding and growth from that point forward, via an analytical relationship that has transitional, mirroring, nonautocratic, and synthetic qualities along with play and experimentation, are necessary steps in such treatment if healthy individuation is to occur. (2002, pp. 469–470)

Note this clinical conception is consonant with regulation theory's formulation that both maladaptive "malignant" and adaptive "benign" forms of regression reflect a return to respectively dysregulated and regulated emotional events of an earlier stage of development. In updated clinical models, regressions within mutual reenactments represent "traumatic repetitions" as well as "new beginnings," and thereby a context for the expression of the right brain creative processing of novelty and a corrective emotional experience. These most difficult moments of the treatment also represent important opportunities for therapeutic change.

NEUROPSYCHOANALYSIS OF TOPOGRAPHICAL
AND STRUCTURAL REGRESSIONS

So far, I have referred to both regressions of mind and of brain. In fact, the earliest ideas about regression came not from psychoanalysis but from neurology. In 1884, John Hughlings Jackson, the father of British neurology, proposed that disorders of the nervous system initially affect the portion of the system with the most recently evolved functions and only later affect the older functions. In this hierarchical model, an evolving higher level of functioning supplanted and inhibited lower levels, which are more automatic and more organized. In the *Interpretation of Dreams*, Freud (1900/1953) incorporated Jackson's hierarchical concept of higher levels inhibiting lower levels of function into both his topographical model of stratified conscious, preconscious, and unconscious systems, and his later structural model (Freud, 1923/1953) of a superego and ego that sit astride the id. These models describe two different mechanisms of regression. Thus, the clinical term of functional psychological regression was derived from neurology's concept of biological regressions within the brain.

In terms of the sequence of neurobiological maturation, note in Figure 3.1 that the brain evolves in a caudal to rostral direction, subcortical to cortical, with the brain stem autonomic and arousal structures maturing earliest, then the emotion-processing limbic system, then the earlier maturing right hemisphere, and lastly the verbal functions of the left hemisphere. This translates into an early evolution of the deep unconscious, then to the unconscious, then preconscious, and finally the higher levels of the conscious mind. In earlier work, I suggested that the deep unconscious represents activity of the subcortical amygdala, unconscious and the anterior cingulate medial frontal system, and the preconscious represents activity of the right orbitofrontal corticolimbic system (Schore, 2003b).

The dual brain, dual mind systems shift from conscious to unconscious functions via the mechanism of regression. A modern neuropsychoanalytic translation of Freud's metapsychological model describes two differ-

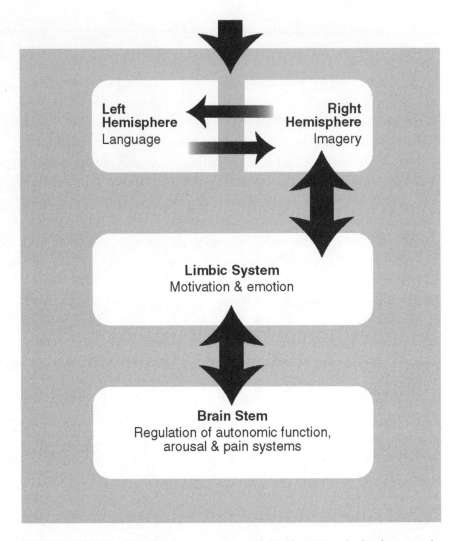

FIGURE 3.1 Unconscious implicit processing of the "lower," early developing right brain and subsequent connections into the "higher," later developing left brain conscious explicit system. Note the vertical axis of the right brain on the right side of the figure. From *The Science of the Art of Psychotherapy*, pg. 82, by Allan N. Schore (2012).

ent mechanisms of regression from the later forming conscious mind to the earlier evolving unconscious right mind. In this hierarchical model, an evolving higher level of functioning supplants and inhibits lower levels, which are more automatic and more organized. *Reversing the sequence in*

Figure 3.1, regression from "higher" to "lower" functional levels represents a *"taking off of the higher"* and *"at the very same time a letting go, or expression of the lower."*

In a further reformulation of Freud's concept of regression, I propose two types of neurobiological regressions: an interhemispheric *topographical* form (a horizontal state switch from conscious left prefrontal cortical to preconscious right prefrontal cortical system), and an intrahemispheric *structural* regression (a vertical hierarchical state switch from higher to lower right brain, downward cortical to subcortical, from preconscious to deeper unconscious levels of the right brain; see the horizontal and vertical arrows in Figure 3.1). A topographical regression thus represents an intrapsychic shift from the later developing conscious "left mind" to the earlier developing unconscious "right mind." In contrast, a structural regression represents a shift from "higher right" to "lower right" levels of emotion-processing unconscious mind.

This neuropsychoanalytic conceptualization of an integration of Freud's topographical and structural models dictates a hierarchical organization of the conscious, preconscious, and unconscious minds. Freud's tripartite taxonomy of a conscious, preconscious, and subliminal unconscious is now reappearing in the scientific literature (Dehaene et al., 2006). In my neuropsychoanalytic models, I am describing a left-lateralized conscious mind and a right cortical preconscious mind behind the left cortical surface mind that is accessed via a shift in hemispheric dominance in a topographical regression. And another mind beneath conscious awareness, the bodily-based unconscious–deep unconscious mind, is accessed via a structural regression. With respect to "horizontal" topographical regressions, Kane (2004) states that the shift in hemispheric dominance in a creative moment of a regression in the service of the ego involves a callosal disinhibition, "a sudden and transient loss or decrease of normal interhemispheric communication, removing inhibitions placed upon the right hemisphere." In the clinical literature, J. Sandler and A. M. Sandler (1986) define regression as "a process of release and disinhibition of past modes of functioning."

This updated integration of Freud's topographic and structural models also can be represented in a neurobiological update of Freud's iceberg

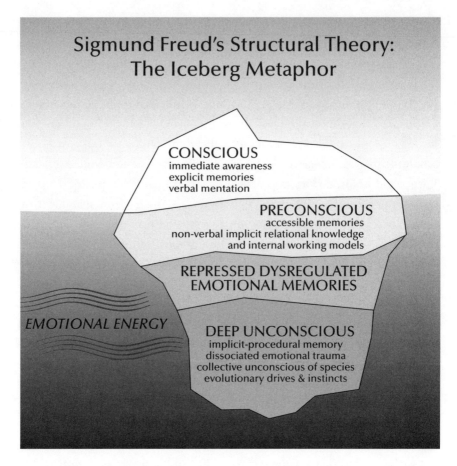

FIGURE 3.2 Revised update of Freud's iceberg metaphor.

visual metaphor (Figure 3.2). The model incorporates the previous discussions of repression, dissociation, internal working models, and implicit functions of the right-lateralized unconscious system.

Why are left brain-to-right brain callosal shifts of hemispheric dominance so essential? Recall Gainotti's (2005) assertion that the "lower" level of the right hemisphere automatically generates experienced "true emotions," while the "higher" level of the left hemisphere consciously analyzes emotions and submits them to *intentional control*. In the journal *Psychosomatic Medicine,* Lane (2008) concludes,

Primary emotional responses have been preserved through phylogenesis because they are adaptive. They provide an immediate assessment of the extent to which goals or needs are being met in interaction with the environment, and they reset the organism behaviorally, physiologically, cognitively, and experientially to adjust to these changing circumstances. (p. 225)

Hartikainen and colleagues (2007) summarize the critical role of nonconscious emotion processing in human survival:

In unpredictable environments, emotions provide rapid modulation of behavior. From an evolutionary perspective, emotions provide a modulatory control system that facilitates survival and reproduction. Reflex-like reactions to emotional events can occur before attention is paid to them. . . . Neuropsychological evidence supports a right hemispheric bias for emotional and attentional processing in humans. (p. 1929)

In order to directly enter into this adaptive right-hemispheric realm, the emotionally focused therapist instantiates, at levels beneath awareness of the conscious left mind, an inversion of hemispheric dominance.

Indeed, this hemispheric left-right shift is described by clinicians. According to Heinz Kohut, "The deeper layers of the analyst's psyche are open to the stimuli which emanate from the patient's communications while the intellectual activities of the higher levels of cognition are temporarily largely but selectively *suspended*." (1971, p. 274, italics added). In the words of Carl Rogers (1989),

As a therapist, I find that when I am closest to my inner, intuitive self, when I am somehow in touch with the unknown in me, when perhaps I am in a slightly altered state of consciousness in the relationship, then whatever I do seems full of meaning. Then simply my *presence* is releasing and helpful. There is nothing I can do to force this experience, but when I can relax and be close to the transcen-

> dental core of me, then I behave . . . in ways that I cannot justify
> rationally, which have nothing to do with my thought processes. But
> these strange behaviors turn out to be *right*, in some odd way. At
> those moments . . . our relationship transcends itself and becomes
> something larger. (p. 137, italics in original)

This shift into the right allows the empathic, intuitive therapist to synchronize her regression with the patient's, and thus form a system of mutual topographical regression and right brain state-sharing. As a result of the right-lateralized interbrain synchronization, both can now co-create a right brain-to-right brain system of nonverbal communication that can send and receive face-to-face unconscious emotional communications (gesture, implicit face, voice) from the subjective self to another subjective self (intersubjectivity). In current clinical writings, Bromberg asserted, "Allan Schore writes about a right brain-to-right brain channel of affective communication . . . as 'an organized dialogue' comprised of 'dynamically fluctuating moment-to-moment state sharing.' I believe it to be this process of state sharing that allows 'a good psychoanalytic match.'" (2011, p. 169). More recently he states, "The interface between my own thinking and his, when linked to the centrality we each place of the mind–brain–body interface, provides the core context that I believe will allow psychoanalysis as psychotherapy to become most genuinely therapeutic" (2017, p. 7).

Mutual topographical regressions, although unconscious, are ubiquitous in all but especially relational, affectively focused psychotherapies. In synchronized left-right shifts, each switches out of the conscious verbal left mind into nonverbal affects and images of the preconscious mind. These events, outside conscious awareness, allow the therapist's right mind to affectively empathize, synchronize, and intersubjectively resonate with the dysregulated or regulated subjective states of the patient's right mind. This synchronization of the therapist's and the patient's right temporoparietal junction (see Figure 1.1 in Chapter 1) is associated with an affective theory of mind that allows the individual to attribute unobservable mental events to others and to self (Saxe & Wexler, 2005), as well as affective empathy

(Decety & Lamm, 2007). This contrasts with cognitive empathy, an intellectual understanding of the patient's state, which represents a synchronization of the therapist's and patient's analytic left minds. In this type of work, both are staying up in the rational left, with no regression down into the intuitive right.

Structural regressions, in contrast, induce a vertical shift from the higher preconscious to deeper unconscious levels of the right brain. This intrapsychic regression can be regulated or dysregulated, adaptive or pathological. But when the empathically resonating therapist remains psychobiologically connected to the patient and implicitly synchronizes with her dysregulating state, synchronized mutual structural regressions facilitate co-creation of an unconscious communication system that can detect and interactively regulate strong unconscious dissociated and unconscious repressed affects. Neuroscience documents "right hemispheric dominance in processing of unconscious negative emotion" (Sato & Aoki, 2006) and "cortical response to subjectively unconscious danger" (Carretie et al., 2005). These interpersonal synchronized mutual regressions of unconscious dissociated affects are activated in therapeutic reenactments of attachment trauma.

In line with a current relational two-person model of psychotherapeutic change, this updated model of Freud's concept of regression reconceptualizes the phenomenon from a solely intrapsychic structural regression to an interpersonal mutual regression whereby both members of the therapeutic dyad experience a synchronized interactively regulated regression, thereby potentially transmuting a pathological regression into an adaptive regression. Mutual topographical regressions facilitate interbrain synchronizations of horizontal right-lateralized cortical-cortical circuits, while mutual structural regressions facilitate interbrain synchronizations of vertical right-lateralized cortical-subcortical limbic autonomic circuits. Both topographical and structural regressions can be rapidly synchronized in milliseconds, at levels beneath conscious awareness, in the intersubjective context of spontaneous emotional communications between the relational unconscious of one individual and the relational unconscious of another. Recent advances in neuropsychoanalysis, the science of unconscious processes, thus describe a "two-person unconscious" (Lyons-Ruth, 1999), a relational unconscious that not only communicates with but also synchronizes and is expanded by another relational unconscious.

These experimental, theoretical, and clinical studies of synchronized mutual regressions elucidate the deeper mechanisms of the invisible, omnipresent unconscious in everyday life and thereby validate and expand upon Freud's enduring and fundamental contribution to science. Regression, "the act of going back; a return to the place of origin," "the process of returning or a tendency to return to an earlier stage of development," needs to be reintegrated into the clinical literature, not solely as an intrapersonal solitary regression but also as an interpersonal mutual regression. The synchronized shifts in hemispheric dominance of the patient and the therapist from the later maturing left-hemispheric into the early developing right-hemispheric "origin of the self" allow for a return to fundamentals and origins that can facilitate a potential reorganization leading to better integration and therefore a creative "new beginning."

The neuropsychoanalysis of left-to-right shifts of hemispheric dominance describes the adaptive role of regressions in facilitating entrance into an earlier stage of development, when only the unconscious mind was (and continues to be) operative. The developmental scholar Ellen Dissanayake (2001) reflects on this continuity of the early developing unconscious mind over all later developmental stages:

> [W]e tend to assume that analytic, abstract, verbalized cognition is dominant. Certainly for scientific and academic investigation and communication it is essential. But *we forget, at our peril, how much of our thinking and communication is imbued with analogical, unverbalizable, unconscious content* . . . our original analogical, nonverbal, intersubjective mind persists after infancy, but it is usually consciously *overridden* by 'cognition' and language (which are necessarily coupled to the real world) so that we are generally unaware of it (pp. 95-96, italics added).

Regressions transiently reverse the left hemispheric overriding of the right hemispheric unconscious mind, allowing us to enter into an awareness of our own intersubjective mind not through controlled voluntary action but by "letting go" of control.

CLINICAL APPLICATIONS OF MUTUAL REGRESSIONS: WORKING WITH DISSOCIATED AFFECT IN SPONTANEOUS REENACTMENTS OF EARLY ATTACHMENT TRAUMA

Recall Kris's healthy regression in the service of the ego and Balint's benign regression describe the output of an adaptive regulated right brain system. Schafer (1958) suggested that regression in the service of the ego applies to scientific and artistic creativity, but also to interpersonal relations, such as empathy, intimacy, and communication. However, the patient who experiences pathological regression and traumatic reenactments in response to even mild to moderate relational stressors seeks therapy because of frequent painful states of affect dysregulation, a failure of integration of mental life, and chronic interpersonal difficulties. These therapeutic reenactments are more common in severe psychopathologic individuals who show histories of early attachment trauma. Borgogno and Vigna-Taglianti (2008) observe,

> In patients whose psychic suffering originates in . . . preverbal trauma . . . transference occurs mostly at a more primitive level of expression that involves in an unconscious way . . . not only the patient but also the [therapist]. . . . These more archaic forms of the transference-countertransference issue—which frequently set aside verbal contents—take shape in the [therapeutic] setting through actual mutual enactments. (p. 314)

Bromberg (2011) articulated the clinical principle that therapeutic joint processing of enactments allows therapists to use their expertise with a wide spectrum of personality disorders often considered "unanalyzable," such as schizoid, narcissistic, dissociative, and borderline personality disorders. According to Sullivan (1953), personality is "the relative enduring pattern of recurrent interpersonal situations which characterize a human life," and so such patients display chronic deficits in their right brain interpersonal functions both outside and inside the therapy.

As a result of chronic relational trauma in infancy and toddlerhood, these early forming severe personality disorders do not attain an efficient right brain system of emotional communication or affect regulation. Indeed, individuals suffering from borderline personality disorder lack internal affect regulatory mechanisms—self-soothing introjects that perform self-consoling and regulatory functions during emotional upheaval (Weinberg, 2000). They also fail to develop a "reflective self" that can take into account one's own and others' mental states, as well as affective empathy, achievements that are essential steps in emotional development. In the clinical context, they frequently access dissociation, a state of mind characterized by a break in the continuity of conscious experience, one associated with detachment, loss of ability for self-monitoring, and emotional blunting (Weinberg, 2000). Thus, such personalities do not developmentally attain a psychic organization that can generate complex symbolic representations of self and other.

Until recently, because of the "primitive" organization of their regulatory structures, these patients were seen to be unable to use cognitive insight and were therefore refractory to "the talking cure." They were also characterized as "difficult patients" because of the not infrequent expressions of dysregulated pathological regressions within the therapy. These spontaneous therapeutic regressions were seen as endogenous expressions of the patient's severe psychopathology. Over the course of my writings, I have offered clinical and research evidence to show that the etiology and developmental traumatology of pathological regressions is associated with early relational trauma. This early, growth-inhibiting socioemotional environment induced severe arousal dysregulations and little interactive repair of frequent traumatic attachment ruptures.

In 1997, I applied the construct of relational trauma to the treatment context. In certain heightened affective moments of the therapy, interpersonal stressors within the transference-countertransference relationship rupture the attachment bond between patient and therapist. This sudden shattering of the therapeutic alliance induces the entrance into consciousness of a chaotic state associated with early traumatic experiences that are stored in implicit procedural memory. I further concluded, "This dialectical mechanism is especially prominent during stressful ruptures of the working alliance that occur during enactments" (Schore, 1997, p. 48).

Psychotherapeutic reenactments of chronic attachment trauma in emotional regressions are expressions of insecure (especially disorganized) working models of attachment that encode unconscious, negatively valenced internal representations of a dysregulated self interacting with a misattuning other as well as defenses against intense painful affect. These are stored in the patient's right brain autobiographical implicit-procedural memory that encodes strategies of affect regulation, including the bottom-line defense against consciously reexperiencing early relational trauma: dissociation (Schore, 2003b). Kalsched described operations of defensive dissociative processes used by the child during a traumatic experience by which "affect in the body is severed from its corresponding images in the mind and thereby an unbearably painful meaning is obliterated" (2005, p. 174). Lane and colleagues (1997) described the defensive function of dissociation in later stages: traumatic stress in childhood leads to self-modulation of painful affect by directing attention away from internal emotional states. The right hemisphere is dominant not only for regulating affects but also for maintaining a coherent sense of one's body, for attention, and for pain processing. And so the right brain strategy of dissociation represents the ultimate defense for blocking emotional bodily-based pain (Schore, 2012).

That said, the characterological use of defensive dissociation comes at a considerable cost. Dissociation is a complex psychobiological process that disrupts the integration of affective, sensory, perceptual, conceptual, and behavioral information and is characterized by a depleted awareness of one's internal state and external environment (Spiegel & Cardena, 1990). Helton, Dorahy, and Russell reported that high dissociators have difficulty in coordinating activity within the right hemisphere, and that such deficits become evident when this hemisphere is "loaded with the combined effects of a sustained attention task and negative emotional stimuli. . . . Thus, the integration of experiences, which rely heavily on right hemispheric activation (e.g., negative emotion, sense of self with reference to the experience) may be compromised in high dissociators leading to dissociative (non-integrated) memory encoding, and therefore later intrusive dissociative phenomena" (2011, p. 700). Spitzer and his colleagues reported that "dissociation may involve a functional superiority of the left hemisphere over the right hemisphere or, alternatively, a lack of an integration in the right hemisphere. This corresponds with the idea that the right hemisphere has a distinct role in establishing, maintaining, and processing personally relevant aspects of an individual's world" (2004, p. 167). Note that while dissociating the patient's right hemisphere is dis-integrating and directing attention away from anticipated emotional pain, the left hemisphere functions may continue to operate in "state of detachment." In moments when the patient's right brain is deflecting attention away from emotional states and from the external environment, his left-lateralized verbal output may continue, but in a detached tone (loss of right-hemispheric prosody). This underscores the clinical importance of reading "beneath the words."

Indeed, a large body of clinically relevant laterality studies now exists on dissociation. According to Enriquez and Bernabeu, "dissociation is associated with dysfunctional changes in the right hemisphere which impair its characteristic dominance over emotional processing" (2008, pp. 272–273). These researchers document that although high dissociators retain an ability for processing left-hemispheric verbal stimuli, they show deficits in right-hemispheric perception of the emotional tone of voice (prosody). This means that while the patient is dissociating, he cannot read the tone of the therapist's voice and is therefore deaf to a comforting tone. Using functional magnetic resonance imaging (fMRI), Elzinga and colleagues (2007, p. 235) documented that dissociative patients showed more activation particularly in the left anterior prefrontal cortex (area 10), dorsolateral prefrontal cortex (areas 9, 46), and parietal cortex (area 40). They point out that the left dorsolateral prefrontal cortex (DLPFC) is associated with verbal working memory, a limited capacity system that provides temporary maintenance and manipulation of information necessary to execute complex tasks. Note the increased activation of the DLPFC, the executive regulator of the left hemisphere in dissociation:

> Dissociative patients may be characterized by *strong executive control capacities*, thereby inhibiting the processing of trauma-related memories . . . this may take place at the expense of other functions that require attention, however, such as a sense of personal iden-

tity, inducing feelings of depersonalization and derealization, as is suggested by the enhanced state dissociation scores and the clinical observations of the dissociative patients when leaving the scanner [some patients, for example, were not able to recognize the experimenter, or assumed (incorrectly) that they had not been performing the task]. (Elzinga et al., 2007, p. 243, italics added)

In light of the fact that verbal interpretations directly impact the left DLPFC, these data raise the question whether the therapeutic intervention of cognitive reappraisal increases left-lateralized dissociation of right brain functions?

Bromberg (2011) asserted that the function of pathological dissociation is to act as an "early warning system" that anticipates potential affect dysregulation by trauma *before it arrives*. These overcontrolling yet fragile personalities use the affect-deadening defense of dissociation that defends against an anticipated pathological regression of affect regulation. The passive avoidance of relational threat and implicit deficit in processing interpersonal novelty occurs at an unconscious level. These patients characterologically automatically trigger intense right brain stress responses at low thresholds of relational stress, frequently experience enduring states of high-intensity negative affect, and defensively dissociate to threat or novelty at lower levels of arousal, thereby interfering with access to interpersonal creativity. This brittle defensive structure too frequently fragments under stress, leading to a reexperiencing of the affective and interpersonal deficits of a "pathological," "malignant" regression. This chronic dysregulating interpersonal neurobiological mechanism underlies what used to be called a traumatic "repetition compulsion." The resulting disorganization in turn increases the individual's affective symptomatology, which brings the patient into psychotherapy. Within the therapeutic relationship, both pathological and adaptive regressions may occur within regulated clinical reenactments of attachment trauma.

SYNCHRONIZED MUTUAL REGRESSIONS
WITHIN THERAPEUTIC ENACTMENTS

The psychotherapy of early relational trauma takes two forms: short-term, symptom reduction/remission, and long-term, growth-promoting treatment of deep psychotherapy. Only the latter can alter the underlying right brain dynamics that drive the affect dysregulation and interpersonal deficits of pathological regression and directly reduce the dissociative defense. The basic clinical principles I outline here refer to both forms of trauma treatment (see Chapter 5 in Schore, 2012). In this work, the clinical focus is not on an explicit reconstruction of an infantile attachment traumatic context but on the effects of early relational trauma on "character structure" and deficits in adaptive right brain functions. Bromberg pointed out that in the treatment, "accessing early trauma is, at heart, personally relational: It does not free patients from what was done to them in the past, but from what they have had to do to themselves and to others in order to live with what was done to them in the past" (2017, p. 32).

Meares (2017) observed that in the developmental histories of various personality disorders,

> The self has been damaged, distorted, and stunted by trauma. In the case of relational trauma, at least, it must be the primary concern of the therapist. Such trauma is not approached by strategies, techniques, interpretations, and so forth, dictated by the agenda of a particular theory. Rather, it is through the establishment of a specific kind of relationship, which is not artificially imposed or manipulated but is allowed to emerge in conversational interplay. (p. 138)

He refers to "a form of therapeutic conversation that can be conceived . . . as a dynamic interplay between two right hemispheres" (2012, p. 315).

Meares's "right brain conversation" is specifically activated in a mutual regression of a traumatic reenactment. This therapeutic conversation related to the (re) processing of early relational trauma, including the patient's own dissociative defenses against such self-awareness, is communicated not verbally, but nonverbally. Dissociation is accessed to blot out the re-evocation of intensely painful right brain autobiographical memories, and so this affect deadening defense is frequently accompanied by left brain cognitive detachment. This means the therapist's contributions to the nonverbal conversation must transiently shift from left to right cerebral dominance, thereby facilitating a shift in the ability to receive what lies beneath the patient's dissociation.

At the beginning of the last century, Sandor Ferenczi (1932), the first of Freud's disciples to formulate groundbreaking therapeutic principles of the treatment of trauma, described the importance of mutual regressions and shifts in the therapist's state:

> It appears that patients cannot believe that a [traumatic] event really took place, or cannot fully believe it, if the analyst, as the sole witness of the events, persists in his cool, unemotional, and as patients are fond of stating, purely intellectual attitude, while the events are of a kind that must evoke, in anyone present, emotions of revulsion, anxiety, terror, vengeance, grief, and the urge to render immediate help. . . . One therefore has a choice: to take really seriously the role one assumes, of the benevolent and helpful observer, that is, *actually to transport oneself with the patient into that period of the past* (a practice Freud reproached me for, as being not permissible), with the result that we ourselves and the patient believe in its reality, which has not momentarily transposed into the past. (Ferenczi, 1932, p. 24, italics added).

In order to promote changes in the patient's subjective, affect regulatory, and relational deficits he concluded, "an abreaction of quantities of trauma is not enough; the situation must be different from the actually traumatic one in order to make possible a different, favorable outcome" (Ferenczi, 1932, p. 108).

McWilliams (2018) offers an evocative description of the object relational emotional change mechanisms that are activated in an optimal therapeutic context, one that can produce *new learnings in the unconscious system*:

Although analytic therapists hope to be ultimately assimilated by their patients as "new objects"—that is, as internal voices that differ significantly from those of people by whom their clients have felt damaged—they appreciate the fact that, because of the stability and tenacity of unconscious assumptions, they will inevitably be experienced as old ones. They consequently expect to absorb strong negative affects associated with painful early experiences and help the client understand such reactions in order to move past them and *learn something new that penetrates to the level of unconscious schemas* (p. 98, italics added).

In the early stages of treatment, the patient begins to share with the empathic therapist the most emotionally salient interpersonal experiences in the outside social world, including her or his subjective dysregulated emotional reactions to these experiences. In ongoing spontaneous psychobiological right brain-to-right brain nonverbal emotional communications, beneath the words, the therapeutic dyad jointly establishes the incipient development of the burgeoning therapeutic alliance. In these emerging emotional communications, the therapist's functional right brain emotional empathy, a key mechanism of psychotherapeutic action, is an emergent property of her structural right-lateralized interbrain synchronization with the patient. This allows for the clinician's "emotional presence," "responsive listening," and "psychological contact" with this particular patient.

On the other side of the therapeutic alliance, the patient's right-lateralized interbrain synchronization allows her to know that, at unconscious levels, she is being perceptually recognized and "feeling felt" by the therapist. In a uniquely well-timed and sufficiently structured early stage of treatment, the patient and the therapist begin to establish an implicit sense of mutual familiarity, to build the positive aspects of the working alliance, to begin to intersubjectively share mild to moderate affects, and to co-construct a system of interactive regulation, the core of the attachment dynamic, thereby increasing the possibility of therapeutic change. That said, it is important to note that this stage may take more time than in patients who begin treatment with more complex psychic structure and more efficient right brains (organized insecure and secure attachment histories).

Over time, due to the developing and strengthening co-created right brain-to-right brain affect communicating and regulating system, the patient's safety and trust, at implicit levels, begins to increase, and this evolving therapeutic mechanism can momentarily suspend, reduce, and alter the affect-blocking defense of right brain dissociation. Thus, the patient can now shift into bringing more intense negative affect in titrated, affectively tolerable doses, into the session, including those that are intersubjectively experienced between them. In this work, the creative therapist's "deep listening" allows for an empathic grasp of the experiential state of the patient. As a result, the patient establishes an "archaic bond" with the therapist and thereby facilitates the revival of the early phases at which his psychological development has been arrested.

The *Oxford English Dictionary* defines archaic as "designating or belonging to an early or formative period," and so the therapeutic archaic bond is a mutual regression to an affective right brain cortical-subcortical attachment bond, a "spontaneous conversation between limbic systems," including communications of right brain trauma and the dissociative defense that blocks critical-period socioemotional integration and growth. The incrementally expanding emotional bond between the patient and the therapist promotes the exploration of the individual's internal experience and affective states. I suggest that due to the cumulative effects of interactive regulation over time, especially after regulated rupture-repair transactions, increases in trust and safety result from co-regulated oxytocin releases that are resonantly amplified by the therapeutic dyad. This hypothalamic neuropeptide is a key modulator of complex socioaffective responses such as attachment stress, anxiety, social approach, and affiliation (Bartz & Hollander, 2006; Meyer-Lindenberg, 2008). Indeed, oxytocin broadly enhances interpersonal rhythmic synchronization, thereby contributing to its prosocial effects on social bonding (Gebauer et al., 2014). This strengthening bond enables the patient to begin to confront dissociated or repressed inner states associated with frightening or shamed aspects of the self. As a result, dissociative defenses against affect are transiently lessened, thereby allowing for attachment trauma to be more easily activated and communicated in a mutual enactment, including "unconsciously strong or even overwhelming, affect" and states of "subjectively unconscious danger" embedded in the patient's right brain traumatic memory.

In the co-constructed enactment, the defense of dissociation occurs not in just the patient, but also in the clinician, where it determines the therapist's ability to receive (or block) the patient's unconscious painful emotional communications associated with attachment trauma. According to Maroda (2010), in the enactment both the therapist and the client need to be unaware of what they are stimulating in each other until some untoward event occurs. This untoward event is frequently a stressful mis-attunement, a breach in transference-countertransference relationship and a rupture of the therapeutic alliance, and thereby an emotional regression. Sands (1997) observed,

> The most empathic breaks (when not the result of some blatant mis-take on the part of the analyst and even sometimes when they are) also signal the reexperiencing of the transference of some important earlier traumatic failure. In this sense, the empathic break, rather than signaling something is "broken" may actually signal that *the therapeutic relationship has reached a new level of safety, one that finally allows for the traumatic transference to be fully experienced.* (p. 662, italics added)

This new level of safety reflects the ongoing co-construction of a regulatory scaffold (an interpersonal "safety net") within the expanding, more efficient therapeutic alliance. The burgeoning sense of safety in the patient is spontaneously expressed in the risk of further implicitly lowering the dissociative defense. Dyadic enactments thus occur in the context of a moment of a synchronized mutual regression of both the patient and the therapist into a state of dysregulating emotional arousal. Both patient and therapist are reenacting a traumatic pathological object relation, an internal interactive representation of a dysregulated-self-in-interaction-with-a-misattuning-object. This transferential traumatic expectation re-instantiates an implicit intense fear that an emotionally close other will imminently trigger a dysregulated intrapsychic pathological regression in the patient, a "malignant regression" (Balint, 1968). Khan (1972) described a dread of surrender to "resourceless dependence."

In classic developmental psychoanalytic writings, Winnicott (1974) discussed working with the patient's "fear of a breakdown," one that has already happened in early development. But Winnicott also considered regression as possibly adaptive, a potentially corrective emotional experience. Recall Knafo's admonition that the move backward in an adaptive regression is risky, "but new and original ideas are not born without risk" (2002, p. 40). Within these "safe enough" contexts, the patient communicates autobiographical memories of attachment trauma to the empathic therapist, who in turn can offer a new object relation, one that acts as an implicit interactive affect regulator of the patient's painful affects and thereby a potentially new, corrective emotional experience.

Recall Krystal's (2002) description of these affectively charged, traumatically overwhelming early memories "that cannot be remembered or forgotten" but can be reenacted in "the *emotional regression* to certain infantile forms of relatedness." Writing in the trauma literature, Nijenhuis, Vanderlinden, and Spinhoven (1998) observed,

> The stress responses exhibited by infants are the product of an immature brain processing threat stimuli and producing appropriate responses, while the adult who exhibits infantile responses has a mature brain that . . . is capable of exhibiting adult response patterns. However, there is evidence that the adult brain may regress to an infantile state when it is confronted with severe stress. (p. 253)

In earlier psychoanalytic writings, Loewald (1960) noted that movement in treatment occurs by the promotion and utilization of regression, and that the clinician must validate the patient's regressive experience so that the patient is not left alone with it. This clearly alluded to the therapist's co-participation in mutual regression. More recently in the traumatology literature, Levine (2010) warned,

> When therapists perceive that they must protect themselves from their clients' sensations and emotion, they unconsciously block those clients from therapeutically experiencing them. By distancing our-

selves from their anguish, we distance ourselves from them and from the fears they are struggling with. To take a self-protective stance is to abandon our clients precipitately. At the same time, we also greatly increases the likelihood of their exposure to secondary or vicarious traumatization and burnout. (p. 41)

This technique also iatrogenically reinforces the patient's dissociative defense. Indeed, this countertransferential reaction may represent an analog of early neglect.

An optimal therapeutic outcome of a spontaneous co-created enactment of dissociated attachment trauma thus depends on the therapist's creative ability to shift from the analytic left-hemispheric surface mind into the deeper levels of the right hemisphere, a mind that specializes in "intense emotions." In this "heightened affective moment," can the clinician creatively initiate an adaptive regression into her own right brain and synchronize with the patient's chaotic dysregulated state in order to perceptually receive the patient's primary process communications and to regulate the patient's intensely strong unconscious affect? Can the therapeutic pair with a shared communication history retain a right brain-to-right brain interpersonal interbrain synchronization? In other words, will the clinician implicitly retain a system of "state sharing" and remain psychobiologically connected to the patient so that she can not only share but also interactively regulate the dysregulated affective state? Can they both "hold in the right?" (For a clinical example, see Sands's creative unconscious communication on pages 176–177 of my 2012 book.)

At the most fundamental level, the implicit change mechanism must include a conscious or unconscious affective experience communicated to an empathic other. Ginot (2009) offered an essential clinical principle for working with the mutual regressions of enactments:

As these interactions might give expression to dissociated painful, angry, and defensive self-states, the empathic aspects in enactments do not depend on the [therapist's] ability to experience empathy for the patient's difficulties. The empathic component is found in the [therapist's] readiness and ability to resonate with what is not verbalized but nonconsciously transmitted nonetheless. (p. 300)

Frequently, this painful self state reflects the patient's unconscious shame. On the matter of these defensive states in the journal *Behaviour Research and Therapy*, Dorahy and his colleagues (2017) now conclude,

> Arguably the most painful socially debilitating and ignored affective experience is *shame*, signaling a threat to the social self. Shame is manifested as an *excruciating psychophysiological affect* with thoughts of worthlessness and inferiority, and an immediate desire to hide, *cover up or transform the feeling (e.g., into anger) to reduce its impact on the self* . . . dissociative phenomena may have affect regulation value, reducing the emotional impact of painful feelings by creating psychological distance. (p. 76, italics added)

Note that shame can be "covered up," that is, held within but defensively blocked from consciousness, yet also that shame can be transformed into anger, the well-known state of "shame-rage" (prominent in narcissistic personality disorders). Indeed, shame has long been known to be associated with anger (Tangney et al., 1992). But what neurobiological mechanism allows for this shift from a passive intrapersonal to an active interpersonal state? A major neurophysiological attribute of the parasympathetic-dominant shame system is its ability to couple with other sympathetic-dominant emotions, including the emotional output of the aggression motivational system: anger.

In other words, in the self-state of shame, aggression can be turned inward to the self (internalizing psychopathologies) or turned outward in an "attack other" shame defense (externalizing psychopathologies). Dorahy observed that "the aggressive response to shame may reflect the uninitiated rage reaction toward the original etiological (humiliating) figure that was never expressed and was subsequently turned toward the self" (2017, p. 386). Especially in cases with a history of relational humiliation, both unconscious nonverbal shame dynamics and unconscious verbal "shame-rage" dynamics will appear in stressful therapeutic transference-countertransference ("bad self") psychodynamics, potentially triggering countertransferential "attack-other" defenses in the therapist (Winnicott's 1949 "hate in the countertransference"). Thus, the therapist's ability to detect (in the patient and himself) unconscious shame and to not dissociate from the patient's communication of overwhelming negative affect is key (see Schore, 2012, pages 97–93, on shame dynamics).

In this traumatic emotional regression, the creative therapist is able to retain an empathic resonance and an interpersonal right brain synchronization with the patient's dysregulation. Note in this moment the emotionally connected therapist remains down in the right (amygdaloidal) limbic system and is not defensively shifting up left. Spezzano (1993) describes this therapeutic context:

> The [therapist] is . . . limited in her ability to make use of the unconscious affective communications of the patient by her ability to hold them in herself—to hold especially those particular blends of disturbing affects that the patient is forced to project, enact, or crumble under and to hold them long enough to be able to identify them, think about them, and say something useful on the basis of them—rather than simply projecting them back between the lines of a resistance interpretation or warding them off through a prolonged blindness to or enactment of them. (p. 212).

The dyadic source of the therapeutic mutual regression of the enactment was the unconscious alignment of both the patient's and the clinician's dissociative defenses to keep the experience of dysregulated strong negative emotions out of the therapeutic relationship. The resolution of the enactment therefore involves each member reducing the affect blocking defense, simultaneously exposing right brain vulnerability and shame in both members of the dyad. Recall Reik's observation, "As rational consciousness gives way to the primary process, it may feel as if 'the ground' is threatening 'to slip away.'" Bromberg (2017) described his own subjectivity when he becomes aware of the defensiveness and the limitations of his left hemisphere within a stressful rupture and repair of a mutual enactment, "surrenders," and then shares this self-disclosure with the patient:

> I could feel my head spinning. Everything that came to mind I discarded, because I could feel my defensiveness and I wanted to hide it from myself as well as from (the patient) . . . [self-conscious shame]. What to do! It was clear that my cupboard was bare. There was nothing left in it that would "work" any better. The problem was ME, not my ideas. So I stopped searching. Strangely, it didn't feel so bad *to give up*. And even more strangely, it was at that moment that I could feel an option that I had not felt earlier: I could share my experience of what was going on in my mind. I could share it just because I wanted her to know it, not because it was supposed to lead somewhere. And so I did; I shared my "formulation," and I also shared my feelings about my formulation—my private awareness. (p. 30, italics added)

Bromberg reflected that he had given up searching because he had run out of ideas in order to *"find a way of just being with the patient."*

Neurobiology and psychoanalysis can offer insights into this process. Heilman, Nadeau, and Beversdorf asserted, "A possible method of resolving a previously unsolved problem is to see the problem 'in a new light' . . . to use a different form of knowledge and a different cognitive strategy that might be mediated by the hemisphere that is opposite to the one previously used" (2003, p. 374). In other words at these critical moments, in order to process something novel, it is necessary to shift dominance and access the other hemisphere. The clinician's creative left brain-to-right brain topographical shift into an "authentic" self-revelation is described by Lichtenberg as a *"disciplined spontaneous engagement"*: " 'Spontaneous' refers to the [therapist's] unexpected comments, gestures, facial expressions, and actions that occur as a result of an unsuppressed emotional upsurge. These communications seem more to *pop out* than to have been planned or edited. The [therapist] may be as surprised as the patient" (2001, p. 445).

Reik (1948) postulated that when unconscious material becomes conscious, it emerges as "surprise" (an "Aha!" inspirational moment of regression). Bromberg (2006) underscored the critical role of "safe surprises" in enactments.

In the negotiation of a spontaneous co-regulated face-to-face enactment, the therapist's creativity is expressed in an authentic right brain-to-right brain novel interpersonal communication that is instantly perceived by the patient's receptive right brain, thereby contributing to "an ambience of safety." Creativity and openness (like emotion) are expressed on the left face (Lindell, 2010), and so the patient implicitly reads authenticity (a "human" response) in the clinician's left face (and in the prosodic musical emotional aspect of her voice). In turn, the patient's instant right brain state switch from implicit danger to implicit safety is also expressed on the patient's left face (right interbrain synchronization). This synchronization underlies improvisation on both sides of the alliance. Wan and colleagues (2014) observed a "let-go" mode in music improvisation, "an instantaneous creative behavior," a shift from a "mechanical" expression of a "technique" to a "more emotionally rich manner."

In classic psychotherapeutic writings, Carl Rogers (1958) emphasized the importance of the emotional congruence of the authentic therapist as a major curative factor in psychotherapeutic change:

> It has been found that personal change is facilitated when the psychotherapist is what he *is*, when in his relationship with the client he is genuine and without "front" or façade, openly being the feelings and attitude which at that moment are flowing *in* him. We have coined the term "congruence" to try to describe this condition. By this we mean that the feelings the therapist is experiencing are available to him, available to his awareness, and he is able to live these feelings, be them, and able to communicate them if appropriate . . . the more the therapist is able to listen acceptantly to what is going on within himself, and the more he is available to be the complexity of his feelings, without fear, the higher the degree of congruence. (p. 61, italics in original)

Levenson (1974) described the emotional aspects of this shared therapeutic landscape:

> Authentic therapy begins by admitting the chaos, plowing ahead, falling on one's face, listening for the feedback, and delineating the patterns of interaction as they emerge from one's mutual experience. A feeling of intimacy, an intense personal commitment, may emerge at the most stormy or unpleasant moments. One risks one's identity in every real therapy. That's enough basis for authentic relationship. (pp. 368–369)

Kantrowitz observed that when both members of the therapeutic dyad are able to overcome resistance to engagement, an intense affective engagement takes place: "When patient and [therapist] are affectively engaged, when the patient has come to trust in the analyst's basic benevolence, and when in this context the patient feels safe enough to lessen defenses, the modification of intrapsychic organization becomes possible" (1999, p. 69). This intense emotional engagement is accompanied by a mutual disengagement of both of their dissociative affect-inhibiting defenses. Whitehead (2006) underscored an essential therapeutic principle of the joint processing of unconscious affects in a mutual enactment:

> Every time we make therapeutic contact with our patients we are engaging profound processes that tap into essential life forces in our selves and in those we work with. . . . *Emotions are deepened in intensity and sustained in time when they are intersubjectively shared.* This occurs at moments of deep contact. (p. 624, italics added)

Interactively regulated mutual regressions co-create this context of deep contact. In this manner, overwhelming events become less traumatic once one can express and communicate emotional reactions to them.

The intersubjective context of the mutual regression of a creative spontaneous enactment provides not only a self-revealing right brain implicit affective communication but also a right brain interactive regulation of a dysregulated intense affective-arousal state, the core of the attachment dynamic. Thus, what was previously a dissociated unconscious overwhelming painful affect that was unbearable and unshareable is now consciously experienced by both and can be shared, interactively regulated, relationally repaired, and thereby bearable. As Bromberg (2011) described,

> A core dimension of using enactment therapeutically is to increase competency in regulating affective states. Increasing competency requires that the [therapeutic] relationship become a place that supports risk and safety simultaneously—a relationship that allows the painful reliving of early trauma, without the reliving being just a blind repetition of the past . . . the [therapist] is communicating both his ongoing concern for his patient's affective safety and his commitment to the value of the inevitably painful process of reliving. (pp. 16–17)

This clinical model mirrors my own work in regulation theory where I assert "a spontaneous enactment can either blindly repeat a pathological object relation through the therapist's deflection of projected negative states and intensification of interactive dysregulation and defensiveness, or creatively provide a novel relational experience via the therapist's auto-regulation of projected negative states and co-participation in interactive repair (Schore, 2012). Note the allusion to the clinician's triggering of an iatrogenic dysregulating pathological regression or a regulated adaptive regression.

DYADIC UNCONSCIOUS PSYCHODYNAMICS
OF AN ADAPTIVE MUTUAL REGRESSION

A key psychopathogenetic mechanism of early relational trauma is not only the frequency, duration, and magnitude of painful ruptures of the developing attachment relationship, but also the lack of relational repair with the caregivers. Encoded in the working model is an implicit expectation that the intrusive/abandoning other will not regulate but dysregulate the emerging self. If a stressful, mutually dysregulating rupture of the therapeutic alliance is a primary driver of a regressive reenactment, then the mutual repair of the right brain emotional bond between the patient and the therapist is a central mechanism of the resolution of the mutual enactment and progression of the treatment. The relational rupture and repair mechanism within an interactively regulated mutual enactment that generates oxytocin amplification and cortisol reduction in the therapeutic dyad can alter defensiveness and bring warded-off affects and motivations into consciousness on both sides of the alliance, so that they can be used to negotiate the mutual repair of a stressed relationship in new and creative ways. The resolution of a mutual regression embedded in enactment is not a cognitive insight but an affectively charged corrective emotional experience and an intersubjective negotiation. Creative adaptive regressions within spontaneous mutual enactments thus represent an optimal intersubjective context of implicit therapeutic change mechanisms.

In an important contribution on the intersubjective dialogues within enactments, Lyons-Ruth (1999) observed that enactments represent important opportunities to gain a window on unconscious motivations and meanings held by the patient that have not been previously recognized or articulated. This therapeutic work "is always involved in the creation of the new and the reworking of the old simultaneously" (p. 608). Therapy involves "both the slow incremental processes" as well as the "sudden emergence of new forms of organization" including a reorganization of the "implicit procedural unconscious." She described the idiosyncratic slow process as an

> extended period of intersubjective encounters between patient and analyst that have increased the complexity and organization of . . . the intersubjective field . . . slowly creating new implicit relational procedures is the work that creates competing and stabilizing mental and behavioral structures. Viewed from a self-organizing systems perspective, as increasingly articulated competing organization emerges, the old organization [of self-regulation] is destabilized, with an increasing subjective sense of creative disorder and internal flux. . . . Once this state of instability and flux is achieved, however, the re-organizing cognitions might also come about through an

emotionally salient series of transactions with the analyst, as loosely captured by the term corrective emotional experience, or through a powerful transaction between the two participants when the analyst is forced somewhat out of his role, as described under the rubric of enactment. (p. 609)

She further noted that this emergence of new implicit relational procedures is not simply about putting unconscious motivations or implicit procedures into words, but about new forms of organization emerging as new forms of *"being with others."*

Here I describe a case example that demonstrates the clinical principles outlined above. The following is a dramatic vignette of a mutual hyper-arousal enactment of a dissociated self-state associated with unregulated aggression and externalizing psychopathology. I remind the reader that other mutual regressions are expressed in a different class of dissociated self-states associated with mutual hypoarousal enactments of early, intensely painful relational loss, as in early depression dynamics and an internalizing psychopathology (Schore, 2012). That said, in all adaptive reenactments of attachment trauma, the mutual regression is triggered by a synchronized release of defensive inhibition in both the patient and the therapist, facilitating dissociated, strong dysregulated affects into consciousness, a mutual Jacksonian "dissolution," a "taking off of the higher" and "at the very same time a letting go, or expression of the lower." An essential mechanism of this description of therapeutic action is thus the synchronized neuroplasticity of the patient's and clinician's defense systems. Listen with your clinical mind, visualize the intersubjective interactions, hear the emotional tone of the voices, and feel the bodily-based affect in this heightened affective moment.

This clinical vignette is documented by the Jungian psychoanalyst Donald Kalsched (2015, pp. 487–489). Like most enactments and consonant with Lyons-Ruth's model, the session occurred some years into the treatment and the establishment of a familiar working alliance. The patient, a 6 foot 2 inch, 220 pound man, would continue to report instances of his road rage despite their effective work. The patient suffered from traumatic humiliation, shame, and helplessness in his early life, so that any frustration would trigger tyrannical rage as a defense to cover up his unbearable vulnerabilities. Kalsched (2015) reports a session in the working-through stage of therapy of a spontaneous mutual enactment and emotional regression that occurred at a crisis of the treatment of a difficult "primitively defended" patient.

Mike came in and confessed superciliously (and with a guilty grin on his face) to yet another incident of road rage in which he had really hurt another man half his size. He was completely activated again, and I could find no regret—no guilt or remorse in him, only the pumped up hyperarousal of this addictive violence. Sensing my discomfort, he changed the subject to some "urgent" issue about his wife. I sat seething, trying to listen with that old familiar feeling of helpless rage. The thought that he was a psychopath crossed my mind—that he was simply too damaged for psychotherapy, etc. Recovering my senses, I suggested that he was avoiding the most important thing we had to talk about and asked him what he was feeling. "About what?" he said with irritation. At that point something snapped in me and I lost my mind—at least my analytic mind. Somewhere from a far-off place inside, I heard myself say to him (with apologies to those of you who may be offended by the language): "Look, you are threatening everything you've created in your life—your profession, your family, your relationship with your wife, the boys, your relationship with me, and that new friendship with that little boy inside you—all for the temporary high of your little shit-fit rages. You think you're getting even or administering some kind of sick justice, but the fact is you're simply indulging yourself like a two-year-old. You're just emotionally incontinent! That's your problem. You can't hold it! When are you fucking gonna learn to hold it?"

[Silence]

"Fuck you!" he said, turning his head away fuming. "I'm outta here!" And he lurched out of his chair, slammed the door behind him and locked himself in the bathroom on the other side of the waiting room. (Fortunately there were no patients waiting.) I sat in stunned silence for a moment, then followed him and stood outside the locked bathroom door and said: "Mike, I am really really sorry. You didn't deserve that outburst from me. It wasn't any better than yours on the highway! Let's not let this wreck our connection. Let me in so we can process this together. We've got too much going for us. There's a lot at stake."

I heard the door unlatched from inside. I went in. He was seated on the toilet lid, head in his hands. I sat on the bathtub and put my hand on his shoulder. Several minutes went by with both of us finally coming back into our bodies. Then I noticed Mike' s eyes begin to tear up. I waited for him to say something, but nothing came. "What're you feeling?" I asked. He looked up at me and saw the tears rimming my eyes also. "I don't know," he said, "Sad . . . about my father I guess." Then Mike really began to sob: "Nobody ever cared! I had to take care of it all by myself. . . . I was always crying out for help in my acting out, but nobody got it. . . . Six felonies before I was 18 and my father never spoke to me about it! All they could do was make me bad. You're not making me bad."

"You're not making me bad." Suddenly I felt a huge upwelling of relief and gratitude inside my chest—relief because I really had "made him bad" in my mind, and I felt terrible about it. I had really hated him for a moment, and it hadn't destroyed him. And it hadn't destroyed us. Both love and hate, the good and the bad, were held together in this moment for each of us, but love was stronger, and hence the relationship was both preserved and deepened. Mike took my hand and we just sat looking at each other in this wet beautiful moment. It was like the Balm of Gilead—healing and reconciliation poured down on us both. Trauma repeated, acted out, but repaired, right there in the session . . . the little boy and the murderous protector (in both of us) present and getting to know each other.

Note Kalsched's creative rupture and repair: synchronized mutual regression, state matching, authentic self-revelations, and interactive regulation. He stated that before the enactment, "Knowing that eruptive anger was a defense against the shame and humiliation he had experienced in childhood . . . I repeatedly tried to help these two dissociated self-states get together." Yet this approach led to no avail. In contrast, in the mutual regression and interactive repair of the dyadic enactment, the dissociated dynamics beneath the conscious aggression, a "not-me" state of unbearable shame and helplessness, was able to come to the surface of consciousness and be communicated to a valued other (a taking off of the higher and letting go of the lower).

Kalsched proposed that in this case history, the relational trauma of unshared emotions of humiliation, shame, and helplessness with the father was too painful for the patient to remember and so was repeated and reenacted in the therapeutic relationship. In light of relational trauma with *both* parents, I suggest the source of shame occurs in later maternal shame and paternal humiliation in the second and third years, but the source of helplessness originates earlier in the first year with a neglectful insecure disorganized mother. Although Kalsched provided no history of the first year, he did describe the patient's memories as a toddler of being driven in a highly dysregulated state to an orphanage where the mother and father threatened to abandon him. On those occasions he'd have inconsolable temper tantrums for which he was shamed, screaming until he couldn't breathe, and then blacking and going numb (dissociating).

In the mutual dissociation preceding the shame enactment, the therapist could not consciously tolerate his own dissociated hatred (helpless rage) and contempt for his patient, which broke through in a creative spontaneous and authentic self-revelation of the regression. Kalsched observed, "Fortunately I did not dissociate my hatred for long. Once enacted, I could own it, and this made my apology possible. That was the beginning of a negotiation towards a different outcome." Note the patient's dissociated right-hemispheric unconscious helplessness and shame beneath left-hemispheric conscious predatory (vs. defensive) aggression. The emotional growth of mutual regression allows the integration of these dissociated self-states of helplessness, shame, and aggression into a blended conscious feeling of shame and remorse about his aggressive road rage. Kalsched observed that shortly after the enactment there was "a major shift in our work together" and a major integration in the patient's psyche. The negotiated enactment of the mutual regression led to a sudden change in the nature of their relationship, a new way of *"being with"* a valued other. The synchronized right brain-to-right brain system now becomes more complex, more intimate.

Kalsched described the enactment: "We get pulled in. Instead of sitting outside the process and providing insight or interpreting defences, we will find ourselves participating in repeated rupture and, hopefully, repairs of our connections with the patient as dissociated pieces of the patient's experience get knit together. . . . Communication is not linear and rational (mediated by the left hemisphere of the brain) but non-verbal and experiential (mediated by the right hemisphere). Allan Schore calls this 'right brain-to-right brain communication'" (2015, pp. 485–486). Indeed, he cited my work on enactments: "When a therapist's wounds are hit, can she regulate her own bodily based emotions and shame dynamics well enough to be able to stay connected to her patient? Can the therapist tolerate what is happening in her own body when it mirrors her patient's terror, rage and physiological hyperarousal. . . . Herein lies the art of psychotherapy (Schore, in Sieff, 2015, p. 132)" (Kalsched, 2015, p. 490).

The mutual regression of the above enactment clearly reactivated aggression on both sides of the dyad, and therefore a therapeutic confrontation. In classic writings, Welpton (1973) described the self-reflective clinician's "empathic confrontation" within a rupture of the therapeutic relationship:

> "Empathic confrontation" is "based on facing myself and my patient with a vivid, here and now, mutually shared experience that has been happening between us in the therapy [p. 261]. I am also confronting myself. I am putting myself on the line about our mutual relationship. . . . I must be examining what I have thought and felt about it as I hold the patient to doing" [p. 262]. If the confrontation was successful, I have found that it deepens my empathy for them and how they have come to be the way they are . . . it is the first-hand experiencing of new ways of being with the therapist that facilitates change [p. 261].

In my 2012 volume, I described in some detail the critical import of heightened affective moments of mutual regressions embedded in therapeutic regulated enactments to the patient's creation of new ways of being with self and other. These corrective emotional experiences of the nonlinear right brain represent essential processes in the therapeutic change mechanism. In the chapter, I cited Hayes and her colleagues (2007) on the distinction of slow, gradual linear change from rapid nonlinear change in psychotherapy:

> Although change can happen in a gradual and linear way, there is increasing evidence across disciplines that it can also occur in discontinuous and nonlinear ways. This latter type of change is often preceded by an increase in variability and a destabilization or loosening of old patterns that can be followed by system reorganization. In post-traumatic growth, life transition, and psychotherapy, destabilization often occurs in the context of emotional arousal which, when accompanied by emotional processing and meaning-making, seems to contribute to better outcomes. (p. 721)

I then concluded that Hayes's description of the discontinuous and nonlinear change process directly applies to the enactments that arise in the psychotherapy of patients with a history of attachment trauma and pathological dissociation.

In a further elaboration of this fundamental nonlinear mechanism of psychotherapeutic change, adaptive affectively charged mutual regressions represent a destabilization or loosening of old patterns that can be followed by system reorganization. Recall Tuttman's (2002) description of regression as the return to fundamentals and origins that might facilitate a potential reorganization leading to better integration. I now suggest that any deep change in the basic personality must involve clinical work that not only "loosens" defenses but also adaptively alters the structure and function of the unconscious character defenses of dissociation and repression. These functional/structural changes of an adaptive mutual regression allow for a new stage in therapy. More complex right brain intimate relational func-

tions are available to the dyad for joint exploration. This important maturational advance of the patient's psychic structure that emerges from regulated
mutual enactments is not only a loosening of the patient's use of defensive
dissociation but also the development of more complex cognitive functions,
namely the emergent adaptive ability to tolerate conflict, the capacity to
access and tolerate two discrepant self-states in the same moment, thereby
overcoming splitting defenses and mutually dissociated self-states.

A key mechanism of therapeutic change underlying an adaptive resolution of a spontaneous enactment is the therapist's creative ability to rapidly
and implicitly enter into and remain synchronized with the patient's regression into the right brain, to co-participate in a mutual regression. As Bromberg's earlier vignette demonstrates during an adaptive mutual enactment,
the therapist's left brain-to-right brain state switch of hemispheric dominance and reduced defensiveness allows for the empathic reception of the
patient's right brain-to-right brain, nonverbally communicated, dissociated
affective state. This callosal shift, a "letting go," a "giving oneself over" to
the regression, is critical to participation in mutual regressions of clinical
enactments. Within this intersubjective context of relational stress, the therapist spontaneously activates a topographical shift from left-hemispheric
control to right-hemispheric vulnerability and uncertainty, subjectively
experienced "as if the ground is threatening to slip away." According to
Erich Fromm, "creativity requires courage to let go of certainties."

Overall, the general interpersonal neurobiological therapeutic principle of working with relational trauma in a mutual enactment and indeed
with any disturbance of affect regulation dictates that the psychobiologically attuned empathic therapist facilitates the patient reexperiencing overwhelming affects in incrementally titrated, increasing affectively tolerable
doses in the context of a safe environment, so that overwhelming traumatic
feelings can be regulated, come into consciousness, and be adaptively integrated into the patient's emotional life. In this manner, adaptive, interactively regulated, spontaneous mutual regressions within synchronized
reenactments "generate interpersonal as well as internal processes eventually capable of promoting integration and growth" (Ginot, 2007, p. 317).

Ann Ulanov (2001) gave an evocative overview of mutual regressions of
early attachment trauma in "deep psychotherapy":

Through . . . counseling . . . we may experience the safe holding that allows us to look into the gaps of dissociation between our bodies and psyches, into the terror of ground falling away beneath us, into the moments of unreality when we feel the flicker of our uniqueness as persons faltering. Looking into such gaps, we may begin slowly, carefully to knit together what was broken apart . . . we must depend on someone holding us in being while we ourselves knit together our broken parts. To heal an early agony resulting from dependency not met and fusion not accomplished, we must depend upon someone present while we do our re-membering of our dismemberment. This is, in Winnicott's phrase, the breakdown that has already happened, which we can now afford to become conscious of and unite with the rest of our personality. But we need someone present, holding the situation, while we undergo regression, the journey back to where we fell apart. It is dependence that escorts us into emptiness, makes us hit the bottom of emptiness, and it is emptiness that opens us to our dependence. We are afraid that no one will be there calling our name, that we alone will know what we are going through. Such regression costs time, money, tremendous energy, and courage if attempted in therapy. (p. 60)

CHAPTER 4

The Growth-Promoting Role of Mutual Regressions in Deep Psychotherapy: Part Two

AFFECT DEFENSES: DISSOCIATION VERSUS REPRESSION

In the preceding section, I discussed the role of the defense of dissociation in synchronized mutual regressions of spontaneous enactments, but before I elaborate a model of working with repressed affect in voluntary mutual regressions, I will offer a more comprehensive discussion of the unique functional and structural aspects of these dual defense systems. Although affective neurobiological structures and emotional functions are now well-studied, one area of the clinical realm continues to attract significantly less attention from both clinicians and researchers—unconscious affect defense systems. Miller's trenchant observation in 1985 still applies: Although "the surface of feeling that we experience—in the case of our own feeling—or hear in another's verbalization, always remains richly communicative . . . the direct experience of feeling may succeed in totally obscuring its defensive aspect unless one has a psychological theory to point the way to those hidden realms" (1985, p. 8). That said, the constructs of unconscious defenses, like regression, have a controversial history in both the clinical and research literatures.

A large body of neurobiological research now confirms that strong affect is generated in the right hemisphere, but mild to moderate in the left hemisphere (see Schore, 2012). Throughout the life span, the bodily-based subjective experience of a strong negative affect can be painful, disorganizing, and even overwhelming and intolerable. This means that in these heightened affective moments of life, the conscious mind in the left hemisphere will be exposed to strong emotional arousal and intense affective states, as well as to the conscious and particularly unconscious defenses associated with these intense emotional states. *Operating at levels beneath conscious awareness, the passive defense of dissociation and the active defense of repression are potential major contributors to the patient's unconscious resistance to psychotherapeutic change, and thus have major intrapsychic impacts on the processes that underlie the psychotherapeutic repair of the self.*

In classic neuropsychological writings on the right brain and the unconscious, Joseph (1992) asserted,

> Just as we have a conscious and an unconscious mind, as well as a right and left brain, we also have two self-images. One is consciously maintained and the other is almost wholly unconscious. The conscious self-image is associated with the left half of the brain in most people. However, this self-image is also subject to unconscious influences. By contrast, the unconscious self-image is maintained within the right brain mental system and is tremendously influenced by current and past experiences . . . the two self-images . . . interact. Indeed, sometimes the conscious self-image is fashioned in reaction to unconscious feelings, traumas, and feared inadequacies that the person does not want to possess, but that nevertheless, are unconsciously maintained. (p. 181)

He further proposed,

> A defense mechanism is a protective strategy most often used by the conscious mind and left brain. Defense mechanisms serve to protect conscious recognition of information that is in some manner threatening to the conscious self-image. However, the conscious mind has to have at least some notion of what is threatening in order to defend against it. Some forms of information are simply

too overwhelming, too threatening, and too difficult to deal with or confront openly. (p. 304)

Expanding upon my own earlier work on defenses (Schore, 1994, 2003b), a central function of repression is to act as a strategy used by the left brain conscious mind to cope with potentially dysregulating intense emotional states that emerge in the subcortical right brain. Recall, regression involves a hemispheric state shift from a left brain mild/moderate surface emotion (anxiety, pleasure, anger) to a right brain strong deep emotion (terror, elation, rage, intense love, grief). As opposed to the role of dissociation in regulating strong negative emotion and traumatic affect and terror, repression, aside from its interhemispheric actions regulating uncomfortable right brain emotion, also controls anxiety. The duality in hemispheric functions of these defenses in seen in a duality of hemispheric structures that regulate strong and even traumatic affect versus anxiety.

Engels and her colleagues (2007) offered fMRI research that differentiates left-hemispheric verbal anxious apprehension from right-hemispheric physiological hyperarousal. These authors provided research evidence indicating that the right-hemispheric state is associated with high *autonomic* arousal, vigilance, and high stress. (In the clinical context, this alteration in right brain subjectivity would be detected by the empathic therapist "beneath the narrative.") In contrast, left-lateralized anxious apprehension is primarily characterized by worry, verbal rumination, and unpleasant thoughts. In addition to worry, physical symptoms often accompany anxious apprehension, including restlessness, fatigue, and muscle tension. The timescale for perceived threat in anxious apprehension ranges into the distant future. Left-hemispheric anxious apprehension is expressed as persistent worrisome thoughts that include personal and emotional threats to the self, physical health, competence at work, or general world problems. These conscious worries are mentally rehearsed repeatedly without resolution and are difficult to dismiss. (In the clinical context, these anxieties would be expressed within the patient's verbal narrative.)

Thus the dual cerebral hemispheres of the brain access different affect regulatory defensive systems. The development of these early and later maturing defense systems parallels the development of right brain implicit-procedural amygdalar memory and unconscious affect regulation that precedes left brain explicit-semantic hippocampal memory and conscious affect regulation. Indeed, a large body of clinical data and research indicates all forms of psychopathology have concomitant symptoms of emotional dysregulation, and that defense mechanisms are, in essence, forms of emotional regulation strategies for avoiding, minimizing, or converting affects that are too difficult to tolerate (Schore, 2003b). I propose that repression represents a left-lateralized defense for regulating left-hemispheric conscious anxiety (anxious apprehension), while dissociation represents a right-lateralized defense for regulating early appearing, right-hemispheric, physiological sympathetic hyperarousal (and parasympathetic hypoarousal). Furthermore, the left-hemispheric defensive signal affect of anxiety anticipates expected upcoming high levels of right-hemispheric sympathetic arousal in the left. This state transition allows for hyperactivation of the inhibitory left dorsolateral prefrontal cortex, which in turn increases left-hemispheric repression. The regulatory defenses of right brain dissociation (CNS-ANS mind-body disconnect) and left brain repression (CNS disconnect between conscious and unconscious minds) against the subjective experience of negative affective arousal, each with a different mechanism of action, contribute to an implicit ubiquitous background (and sometime foreground) yet central feature of all clinical interventions in both symptom-reducing or growth-promoting psychotherapies.

Recall, research now describes the neurobiology of "unconscious negative emotion" and "subjectively unconscious danger." Both the dissociative and repressive defenses are involved in blocking affect from reaching consciousness and in the generation of unconscious states. That said, in recent writings authors have differentiated the defense of dissociation from the defense of repression. According to Diseth (2005):

> As a defense mechanism, dissociation has been described as a phenomenon quite different from repression. Repression has been considered an unconscious mechanism, placing unwanted feelings away from the conscious mind because of shame, guilt, or fear. . . . However, in order to repress, you must to some degree have processed

the feelings. Dissociation is about not having processed the inputs at all. (p. 82)

For Donnell Stern, dissociation is not the action of putting out of mind what we cannot bear knowing, the disavowal of psychic conflict, but rather "the subjectivity we never create, the experience we never have" (1997, p. 95). This dissociated dreaded *not-me* state has never been symbolized, and although it originates in a fear of annihilation, it remains as "a vaguely defined organization of experience; a primitive, global, nonideational affective state" (1997, p. 119). Spiegel and Cardena referred to a distinction in which repression is seen as "a pushing (or pulling) of ideas deep into the unconscious where they cannot be accessed" and dissociation as "a severing of the connection between various ideas and emotions" (1991, p. 367). According to Nemiah, "In Janet's view dissociation resulted from the *passive* falling away of mental contents from an ego that was too weak to retain them in consciousness, whereas, for Freud, repression was described as 'the result of the *active* repression of undesirable and emotionally painful mental contents by an ego that was strong enough to banish them from conscious awareness'" (1989, p. 1528).

Although in his 1891 volume *On Aphasia*, Freud accepted Janet's concept of dissociation, by 1900 in *The Interpretation of Dreams* and the elaboration of his topographic theory, he rejected and replaced it with preconscious repression as the central psychoanalytic defensive construct. In 1915, Freud asserted that repression, established in the latency period, allows for barriers to the representations of sexual drives, thereby preventing particular *thoughts* from becoming conscious (Freud, 1915b/1957). Yet in that same year, Freud also described the repression of what he termed the "*charge of affect*" attached to sexual drives and concluded (Freud, 1915c/1957):

We have learned from psychoanalysis that the essence of the process of *repression* lies, not in putting an end to, in annihilating, the idea that represents an instinct, but in *preventing it from becoming conscious*. When this happens we say of the idea that it is in a state of being "unconscious," and we can produce good evidence to show that *even when it is unconscious it can produce effects, even including some which finally reach consciousness.* Repression, has to do with an active removal from consciousness of material or contents that have undergone a process of repression by a subject. (p. 166, italics added)

In the middle of the century, Winnicott proclaimed "an instinct repressed along abnormal paths is liable to be *shoved down deep into the subconscious* and there act as a foreign body: this 'foreign body' may remain in the subconscious for a whole lifetime and completely control the life of the individual who has not control over this curious tendency since it is not known to him even to exist" (qtd. in Rodman, 2003, p. 43, italics added). At the end of the century, Jones (1993), citing Brenner's (1957) classic definition of repression proper, the hallmark of the dynamic unconscious, asserted that "events, feelings, or wishes which were unquestionably *at one time in conscious awareness and accessible to verbal representation came to be excluded from consciousness or memory.* As Freud pointed out, this exclusion of memories from conscious recall appears to be due to the mobilization of guilt, shame or disgust which are aroused by the event, feeling, or wish in question" (1993, p. 88, italics added).

Consonant with these clinical ideas and with neuroscientific studies, Bromberg (2011) offered a fundamental distinction between these two defenses: "Repression as a defense is responsive to anxiety—a negative but regulatable affect that signals the potential emergence into consciousness of mental contents that may create unpleasant, but bearable intrapsychic conflict. Dissociation as a defense is responsive to trauma—the chaotic, convulsive flooding by unregulatable affect that takes over the mind, threatening the stability of selfhood and sometimes sanity" (p. 49). For an excellent discussion of differences between repression and dissociation I refer the reader to Mucci (in press). In my own developmental neuropsychoanalytic work differentiating these two defensive systems, I have suggested that early appearing dissociation acts a postnatal preoedipal defense against traumatic affects such as terror, rage, and hopeless despair that are generated subcortically in the right brain, while repression is a developmentally more advanced left brain defense against affects that are represented at the cortical level of the right brain (Schore, 2003b).

Furthermore, I have offered research indicating that dissociation, the right brain defense against overwhelming infantile trauma, appears in the prenatal and postnatal periods, what was previously referred to as the preoedipal stage of development, while repression appears later in early childhood, previously described as the oedipal stage. In contrast to later developing repression and its actions on lateral shifts in interhemispheric processing and cortical disconnectivity between higher frontal structures, the survival strategy of dissociation represents a loss of vertical connectivity between cortical and subcortical limbic-autonomic areas within the right hemisphere that appears well before the frontal areas of the cerebral cortex are myelinated and before callosal connections are functional (Bergman, Linley, & Fawcus, 2004; Schore, 2001. Indeed, dissociation is seen in the hypoxic human fetus (Reed et. al., 1999) and soon after birth (Bergman et al., 2004).

In earlier work, I cited developmental neurobiological data indicating that although the right hemisphere's growth spurt precedes that of the left, at the middle to end of the second year when it ends, the left enters its own critical-period growth spurt (Schore, 1994, 2003b). Thatcher's (1997) electroencephalography (EEG) coherence research shows that this left-hemispheric growth spurt that commences in the latter half of the second year continues through the third year. In early neuropsychoanalytic theoretical writings, Levin cited extant research indicating that left-to-right interhemispheric commissural transmission is clearly defined at 3½ years, a time period of intense interest to Freud. Levin observed "the beginning of the oedipal phase, a psychological and neuroanatomical watershed in development, coincides with the onset of the ability (or inability) of the hemispheres to integrate their activities" (1991, p. 21). Synthesizing classical developmental psychoanalytic conceptions of repression with extant neuroscience, Levin proposed that in this time frame of human childhood, "a system of two properly functioning cerebral hemispheres with a high level of interhemispheric (i.e., left-right and right left) connectedness comes into being. It is speculated that the resulting integrative tendency of affective-cognitive processing that results from the integration of the two hemispheres makes a further contribution to the cohesiveness and to the early formation of the repression barrier" (1991, pp. 193–194).

Expanding this theme, Levin (1991) proposed,

> With the further refinement of the system of right cerebral hemi-
> sphere and limbic system (which have intimate connections with
> each other) it is known that affects are better regulated . . . the
> repression barrier further matures on this basis. It is speculated
> that the remainder of the development of this defensive function,
> which Freud called the repression barrier, is accomplished by the
> increasing and *reversible dominance* of the left over the right hemi-
> sphere, which is known to occur during brain maturation. That is,
> the assumption of left-hemispheric dominance provides us with
> improved control over sexual and aggressive impulses. (p. 194, ital-
> ics added)

On this matter, Levin cited earlier clinical studies of Basch, who suggested that "in repression it is the path from episodic to semantic memory, from right to left brain, that is blocked" (1983, p. 151). In more current neuro-psychoanalytic studies, Solms and Turnbull assert what is blocked from consciousness is specifically right-hemispheric affect: "Thus we seem to have rediscovered, from a neuroscientific standpoint, the obvious fact that what we feel about our experience is what renders them susceptible to 'repression'" (2002, p. 162).

The current expanding body of knowledge of neuropsychoanalysis and neuroscience thus suggests two major alterations in the conceptualization of repression. Indeed, repression, which Freud early in his career described as "the psychical mechanism of (unconscious) defense" and later as "a topographical-dynamic conception" equated with the "dynamic uncon-scious," still remains a central construct of psychoanalysis, "the science of unconscious processes." In classic writings, Freud emphasized, "Every-thing that is repressed must remain unconscious; but let us state at the very outset that the repressed does not cover everything that is uncon-scious. The unconscious has the wider compass: the repressed is a part of the unconscious" (1915c/1957, p. 166) (see Figure 3.2). In my earlier neuropsychoanalytic studies, I offered the following update of this "wider compass": Freud's seminal model of a dynamic, continually active unconscious mind describes the moment-to-moment operations of a hierarchical, self-organizing, implicit-procedural regulatory system that is located in the right brain (Schore, 2003b). In support of this, Mancia (2006) also described the implicit functions of an early forming "unrepressed unconscious," which he also located in the right hemisphere.

In another earlier neuropsychoanalytic revision, I proposed a second conceptual alteration:

> Freud's concept of the dynamic unconscious is usually interpreted to refer to the self-regulatory capacities of an unconscious system which operates via the process of repression in order to bar access of anxiety and sexual and aggressive wishes into consciousness. This characterization describes the left hemispheric horizontal inhibition of right hemispheric cognitive-emotional representations. (Schore, 2003b)

Neurobiologically, repression represents the left frontal verbal cognitive callosal inhibition of right frontal nonverbal emotional functions. McGilchrist (2015) cites a body of research indicating that the left-right interhemispheric callosal action is mutual inhibition, yet the left hemisphere is better able to inhibit the right than the right hemisphere is able to inhibit the left. The repression defense that blocks entry into left-hemispheric consciousness is more effective than conscious suppression or distraction. And yet this left callosal inhibition has its limits, and at times results in "a return of the repressed." Carter observed, "Our conscious control over emotions is weak, and feelings often push out thinking, whereas thinking fights mainly a losing battle to banish emotions. . . . The connections from the emotional systems to the cognitive systems are stronger than the connections that run the other way" (1999, p. 98).

In this work, I expand the neuropsychoanalytic model by defining repression as a strategy used by the left brain conscious mind to cope with potential emotional-energetic stressors that emerge in the right brain, which is dominant for the unconscious processing of relational-emotional stress and intense emotional arousal. As opposed to mild to moderate conscious stressors that trigger left brain conscious emotion regulation strategies (dorsolateral prefrontal cortex suppression and cognitive reappraisal; Anderson et al., 2004; Goldin et al., 2008), defensive repression regulates the impact of potentially strong levels of right brain emotional energy (very high or very low) on the conscious left-hemispheric mind (which operates in an "inverted U" mid-range of physiological arousal). The hierarchical "bottom-up" relationship of the right to the left cerebral hemispheres is described by Buklina (2005):

> The right hemisphere . . . performs simultaneous analysis of stim-
> uli . . . the more "diffuse" organization of the right hemisphere has
> the effect that it responds to any stimulus, even speech stimuli, more
> quickly and, thus *earlier*. The left hemisphere is activated *after this*
> and performs the slower semantic analysis and synthesis . . . the
> arrival of an individual signal initially in the right hemisphere and
> then in the left is more "physiological." (p. 479)

Note the deep right brain source of emotional arousal, which then arises from the right into the left hemisphere (see the vertical arrows in Figure 3.1).

It is important to emphasize that Freud's construct of repression, grounded in oedipal dynamics, underlies his clinical model of therapeutic action anchored in the topographical model—the undoing of repression and making the unconscious conscious. In my past book (Schore, 2012), I offered an updated model of therapeutic action of working with affect defenses wherein the clinician co-creates a right-lateralized therapeutic alliance with the patient in order to empathically resonate and regulate not only the patient's conscious but also unconscious (dissociated or repressed) dysregulating affects. Relational therapeutic work with repressed affect involves synchronized mutual regressions from the patient's and the therapist's left brain conscious minds into both of their right brain unconscious minds. Thus, not the words of a mutative interpretation nor cognitive insight but regulation is the central mechanism for working with both dissociated, intense unconscious affects and repressed, moderately stressful unconscious affects in mutual regressions.

Furthermore, we need to expand the construct of repression (like dissociation) from solely a one-person model of intrapsychic repression to also include a two-person model of mutual repression and its release. At the most fundamental level, interactively regulated mutual regressions enable the psychobiologically attuned therapist to monitor, enter into, and regulate the patient's affective states of emotional arousal. Indeed, regulation is at the core of the psychotherapy change mechanism (Schore, 1994, 2003b, 2012). A comprehensive overview of psychoanalytic theories of psychotherapy concluded, "There has been a shift involving a relative deemphasis on the therapeutic role of [mutative] interpretation and [cognitive] insight and an increasing emphasis on the importance of the therapeutic relationship as the effective therapeutic agent" (Wolitsky & Eagle, 1999, p. 86).

That said, the construct of interpretation has shifted in psychodynamic theory from an emphasis on left brain objective, mutative, genetic, and resistance interpretations to more right brain interpretations that directly impact the patient's subjective state. The latter form is not authoritative but inquisitive and curious. Writing on revised contemporary models of interpretations, Blum asserted that "interpretations are more likely to be regarded as trial balloons, tentative proposals, rather than definitive statements" (2016, p. 43). Thus, their clinical value is less in their explanatory power than in their capacity to encourage further exploration (Clulow, 2017). Recent neuroscience research clearly demonstrates that the right and not left prefrontal areas are active when decisions are required in incompletely specified situations, and that this adaptive role "involves the maintenance of ambiguous mental representations that temper premature overinterpretation by the left hemisphere" (Goel et al., 2007, p. 2245).

In parallel, reformulations of the role of language in interpretations are now being informed by current neuroscience, which documents that the traditional concept of language being a dominant and lateralized function of the left hemisphere is no longer tenable (Ross & Monnot, 2008). These authors demonstrate that the right hemisphere is essential for communication competency and psychological well-being through its ability to modulate affective prosody and gestural behavior, make thematic inferences, and process complex linguistic relationships and metaphor. Note each of these abilities are involved in an intersubjective (rather than objective) interpretation.

Integrating these advances, Stevens (2005) describes a "vital" interpretation as opposed to an interpretation that is rote and not linked to moment-to-moment subjective experience. In contrast to the left-lateralized literal or semantic meaning of words, this right-lateralized interpretation is linked both to the metaphoric content of the language and to the nonverbal communication from the patient. The functions of a vital interpretation include an expansion of the patient's ability to tolerate feelings, the capacity to recognize and think about these feelings, the ability to be creative, and the awareness of what was previously unconscious. Thus, vital interpretations are an essential mechanism in patients with fully developed object relations who can access symbolic and metaphoric capacities in order to work with the defense of repression. In line with the previous discussion of dissociation versus repression, Andrade asserts the clinical principle, "As a primary factor in psychic change, interpretation is limited in effectiveness in pathologies arising from the verbal phase, related to explicit memories, with no effect in the pre-verbal phase where implicit memories are to be found" (2005, p. 677). In the next section, I elaborate a model of working with mutual regressions in more developmentally advanced patients that includes the therapist's own psychodynamic, deep psychotherapy.

CLINICAL APPLICATIONS OF MUTUAL REGRESSIONS: WORKING WITH REPRESSED AFFECT IN VOLUNTARY MUTUAL REGRESSIONS

Until recently, psychodynamic models of treatment have been anchored in the late developing defense of repression and its central role in inhibiting not just anxiety, drives, and sexual and aggressive fantasies, but more fundamentally unconscious negative affect. As mentioned, for most of the past century, the mechanism of therapeutic action centered on undoing repression and making the unconscious conscious through the therapist's interpretations that stimulate the patient's conscious cognitive insight. However, with the expansion of modern trauma theory and incorporation of an interpersonal neurobiological model of early relational trauma into clinical theory, there is now a focus on therapeutic work with the earliest developing defense, dissociation, a strategy for coping with traumatic intense negative affect. In the previous section, I discussed my work with personality disorder patients who present with early attachment trauma, interpersonal deficits, severe affect dysregulation while under relational stress, and a failure of integration of mental life.

In contrast to severe personality disorder patients who access dissociation under even mild stress, what was previously termed "neurotic" patients who access repression in general present with an attachment history of more efficient repairs of relational ruptures. Echoing early emotional development, alliance ruptures are not as severe, and therapeutic misattunements are not responded to with extremely intense negative affect or with dissociative disengagement. As opposed to more archaic forms of transference-countertransference mutual enactments of preverbal trauma associated with dissociation, these patients can access verbal mechanisms to express affective dysregulation of early misattuned relational experiences. In contrast to using dissociation as a characterological defense against the subjective bodily-based experiencing of negative affect, these more developmentally advanced patients use repression to block unconscious painful affects from becoming conscious. Although the body of my studies focuses on the affect-regulating aspects of the early defense of dissociation, I now expand my work and offer a more complex neuropsychoanalytic conceptualization of later forming repression as a defense against negative affect.

Before the recent advances in trauma theory and dissociation, Wolberg asserted that "Any material that is emotionally disturbing will be suppressed or repressed by the patient until enough strength is gained to handle the anxieties evoked by the verbalization. . . . It is essential to remember, however, that it is not so much the events or ideas that are disturbing, but rather *the emotions that are related to them*" (1977, p. 610, italics added). Wolberg (1977) further postulated,

> Among repressed and repudiated aspects of psychic activity are fears and fantasies . . . and sexuality. There are hostile and destructive impulses directed toward other persons and the self. . . . There are incestuous desires and other unresolved oedipal elements. . . . There are such normal strivings as desire for love, companionship, recognition, self-esteem, independence of self-fulfillment, which have developed incompletely, or, for anxiety reasons, been abandoned.

There are, in addition, rejected neurotic drives for affection, dependence, superiority, dominance, ambition, power and detachment as
well as conflicts that these drives initiate. (pp. 574–575)

Wolberg described "first-line defenses," conscious efforts at maintaining
control through manipulating the environment, which are then supple-
mented by activation of the "repressive defense." Yet he pointed out that
"These efforts directed at reinforcing repression are usually associated with
a constant failing of repressive barriers with a breakthrough and release of
repressed material" (1977, p. 413). Indeed, Freud suggested that repressed
material retains its impetus to penetrate into consciousness.

Utilizing a neuropsychoanalytic perspective, I now offer a clinical
model for working with more stable personality organizations and more
complex character structures, especially those who use excessive repression,
a major force of inhibition of affect, cognition, and behavior. Repression
can be either rigid and pathological or adaptive and resilient. A large body
of studies indicates that individuals with a heavily repressive personality
style, who habitually repress negative affects, are at risk for psychological and physical disorders. In the following, I describe an interpersonally
creative therapeutic context that can facilitate a more adaptive repressive
defense. As opposed to spontaneous reenactments of dissociated terror,
rage, and hopeless despair of attachment trauma in the early part of the
first year through the middle of the second year, in modeling repression I
focus on later developmental relational stressors that commence after the
latter part of the second year and into the third year, especially unrepaired
dysregulating nonverbal shame, verbal sexual trauma, aggression, and verbal humiliation. As opposed to shame's right brain attachment dynamics,
humiliation is driven by left-hemispheric power dynamics and an intentional conscious action that targets the deficits or disabilities of the verbal
conscious self.

Patients with these more developmentally advanced early histories can
access affects and conflicts via right-hemispheric regulatory, symbolic,
imaginative, and self-reflective functions, but also via left-hemispheric
volition and voluntary behavior, verbal secondary process cognition, metacognition, mentalization, abstraction, and, most importantly, by the later

forming defense of repression against negative affect. These complex cognitive functions are available to the patient during the (re-) experiencing
of distressing affect, which is regulated by the defense of repression. As
mentioned, the following model of growth-promoting long-term deep psychotherapy also apples to *the clinician's own therapeutic work*, which is
essential to clinical efficacy, especially working with intense emotions and
their unconscious defenses.

In further contrast to dissociative patients, these individuals can utilize
the psychic mechanism of regression in the service of the ego, or in modern terms regression in the service of the growth of the subjective self. In
classic writings, Gill and Brenman (1959) characterized this adaptive form
of regression as voluntarily sought by the individual; entered only when the
person judges the situation to be safe; being active rather than passive relative to pathological regression; having a definite beginning and end; and
being terminable and reversible, with a sudden and total reinstatement of
the previous ego organization. Bach stressed the active role of the patient:
"He submits himself voluntarily to regression because he has some confidence that it is, in fact, reversible. With these patients it is of the utmost
clinical importance that the regression be engaged voluntarily and that
they feel free to discuss their anxieties and to control the situation" (1985,
p. 185). An update of this model transforms it to a mutual adaptive regression and underscores the importance of this submission to the reduction of
the repression defense on both sides of the therapeutic dyad.

The construct of a synchronized interpersonal mutual repression contrasts with the classical intrapsychic regression, wherein as the patient
regressed and dropped down right into a state of ego-dystonic affect, the
therapist remained up left, interpreting the regression in order to ostensibly
increase cognitive insight and reduce repression. Frequently this would
take the form of a resistance interpretation, which often either shamed and
dysregulated the patient into an iatrogenic negative therapeutic reaction
or intensified the repression defense. Valliant observed, "By thoughtlessly
challenging irritating, but partly adaptive, immature defenses, a clinician
can evoke enormous anxiety and depression in a patient and rupture the
alliance" (1994, p. 49). Recall Spezzano's description of the therapist's (left

hemispheric) resistance interpretation when she cannot hold the patient's projected disturbing affects. Epstein (1994) described the iatrogenic effects of this inability to "take the transference":

> The projected affects often involve the therapist's hidden feeling of shame, envy, vulnerability, and impotence. The hidden shame is signalled by the therapist's use of "attack other" defenses such as sarcasm, teasing, ridicule, and efforts to control the patient in some way. Later on, the tragic projection comes full circle when the patient feels humiliated, exploited, betrayed, abandoned, and isolated. (p. 100)

In a classic misattunement, the members of the therapeutic dyad are in different hemispheres, different minds. Especially in a context involving the patient's aggression, the therapist's left brain now inadvertently implicitly shames the patient by offering a genetic interpretation that his regressed behavior is a repetition or transference of an immature defense mechanism used by the patient during his childhood. Or an emotionally detached therapist interprets the patient's dependency ("need for gratification") as the best possible solution to his difficulties in childhood, even if no longer useful, also implicitly shaming the patient's regression. This iatrogenic shame is intensified by the clinician's tone of voice and facial expression, beneath conscious awareness.

Loewald (1986) offered a clinical example of this process and pointed out that this defensive countertransferential strategy, if not recognized and processed by the clinician, can cause gross interference with the therapeutic process. He noted,

> Less spectacular but more insidious and more damaging, are behaviors of the [therapist] that are the results of inner defense against his countertransference reactions, such as rigid silences, unbending attitudes, repression or isolation of troublesome impulses, fantasies, or memories [p. 282]. . . . The [therapist] . . . in his effort to stay sane and rational is often apt to repress the very transference-countertransference resonances and responses induced by the

patient that would give him the deepest but also the most unsettling understanding of himself and the patient [p. 283].

Note the direct description of the defensive use of repression, conscious suppression, and distraction by the therapist and the allusion to countertransferential strains on the therapist's rational left hemisphere by the patient's dysregulating right hemisphere affect.

Indeed, Russell pointed out the importance of not just the patient's but also the therapist's defenses, clearly alluding to a two-person psychology of mutual defense: "The most important source of resistance in the treatment process is the therapist's resistance to what the patient feels" (1998, p. 19). In this paradigm shift, what is needed in a relational, intersubjective model of affect defenses is one that addresses how the patient's and the therapist's defenses interact with each other, communicate with each other, and synchronize or desynchronize with each other. Like mutual dissociation defenses, mutual repressive defenses of both the patient and the therapist need to be lifted in order to activate adaptive, co-created, synchronized psychotherapeutic mutual regressions.

Balint (1968) described the therapeutic use of these adaptive "benign" regressions:

> Thus, the first task of the understanding analyst, who has determined that therapeutic regression is indicated, involves the facilitation of a trusting therapeutic partnership that encourages the *dissolution of resistances to that regression*. Once this is accomplished, the function of the treatment is to allow the patient to experience acceptance and recognition. In this way, the treatment provides what was unavailable during the patient's early life. (p. 469, italics added)

In her book *The Analyst's Preconscious*, Hamilton (1996) cites the clinical approach of Matheson on the value of adaptive mutual regressions:

> I think in Winnicottian and Balint's terms, which are very similar . . . that is, in terms of the basic fault and therapeutic regression where, in the analysis, the patient gets back to much earlier states of

development, perhaps to traumatic or pretraumatic states. And working with these states, both in terms of experiencing and in terms of interpretation. Very often, it is the noninterpretation that is as important, the experience of the analytic situation. And also it can be very important not to interpret because interpretation, particularly transference interpretation, can take the patient out of a state of regression. *It is better to allow the patient to experience what it is like to be in that state and for you to be in the regression with them. . . .* You should do everything you can to keep yourself as "unobtrusive," in Balint's phrase, as possible. (p. 259, italics added)

Note the direct allusion to a relational two-person model of mutual regression into an early traumatic state. Also note the emphasis on not left-hemispheric language but on shared right-hemispheric emotional experience in the synchronized down shift of state. In these regressive moments, the therapist's creativity is critical. Giovacchini described the creative process as "a broad range of functioning [that] traverses various levels of the psyche, frequently reaching down to the very earliest, primary process-oriented parts of the self. Ego boundaries, in turn, can become quite fluid and permeable, even though they are ordinarily firmly established and well structured" (1991, p. 187).

REPRESSION PSYCHODYNAMICS: NEUROPSYCHOANALYSIS OF LEFT-RIGHT FRONTAL STATE SHIFTS

An essential task of the burgeoning therapeutic relationship, at certain well-timed moments, is that both the patient and the therapist begin to suspend the left-hemispheric repression of right-hemispheric affect. In the early stages of treatment, the therapist takes the lead in this reversal of hemispheric dominance, and her own ability to overcome not only the patient's but also her own resistances to an adaptive regression requires a creative response in order to "mistrust sweet reason" and "abandon" oneself to the emerging unconscious when the barriers separating conscious from preconscious have been transiently "loosened."

Translating this clinical description into neurobiological terms, in order to empathically attune to the patient's conscious and especially unconscious negative affective state, especially during a stressful therapeutic impasse and alliance rupture, the creative clinician initiates an intrapsychic topographical regression, a horizontal switch from a conscious left prefrontal cortical into a preconscious right prefrontal cortical system, a left-hemispheric to right-hemispheric shift in dominance from the rational conscious mind into the intuitive preconscious mind (see the horizontal arrows in Figure 3.1). According to Mihov and colleagues (2010), creativity, a right-hemispheric function, is the ability to "think outside the box." In the therapeutic context of a mutual defensive impasse, the clinician's most successful strategy to create a novel solution to the dyadic misattunement would be to instantiate a regression from left-hemispheric secondary process convergent to right-hemispheric primary process divergent thinking and the creation of new ideas. The therapist's state shift from rational to intuitive cognition is expressed in the ability to feel and not think her way through a therapeutic stalemate of mutual repressive defenses. Mayer stated "we have to lose what's familiar in order to see what's new. . . . Giving up our habitual grounding in rational thought to see something new, even for just a moment—that's anything but easy for most of us" (2007, p. 138).

Indeed, Popper emphasized the unique role of intuition and not rational thinking in the processing of something new: "There is no such thing as a logical method of having new ideas, or a logical reconstruction of this process. My view may be expressed by saying that every discovery contains 'an irrational element,' or 'a creative intuition'" (1968, p. 32). Within an emerging deep psychotherapy, something "new" describes the sudden encountering in a relational context of nascent parts of the patient's self and new ways of *being with* another. The clinician's left-right frontal shift that reduces repression and releases a creative intuition facilitates the patient's self-discovery. This topographical shift allows the therapist to access primary process cognition and primary process communication. Rogers's (1954) construct of "constructive creativity" applies to a therapist's preconscious countertransferential ability for divergent thinking about self and other via an adaptive intrapsychic regression:

Associated with the openness and lack of rigidity . . . is the ability to play spontaneously with ideas, colors, shapes, relationships—to juggle elements into impossible juxtapositions, to shape wild hypotheses, to make the given problematic, to express the ridiculous, to translate from one form to another, to transform into improbable equivalents. It is from this spontaneous toying and exploration that there arises the hunch, the creative seeing of life in a new and significant way. (p. 255)

This right-lateralized intuitive generation of a therapeutic hunch also allows for not only seeing the patient in a new way but also promoting the therapist's spontaneous authentic self-disclosure.

These resilient alterations of reversible callosal dominance of the left over the right hemisphere underlie the previously mentioned clinical descriptions of the therapist's entrance into a creative regression by a passively "letting-go" out of the left hemisphere, dominant for control, into the right hemisphere, dominant for both vulnerability and creativity (Hecht, 2014). McGilchrist (2009) described this hemispheric relationship, "We must inhibit one in order to inhabit the other," clearly implying that the left prefrontal must be inhibited (taken "off-line") to bring the disinhibited right prefrontal from the background to the foreground of consciousness. Even more specifically, these reversible shifts in dominance occur between dual prefrontal systems. A recent neuroimaging study by Huang and colleagues (2013) reported that the left frontal lobe is negatively related to creativity, that the right hemisphere's predominance in creative thinking may be inhibited by the left part of the brain in normal people, and that removal of this inhibition can facilitate the emergence of creativity.

In earlier writings, I offered evidence to show that the prefrontal executive functions of the right and left hemispheres are respectively mediated by the early maturing orbital frontal (and ventromedial) and later maturing dorsolateral (and dorsomedial) prefrontal cortices (Schore, 1994). These systems reciprocally inhibit each other's functions; their callosal connections are centrally implicated in interhemispheric relationships. Thus, the empathic clinician's topographical left-right shift is initiated by temporarily taking the left-hemispheric dorsolateral rational system connected into the left hippocampal memory system off-line, thereby disinhibiting the right-hemispheric orbitofrontal emotional system and its direct corticolimbic connections into the right amygdala. According to Cavada and colleagues, "the anterior sections of the corpus callosum which include axons of the orbitofrontal areas participate in interhemispheric integration on a broad scale" (2000, p. 229).

Furthermore, this shift between left-lateralized prefrontal and right-lateralized prefrontal executive functions represents a shift not only from narrow to broad attention, but also in states of consciousness, unique to each hemisphere. Edelman (1989) stated that *primary consciousness* relates visceral and emotional information pertaining to the biological self to stored information pertaining to outside reality, and that it is lateralized to the right brain. This right limbic–driven state is equated with Jackson's (1931) *"subject consciousness,"* an "experience-near" preverbal mode that organizes perceptions and memories automatically and nonconsciously, according to similarity and affective valence. Jackson contrasted this with *"object consciousness,"* which is more "experience-distant." Research now shows that the dorsolateral prefrontal system is fundamentally involved in *self-reflective consciousness* and abstract thinking (Courtney et al., 1998; Dehaene & Naccache, 2001; Posner, 1994). Note the transient loosening of the self-reflective consciousness of the left mind allows for the transient dominance of the primary consciousness of the right mind. Recall the previous description of Rogers's (1989) shift into an intuitive "slightly altered state of consciousness" in the therapeutic relationship. This conception suggests that regression in the service of the ego fundamentally involves a regression from the later forming executive functions of the left hemisphere to the earlier forming executive functions of the right hemisphere.

The left dorsolateral system is also activated during cognitive reappraisal, the changing of the interpretation of emotion-generating events via a cognitive-linguistic strategy that alters the trajectory of emotional responses by reformulating the verbal meaning of a situation (Schore, 2012). Fonagy and his colleagues reported an fMRI study showing mentalization, the ability to *interpret* the mental states of others is associated with specifically left-hemispheric activation (Nolte et al., 2010). Note that in the moment of a topographical left-right shift, the clinician's cognitive appraisal and mentalization functions are deactivated. The analytical left brain meaning system now switches to an emotional right brain bodily-based meaning system. In an intrapsychic topographical shift, the emotion-processing right orbitofrontal cortex is now dominant over verbal cognitive left dorsolateral prefrontal cortex.

Kris's (1952) definition of regression in the service of the ego thus describes a partial, temporary, controlled lowering of the level of psychic functioning of the left dorsolateral cortex executive system that releases the dominance of the orbitofrontal executive system, the "thinking part of the emotional brain" (Goleman, 1995). This left dorsolateral prefrontal to right orbital prefrontal shift represents a shift from secondary to primary process functions, an essential mechanism of a regression. Acting at levels beneath conscious awareness, the orbitofrontal system acts to "integrate and assign emotional-motivational significance to cognitive impressions; the association of emotion with ideas and thoughts" (Joseph, 1996) and in "the processing of affect-related meanings" (Teasdale et al., 1999). Because its activity is associated with a lower threshold for awareness of sensations of both external and internal origin, it functions as an "internal reflecting and organizing agency" (Kaplan-Solms & Solms, 1996).

In a description of the unique functions of the orbital prefrontal cortex that mirror the processes of psychotherapy, Andreasen and colleagues (1995) reported that during focused episodic memory, the *recalling and relating of a personal experience* to another, an increase of blood flow occurs in the orbitofrontal areas. Right frontal activity specifically occurs when the brain is actively retrieving this personal event from the past. Even more intriguingly, this same inferior frontal region is activated when the subject is told to allow the mind to "rest." They observed that in this condition of uncensored and silently unexpressed private thoughts, the individual's mental activity consists of loosely linked and freely wandering past recollections and future plans. The authors concluded that this orbitofrontal activity reflects "free association" that taps into primary process.

In my earlier work, I cited research indicating that the right orbitofrontal cortex, the apex of the limbic system, plays a fundamental role in preconscious functions, specifically acting as a dynamic filter of emotional stimuli, providing a panoramic view of the entire external and internal environment

associated with motivational factors, and formulating a kind of affective decision making (Schore, 2003b). In classical psychoanalytic conceptualizations,
Freud's notion of repression is understood to represent the brain's capacity to
recognize and filter affects at an unconscious level. The right orbitofrontal
preconscious subjective self-system thus acts as a major determinant factor
in which subcortical affects that support different self-states can reach right-
subjective and then left-hemispheric objective consciousness.

The preconscious has been classically defined as that part of the mind
below the level of immediate conscious awareness, from which memories
and emotions that have not been repressed can be recalled. The patient's
excessive reliance on the repression defense is used to actively block right
orbitofrontal preconscious distressing negative affects—the intensity of emotional arousal, which in turn potentially interferes with left-hemispheric
functions—from entering consciousness. Thus, the conscious mind, the
left hemisphere, whose window of tolerance is optimal in a mid-range of
arousal ("inverted U"), can actively "push out," can repress strong (high or
low) negative emotional arousal that would dysregulate its function, back
into the right brain preconscious. In this manner, the preconscious mind
contains repressed affects that do and do not reach conscious awareness.
Furthermore, explicit cultural taboos are a major source of what is expelled
from the conscious mind.

In a neuropsychological reconceptualization of Freud's repression,
Joseph postulated, "The preconscious contains information and memories
that exist *just below the surface of consciousness*, and in this respect, it is
part of the unconscious. Once information reaches the preconscious, it
becomes relatively accessible to the conscious mind. However, *the preconscious also contains information that is pushed out of consciousness*" (1992,
p. 19, italics added). These repressed unconscious affects can however be
communicated to another preconscious system in a right brain-to-right
brain communication. Intuitive intrapsychic topographical regressions into
the right orbitofrontal preconscious system allow the clinician to receive
and regulate repressed unconscious negative affects that are embedded
in preconscious communications. This intrapsychic regression into the
therapist's right hemisphere now allows for an alignment and interbrain
synchronization with the patient's right hemisphere and co-participation

in a mutual regression that creates a right brain-to-right brain communications system. Kantrowitz suggested, "It is in the realm of preconscious communication that the interwoveness of intrapsychic and interpersonal phenomena becomes apparent" (1999, p. 72). This interpersonal neurobiological mechanism thus mediates the co-creation of an adaptive creative topographical mutual regression that can potentially transform repressed unconscious negative affect into a domain of the preconscious where it can enter consciousness as a discrete feeling, one that can be communicated to both the patient's subjective self and to the therapist.

In classic writings, Kubie (1958) proposed that creative activity is the outcome of the free interplay of specifically preconscious processes, a natural and universal activity of the human organism. These processes are presymbolic, and they reshuffle learned experiences into new constellations on the basis of analogic characteristics. Yet they may become accessible symbolically on the conscious level, especially in free associations and adaptive instances of regression in the service of the ego. Alluding to preconscious functions, Welling described intuition as "a factory of pieces of thoughts, images, and vague feelings, where the raw materials seem to "float around half formless, a world so often present, though we hardly ever visit it. However, some of these floating elements come to stand out, gain strength, or show up repeatedly. When exemplified, they may be easier to recognize and cross the border of consciousness" (2005, p. 33). Recall Reik's primary process refers to a level of mentation in which "sounds, fleeting images, organic sensations, and emotional currents are not yet differentiated." Epstein described the salience of "the preconscious level of awareness," where preconscious cognitions play an essential role in structuring experience, particularly "emotions and moods." He further stated, "Freud believed that unconscious motivation is the most significant source of human behavior. I submit that the preconscious level of functioning deserves the honor because it is here that the implicit beliefs and values reside, which automatically organize and direct our everyday experience and behavior" (1983, p. 235).

These clinical data indicate that the preconscious system stores and generates "implicit relational knowledge" (Stern et al., 1998). In earlier work, I offered interdisciplinary evidence supporting the idea that the right orbitofrontal system is isomorphic to Bowlby's control system of attachment (Schore, 2001). Further elaborating the model, I now suggest Freud's preconscious represents the neurobiological orbitofrontal locus of Bowlby's unconscious internal working models that encode strategies of affect regulation (see Figure 3.2). Recall, Bowlby proposed that psychotherapy is directed toward altering these internalized representations of early relationships. This conceptualization clearly implies that *the mother's right hemisphere imprints the toddler's emerging preconscious system in the second and third years.*

Mutual synchronized topographical regressions, operating at levels beneath conscious awareness, are ubiquitous in all relational, psychodynamic, affectively focused psychotherapies (while the cognitive behavioral therapist attempts to stay up left and work with cognitive reappraisal, lateralized in left prefrontal cortex). In these synchronized left-right hemispheric shifts, each simultaneously switches out of the conscious verbal left mind into nonverbal affects and sensorial images of the preconscious right mind. These events allow the therapist's right mind to affectively intuit, empathize, and intersubjectively resonate with repressed unconscious dysregulated states of the patient's right mind. Mutual structural regressions are also accessed as the dyad moves into working with the subcortical deep unconscious. In these moments, the right orbitofrontal cortex may be transiently taken off-line to allow for a reorganization of its reciprocal connections with the right amygdala (and then to the higher corticolimbic right frontal system coming back online). Thus as opposed to topographical horizontal regressions, right-hemispheric hierarchical structural regressions represent right cortical-subcortical synchronizations that allow for working with dissociated affects, "not me" states.

Indeed, mutual structural regressions may also be activated in enactments with these more developmentally advanced patients who can access symbolic and verbal functions (see Bromberg, 2011 on what I would term late "developmental trauma," especially shame trauma, in the second year as opposed to the early relational trauma of abuse and/or neglect in the first year). For Bromberg "developmental trauma" is a core phenomenon in the shaping of personality that is expressed in "the trauma of nonrecognition that is an inevitable part of everyone's early life to one degree or another"

(p. 69). This clearly implies that "developmental trauma," relational trauma in the second year (and therefore interferes with autonomy) is an essential area of therapeutic exploration in all cases of "deep" psychotherapy, even with those more regulated patients who have not experienced early chronic attachment trauma (organized insecure and secure attachments). Bromberg (2011) concluded that therapeutic joint processing of enactments allows one's work with so-called "good" patients to become more effective because it provides a more experience-near perspective from which to engage clinical phenomena that are immune to interpretation, such as the mutual patient-therapist regressions that mediate "intractable resistance" and "therapeutic stalemate." These jointly constructed, highly defended unconscious states need to be brought into consciousness in both members of the therapeutic alliance through the mutual regression of a joint enactment,

Note the right preconscious system is activated in both topographical and structural regressions. Indeed, the right orbitofrontal system is centrally involved in not only the preconscious horizontal transmission of regulated and dysregulated affective states to the conscious left hemisphere, but also in the preconscious hierarchical regulation of lower levels of the right brain unconscious system that generates intense negative and positive affect. A body of studies now indicates that the right orbitofrontal preconscious system plays a fundamental role in processing of emotion-evoking stimuli without conscious awareness and controlling the allocation of attention to possible contents of consciousness, but also in the homeostatic regulation of body and motivational states via its monitoring and regulation of the duration, frequency, and intensity of repressed (and dissociated) unconscious affective states (Schore, 2012). Northoff and his colleagues (2007) assert that the orbitofrontal cortex is involved in constituting a more mature and cognitively guided defense, and that dysfunction in this region make the constitution of higher defense mechanisms impossible. Indeed in contemporary neuropsychoanalytic research, these researchers describe repression as "moving thoughts unacceptable to the ego into the unconscious, where they cannot be easily accessed."

Affectively focused psychodynamic psychotherapy that utilizes left-right frontal shifts in order to induce mutual regressions to access unconscious affects can thus potentially bring repressed affects into conscious awareness. In this work, the empathic clinician's right-lateralized preconscious creativity is expressed in her ability to remain subjectively and psychobiologically connected to the patient during a synchronized mutual regression so that she can facilitate a relational context that can implicitly co-regulate unconscious affect into subjective awareness. The *Oxford English Dictionary* defines creativity as "bringing into being." The therapist's interpersonal creativity relationally catalyzes unconscious, undeveloped repressed aspects of the patient's self to "come into being."

MUTUAL REGRESSIONS IN THE EARLY STAGE OF DEEP PSYCHOTHERAPY

An interpersonal neurobiological model of mutual regression can be applied to working with unconscious affects over different stages of the psychotherapeutic process, especially in "deep" psychodynamic explorations, including the clinician's own long-term psychotherapy. Over the course of the treatment, the therapeutic dyad creates changes in both process and content. This model emphasizes the primacy of the processes of affect, affect dysregulation, and affect regulation. A long-standing, cardinal tenet of clinical psychodynamic models dictates that the treatment must match the developmental level of the patient. From the first point of contact, the therapeutic inquiry centers not only on the affective and relational underpinnings of the patient's symptomatology and dysfunctional behavior, but also on the past history and character structure, the patient's conscious and unconscious minds, and both the external and internal world.

Recall the central psychoanalytic concept of an unconscious internal object relation. Greenberg and Mitchell (1983) observed, "People react to and interact with not only an actual other but also an internal other, a psychic representation of a person which in itself has the power to influence both the individual's affective state and his overt behavioral reactions" (1983, p. 10). Kernberg (1976) clinically demonstrated the importance of the conception of internalized representations of the self affectively transacting with objects in the social environment as an explanatory mechanism of various psychopathological conditions that originate in very early development. In my own neuropsychoanalytic work I have described a pathological object relation, an internal representation of a dysregulated self affectively interacting interaction with a misattuning-object, which is re-activated in a mutual enactment. Psychoanalytic clinicians thus explore the dynamic interplay between these unconscious internal emotion transacting object relational images of self and other within the therapeutic relationship.

I now offer a dynamic conceptualization of the unconscious nonverbal affective communications that lie beneath the conscious verbal conversations transacted between the patient and the therapist *over the stages of treatment*. This two-person psychoanalytic psychology of the therapeutic development of *unconscious functioning of the patient and the therapist* in psychodynamic psychotherapy focuses on synchronized affect state shifts, spontaneous transitions between self-states that take place in the present moment, a time frame of fractions of a second to 2 to 3 seconds. These rapid, implicit, short-term synchronized *regressions* do have significant effects at longer time frames, especially on *progressions* of the patient's unconscious "right mind" and conscious left mind. This adaptive developmental advance is neurobiologically expressed in more flexible repression defenses and a rebalancing of the hemispheres.

Psychodynamic psychotherapy differs from cognitive behavioral therapy from the outset of the treatment. Cognitive behavioral therapy's focus on a self-control form of emotion regulation involves higher levels of cognitive executive function that allow individuals to change the way they feel by consciously changing the way they think. This explicit form of affect regulation is performed by the verbal left hemisphere, and *unconscious bodily-based emotion is usually not addressed*. In contrast to this conscious emotion regulation system, psychodynamic psychotherapy focuses on more fundamental implicit affect regulatory functions performed by the right hemisphere, the biological substrate of the human unconscious. This right-lateralized system rapidly and automatically processes facial expression, vocal quality, eye contact, and bodily changes in a relational context. Psychodynamic therapy thus attempts not control but the acceptance or facilitation of particular emotions, including *defensively avoided repressed emotion* in order to allow the patient to tolerate and transform them into adaptive emotions. Thus from the beginning, the patient's attentional focus is shifting from conscious cognition to (avoided and repressed) unconscious affect, and from the cognitive left to the emotional right hemisphere.

Ackerman, Hilsenroth, and Knowles (2005) offered a description of the early stage of treatment:

> The therapist's use of psychodynamic-interpersonal activities in the beginning of treatment (e.g., encouraging the experience and *exploration of uncomfortable feelings,* allowing the patient to initiate discussion of salient themes, and focusing on in-session relational themes between the therapist and the patient) may inform the patient that the therapist is willing (and able) to help address issues that have been previously *avoided.* The willingness of the patient to experience and explore affect, as well as initiate discussion, may broaden the therapist's perception of the patient as even more actively engaged and *lend momentum to the developing therapeutic alliance.* (p. 229, italics added)

Note the unconscious avoidance of uncomfortable feelings directly implies a focus on defenses such as repression. Also note the emphasis on the patient's autonomy, and that the patient plays an active relational-emotional role in the treatment and is not just a passive recipient of a talking cure.

On the other side of the burgeoning therapeutic alliance, at the beginning of the therapy, "It remains the first aim of treatment to attach him [the patient] to it [the process of therapy] and to the person of the doctor" (Freud, 1913/1958, p. 139). In modern terms, from the outset of this joint exploration, the empathic clinician co-creates a therapeutic alliance, a spontaneous right brain-to-right brain attachment communication system that can psychobiologically attune, synchronize, and regulate the patient's conscious and unconscious repressed affective states, especially those that contribute to the presenting symptomatology. In order to participate in co-creating the emotional bond of the developing therapeutic relationship, the clinician enters into a receptive state of what Leslie Greenberg (2014) terms "therapeutic presence":

Therapeutic presence involves therapists being fully in the moment on a multitude of levels, physically, emotionally, cognitively, spiritually and relationally. The experience of therapeutic presence involves (a) being in contact with one's integrated and healthy self, while (b) being *open and receptive,* to what is poignant in the moment and immersed in it, (c) with a larger sense of spaciousness and expansion of awareness and perception. This grounded, immersed, and expanded awareness occurs with the intention of *being with and for the client,* in service of his or her healing process. (p. 353, italics added)

Citing my work, Greenberg (2014, p. 351) asserts that this therapeutic stance is directed toward promoting implicit affect regulation rather than explicit self-control of emotion: "The type of implicit affect regulation that results from a good therapeutic relationship occurs through right hemispheric processes, is not verbally mediated, is highly relational, and is most directly affected by such things as emotional communication, facial expression, vocal quality, and eye contact (Schore, 2003)." This clinical model is supported by personality and social psychology research that shows "*intuitive affect regulation*" is highly sensitive to context and is nonrepressive, because unlike defensive repression it does not interfere with automatic vigilance for negative affect and is accompanied by a highly accessible self (Koole & Jostmann, 2004).

In order to access these right brain functions, the creative clinician intuitively instantiates topographical left-right hemispheric shifts to match the patient's right brain affective state patterning. This state shift allows the therapist to adopt a therapeutic stance of "regressive openness and receptivity." Indeed, research demonstrates that "openness to experience" is associated with tolerance for regressive experiences such as affects, fantasy and daydreaming, emphasis on richness of creative imagination and inquisitiveness into the unusual or the subtle nuances of the commonplace, and less use of sustained effort and conventional categories of thought (Fitzgerald, 1966). This state of "openness to experience" that results from a transient reduction of unconscious defensiveness allows for "free association," asking patients to report "what comes into their heads, even if they think it is unimportant, irrelevant, or non-sensical" (Strachey, 1953). According to Kubie, "Free associations are essential to creativity; because they free the sensitive, fluid, and plastic preconscious system from the rigidity imposed at the conscious and of the symbolic spectrum" (1958, p. 57). From the outset of the therapy, the patient is implicitly learning how to tolerate reducing defenses to negative and positive affect, and how to be more open to his own and others' affective state. According to Rotenberg (1993), the creative right hemisphere is "open" to real-life occurrences as opposed to the openness of the left hemisphere to constructing logical structures that are shut off from the outside world.

Thus, left-to-right regressive state shifts are key to a psychodynamic formulation of how to listen to the patient, especially how to use free-floating attention and "the third ear" to listen "beneath the words" to the patient's free associations. In classic psychoanalytic writings, Spiegel (1975) noted that both the therapist and the patient were operating in similar states of mind (free-floating attention and free association, respectively), and that this results in a type of "conversation" unique to psychoanalysis. Balter, Lothane, and Spencer proposed that "the analyzing instrument" within the clinician "is more likely to perceive connections between words, ideas, and images which are the products of the patient's primary process, because the subsystem is itself part freed from the constraints of secondary process thinking, reality testing and so on" (1980, pp. 490–491). In the next decade, Boyer (1990) described the importance of a *"complimentary regression of patient and therapist"*:

> The analyst's awareness of his own fantasies, emotional states, and physical sensations that occur during his free-floating attention (and at times subsequent dreams) enables him to be more in tune with his patient's communications, and that such awareness is especially useful in working with the regressed patient. The analyst's tolerance of the patient's primitive regressions . . . as they are relived in the analytic situation, entails his capacity to regress concomitantly with his patient, while simultaneously retaining the observing function of his ego. (pp. 209–210)

In current relational psychoanalytic models authors are now emphasizing not only the clinician's awareness of the inner workings of his/her own mind, but the importance in specific moments of disclosing and sharing these primary process emotions, sensations, and fantasies with the patient. Alluding to a reciprocal, open, nondefensive, implicit mutual regression Sheldon Bach advocates,

> I allow the patient to witness my mind at work in the process of free-associating or making formulations, so that the interpretation becomes a *mutual* endeavor and is thereby much improved. It is especially useful for such patients to experience the analyst as he/she tries to deal with doubt and ambiguity, or as he/she tries to hold two ideas or two roles in mind at the same time, for it opens up the possibility of their doing the same thing. Most importantly, since I am implicitly asking my patients to trust me with their minds, I struggle to attain a position where I can trust them with my own mind and feel that I have nothing to hide from them (Bach, 2003, pp. 403–404, italics added).

In my own neuropsychoanalytic studies I am describing how during a creative mutual regression the receptive clinician enters into a state of "evenly suspended attention" or what McGilchrist (2016) terms a right hemispheric state of "active passivity," an open attendant disposition in which one is ready to respond to what emerges from the inner workings of the right lateralized unconscious intersubjective mind. In this "quiet alert state" the clinician can subjectively attend to "barely perceptible cues that signal a change in state" in both the patient and herself, and to intersubjectively detect the patient's "nonverbal behaviors and shifts in affects," including the patient's right brain communications of sudden defensive shifts that block or release preconscious affects just beneath conscious awareness. This right brain state sharing allows the therapist to enter into the patient's changing feeling state. The empathically resonating therapist's synchronized matching of the rhythmic crescendos and decrescendos of the patient's psychobiological state represents the psychobiological attunement of her felt sense with the patient's felt sense. In this moment-by-moment state matching, both partners increase their degree of engagement. The emergent therapeutic conversation between two aligned right hemispheres initiates a right-lateralized interbrain synchronization between the patient's and the therapist's preconscious systems (see Figure 1.1 in Chapter 1).

In earlier writings (Schore, 2001, 2003b), I described the expanded awareness that ensues from interpersonal synchronization. In the session during a "heightened affective moment" of right brain-to-right brain communication, a bodily-based affective experience and a preconscious image of self and other is automatic and fleeting. But when such synchronized expressions of "nonconscious affect" are interactively regulated, dyadically resonated, amplified, and held in working memory long enough to be felt and recognized, they can be expanded in awareness and shape the subsequent conscious processing of an emotional stimulus. Lou Sander (1992) stated that "moments of meeting" between patient and therapist occur when there are matched specificities between two systems in resonance, attuned to each other. Elaborating this idea, when a psychobiologically attuned dyad co-creates a resonant context within an emotional transaction, the behavioral manifestation of each partner's internal state is monitored by the other, and this results in the coupling between the output of one partner's loop and the input of the other's to form a larger feedback configuration. This *larger* feedback configuration is an emergent function of a right-lateralized interbrain synchronization, one that allows for communications between the relational unconscious of a subjective self and the relational unconscious of another subjective self. When the patterns of synchronized rhythms are in interpersonal resonance, this right brain-to-right brain "specifically fitted interaction" generates amplified energetic processes of emotional arousal, and this interactive affect regulation in turn co-creates an emotional energy transmitting intersubjective field (see pages 92–100 in Schore, 2012).

This dyadic amplification of emotional energy (arousal-intensity) generated in a resonant right brain-to-right brain mutual topographical regression facilitates the intensification of the felt sense of the preconscious and now conscious affect in both therapist and patient. Recall, in a mutually synchronized attunement of emotionally driven behaviors, the dyad co-constructs a mutual regulatory system of arousal that contains a *"positively amplifying circuit mutually affirming both partners"* (Schore, 2003b). In the early developmental context the primordial expression of this mechanism is described by the research of Trevarthen on intersubjectivity, and by Tronick on dyadically *expanded* states of consciousness generated between mother and infant, and between therapist and patient.

According to Tronick et al. (1998) the *relational expansion* of "these states of consciousness emerge from the mutual regulation of affect between the patient and the therapist. When these dyadic states are achieved, the state of consciousness of the patient expands and changes" (p. 298). In this moment of mutual co-creation, the patient's emergent state of consciousness becomes more coherently organized and more complex. In earlier writings I suggested that Tronick is describing an expansion of what Edelman (1989) called right brain *primary consciousness,* which relates visceral and emotional information pertaining to the biological self to stored information processing pertaining to outside reality. Furthermore Tronick hypothesized that "the capacity to create dyadic states of consciousness with another, and the quality of those states, depends in part on the history the individual had in creating these states early in development with his or her mother (and others)" (p. 298–299).

Tronick proposed that dyadically expanded states of consciousness represent an "unconscious force driving social engagement" (1998 p. 296). From the perspective of regulation theory the interpersonal neurobiological mechanism of mutual right brain-to-right brain synchronization underlies a relational "expansion" of a state of affective consciousness, especially at moments when an unconscious affect comes into primary consciousness. This interpersonal neurobiological mechanism sustains the affect in time; the unconscious affect is "held" within the intersubjective field long enough for it to reach conscious awareness in both members of a psychobiologically attuned dyad. Whitehead (2006) asserted, "Emotions are deepened in intensity and sustained in time when they are intersubjectively shared. This occurs at moments of deep contact." In line with the principle that affect acts as an "analog amplifier" that extends the duration of whatever activates it, the clinician's resonance with the patient's preconscious affect state allows for an energetic amplification of an unconscious negative (or positive) affect into consciousness, expanded into awareness in both patient and therapist. In the psychoanalytic literature, Loewald (1986) described "resonances between the patient's and the analyst's unconscious." Recall his proposal that resonances between the patient and the therapist can give the deepest but also the most unsettling understanding of himself and the patient.

In clinical research, Kuhl, Quirin, and Koole (2015) reported,

> Sustainable coping with negative emotions is presumably only possible when individuals confront themselves with those emotions through right-hemispheric processing. By contrast, mere verbalization of unpleasant circumstances without experiencing concomitant emotions *constitutes defensive rather than integrative coping.* . . . There is also evidence that the type of emotion regulation supported by the right prefrontal cortex is integrative rather than defensive and unconscious rather than conscious. (p. 124)

In light of the well-documented clinical observation that physical containment by the therapist of the patient's disavowed experience needs to precede its verbal processing, the interactive regulation of the patient's state enables him or her to now begin to verbally label the affective experience. In this affective moment of a "genuine dialogue," the therapist accesses a "focusing attitude" of waiting patiently in the *presence* of "the not yet speakable, being receptive to the not yet formed," an intersubjective context that facilitates the patient's capacity to raise to an inner word and then into a spoken word what he needs to say at a particular moment but does not yet possess as speech. Note the patient (and not the therapist's interpretation) establishes the creative moment and (re-) discovers the personal meaning, thus reinforcing the subjective agency of the creation of a novel self-state.

But in addition, the patient must experience that this verbal description of an internal affective state is heard and felt, "witnessed" by an empathic, emotionally present other. It is now well established that the right hemisphere is involved in language functions, not only in expressing emotional prosody (Godfrey & Grimshaw, 2016), but also in generating idiomatic expressions, in making thematic inferences, and in processing novel metaphors, and indeed verbal creativity (Ross & Monnot, 2008). The research of Kuchinke and his colleagues (2006) documented that the processing of both positive and negative emotional words activates the right and not left prefrontal cortex. Attachment words, especially those associated with positive interpersonal relationships, are more efficiently processed by the right hemisphere (Mohr, Rowe, & Crawford, 2007). In neuropsychological terminology, subsequent to this transformation within the right-lateralized preconscious, the patient's affectively charged but now regulated right brain experiences can then be communicated to the left brain for further conscious processing. The objective left hemisphere can now process subjective right brain communications, allowing for a linkage of the unconscious nonverbal and conscious verbal representational realms. This facilitates the evolution of affects from their early form, in which they are experienced as bodily sensations, into subjective states that can gradually be verbally articulated and semantically encoded by the left mind.

In writings in the social and personality psychology literature on the right-hemispheric integrated self, Kuhl and colleagues (2015) conclude,

> Expressing emotional contents through language may be one way in which communication between psychological systems may be facilitated . . . such verbalizations may facilitate a transfer of the right hemisphere's implicit information into the analytical left hemisphere. This transfer may be crucial for nurturing integrative competencies, especially when verbalizations are accompanied by emotional and self-related feelings. (p. 124)

There is now agreement among both clinicians and researchers that the ability to express oneself in words during states of high emotional arousal is an important achievement in self-regulation. Not uncommonly after the relational processing and regulation of a disavowed repressed (or dissociated) affect, the dyad now goes "up left" (a synchronized upward state shift) for a more objective, abstract, cognitive understanding of the subjective emotional dynamics that have just played out. This synchronized left brain-to-left brain conversation, usually at end of the session, invokes the dyad's more detached abstracting left dorsolateral mechanisms of mentalization and cognitive reappraisal. In this manner "psychodynamic work is the repetitive moving back and forth, trying to go inside the patient's subjectivity and then trying to come out and reflect on that immersion" (McWilliams, 2018, p. 94). Note the left-right-left sequence, the synchronized downward and then upward state shift, and the move from regression to progression.

These interpersonal neurobiological events are repeated in an increasing number of affective interchanges in the early stages of the therapeutic relationship, building and strengthening both the implicit nonverbal and explicit verbal therapeutic alliance. The formation of the co-created therapeutic alliance proceeds more rapidly with these patients who can access higher right brain self-reflective, symbolic, and imaginative functions, as well as left brain volition, metacognition, secondary process cognition, mentalization, and abstraction than it does with those patients who have severe personality disorders. Yet, in both by the end of a sufficiently relationally structured and regulated early stage of treatment, the patient and the therapist establish an implicit sense of mutual familiarity and trust, build the positive aspects of the working alliance, continue to not avoid but to share mild to moderate affects, and co-construct a system of interactive regulation, the core of the attachment dynamic. This therapeutic attachment mechanism accounts for a reduction in the patient's emotional symptomatology of affect dysregulation, a common outcome of short-term psychodynamic psychotherapy. Because of the cumulative strengthening of the therapeutic communication system over time, both the patient and the therapist can now implicitly and explicitly access more efficient right-lateralized cortical-subcortical interbrain synchronization and thereby co-create even more complex mutual regressions, further reducing repressive defenses on both sides of the dyad.

MUTUAL REGRESSIONS IN THE LATER STAGES
OF DEEP PSYCHOTHERAPY

These emergent functions of the therapeutic alliance allow the dyad to transition into the next and most prolonged "middle" stage of long-term therapy, "working through" (Freud, 1914/1958), a mutual exploration of what Jung (1961) termed "to become conscious of the contents that press upward from the unconscious." The central theme of the working-through stage of mutual exploration is expressed in Joseph's (1992) title *The Right Brain and the Unconscious: Discovering the Stranger Within*. This right brain self-discovery of the unconscious includes continued work with defenses that block awareness of repressed (and dissociated) unconscious affects. In light of the well-established concept of the multiplicity of self-states I suggest these therapeutic encounters are a familiarization of the self with a number of "strangers" in the internal world, self-states that are hidden behind unconscious repression and dissociative defenses. These unconscious defenses determine the rate of development of the establishment of the therapeutic alliance (they also play a significant causal role in the patient's sudden discontinuance of treatment and in the high drop-out rate of subjects in clinical research). Indeed, Guntrip held that "Only when the therapist finds the person behind the patient's defences, and perhaps the patient finds the person behind the therapist's defences, does true psychotherapy happen" (1969, p. 352).

In deep psychotherapy, the further mutual reduction of affect defenses reflects an expansion of the dyad's capacity for both types of mutual regressions. In the early stage, as the patient explicitly or implicitly expressed affect dysregulation, the resonating therapist responded with a topographical regression out of the left and into the right, so that she could match, synchronize with, and then interactively regulate the patient's emotional arousal and affective self-state. The creative clinician, sensitive to even low levels of the patient's defensive shifts when encountering repressed unconscious affects, learned how to synchronize these shifts in hemispheric dominance with patient shifts, co-creating adaptive mutual regressions.

Now in "working through" as a result of the emerging, strengthened therapeutic alliance, the patient acquires not only more of a sense of safety but also an increasing *positively charged curiosity, wonder, and surprise* that fuels the burgeoning self's exploration of novel socioemotional and physical environments. McWilliams observed, "The curiosity about how any individual's unconscious thoughts, feelings, images, and urges work together is the engine of the therapist's commitment and the bulwark of the patient's courage to be increasingly self-examining and self-disclosing" (2018, p. 90).

Toward that end at this stage of the work, the patient can initiate topo-graphical and structural regressions himself and can take the left control center off-line in order to voluntarily attempt a deeper exploration of the right brain bodily-based emotional unconscious. This more fluid reversal of hemispheric dominance represents a resilient ability to shift from left brain convergent cognition to right brain divergent cognition associated with the creative processing of novelty. Frequently, this left-right state shift is now subjectively experienced as some thought or question that spontaneously "pops" into the patient's mind (the inspiration mode of a creative free asso-ciation). A further progression of right brain activities is also seen in the patient's capacity to more easily read the therapist's right brain signals and synchronize with the therapist's regressions, thereby forming a more effi-cient and intimate system of a right brain-to-right brain communication.

This interpersonal neurobiological advance strengthens the patient's ability to join with the therapist to move even more deeply into working with what Bollas (1987) termed "the unthought known:"

> This concept speaks to experiences that are in some way known to the patient but about which she has not yet thought, that is, expe-riences that are in some way [intuitively, implicitly] known to the patient but are waiting to be [rationally, consciously, explicitly] found. In other words, the unthought known speaks to early sche-mata (or templates for interpreting the object world) that will then *preconsciously* determine the individual's subsequent life expecta-tions. (p. 60, italics added)

This domain of "the unthought known," generated in right brain inter-nal working models of attachment, is accessed in regulated mutual regres-sions. The preconscious transformation of unconscious implicit-procedural self-knowledge into conscious explicit self-knowledge parallels the elevation of emotions from a primitive presymbolic sensorimotor level of experience to a mature symbolic representational level, a functional advance that is medi-ated by an increased flexibility of the patient's emotional control structures. That said, it is important to point out that the affective and imagistic right hemisphere is better able than the left to understand the meaning of symbols with implicit, multiple meanings (McGilchrist, 2015). This "evolution" of an emotion from a presymbolic to a symbolic level occurs in the right preconscious mind. Therapeutic creative mutual regressions, both cortical topographical and cortical-subcortical structural, thus enhance the development of the patient's right brain capacity for symbolization, metaphor, fantasy, imagination, and play (Schore & Marks-Tarlow, 2018). These higher right functions evolve to more complexity over the stages of treatment.

In more recent work, Bollas (2013) described this progression in the deepening therapeutic relationship between patient and therapist (note the increase in right-lateralized interpersonal synchronization over time):

> If the [therapist] has worked with the patient for a year or more they will have begun to internalize their character form. It is hard to define this, but think of how after listening, over some time, to the music of a particular composer we begin to feel within ourselves the shape of their musical personality. *Our unconscious receives, organizes and recognizes patterns, and these patterns constitute the form that any content may take.* (p. 20, italics added)

Bollas noted that therapists are trained to be "impressionable," allowing the patient's "way of being and of relating to affect them":

> They need to be open to this as possible and even they may begin to notice patterns early on, they should suspend early judgments in order to continue to be open to the form of a person's character. When the [clinician's] unconscious communicates to the patient's unconscious that the other is *open* in this way to character communication, the patient will become more expressive, often more difficult, certainly more specific in the release of personal idioms of being and relating, and over time, the [clinician] will begin to feel the shape of the patient within himself . . . we know the feel of the many impressions created by the impact of the patient. (pp. 20–21, italics added)

The mutual expansion of right brain-to-right brain synchronization over the stages of therapy and the lessening of the repression defense now allows for intersubjective communications from the lower levels of the patient's preconscious system and its direct connections to the deep unconscious (see Figure 3.2). For a clinical example of such a deep communication within a mutual structural regression, see the clinical vignette of Susan Sands in Schore (2012, pp. 176–177).

I suggest that this significant alteration in the patient's subjective openness to experience in a mutual regression reflects a further disinhibition of the patient's defense systems, a "taking off of the higher" and "at the very same time a letting go, or expression of the lower." This results in a more permeable dynamic within the patient's deeper preconscious system that contains repressed negatively charged affective cognitions (fantasies) that have been expelled from consciousness of the left mind in the patient's early relational history (during the critical period of the initial establishment of hemispheric balance at 3 to 4 years). This change mechanism, an emergent function of the expanding therapeutic alliance, allows for more direct work with the unblocking of repression; that is, a more fluid and sudden access into consciousness of right frontal Aha! moments of intuitive emotional (as opposed to a cognitive) insight (Rosen & Reiner, 2016; Schore, 2012). These heightened affective moments represent a creative transition of the "unthought known" in which unconscious repressed affects can come into consciousness.

In the middle period of therapy, "working through," the therapist now is able to acquire a felt sense of the patient's unconscious affects not just beneath the surface of the preconscious, but repressed affects deeper within the patient's preconscious mind. These repressed affects may be activated when the patient is reexperiencing and recounting emotionally difficult, stressful, painful, and highly conflictual past experiences in right-lateralized episodic autobiographical memory. The ability to tolerate the phenomenological pain experienced upon the emergence of repressed material (negative affect-laden cognition stored in unconscious episodic memory) is critical to growth-promoting psychodynamic treatment. The psychotherapeutic exposure, confrontation, and uncovering of defenses that facilitates the breakthrough of repressed ego-dystonic unpleasant emotional distress into consciousness has been shown to be directly correlated with elevated corticosteroid levels (Sachar et al., 1968).

Although various affectively charged self-states can be repressed, such as aggression, fear, depression, disgust, joy, sexuality, and so forth, frequent and intense early shaming without repair has a particular association with the repression defense. In addition to the developmental trauma of non-verbal shame in the second year, later traumatically painful memories of verbal humiliation may be a potent source of repressed affects. Dorahy suggested that in humiliation, the uninitiated rage reaction that was never expressed to the other and the aggression was subsequently turned toward the self. Thus, "rage is not acknowledged toward the other, or only faintly" (2017, p. 386) (internalized "shame-rage").

Shame is associated with a sudden, rapid, painful implosion of the subjective self that is beyond conscious control (Schore, 1991, 1994, 2003b, 2012). This negative affect inhibits the expression of any specific emotion (Tomkins, 1987), and indeed the expression of emotion *per se* (Kaufman, 1992), and at continual high levels produces a constriction of the affect array. Davis (1987) concluded that repression is motivated, in particular, by affective experiences of heightened self-consciousness in which the self is exposed to a negative evaluation, specifically citing shame. Unrecognized and unaccepted (repressed) shame is thus a growth-inhibitory force to emotional development, because it paralyzes the "self-generating" maturational drive. It therefore must be confronted, consciously recognized, and understood in psychotherapeutic interventions that attempt to facilitate growth and expansion of the self. Dysregulated shame has been proposed to be a potent motive force for not only dissociation but also repression. The avoidance of the recognition of shame "directly opposes derepression and the integration of unconscious material within the conscious ego" (Ward, 1972). Note not conscious but repressed unconscious shame blocks integration into consciousness.

Unconscious dysregulated shame is a central mechanism of psychopathogenesis. It can be accessed by synchronized mutual regressions. At the end of the past century, Wolitzky and Eagle (1999) asserted,

> Both Winnicott (1958b) and Guntrip (1969) refer to the importance
> of the patient returning to an earlier point at which psychological
> development went askew and to that point at which development

turned in the direction of a "false self." The basic idea behind these various formulations seems to be that under the impact of trauma, certain defensive and defective structures (e.g., false self, a pseudo-adult self masking an underlying ego weakness) developed that are at the heart of the patient's pathology. According to this view, what needs to be accomplished in treatment is a regression to the point at which these structures developed and a resumption of developmental growth along *new* and better pathways. (pp. 60–61, italics added)

Since that writing, over the past two decades we now have access to a theory of early relational trauma to the early evolving "true self" and the psychopathogenesis of the later maturing "false self," as well as an interpersonal neurobiological model of both the underlying mechanisms of early emotional development and psychotherapeutic change. In classic developmental psychoanalytic writings, Winnicott (1960) differentiated a "true self" and a "false" or "caretaker self" designed to protect it. This caretaker self usually becomes identified with the conscious mind, leaving the true self languishing in the body, potentially causing psychosomatic illness. In modern neuropsychoanalytic terms, early developmental trauma generates an underlying weakness of the bodily-based right brain "true self" that is masked by a left brain pseudo-adult "false self." In light of the fact that the nonverbal right hemisphere matures before the verbal left hemisphere starts its growth spurt in the second year of life, this clearly implies that the true self evolves before the false self, one associated with a developmental shift in dominance in early childhood from the right to left hemisphere.

Furthermore, the second year is also a time when the primary attachment figure shifts from caregiver to socialization agent, and therefore the onset of shame dynamics (Schore, 1991). This socialization of the child's instinctual (right brain) behavior is tightly associated with the affect of shame. When shame, a major dampener of positive emotion, is intense, and when there is no or little repair of shame misattunements, the emotional responses to continual relational shame-dynamics is painful (see Schore, 1994, pp. 485–487 on "Shame and the Emergence of the 'Bad Self'" and on disgust, a response to a "bad other" that terminates intimacy). I suggest the internalization of the painful intersubjective nonverbal and verbal shaming and humiliating assaults with one or both caregivers in the second and third years represents the object relational source of Jones's description of repression as events, feelings, or wishes that were unquestionably at one time in conscious awareness and accessible to verbal representation but came to be excluded from consciousness or memory. Indeed, at 18 months the child becomes able to conceptualize the self in terms of symbolic "good" and "bad" self-representations (Sander, 1975). Importantly, split-brain research indicates that the right hemisphere is responsible for the generation of single words such as "no," "good," and "bad" (Sperry, Zaidel, & Zaidel, 1979).

Although the early forming right-lateralized automatic "ventral" implicit regulation system including the amygdala, anterior cingulate, insula, and orbitofrontal cortex is operating at this time, when the onset of the left-lateralized growth spurt in the second and third years occurs, the nonlimbic "dorsal" system in the hippocampus and dorsolateral cortex (involved in the explicit processing of the verbal components of emotional stimuli) matures. It is well established that the amygdala matures before the hippocampus, and that developmentally the implicit amygdala memory system is superseded by the explicit memory system in terms of access into consciousness. Thus the emerging hippocampal hierarchical inhibition of the amygdala's role in processing painful affect may account for the repression of conscious shame. What appeared in affective consciousness as right-hemispheric shame at 2 and 3 years, by age 4 (a milestone in maturation of left callosal inhibition of the right hemisphere) is now blocked (including memories of oedipal, sexual wishes toward and aggressive verbal or physical assault by the parents) and replaced by a left-hemispheric, idealized, positively valenced false self that counterbalances the down-regulation of positive affect by right hemispheric shame.

This bi-hemispheric dynamic is overexpressed in those who experience early intense unrepaired shame, and therefore in the psychopathogenesis of narcissistic personality disorder (see Schore, 1994). In such, note the discrepancy between Joseph's (1992) left-hemispheric, superficial, positive conscious self-image and a split-off right-hemispheric, deeper, negative unconscious self-image. Joseph also observed "early emotional learning occurring in the right hemisphere unbeknownst to the left; learning and associated emotional responding may later be completely unaccessible to the language centers of the brain" (1982, p. 243). This is especially so in highly repressed personalities.

And yet the shame-based self remains in implicit-procedural memory as unconscious shame, disgust, and guilt being internally transacted between a dysregulating self and a misattuning object, frequently taking the form of a harshly critical, persecutory, and humiliating verbally aggressive internal object attacking a vulnerable self, or what Mucci (in press) terms an internalized object relation of a "persecutor-victim." Mentally, this splitting between one objective self standing off in the distance observing a second, separate, estranged, experiencing self takes the form of a detached, excessively self-critical internal voice within the resting mind, directing subvocal left hemispheric verbal aggression towards a vulnerable, weak, and shamed right brain, an internal attack on the subjective bodily-based self. In "thin-skinned" (Rosenfeld, 1987), "covert" (Cooper, 1998), "vulnerable" narcissism the aggression is directed inwardly toward the victimized unconscious self, attacks on both the subjective mind and the psychosomatic body (internalizing psychopathology). In "overt," "thick-skinned," "grandiose" narcissism this unconscious object relation is projected out onto external objects (externalizing psychopathology).

This internal object relational mechanism also applies to my previous description of Winnicott's conception of repression (an instinct repressed along abnormal paths is liable to be shoved down deep into the subconscious and there act as a "foreign body," one that may remain in the subconscious for a whole lifetime and completely control the life of the individual who has not control over this tendency because it is not known even to exist within). Bringing this unconscious, internal dyadic object relation into awareness in therapeutic mutual regressions is a central mechanism of psychodynamic psychotherapy (see "Unconscious Object Relations as a Focus of the Psychotherapeutic Treatment of Developmental Disorders" in Schore, 1994, pp. 445–448).

According to Ogden (1994), Winnicott's (and Fairbairn's) theory represents steps in the development of an internal object relations theory in which unconscious aspects of the person, each with a capacity to generate meanings according to its own patterns of linkage, engage in internal relationships with one another (different affective self states dialogues):

> Donald Winnicott's major contribution to the development of a theory of internal object relations was his theory of multiple self-organizations functioning in relation to one another within the personality system. Winnicott envisioned the infant as born with the potential for unique individuality of personality (termed a True Self personality organization) which can develop in the context of a responsive holding environment provided by the good enough mother. However, when a mother substitutes something of herself for the infant's spontaneous gesture (e.g., her own anxiety over separateness for the infant's curious exploration), the infant experiences traumatic disruption of his developing sense of self. When such "impingements" are a central feature of the early mother-child relationship, the infant will attempt to defend himself by developing a second (reactive) personality organization (the False Self organization). This false self vigilantly monitors and adapts to the conscious and unconscious needs of the mother and in so doing provides a protective exterior behind which the true self is afforded the privacy that it requires to maintain its integrity. (p. 231)

Furthermore,

> The false self is . . . a caretaker self that energetically "manages" life so that an inner self might not experience the threat of annihilation resulting from excessive pressure on it to develop according to the internal logic of another person (the mother). The dread of annihilation experienced by the true self results in a feeling of utter dependence on the false self personality organization. This makes it extremely difficult for a person to diminish his reliance on this false self mode of functioning despite an awareness of the emptiness of life that devolves from such functioning. Functioning in this mode can frequently lead to academic, vocational, and social success, but

over time, the person increasingly experiences himself as bored, "going through the motions," detached, mechanical and lacking spontaneity. (p. 231)

This dystonic symptomatic state is frequently a major motivator of the patient's entrance into deep psychodynamic psychotherapy.

In his essential contribution to object relations theory, "The Repression and Return of Bad Objects (with Special Reference to the 'war neuroses')," Fairbairn postulated, "I now venture to formulate the view that what are primarily repressed are neither intolerably guilty impulses nor intolerably unpleasant memories, but intolerably bad internalized objects. If memories are repressed, accordingly, this is only because the objects involved in such memories are identified with bad internalized objects" (1943, p. 62). Fairbairn postulated that the child represses not an impulse to hurt the parent but the awareness of the "badness" that was in the parents. In recent psychoanalytic research on "pathological identification," Foreman asserted, "Children repress awareness of *hurtful things the parents actually did (in reality)* to promote and protect their parents from multiple real threats, including the consequences of their own feeling of hurt, anger, and disdain" (2018, p. 27). Guntrip (1969) described how the innocent child, growing up in a severe parental environment, a neglectful or abusive environment, comes to hate his own immaturity, identified with the "bad" (shaming) parent until a split occurs, and a "lost heart of the self" disappears into the unconscious, tormented by an internal saboteur.

Davies pointed out the importance of mutual regressions in this therapeutic work: "It seems to me intrinsic to relational thinking that these 'bad object relationships' not only will but must be reenacted in the transference-countertransference experience, that indeed such reenacted aggression, rage, and envy are endemic to psychoanalytic change within the relational perspective" (2004, p. 714). Alvarez, another master clinician, articulated the clinical principle that "patients have the right to bring us the bad objects in their emotional baggage and explore them and experience them with us" (2006, p. 214). Mendelsohn (2002) stated, "These manifestations of [the therapist's] 'badness,' as long as they are honestly considered and creatively used, are expectable, and even therapeutically essential, aspects of analytic relatedness" (p. 331).

More specifically, rupture and repair re-enactments embedded in mutual regressions represent a relational context in which the misattuning, dysregulating therapist, analogically acting as a "bad object" in the eyes of the patient, can be rapidly, sequentially followed by a regulated emotional experience with a reparative "new object." In this growth-facilitating inter-subjective context, the creative therapist now authentically co-participates in a novel dyadic re-establishment of an interactively regulated attachment bond of emotional communication. Note the sequence of these two forms of object relationships. The initiating event of this regression-progression thus involves the clinician spontaneously enacting the countertransferen-tial "bad object," inducing an interactive regulatory failure in the patient. The critical role of rupture and repair of the dyadic right brain-to-right brain communication system is well documented in both the research and clinical literatures (see Schore, 2012). Therapeutic enactments may thus be central mechanisms in J. R. Greenberg's (1986) observation that if the ther-apist is not taken in as a new, good object, the treatment is never launched, but if the therapist is not also experienced as the old, bad one, the treatment may never end.

That said, these events are the most emotionally stressful for a psy-chotherapist. Clinical studies of the negative therapeutic interaction cited by Gorney (1979) show that the therapist's technical competence may specifically deteriorate when the patient attempts to transform the ther-apist into someone "bad," clearly involving the reception of the patient's unconscious projective identification of shame. Alluding to the difference between repressed and dissociated shame, DeYoung differentiated "*bad-me* shame that can be brought out of dark psychic hiding places into the light, and *not-me shame* that must remain dissociated and unknowable" (2015, p. 154; see DeYoung's superb volume for working with dissociated chronic shame). She also pointed out that although "not-me" states have never been symbolized, "bad-me" states have been symbolized (and are thus accessible to affectively, relationally focused repression psychodynamics).

In these mutually stressful transferential-countertransferential transac-tions, the interactively regulating therapeutic relationship supports bringing the unconscious "bad-me" shame state out of hiding and, with a lowering of defenses, exposed to the eyes of and shared with an emotionally present other (see Schore, 2012, p. 97). At this moment, the "open" therapist "takes" the transferential "bad-self" shame communication (see the earlier discussion of the unconscious communication of internalized shame and externalized shame rage within the therapeutic relationship). In this heightened affective moment, the key is not to offer a resistance interpretation but to resonate with the shame or fear that lies beneath the "attack other" defensive aggression.

In these "heightened affective moments," the patient with a history of relational shame dysregulation frequently employs a "splitting defense," an unconscious process in which the individual fails to integrate both the positive and negative qualities of the self or others into a cohesive whole and splits the mental representation of self and other into two opposing realities (e.g., "good mother" and "bad mother"). Splitting typically results in great distress and unstable, tumultuous relationships. Within the transference-countertransference relationship, this defense is manifest in overidealizing the therapist at one point in time and devaluing her at another point, with repeated spontaneous shifts between these two irreconcilable views. In the therapeutic relationship, this triggers an instant evaporation of the positive and intensification of the negative transference. In such, dyadic repair of the attachment bond rupture involves the clinician staying in the right hemisphere, which utilizes a creative strategy of thinking that is adaptive "when the information itself is complex, internally contradictory and basically irreducible to an unambiguous context" (Rotenberg, 1994, p. 489). Creativity is central to accommodating apparently opposite or conflicting traits in one's self-concept (Barron & Harrington, 1981). Indeed, creativity is finding unity in what appears to be diversity (Bronowski, 1972).

Regarding this relationally stressful collaborative work, Rycroft (1985) offered the clinical observation,

> Psychoanalytic treatment is not so much a matter of making the unconscious conscious, or of widening and strengthening the ego, as of providing a setting in which healing can occur and connections with previously repressed split-off and lost aspects of the self

can be re-established. And the ability of the analyst to provide such a setting depends not only on his skill in making "correct" interpretations but also on his capacity to maintain a sustained interest in, and relationship with his patients. (p. 268)

Psychodynamic psychotherapy focuses on bringing this repressed unconscious internal object relational dialogue into awareness, especially as it is affectively played out in mutual regressions of right brain-to-right brain transferential-countertransferential aspects of the continually developing therapeutic relationship. In such, projective identifications are a universal feature of the externalization of an internal object relation (see Chapter 3, "Clinical Implications of a Psychobiological Model of Projective Identification," in Schore, 2003b).

The patient's intersubjective right brain communications of repressed affects first appear in the therapist's preconscious, but the central question is how can an unconscious affect emerge into conscious awareness in the patient's right-lateralized preconscious mind? The clinician facilitates this alteration in the patient's subjective consciousness not so much by offering explicit left brain mutative interpretations to make the unconscious conscious, but by co-constructing a right brain context in which the patient begins to feel enough implicit safety and trust in the developing therapeutic relationship to risk taking the left hemisphere off-line. This regression potentially allows right hemispheric affects, including repressed unconscious affective states that are shared with the therapist to emerge into the patient's conscious awareness. The clinical dictum "safe but not too safe" means not staying entrenched in the left mind, which processes the familiar, versus the right mind, which processes the novel, the unexpected. Bromberg (2006) described the critical role of "safe surprises," stating it is through the novelty and surprise of this reciprocal process that the therapeutic action takes shape. In this moment, the patient and the therapist need to synchronously lower defenses and take more risk.

This clinical principle also applies to the therapist's creative emotional involvement in mutual regressions, unexpected moments of surprise to both members of the dyad. Bruner (1962) stated the hallmark of the creative experience is its ability to produce "effective surprise," in addition to a "shock of recognition," and that the product of the response, although novel, is entirely appropriate. The *Oxford English Dictionary* defines surprise as "the emotion aroused by something unexpected." Reik (1948) observed that when unconscious material becomes conscious, it emerges as "surprise." Note the emotionally marked moment when what's defensively unconscious becomes conscious, a moment of right brain "Aha!" self-recognition. In a shared creative "Aha!" experience, these unconscious affects are communicated and relationally shared *between* the patient and the empathic therapist, as well as intrapsychically transferred *within* the patient's right and left implicit-unconscious and explicit-conscious self-systems.

Kris postulated, "The coming to consciousness in the case of creative effort presupposes a long unnoticed process of shaping: it is this process which, entrusted to preconsciousness, is geared to integration and communication" (1952, p. 344). Kris stated that this transformation is expressed in a "sudden and inspirational phase" of creativity. He also observed that a creative regression facilitates an adaptation so long as there is sufficient ego strength and that the inspirational content does not release large amounts of anxiety that trigger repression. Note that in this moment of passively "letting go," the creative process is unblocked by repression.

Sands (1997) offered a clinical example of "a return of the repressed" in a voluntary mutual regression. In this working through of repressed aggression, note the elevation of emotion from a primitive presymbolic sensorimotor level to a mature symbolic representational level.

> Almost from the beginning of the three-year-long therapy, I had had the persistent feeling that I was never "doing enough" for this particular patient. It was not clear to me why this should be so, for the patient was very bright, verbal, responsive to and interested in me, and able to use the therapy well.
>
> But as I focused in more and more on my experience of him, I became aware of a "pull," like something tugging on the center of my chest. As this bodily experience became more conscious, I realized that I had in fact felt this pull from the first moment I met him. I also became more aware of a subtle countermovement in myself to resist this pull, to dig in my heels. One day the patient started

(as he often did) with, "I'm not sure what I want to do today," and we both sat there for a while in silence, staring at each other, my feeling the pull more and more. I felt myself becoming irritated and resistant. I told him, "I am feeling a strong pull to do something, and yet I'm not sure what there is to do." He responded immediately that he felt resentful about having to have all the responsibility for this relationship.

He felt I was withholding, and he wanted to "demand—no, *command*" me to do what he wanted. Then he said, his eyes filling with tears, "When's it going to be my turn?" At this point we both felt a major shift in the therapy, that we had uncovered something that had been going on forever but had never before been made conscious.

Suddenly it was easy for both of us to make the connections to his childhood, where his depressed and self-doubting mother had relied on him not only to guide himself but also to guide her and reassure her that she was being a good mother. He had felt this impossible pull all his life—as well as his resistance to it.

The most striking evidence to me that we had reached a new, more fundamental level of understanding was that, after this series of interchanges, for the first time since the beginning of therapy, my own sense of "pull" completely disappeared." (pp. 652–653)

During working through, synchronized mutual regressions that release left-hemispheric defensive repression of "more difficult" right-hemispheric affect and allow for a coming into consciousness of repressed material act as a central mechanism in the progression of the therapeutic relationship. Creative mutual topographical regressions thus represent the interpersonal neurobiological mechanism by which repressed material can generate original insights (Reik, 1948) and by which the coming into consciousness of creative effort is shaped by activities of the preconscious (Kris, 1953). According to Downey, "Therapeutic change is analogous to developmental change in that both involve the crucial presence of another to release energies. In therapeutic change these are energies that have been repressed beyond the reach of developmental dynamics" (2001, p. 56).

This metapsychological principle can now be understood from a neu-robiological perspective. The therapeutic change mechanism of a topo-graphical regression and "reversible dominance" allows the patient's energy-expending left hemisphere to reduce its active over inhibition of the right hemisphere, thereby increasing right-lateralized emotional energy being used for creativity. Neuroscience thus mirrors the common intuitive notion that repression inhibits creativity. Indeed in repression, the path from right to left brain is blocked (Basch, 1983), while the illumination stage of creativity represents "a sudden, temporary increase above normal in the flow of information from right to left" (Kane, 2004, p. 52). These clinical and research data also support the clinical proposition that inter-personally regulated voluntary mutual regressions in the service of the self can alter repression dynamics.

PSYCHOTHERAPEUTIC REGRESSIONS AND THE CREATIVE REBALANCING OF THE CEREBRAL HEMISPHERES

In synchronized, interactively regulated mutual regressions, the dyad repeatedly revisits relational and emotional themes with greater levels of awareness and integration of the right brain unconscious and left brain conscious self-systems. Recall regressions allow for "reorganization leading to a potential integration" (Tuttman, 2002). These adaptive creative mutual regressions may facilitate structural alterations of the relationships of the hemispheres to each other, including a transformation from excessive left-hemispheric repression and inhibition of right-hemispheric functions to a more balanced interhemispheric inhibition. McGilchrist (2015) described the cost of excessive repression to the subjective inner world:

> Interaction with the world requires the right hemisphere's broad attention, which is inclusive and opens up into possibility, coupled with the left hemisphere's narrow attention, which collapses the world we experience into specificity. If the left hemisphere collapses the world too quickly into what is specific, however, it precludes the possibility of knowledge that transcends what is already famil-iar. (p. 1583)

Note the relationship between repression and the untoward effects of premature interpretations. Highly repressed systems prevent novel insights to an emotional problem, the product of not left-hemispheric but right-hemispheric activity. An inability in solving social problems with right brain implicit emotional regulating functions is frequently accompanied by an overreliance on left brain explicit analytic reasoning. The limitation of this hemispheric strategy is described by Keenan and colleagues: "The left hemisphere often fills in information that it is unaware of. . . . However, the filling in of left hemisphere does not require insight, self-awareness, or any higher-order state. The left hemisphere appears to do so in a rather blind manner" (2005, p. 702). Indeed, research demonstrates that verbal activity interferes with insight (Schooler, Ohlsson, & Brooks, 1993). Rotenberg asserted that the left-hemispheric strategy of thinking generates "a pragmatically convenient but simplified model of reality" (1994, p. 489).

Repression represents a characterological overreliance of explicit left dorsolateral control over implicit right orbitofrontal-ventromedial affect regulation. The focus of the therapy is thus on right-hemispheric deficits *and* left-hemispheric "compensation." Recall excessive left dorsolateral activation is also seen in dissociation. Over the course of the treatment, the more the patient in day-to-day life uses topographical regressions that shift dominance into adaptive right-lateralized relational and subjective functions, the more he or she accesses synchronized mutual structural regressions to activate moments of oxytocinergic and opioidergic intimate "deep contact" with emotionally salient close others, the more the characterological "highly repressed" affect blocking defense is reduced. In the "slow growth" of psychotherapy, this move to more flexible hemispheric defenses is expressed in increased subjective safety and trust within the dyad. Thus, mutual regressions allow for the lessening of both dissociative and repressive defenses.

As the therapy progresses, the patient brings diverse affective exchanges and novel relational experiences in the outside social world into the therapeutic relationship for mutual symbolic reflection. Therapeutic, interactively regulated mutual regressions allow the patient to implicitly learn not only how to "internalize" the therapist's adaptive regression functions, but also how to unconsciously coordinate and synchronize with the hemispheric shifts of an emotionally valued other. This transformation includes synchronized regressions of not only strong negative but also strong positive affect and thereby facilitates the patient's capacity for mutual play. These shared experiences of positive arousal increase over the later stages of treatment. Recall Winnicott's dictum, "Psychotherapy is done in the overlap of two play areas, that of the patient and that of the therapist. . . . The reason why playing is so essential is that it is in the playing that the patient is being creative" (1971, p. 54). In other words, the dyad increasingly co-creates more *synchronized mutual regressions in the service of the ego*, shifting from secondary to primary process, which Kris (1952) described as a generator of fantasy, imagination, and the appreciation of wit and humor.

Furthermore, this emergent creative context that amplifies positive arousal, safety, and trust also forges deeper bonds of intimacy within the dyad (see Schore and Marks-Tarlow, 2018, on the relationship between creativity and mutual love). This enhanced ability to nondefensively align, synchronize, and intersubjectively communicate within right brain-to-right brain intimate relationships represents an expansion of the "relational unconscious" and the "creative unconscious." Indeed, according to Geller,

> During the ending phase of therapy, self-disclosures are called upon to serve a different constellation of tasks than those that predominated during earlier stages. During the middle phases of therapy, self-involving statements play a vital role in identifying those problematic aspects of the therapeutic relationship that prevent the realization of treatment goals. It is quite a different order of things to self-disclose to celebrate the achievement of these goals, to reciprocate the tender feelings expressed by an appreciative patient, and to say good-bye. Intimacy replaces power and authority as the focal point of therapist self-disclosures during termination. (2003, p. 552)

Earlier I described Wolberg's (1977) clinical description of the essential role of clinical work with the repression defense, one involved in many essential aspects of the basic personality structure including repressed strivings for not only independence, dominance, ambition, and power, but also love, companionship, and affection. Each of these fundamental human, affectively-driven motivational systems can become a clinical focus of the working-through and ending phases of a psychotherapeutic joint exploration. In long-term treatment, the transformation of rigid and pathological repression to adaptive and resilient repression can allow for a creative rebalancing of the right and left hemispheres. The conscious mind can now tolerate even higher intensities of both negative and positive affects generated by the unconscious mind. Mayseless and Shamay-Tsoory (2015) demonstrate that altering the balance between the right and left frontal lobes can modulate creative production. Reducing left frontal and enhancing right frontal activity reduces cognitive control, allowing for more creative idea production. This interpersonal neurobiological rebalancing of the explicit objective self with the implicit subjective self promotes enhanced access to unique adaptive functions of each of the cerebral hemispheres. Recall, Joseph's (1992) unconscious self-image is located in the right hemisphere, while the *conscious self-image, which is subject to unconscious influences,* is in the left.

According to McGilchrist (2009), the right and left hemispheres create coherent, utterly different, and often incompatible versions of the world with competing priorities and values. Following up on earlier clinical research by Kuhl and Kazen (2008), Hecht (2014) cited a large body of neuroscience research indicating that the right hemisphere mediates affiliation motivation, and the left hemisphere mediates power motivation.

> Psychological theories on motivation postulate that human beings have an intrinsic need for *affiliation*—being connected with and accepted by other people. This fundamental need motivates people to seek warm, stable and intimate interpersonal relationships, form friendships, and affiliate with specific groups. . . . On the other hand humans also have an innate need to maintain their *individuality and independence.* This need motivates people to acquire power in order to achieve autonomy and freedom that will enable them to master and influence their environments and social relationships, instead of being influenced by them. Ideally, these two coexisting needs—for affiliation and power—would complement and balance each other. Nevertheless, oftentimes they are in conflict and lead to opposite directions. (p. 1, italics added)

Individual cultures can shape not only the degree of repression but also the balance of affiliation and power motivations in each gender (becoming connected and *getting along* by relatedness versus becoming individuated and *getting ahead* by autonomy and control).

Regulated mutual regressions promote "bearable intrapsychic conflict" between the power and affiliation motives, between autonomy and intimacy. The therapeutic rebalancing of the explicit, conscious objective self with the implicit, unconscious subjective self allows for a more harmonious relationship, yet one that can also process the intrinsic tensions and conflicts of left-hemispheric autonomy functions and right-hemispheric interpersonal functions. This developmental advance is expressed in a more complex capacity for tolerating conflict between the dual modes of self-regulation, autoregulation in autonomous contexts, and interactive regulation in interconnected contexts. Therapeutic synchronized regressions, especially those that are mutually repaired and negotiated, thus enhance the patient's creative approaches to conflicts, which represent the complementary different perspectives and motivational systems of the left and right hemispheres. As opposed to the rigid left-hemispheric repression of right-hemispheric functions, this adaptive capacity is enhanced in more fluid access to the unique specializations of both hemispheres, including increased tolerance for left-hemispheric anxiety and right-hemispheric novelty and creativity. This psychoneurobiological model of psychotherapeutic mutual regressions suggests that left-to-right and right-to-left callosal growth, especially synaptogenesis between the left-hemispheric dorsolateral and right orbital prefrontal (including right ventrolateral) regions, is a potential outcome of effective long-term psychotherapy. The right ventrolateral areas are involved in the non-conscious detection and regulation of death-related threats and mortality concerns, as well as social rejection (Yanagisawa et al., 2013).

McGilchrist (2015) described the adaptive functions of the right brain intuitive "creative unconscious" in contrast to the left brain analytical conscious mind. He referred to the unique specializations, "tools" of "the right hemisphere, including being on the lookout for what is not suspected by the left hemisphere:

All the evidence is that the right hemisphere "sees" more than the left hemisphere. Perhaps it is for this very reason that it is more aware of the limitations of its knowledge. In neuropsychological studies, the right hemisphere exhibits a more tentative and self-depreciating style, whereas the left hemisphere is confident about matters of which it is ignorant, and overestimates its capacities. . . . It seems that the cognitive processes of the *right hemisphere* allow it to appreciate *the importance of what it does not know,* whereas those of the left hemisphere do not permit such insight. And indeed, insight into one's capabilities is largely dependent on the right frontal region. (p. 1592, italics added)

The right frontal tentative style allows the right hemisphere to know something it does not yet know, something new.

More recently McGilchrist (2016) points out the unique specializations of the "open" right hemisphere over the "defensive" left hemisphere that are specific to *new* learning (especially new alterations of unconscious internal working models of attachment):

The right hemisphere, with its understanding of possibility, change, and flow, is far better than the left hemisphere at incorporating new information into a schema, without having necessarily to abandon it, while the left hemisphere, with its attachment to the fixed and certain, sticks stubbornly to what it 'knows' at all costs, in the teeth of evidence to the contrary (pp. 205-206).

In light of his assertion that "the right hemisphere first grounds, and ultimately interprets, what the left hemisphere unpacks at an intermediary stage" (2016, p. 210), he concludes that "newness" is "the return from left-hemisphere familiarity to right-hemisphere familiarity, from inauthenticity to authenticity. It cannot be willed, though it might be much desired; it requires an (apparently passive) patient openness to whatever is, which allows us to see it as if for the very first time" (2009, p. 173). He further suggests,

Where the left hemisphere tends to see linear chains of cause and effect, the right hemisphere sees reverberative, responsive relations in which all exists in 'betweenness'—not the space between two entities, but the new whole that is made by their coming together, in which each party and the 'space' between is taken up into *something radically new* (pp. 202-203, italics added).

Note this description also characterizes the new transitional space within a co-created intersubjective field.

Earlier I stated that in contrast to left brain-to-left brain linguistic interpretations, the mutual generation of dyadic states of consciousness involve synchronized right brain-to-right brain emotional communications. According to Tronick and his colleagues, they occur in "moments of meeting" that induce significant new changes in the therapeutic relationship:

The future relationship between the patient and the therapist will be changed from what it was because this *new experience* will be part of their connection . . . From a subjective perspective, the patient experiences "something new, something expanded and something singular" . . . With the achievement of the patient and therapist of a more coherently organized and complex state of dyadic consciousness, *old elements of consciousness need to be reintegrated into this new state of consciousness* (Tronick et al., p. 298, italics added).

I would add that for this adaptive new integration of states of consciousness as well as new perceptions of the subjective self, the therapeutic context needs right hemispheric creativity, the product of a psychic regression in the service of the self.

As I stated at the beginning of this chapter, over the course of the past century the concept of clinical regression was controversial. Although Sigmund Freud first articulated the psychoanalytic theory of regression in 1900, Carl Jung was the first discoverer of clinical regressions. In 1912, Jung described the importance of supporting the patient's therapeutic regressions back to the earliest stages of life in order to make contact with a vital generative core of the self that was hidden in the unconscious, the "lost heart to the self." In surprisingly modern terms, Jung (1912) proposed,

> As against this idea [that regression is pathological], therapy must support the regression, and continue to do so until the "prenatal" stage is reached. . . . Hence the regression leads back only apparently to the mother . . . but goes back beyond her to the prenatal realm . . . [to] the germ of *wholeness*. . . . It is [the] inherent possibilities of "spiritual" or "symbolic" life and of progress which form the ultimate, though *unconscious goal of regression*. (paragraphs 508–510, italics added)

Jung (1961) also concluded that "Man's task is . . . to become conscious of the contents that press upward from the unconscious . . . his destiny . . . is to create more and more consciousness."

Long-term work with the emergence of dissociated self-states into consciousness can restructuralize the right hemisphere, while working with lifting repression of the dynamic unconscious can rebalance the right and left hemispheres. This balanced hemisphericity structurally underlies a unitary sense of self. And yet within this dual system, the left hemisphere acts as the "conceptual self" while the right hemisphere represents the "integrated self" (Kuhl et al., 2015). According to these authors, "the integrated self is supported by parallel-distributed processing in the right anterior cortex," and its adaptive functions are specifically expressed in "emotional connectedness, broad vigilance, utilization of felt feedback, unconscious processing, integration of negative experiences, extended resilience, and extended trust" (2015, p. 115). Furthermore, "the unconscious nature of the integrated self implies that *self-access may be facilitated when people relinquish conscious control and give the self's unconscious intelligence more room*" (2015, p. 123, italics added).

The loosening of "top-down" left-hemispheric control of the right hemisphere and rebalancing of the hemispheres allows for the ongoing development of the subjective self of the right brain, which enters into later growth spurts on a timescale different from that of the later growth spurts of the left hemisphere (Thatcher, 1996). The essential importance of adaptive "bottom-up" access of the early maturing deeper levels of the unconscious "core self" over the life span was elegantly described by Hans Loewald in the middle of the past century (in light of the shift in emphasis from a prior psychology of the ego to a current psychology of the self, I have taken the liberty of substituting "self" for "ego" in the following):

> It is not merely a question of survival of former stages of self-integration, but that people shift considerably, from day to day, at different periods in their lives, in different moods and situations, from one such level to other levels. In fact, it would seem that the more alive people are (though not necessarily more stable), the broader the range of their self-integration levels is. Perhaps the so-called fully developed, mature self is not one that has become fixated at the presumably highest or latest stage of development, having left the others behind it, but is a self that integrates its reality in such a way that the earlier and deeper levels of self integration become alive as dynamic sources of higher organization. (Loewald, 1949, p. 20)

A central theme of these two chapters dictates that *interactively regulated, mutually synchronized right brain regressions are a central mechanism of therapeutic action, and that these affective-relational growth-promoting experiences can lead to progressions of emotional development.* This developmental advance of the emotional right brain is reflected in an "expansion in the affect array," which is expressed in the emergence of more intense discrete affects and then a blending of these affects into more complex emotions. Emotional development evolves through a series of stages culminating in the capacity to experience blends of feelings and finally blends of blends of feelings (Schore, 1994). Across the life span, this ability to share mutual regressions with valued others allows for an expansion of the unconscious subjective self, expressed in a dynamic system that is capable of efficiently modulating a broad range of affects, integrating these discrete emotions into a variety of adaptive motivational states, utilizing affects as signals, and linking coherent behavioral states to appropriate social contexts. Note the potential growth of right brain emotional intelligence over the Eriksonian stages of life, an adaptive capacity to flexibly cope with the successive emotional and social challenges to the right brain integrated self over different life stages, within changing cultural and social environments.

In fact, the highest human functions—intersubjectivity, empathy, compassion, humor, morality, mutual love, and artistic, scientific, and personal creativity—are all right brain functions that operate via a regression in the service of the self. According to Weinberg, "Only the right hemisphere enables one to sustain experiences in their complexity and in interactive and mutually enriching connections between their various components. Furthermore, this ability to represent the experiences in a multi-dimensional way generates a *need for new experiences* in order to further enrich, deepen, and organize them" (2000, p. 807, italics added). Recall, creativity, an emergent property of regression in the service of the self, "gives value and purpose to human experience," allows the individual to "respond efficiently and effectively to a constantly changing and regularly challenging environment," and is expressed in "discovering *new* forms of human relationship."

In classic clinical writings, Masterson concluded that creativity is an essential function of "the real self," where it is used specifically "to change old familiar patterns into *new*, unique, and different patterns" (1985, p. 27). Indeed, over all stages of life, access of the self-system to creativity represents a central mechanism for self-actualization and self-expression of one's inner being (Maslow, 1973; May, 1976; Rogers, 1961). Mutual regressions embedded in long-term psychotherapy can facilitate an expansion of not only creative self-expression but also interpersonal creativity, the adaptive use of creativity in synchronized interpersonal relationships, and therefore in relatively effective emotional communication and efficient interactive affect regulation with other humans.

As Ulanov (2001) pointed out in creative therapeutic mutual regressions, "we need someone present, holding the situation, while we undergo regression." In that same work, she described the growth-promoting effects of deep psychotherapy:

> When true, our self at the core feels real in the world. We can hold
> ourselves in being, inhabit our bodies, and touch others. We can
> imaginatively elaborate our experiences and arrive at new percep-

tions. We feel able to be ourselves, glad in others' company and intimacy, grateful for work we find exciting. This being of ours proves durable, even in the face of suffering. The sense we possess of the real, that we can carry our lot, know some measure of room to change and improve it, and share it with others, confers on us aliveness, a feeling that whatever happens, this living is worth it. . . . We can go on being, sustaining a sense of continuity through time and space, acquiring a history, a narrative thread to our identity. Above all we enjoy living creatively. Presence of self shines through. (p. 46)

CHAPTER 5

How Love Opens Creativity, Play, and the Arts through Early Right Brain Development

Allan N. Schore and Terry Marks-Tarlow

OUR VIEW OF HUMAN NATURE is intimately tied to our view of human love. Philosophers, poets, and psychologists have adopted one of two basic stances: either people are seen as inherently selfish and out for the good of themselves or people are seen as inherently altruistic and out for the good of each other and society. Love has been slow to enter the psychological dialogue partly because Freud epitomized the former stance. In *Civilization and Its Discontents*, Freud hypothesized that the very origins of civilization arose from a collective need for checks and balances to counteract otherwise selfish motives. Only an authoritative, hierarchical structure of customs and laws could keep things fair for everyone.

The humanistic revolt of the 1960s rebelled not only against authoritarian and paternalistic aspects of Freud's model but also against his very model of human nature, as did some of Freud's own disciples including Donald Winnicott and Sándor Ferenczi, who boldly asserted the essential importance of love in early development. The contemporary fields of modern attachment theory, regulation theory, and interpersonal neurobiology weigh in on this issue of human nature. The two opposing views of human nature represent the primary motives of each of the two hemispheres of the human brain. At a conscious level, the left side of the brain concerns itself primarily with power motives, while the right side of the brain is steeped in affiliation drives (Hecht, 2014; Kuhl & Kazén, 2008). Only one perspective can press forward into consciousness at a time, and as this occurs, the other perspective recedes into the background (McGilchrist, 2009). Schore's modern attachment theory (Schore, 2017; J. Schore & A. Schore, 2008) and regulation theory (Schore, 1994, 2012) add an important developmental dimension to which set of motives is more primary in a particular social context. In a nutshell, from the start of life, infants thrive on mutual love, and the social, emotional, relational right brain is the cradle for a healthy brain. If a baby is adequately cherished, soothed, stimulated, and respected by receiving attuned response during the first 2 years of life, the right brain—the relational, emotional, social, somatically grounded side—becomes a healthy regulator for the more individualistic motives of the left brain.

In this chapter, we propose a two-person relational model of love, play, and creativity. We suggest that maternal love and mutual love are primary motivational forces from the start of a baby's life. Love is capable of energetically jump-starting all of the positive emotions and behaviors—including interest, excitement, joy, curiosity, exploration, and play—in babies. The mutual exchange of love fuels a young child's desire to explore the environment, drink in novelty, and eventually to fire up imagination in service of creativity. As children grow and develop, this initial dose of love gets internalized into passionate engagements throughout life, including a love for life itself.

The early origins of the relational capacity to engage in mutual love and for creativity are generated in the early developing right hemisphere. The most rapid development of the right brain over the first 2 years of life occurs over a period when the child is processing enormous amounts of socioemotional information, much of which is *novel* and increasingly complex. According to McGilchrist (2009), at all points of the life span what is *new* must first be present in the right hemisphere before it can come into focus for the left. It begins in wonder, intuition, ambiguity, puzzlement, and uncertainty on the right. Integrating interdisciplinary data, Schore (2012) is now documenting that current neuroscientific models view creativity as the production of an idea that is both *novel* and useful in a particular social setting. Although the left hemisphere is specialized for coping with predictable representations and strategies, the right predominates for coping with and assimilating novel situations and ensures *the*

formation of a new program of interaction with a new environment. Indeed,
the right brain possesses special capabilities for processing novel stimuli. The
experience-dependent growth of this hemisphere, which is promoted in
right brain-to-right brain intensely emotional attachment communications
embedded in mutual love transactions, thus allows the maturing infant to
process novel intrapersonal and interpersonal information, an essential
functional aspect of creativity.

In the first part of the chapter, we examine historical precedents of love's
investigation before turning to neurobiological and developmental origins
of love as the guiding force for attunement, synchrony, and coordinated
response. We argue that the paradigmatic expression of how the mother
shapes the baby's brain *for the better* is expressed in an early bond of mutual
love, and that this growth-promoting early emotional experience acts as a
relational matrix for the emergence of the capacity to play as well as the
lifelong capacity for creative self-expression. We suggest that two kinds
of maternal love—quiet and excited—help to expand affect tolerance in
babies for high-intensity positive *and* negative emotions, preparing young
children for the highs and lows of playful explorations that generate self-
constituting creativity. In the following, we discuss recent neurobiological
studies of mother-infant love, describe a developmental model of three
stages of mutual love, highlight the central role of the right brain in primary intersubjectivity and the onset of mutual love, interpersonal play, and
creativity, and offer support for Ellen Dissanayake's artification hypothesis,
that art springs directly from the intimacy of the mother relating lovingly
to her infant. The chapter ends by addressing some clinical implications of
the importance of transferential-countertransferential mutual love within
psychotherapy.

LOVE'S HISTORICAL SCIENTIFIC INVESTIGATION

Love is mostly thought to be the province of the arts, poets and writers,
actors, dancers, and musicians, yet from the very beginnings of modern
biology and psychology, science has also explored its origins and emotional
expressions. Indeed in his seminal work *The Expression of the Emotions in
Man and Animals*, Charles Darwin (1872/1965) proposed,

The emotion of love, for instance that of a mother for her infant, is one of the strongest of which the mind is capable. . . . No doubt, as affection is a pleasurable sensation, it generally causes a gentle smile and some brightening of the eyes. A strong desire to touch the beloved is commonly felt. (pp. 224–225)

Specifically referring to the origins of perhaps this most essential expression of the human species, he speculated, "The movements of expressions in the face and body . . . serve as the first means of communication between the mother and her infant; she smiles approval and thus encourages her child on the right path or frowns disapproval" (p. 385).

At the end of the 19th century, Sigmund Freud (1895/1953) began his pioneering studies in psychoanalysis and initiated the field's long history of interest in the essential role of love in human function and dysfunction. Referring to Freud's evolving position on the developmental origins of love, Schore (2003b, p. 256) has suggested, "Although for much of his career [Freud] seemed ambivalent about the role of maternal influences in earliest development, in his very last work he stated, in a definitive fashion, that the mother-infant relationship 'is unique, without parallel, established unalterably for a whole lifetime as the first and strongest love-object and the prototype of all later love relations' (Freud, 1940)."

Donald Winnicott, an important follower of Freud, studied the deepest origins of the capacity to love. He observed, "The early management of an infant is a matter *beyond conscious thought and deliberate intention*. It is something that becomes possible only through love" and that the mother "by expressing love in terms of physical management and in giving physical satisfaction enables the infant psyche to begin in the infant body" (1975, p. 183, italics added). Thus the early origins of love are expressed in the mother-infant experience of mutuality. Furthermore, Winnicott (1963) described two forms of love in the developing infant. On one hand, "quiet love" (Figure 5.1) is seen in moments when the mother holds and handles (soothes, comforts, caresses) the infant. Quiet love has been characterized as "a mutual dwelling of baby and mother where one and one make not two but one" (Ulanov, 2001, pp. 49–50).

FIGURE 5.1 Quiet love. Courtesy of Sharon Austin.

On the other hand, "excited love" (Figure 5.2) occurs in moments of thrilling excitement and intense interest in interaction with the mother and contains an energetic potential.

In the middle of the past century, another of Freud's followers, John Bowlby (1953), began his seminal writings on what would become attachment theory with his book *Child Care and the Growth of Love*. In that volume, he asserted that a mother's love in infancy and childhood is as important for mental health as are vitamins and proteins for physical health. Following this explicit association of the origins of attachment and love, Ainsworth (1967) offered her classic *Infancy in Uganda: Infant Care and the Growth of Love*. In his later writings, Bowlby concluded,

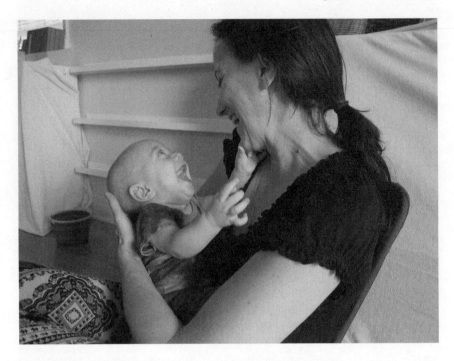

FIGURE 5.2 Excited love. Courtesy of Ruth Anne Hammond.

"Many of the most intense emotions arise during the formation, the maintenance, the disruption, and the renewal of attachment relationships. The formation of a bond is described as falling in love, maintaining a bond as loving someone, and losing a partner as grieving over someone" (1969, p. 130).

Also in mid-century, another of Freud's disciples, Erich Fromm (1956), wrote the classic *The Art of Loving*, in which he described love as "the experience of union with another being" and "becoming one with another." In that volume, Fromm described what he deemed to be the central problem in individual development: "What meaning—in both women as well as men—does our longing for a mother have? What constitutes the bond to the mother?" (pp. 26–27). He stated that motherly love is an unconditional affirmation of the child's life and needs, and that it is expressed in two different aspects:

One is the care and responsibility absolutely necessary for the preservation of the child's life and his growth. The other aspect goes further than mere preservation. . . . Motherly love, in this second step, makes the child feel: it is good to have been born; it instills in the child the *love for life* and not merely the wish to remain alive. . . . Mother's love for life is as infectious as her anxiety. (pp. 46–47, italics added)

Note the overlap between maternal "care" and Winnicott's "quiet love" and between Fromm's maternal support of the child's love for life and Winnicott's "excited love" that contains an energetic potential. Winnicott and Fromm understood the significance of the mother's loving attitude for instilling emotional resilience plus a passionate stance in children that lasts a lifetime. Thus the major pioneers in the field conceptualized love as an "intense" emotion, indeed "one of the strongest of which the mind is capable," which when shared by another forms an "intense emotional union" that persists as an intrapsychic stance toward life itself.

LOVE, ATTACHMENT, AND EMOTIONAL REGULATION

The *Shorter Oxford English Dictionary* defines love as "a state or feeling," "*deep affection, strong emotional attachment.*" This raises the matter of the relationship of love to attachment, especially in light of the transformational impact of the shift of modern attachment theory from behavior and cognition to affect and an emotional bond between intimate individuals (Schore, 2017; J. Schore & A. Schore , 2008). Love is defined as (1) a noun: a feeling of tenderness, passion, and warmth; and (2) a verb: to feel love for another person—actions including expressions of physical affection, tenderness, and acts of kindness. The first usage implies love as an intense intrapersonal emotion, the second as a strong interpersonal emotional communication. The contrast in these two definitions mirror the ongoing shift from a "one-person" intrapsychic to a "two-person" interpersonal perspective in psychology, the latter including the most prominent theory in developmental psychology: attachment theory.

Although the humanities have a long history of exploring this deepest expression of the human heart and mind, the idea that the brain sciences can be used to explain the subtleties and depths of human love has been controversial. In the humanities, many feared that a reductionist science would simplify the complexities of love to a neural synapse or to a collection of neurochemicals. This idea is disputed by Schore's ongoing interdisciplinary work on emotion, a central component of love, which conceptualizes brain/mind/body well-being to emerge from early healthy relationship dynamics. To understand the attachment origins of the capacity to receive, feel, and express the emotion of love with another, the perspective of *interpersonal* neurobiology elucidates the biological *and* psychological development of the early bonds of *mutual* love. The mutual love between a mother and her infant is embedded in an optimal co-created, reciprocal, synchronized, bodily-based, emotion-transacting attachment relationship. In this manner, the relational mechanism of mutual love, "*strong emotional attachment*," is mediated by the mother's right brain interacting and resonating with the infant's right brain, amplifying intense positive arousal in both (Schore, 1994).

After 9 months of gestation within the womb, a newborn human is quite helpless, requiring care from adults for years, a period that extends much longer than that for any other primate. It appears that "intense maternal care" or "intensive parenting" arose as early as 1.8 million years ago (Falk, 2004; Flinn & Ward, 2005, p. 31; Leakey, 1994; Rosenberg, 1992). The mother-infant interaction is an evolved adaptation, because all healthy infants are born ready to recognize, respond to, and coordinate their behavior with the signals and responses of primary caretakers.

Infants are much less responsive to adult-style discourse than to what Dissanayake (2017) calls "extra-ordinary" signals in the form of exaggerated facial expressions and vocal tone, to which babies respond with "beguiling wriggles, coos, and smiles." As Dissanayake noted, babies are not *taught* to engage with caretakers in this way, and if anything are more the teachers, who by their positive and negative reactions let caretakers know which movements, expressions, and sounds they prefer. Babies are not passive beings, but instead use their own positive and negative emotional experiences to actively elicit responses and shape the pace, intensity, and variety of signals that adults, especially loving adults direct toward them.

All emotion is composed of two dimensions: valence (positive-negative, pleasant-unpleasant, approach-avoidance of discrete emotions) and arousal (intensity, energy, calm-excited). Furthermore, left-hemispheric activity is associated with moderate levels of cortical arousal, while right-hemispheric activity accompanies either high or low levels of cortical arousal. Shared right brain states of reciprocated mutual love thus generate the most intense states of emotional arousal and positive affects in the human experience.

On the matter of a centrality of a mother's love, we would go so far as to say that most if not all mothers have the conscious intention of loving their babies. Yet one of the major findings of science is that many of the essential processes involved in love operate at rapid time frames, unconsciously, at levels beneath awareness. For this reason, the relational psychobiological mechanisms that underlie mutual love can best be described by integrating observations and data from neurobiology and psychoanalysis, the science of unconscious processes.

Toward that end, rather than describing love as an ideal mental state, we will suggest that love is embedded in a basic evolutionary mechanism located in the early developing, emotion-processing right brain. A central purpose of this chapter is to highlight the structural and functional onto-genetic development of this evolutionary system, all of which takes place at nonverbal levels. In light of modern conceptions of nature-nurture inter-actions, we now understand how a loving early beginning can optimally epigenetically shape the basic evolutionary processes that are expressed in human infancy.

In terms of regulation theory, the calming and soothing, dyadic context of Winnicott's "quiet love" represents a transition of strong negative affect from a high-arousal, sympathetic-dominant, energy-expending state to a low-arousal, parasympathetic-dominant, energy-conserving psychobiologi-cal state expressed in comfort and relief from stress and distress. In contrast, Winnicott's "excited love" contains an energetic potential that represents a transition from a calm, alert state into a regulated, high-arousal, mutu-ally accelerating, sympathetic-dominant, energy-expending emotional state expressed by expanding joy and excitement. In other words, Winnicott's quiet love describes the down-regulation of intense, negatively valenced emotional arousal into a positively valenced, calm, intensely pleasant state, while excited love describes the up-regulation of emotional arousal from open engagement into an intensely positive, excited, and joyful state. Ultimately, quiet love and excited love need to be integrated into the personality structure.

THREE STAGES OF MUTUAL LOVE

A central thesis of this chapter is that during development, the emergent capacity for mutual love evolves in three stages that correspond roughly to MacLean's (1985) three layers of the brain: reptilian, mammalian, and neo-cortical. For the first several months after birth, a mother's quiet love is dominant, exquisitely monitoring and attuning her to the physical and emotional needs of her baby. During this stage, both mother and baby are primarily engaged at the subcortical level of the amygdala, which mediates basic emotions and corresponds to Freud's deep unconscious and to MacLean's reptilian level of basic safety and trust.

Barrett and colleagues (2012) reported a functional magnetic resonance imaging (fMRI) study that demonstrates the importance of the mother's subcortical amygdala in response to the facial affective signals of her very young infant. Referring to the emotional parenting tasks specific to this early postpartum period, they noted that giving birth and becoming a mother is a "profound experience":

> Over the course of pregnancy and throughout the postpartum period, changes in levels of certain hormones likely influence the function of key brain regions to increase the likelihood that a mother is attracted to her baby, is attentive and sensitive to her baby's needs, learns from her experiences, and behaves appropriately . . . the early postpartum period is an inherently emotional and challenging time, associated with both positive and negative affect. (p. 253)

The second stage of maternal-infant mutual love first appears at about 2–3 months, when the attachment system common to all social mammals comes online. Now mother and child are engaged with one another at the level of the anterior cingulate cortex, which mediates both engaged attachment and separation anxiety. In classic research, Stern (1985) described the transition from an early forming "emergent self" at birth into a "core self" at 2–3 months. He observed, "At the age of two to three months, infants begin to give the impression of being quite different persons. When engaged in social interaction, they appear to be more wholly integrated. It is if their actions, plans, affects, perceptions, and cognitions can now all be brought into play and focused, for a while, on an interpersonal situation" (p. 69).

As mother moves from quiet love in the earliest phase to excited love that is mutual, she naturally starts to play in intimate and affectionate ways that express reciprocal and intense engagement (Miall & Dissanayake, 2003). Daniel Stern (1971, 1974), Beatrice Beebe (Beebe & Stern, 1977; Beebe, Stern, & Jaffe, 1979), Colwyn Trevarthen (1979), and Ed Tronick (Tronick, Als, & Adamson, 1979) have provided essential basic research on the extraordinary abilities of young infants to engage with their mothers in mutually improvised, spontaneously choreographed interactions. The mother-infant pair employ rhythmic head and body movements, hand gestures, and facial expressions plus vocal sounds to co-create and maintain exquisitely patterned temporal and communicative sequences. As Beebe (1986) demonstrated, even newborns show sensitivity to temporal sequence and pattern. Babies are ready to engage in behavioral turn-taking as early as 8 weeks of age, when they expect social contingency, which consists of predictable back-and-forth interactivity. Infant research has established the importance of timing (Murray & Trevarthen, 1985; Nadel et al., 1999).

Ellen Dissanayake (2017) suggested that the usual labels for the interaction (i.e., "baby talk," "infant-directed speech," or "motherese") fail to sufficiently emphasize two important features: its *dyadic* nature, where both partners influence each other, and its *multimodality*, where multiple senses are involved. Frame-by-frame microanalyses of videotaped mother-infant interactions that show the faces and upper torsos of both partners side by side reveal that *facial expressions* and *head-and-body movements* are as significant in the interaction as vocalizations (Beebe et al., 1985; Beebe & Lachmann, 2014, Murray & Trevarthen, 1985; Stern, 1971). Dissanayake emphasized how much all three sensory modalities or "languages" of the engagement—body, facial, vocal—are processed as a whole in the infant's brain during these interactions (Beebe & Lachmann, 2014; Stern et al.,

1985). Schore (1994, 2003a, 2012, in press) has provided a large body of evidence that gestural, facial, and auditory signals are processed in the infant's right brain.

The third stage of maternal-infant mutual love spans from 10–12 to 16–18 months, as the baby's neo-cortical, emotion-regulating area of the orbitofrontal cortex traverses a critical period of growth. In 2008, Noriuchi, Kikuchi, and Senoo published "The Functional Neuroanatomy of Maternal Love: Mother's Response to Infant's Attachment Behaviors" in *Biological Psychiatry*. In this study, mothers of 16-month infants were shown two videos of infant attachment behavior. In the first situation, the infant was smiling while playing with his or her mother, and in the second video, the infant was asking for her while being separated from his or her mother. Note this use of both a play and a separation context parallels infant studies in the psychological sciences for evaluating attachment as maternal up-regulation of positive states and down-regulation of negative states.

In the video of the play context, the smiling mother blew bubbles toward her infant, while in the video of the separation context, the mother leaves the room and the infant is left alone "unduly distressed," crying and calling for mother. Noriuchi and colleagues noted, "While mothers may feel joyful by watching video clips of their own infant in the first situation, they may feel anxious and protective when shown video clips of their own infant in the second situation" (2008, p. 415). They posited maternal love and strong emotional attachment would be invariant regardless of whether she was expressing affectionate behavior or vigilance and protectiveness.

Noriuchi and colleagues reported that maternal love is associated with activation of the mother's right anterior cingulate and periaqueductal gray, areas "involved in maternal response to infant's pain of separation" (2008, p. 421). They interpreted this as indicating that the mother is paying attention to her infant, who is expressing strong attachment behaviors, and that she recognizes her infant's emotional and mental *states evoked by separation from herself.* They therefore concluded, "Positive emotions such as love and motherly feeling coexisted with negative ones such as anxious feeling and worry in the mother herself. In this complicated situation, the mother's emotional responses to her own infant might be appropriately regulated by monitoring her own emotional states and by inhibiting her excessive negative affects so as not to show negative expressions to her infant who is in distress" (2008, pp. 422–423). Note the emphasis on the autoregulation of negative states in a loving mother and also her ability to hold ambivalent feelings for the infant (see Schore, 1994, 2012).

In line with earlier cited studies, these researchers documented that feelings representing maternal love were elicited when the mother viewed her own infant, regardless of the situation, and that activity in her orbitofrontal cortex was associated with this. Maternal love activates the mother's right orbitofrontal cortex, the highest level of the limbic system that regulates both positive and negative affect. They stated that the orbitofrontal cortex plays an important role in the positive reward system (it receives ascending dopamine projections from the ventral tegmental area), and at the same time its activation reflects selection of appropriate strategies to reduce the negative distress of her infant. This finding fits nicely with Schore's ideas about the right orbitofrontal system acting as the control system of attachment that encodes strategies of positive and negative affect regulation in the mother's internal working model of her relationship with her infant. In summary, they concluded "the amount of love with which a mother interacts with her infant is highly influential on the stability of the mother-infant relationship and the quality of the mother-infant attachment" (Noriuchi et al., 2008, p. 415).

Brown and Dissanayake (2009) speculated that the functional properties of orbitofrontal cortex provide important insight into the multimodal processing so central to the components of ritual behaviors, whether in mother-infant interactions or participation in group-wide rituals. In both contexts, one finds entrainment, joint action, emergent coordination, planned coordination, chorusing, turn taking, imitation, complementary joint action, motor resonance, action simulation, and mimesis (Phillips-Silver & Keller, 2012).

These studies indicate that loving affiliative behaviors and emotions, such as those created and reinforced by the operations of mother-infant interaction and participation in temporally coordinated and integrated multimodal (facial, vocal, gestural) behaviors, make lasting imprints in the orbitofrontal cortex and its connections into the ventral tegmental dopamine system and reward centers of the brain, and the periaqueductal gray involved in emotional pain of separation (Carter, Lederhandler, & Kirkpatrick, 1999; Miller & Rodgers, 2001). In their groundbreaking study "The Neural Correlates of *Maternal and Romantic Love*," Bartels and Zeki (2004) describe these enduring effects:

> The tender intimacy and selflessness of a mother's love for her infant occupies a unique and exalted position in human conduct . . . it provides one of the most powerful motivations for human action, and has been celebrated throughout the ages—in literature, art and music—as one of the most beautiful and inspiring manifestations of human behavior. It has also been the subject of many psychological studies that have searched into the *long-lasting* and pervasive influence of maternal love (or its absence) on the development and future mental constitution of a child. (p. 1155, italics added)

PRIMARY INTERSUBJECTIVITY: ONSET OF MUTUAL LOVE, CREATIVITY, AND INTERPERSONAL PLAY

Love is a strong motivating and growth-promoting force, both in caretakers and in their children, because love is intrinsically rewarding. Love fuels self-sacrifice and hard work because it is inherently emotionally powerful, and thereby meaningful. Like love, play and creativity also involve intrinsic motivation that is connected to inherently meaningful states of being and doing. Subjectively speaking, love, play, and creativity are undertaken voluntarily; that is, freely for the sake of their own pleasure, reward, and satisfaction. Mutual love between mother and child carves out a dopamine-rich, oxytocin-laden landscape of passion, joy, curiosity, intrinsic motivation, and self-evident meaning that becomes preserved throughout life through other playful, passion-filled, and creative pursuits.

Indeed, Ellen Dissanayake (1991) observed that at 2–3 months, the initiation of a critical period of mutual love, there is a significant change of infant facial expressions, voice, and gesture.

What mothers convey to infants are not their verbalized observations and opinions about the baby's looks, actions, and digestion—the ostensible content of talk to babies—but rather positive affiliative messages about their intentions and feelings: You interest me, I like you, I am like you, I like to be with you, You please me, I want to please you, You delight me, I want to communicate with you, I want you to be like me. (p. 91)

This same time period represents the onset of right brain-to-right brain protoconversations within the dyad (Trevarthen, 1979). In these initial transactions of "primary intersubjectivity," the baby, attracted to the mother's voice, facial expressions, and gestures, replies *spontaneously and playfully* with affection, while the mother replies *spontaneously and playfully* to the baby's nonverbal communications. A traffic of visual, auditory-prosodic, and tactile signals induce instant emotional effects; namely, dyadically amplified excitement and pleasure (*"excited love"*) builds within the dyad. These expressions of increasing accelerating positive emotional arousal represent products of "primary process communication" expressed in "both body movements (kinesics), posture, gesture, facial expression, voice inflection, and the sequence, rhythm, and pitch of the spoken words" (Dorpat, 2001, p. 451). The loving mother's and infant's right brain-to-right brain nonverbal communications expose the infant's rapidly developing right brain to high amounts of *spontaneous* interpersonal and intrapersonal *novelty*, allowing for the multimodal *integration* of external and internal sensations (see the earlier description of the appearance of Stern's core self at 2–3 months).

These same interpersonal neurobiological mechanisms contribute to the interpersonal origins of creativity. In the neuroscience literature, Chavez-Eakle and colleagues (2007) concluded, "Creativity means *bringing into being*; it involves generation of *novelty* and transformation of the existent [p. 519] . . . creativity involves *spontaneity* and the production of unusual and original responses to the environment [p. 525]." Documenting right-lateralized activity in these processes, they observed that *"inspiration,"* the first and deepest initiatory stage of creativity, involves sensorial, affective, and cognitive integrations that take place rapidly at unconscious levels. In neuropsychological research, Martindale and colleagues (1984) demonstrated that creativity is associated with right-hemispheric primary process cognition. In early psychoanalytic studies of creativity, Reik suggested that creativity specifically activates unconscious primary process mentation, which involves "sounds, fleeting images, organic sensations, and emotional currents" (1953, p. 9).

Mutual love, an interpersonal context of right brain–accelerating positive emotional arousal, thus is the source of right brain intrapsychic creative inspiration, a function that occurs rapidly, "beyond conscious thought." The *Shorter Oxford English Dictionary* defines inspire as "arouse in the mind, instill (a feeling or impulse)." Discussing Reik's proposal of "the origin of inspiration in childhood," Arnold (2007) describes the adaptive functions of "the creative unconscious." Creativity has long been associated with a feminine muse, which may be derived from an unconscious representation of mother's love, which Bartels and Zeki (2004) describe as "one of the most beautiful and *inspiring* manifestations of human behavior."

Indeed, there is now agreement across disciplines that creativity is important for social survival and individual well-being. Recall this adaptive function involves the production of an idea that is both *novel* and useful in a particular social setting, and that the right hemisphere predominates in coping with and assimilating novel situations and ensures the formation of a new program of interaction with a new environment, a description of the infant's socioemotional development over the first 2 years. Attachment transactions directly influence the "early life programming of hemispheric lateralization" (Stevenson et al., 2008, p. 852), and thus the creative loving mother's excited love and quiet love provide novel and more complex social and emotional stimuli that facilitate the growth and development of the infant's rapidly maturing, right brain–emergent functions. In this manner, the right brain-to-right brain intersubjective communications that begin to structuralize the core self at 2–3 months represent the primordial developmental crucible of mutual love, creativity, and play.

Along with being intrinsically motivating, love, creativity, and play also share emotion-regulating functions. Just as love permits the mother to endure hardship and willingly self-sacrifice in the face of adversity, as noted in the previous section, love also helps to stretch affect tolerance in young children, thereby permitting safety in novelty-seeking activities. Marks-Tarlow (2010, 2012) described the emotion-regulating aspects of early play, designed by nature to implicitly carry babies to the brink of regulatory boundaries. Early games of peek-a-boo and later versions of hide-and-seek tap into the edges of abandonment fears. Throwing baby high up in the air becomes gleeful due to fears of falling and necessary trust of being caught instead of perishing. In all of these early games, the line between safety and danger, joy and distress is a thin one. Tickling so easily turns into painful distress if not conducted in an attuned fashion. By playing on the edges of what is intolerable again and again young children learn to stretch those regulatory boundaries, such that later in life they can engage in passionate and creative pursuits that may be difficult, risky, and not always fun, yet nonetheless rewarding.

We suggest that excited mutual love in the form of play is the apex that drives the heights and breadth of the developing child's positive emotions, which in turn expand joy, broaden the attentional landscape (Frederickson, 2001), and enhance creativity (Estrada, Young, & Isen, 1994). Love signals the safety to be vulnerable and to take risks. Love drives open perceptual doors through which children soak in novelty, revel in spontaneity, and tolerate frustration. Love inspires mutual play and creativity that continue throughout the life span, preserving open-hearted engagement with others and the world at large.

THE ARTIFICATION HYPOTHESIS

Another central thesis of this chapter is that in young children, the neurobiology fostered by maternal love boosts a lifelong engagement with play and the arts, partly by fueling the physiology of passion, joy, curiosity, and full engagement with both negative and positive emotions. In this section, we explore a direct link between mutual love, play, and the arts. One reason a mother's love has been so celebrated in literature, art, and music may be because a mother's love resides at the very origin of art-making itself. This is the "artification" hypothesis put forth by Ellen Dissanayake (2017).

Dissanayake traced the evolution of the arts back to early mother-child relations within hominin culture. By artification, she refers to "the behav-

ior, observed in virtually all human individuals and societies, of intentionally making parts of the natural and manmade environment (e.g., shelters,
tools, utensils, weapons, clothing, bodies, surroundings) extraordinary or
special by marking, shaping, and embellishing them beyond their ordinary natural or functional appearance" (p. 148). The same term can apply
to behaviors within vocal, gestural, and verbal modalities that translate
to what we call song, dance, poetic language, and performances of various types.

Because of unprecedented helplessness of human infants and their need
for protracted maternal care after birth, Dissanayake suggested that multimodal intimate maternal practices that solidified the mother-child bond
carried an evolutionary advantage and so became amplified. She described
how maternal behavior became ritualized, in a fashion first described by
ethologists for birds and other animals, such that vocalizations and body
movements from ordinary contexts became altered to enhance communication (Dissanayake, 2017). Often occurring in playful contexts, such
behaviors were characteristically stereotyped or formalized, repeated, exaggerated, elaborated, as well as temporally manipulated in order to create
suspense and surprise. Dissayanake also speculated that facial expressions
and body movements that convey social affiliation and accord between
adults became co-opted into extra-ordinary and noteworthy signals to
attract attention, sustain interest, and to create and mold emotion. Indeed,
Chong and her colleagues (2003) presented a typology of exaggerated facial
expressions universally employed by mothers, including a trio of facial
expressions of love that is completely unique to maternal-child interactions.

Much like Winnicott, Dissanayake described an early, quiet kind of
love, when a mother's vocalizations, movements, and facial expressions are
primarily concerned with regulating the emotional state of her infant—
soothing, showing endearment, or modulating distress. As an infant's
autonomic and central nervous systems mature, excited love emerges at
3 months, and the infant now desires and seeks not just calmed, soothed
states but also suspense, surprise, and fun. Over the first year, early exploration heightens into action games through play and songs or nursery rhymes
like peek-a-boo or "This Little Piggy." Repetition in a mother's vocal utter-
ances, facial expressions, and body movements coordinates the two bodies,

minds and brains, serving to regulate the infant emotionally and unite the pair temporally. Dissanayake described how repetition also enables manipulation of expectation during mother-infant interaction, which occurs by delaying what the baby anticipates. Sensitivity to regular repetition leads to prediction of what will come next, while manipulations in timing and beat induce pleasurable release of emotion (Kubovy, 1999). Consider how a mother playing peek-a-boo will delay the removal of her hands from her eyes in order to provoke amusement and laughter from her baby or similarly when reciting "This Little Piggy" will wait to utter what the fifth piggy squeals—"wee, wee, wee, all the way home."

These games illustrate why early mother-infant interaction is often described, thought of, and experienced as a kind of play (Stern, 1977). It is spontaneous, improvised, and self-rewarding, with both partners actively showing how much they are enjoying themselves. Spontaneous play transforms a context into an enriched environment, one that facilitates processing of novel information and thereby improves learning capacity, including socioemotional learning (Schore, 1994). Play is common in all social animals (Burghardt, 2005; Panksepp, 1998). Humans and other animals tend to display special facial expressions and body postures to indicate their play-actions are not real-life behavior. In humans, this "as if" behavior morphs through play first into embodied metaphor and later into creative uses of the imagination. Marks-Tarlow (2012) details a two-stage neurobiological model by which free play of the imagination during childhood establishes a bodily, social, and emotional form of exploration that later permits intuitively grounded navigation of social space "from the inside out."

Dissanayake (2017) noted that ritualized maternal-child sequences that are patterned in time foster mutual temporal coordination, or interpersonal synchrony that includes a release of oxytocin ("the love hormone") and other endogenous opioids in both parent and child. Oxytocin is produced in the hypothalamus and serves as a key modulator of complex socioaffective responses such as affiliation, social approach, and attachment stress and anxiety (Bartz & Hollander, 2006; Meyer-Lindenberg, 2008). Release of these neuropeptides creates feelings of intimacy and trust and relieves feelings of anxiety. Just as right brain prosody, the musical dimension of maternal care, enhances emotional regulation and creates strong mother-infant bonding, so too in adults does music create strong social bonds, partly by synchronizing movements, emotions, and physiological responses. Dissanayake (2008) suggested a dual function of oxytocin: It both drives participation with others in coordinated music-making, as in the songs and dances of ritual practice, and relieves individual anxiety and emotional tensions in the process. Not only does group singing and individual music listening release oxytocin, but also oxytocin enhances interpersonal rhythmic synchronization broadly, thus contributing to its pro-social effects (Gebauer et al., 2014).

Neurobiological studies of the right brain now confirm Dissanayake's artification and Schore's regulation hypotheses. An fMRI study of 1- to 3-day-old newborns reported that music evokes activation in the right auditory cortex (Perani et al., 2010). In adults, the right somatosensory cortex is involved in subjective reports of emotional experience induced by music, one of the most potent and universal stimuli for emotional mood induction (Johnsen et al., 2009). More recently, Swart offered interdisciplinary evidence to conclude, "as regards the emotional aspects involved, the right brain appears to contribute most to the emotional meaning of music as well as of speech (2016, p. 7). Referring to the developmental model of Schore and Schore (2014), she described the communicative and relational aspects of "music's ability to process emotion—both in terms of intensifying as well as releasing emotion, and particularly in terms of its ability to bypass the conscious mind (Montello, 2002) and to 'pierce the heart directly,' to borrow the words of Oliver Sacks (2008)" (2016, p. 14).

Further support for Dissanayake's proposal that maternal love is an essential origin of the arts is found in neurobiological research on artistic creativity. Julian Jaynes speculated that the "pre-literate" right mind is dominant "during periods when consciousness is significantly altered, such as during literary or musical creativity" (1976/1999, p. 223). More recently, Wan, Cruts, and Jensen (2014) offered an electroencephalography (EEG) study of improvisation, an instantaneous creative behavior associated with different forms of art such as music and dance. They documented the right frontal region plays a central role in a "let-go" mode of improvisational playing in a less technical, more emotional manner. Citing both Dissanayake's and Schore's developmental models, Platt (2007) linked poetry to the right hemisphere.

Indeed. a large body of research demonstrates that the right prefrontal cortex is centrally involved in artistic creativity (e.g., Bhattacharya & Petsche, 2009; Drago et al., 2009; Finkelstein, Vardi, & Hod, 1991; Kowatari et al., 2009). Mihov, Denzler, and Forster (2010) reported a meta-analytic review of lateralization studies that support right-hemispheric superiority in creative thinking. Furthermore, research is now revealing the underlying neurobiological mechanisms of creativity. Mayseless and Shamay-Tsoory (2015) offered evidence to show that the early developing right frontal area mediates creativity, while the later developing left competes with or interferes with an original creative response. They suggested, "Altering the balance between the right and the left frontal lobes can be used to modulate creative production . . . reducing left frontal activity and enhancing right frontal activity reduces cognitive control, thus allowing for more creative idea production" (2015, p. 173). Indeed, Kane suggested that the creative moment involves "a sudden and transient loss or decrease of normal interhemispheric communication, removing inhibitions placed upon the right hemisphere" (2004, p. 52). These observations are relevant to creativity in the caregiving of infants and in the psychotherapeutic context.

THE EMOTION OF LOVE IN PSYCHOTHERAPY

In the sections above, we explored how maternal love expresses itself initially through facial expression, soothing, affective touch, and lullabies as quiet love. The excited form of mutual love subsequently builds to a crescendo through spontaneous play that includes coordinated exploration, novel pursuits, emergent interaction, turn taking, and synchronized pleasure. In these ways, mutual love, play, and creativity are yoked together in multimodal expression that dovetails with early interactive regulation and development of self and cascades into lifelong and collective creativity at a societal level.

According to Schore (2014), right brain processes are dominant in psychotherapy. There is now agreement that right brain creativity, a fundamental aspect of clinical expertise, is an essential contributor to treatment, both in establishing and maintaining the therapeutic alliance and in reestablishing it after ruptures, especially in reenactments of attachment trauma (see Schore, 2012). He observed that a spontaneous enactment can either blindly repeat a familiar pathological object relation or creatively provide a novel relational experience via the therapist's co-participation in interactive repair and the regulation of the patient's affective states. Regulated enactments also include moments of intimate intersubjective play. Indeed, play has a long history in psychotherapy, championed by Winnicott, who argued, "Psychotherapy is done in the overlap of the two play areas, that of the patient and that of the therapist. . . . The reason why playing is essential is that it is in playing that the patient is being creative" (1971, p. 54). Contemporary neuroscience now emphasizes the adaptive value of creativity, which is also an outcome of a successful psychotherapeutic experience. Lindell observed, "Flexibility of thought . . . when coupled with originality . . . allows a creative individual to respond efficiently and effectively to a constantly changing, and regularly challenging, environment" (2011, p. 480). Directly relevant to psychotherapeutic mechanisms of change, Abraham concluded, "The immense capacity of human beings to be creative can be gleaned from virtually all realms of our lives whenever we generate original ideas, develop novel solutions to problems, or express ourselves in a unique and individual manner" (2013, p. 1).

On the other hand, the right brain functions of love have had a long and controversial history in psychotherapy. In classical psychoanalysis, love was considered a natural aspect of the transference dynamic on the part of patients, yet was discouraged, if not forbidden within psychoanalysts by Freud, who tended to eroticize all forms of adult love. In an early essay on the matter of love within psychotherapy, Eric Fromm (1958) observed Freud's implicit mistrust of *all* emotions. Because Freud considered emotions to be irrational and inferior to thought and objective interpretation, affectively charged non-erotic love on the part of the psychoanalyst had no place in Freud's clinical methodology or in "the talking cure."

In the same essay, Fromm described how Freud's fallout with his early

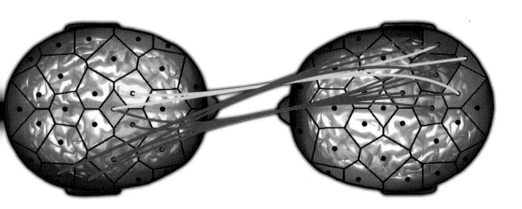

FIGURE 1.1 Right-lateralized interbrain synchronization of a spontaneous nonverbal communication. Adapted from "Toward a Two-Body Neuroscience" by Dumas (2011). Copyright 2011 by Landes Bioscience. Adapted with permission.

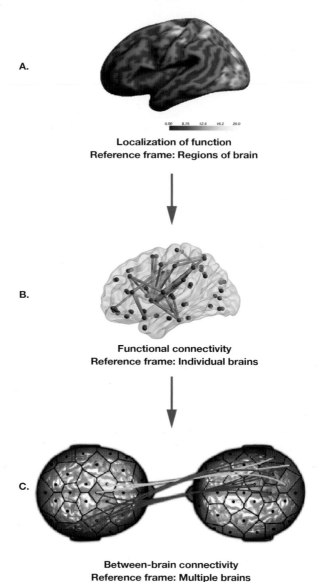

A.

5.00   8.75   12.5   16.2   20.0

Localization of function
Reference frame: Regions of brain

B.

Functional connectivity
Reference frame: Individual brains

C.

Between-brain connectivity
Reference frame: Multiple brains

FIGURE 1.2 (*opposite*) © 2017 Ray D, Roy D, Sindhu B, Sharan P and Banerjee A l Front. Psychol., 28 September 2017 | https://doi.org/10.3389/fpsyg.2017.01627
    Functional neuroimaging: evolution of reference frame. (**A**) In its early years, the sole focus of functional neuroimaging techniques (e.g., fMRI) was to localize brain functions to discrete regions. (**B**) The first paradigm shift took place with experimental validation of functional integration over distinct brain areas using measures of functional connectivity and shifting of the reference frame to the whole of the brain. Adapted from "Decreased Functional Brain Connectivity in Adolescents with Internet Addiction" by Hong et al. (2013). Copyright 2013 by Hong et al. Used under Creative Commons Attribution license. (**C**) The emerging techniques to assess between-brain functional connectivity calls for a second paradigm shift from a single brain to a multi-brain reference frame. Copyright 2011 by Landes Bioscience. Adapted with permission. Adapted from Guillaume Dumas, Communicative & Integrative Biology Vol 4:3 pp. 349-352 (2011).

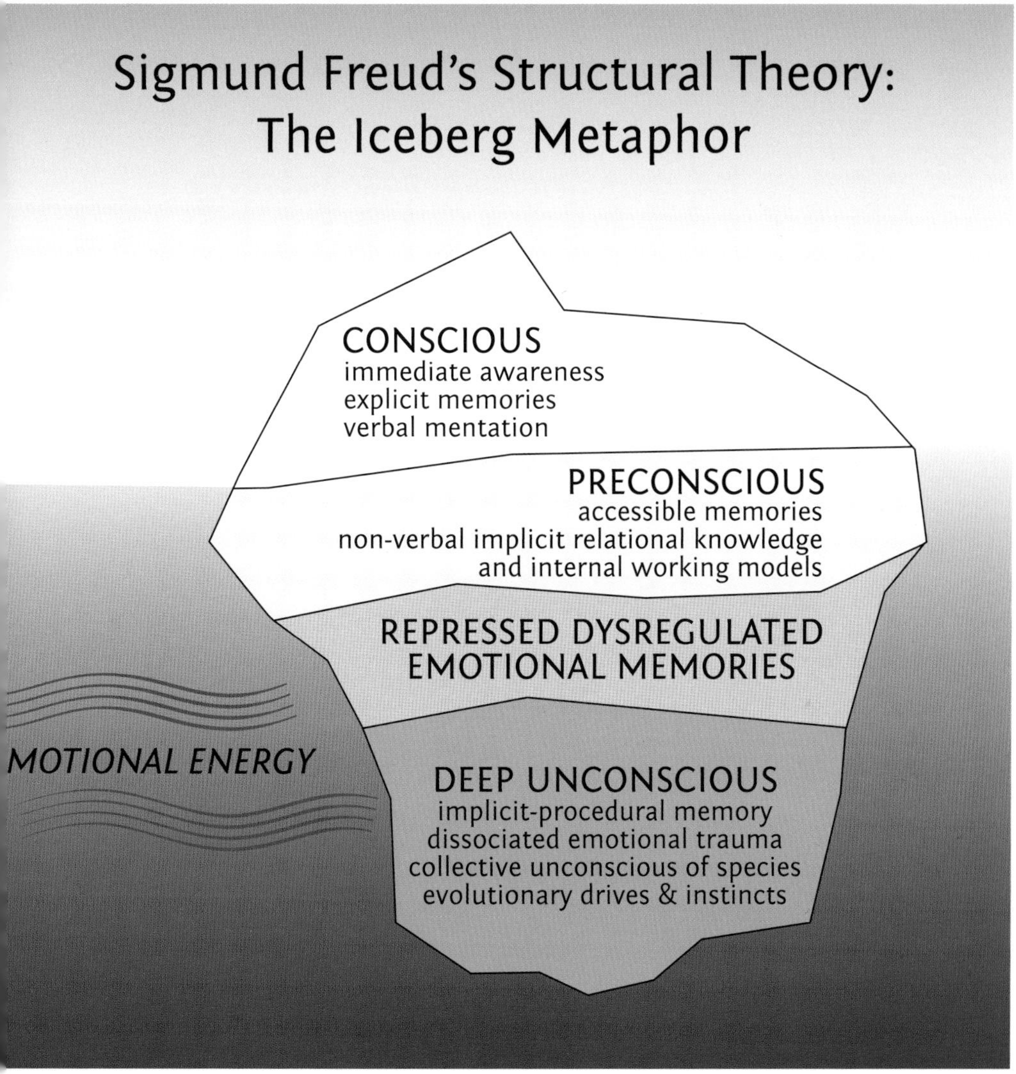

Sigmund Freud's Structural Theory:
The Iceberg Metaphor

CONSCIOUS
immediate awareness
explicit memories
verbal mentation

PRECONSCIOUS
accessible memories
non-verbal implicit relational knowledge
and internal working models

REPRESSED DYSREGULATED
EMOTIONAL MEMORIES

EMOTIONAL ENERGY

DEEP UNCONSCIOUS
implicit-procedural memory
dissociated emotional trauma
collective unconscious of species
evolutionary drives & instincts

Figure 3.2 Revised update of Freud's iceberg metaphor.

Increasing sympathetic hyperarousal
Dysregulated rage, violence, fear, panic.
Fight-flight and explosive fragmentation of self.

**Zone of moderate emotional arousal
in which we can tolerate our emotions**

Increasing parasympathetic hyperarousal
Dysregulated shame, disgust, despair.
Dissociation and implosive collapse of self.

FIGURE 7.1 Adapted by Daniela Sieff. Source: On the same wave-length: How our emotional brain is shaped by human relationships. Interview by Daniela Sieff. Understanding and Healing Emotional Trauma: Conversations with Pioneering Clinicians and Researchers, 2015. Routledge, UK.

disciple, Sándor Ferenczi, arose precisely over the issue of love. Ferenczi was an early proponent of leveling the playing field between psychoanalyst and patient. Through a process he called "mutual analysis," Ferenczi established the centrality of mutual emotional experience generally, and love specifically. For Ferenczi, the essential characteristics of parenthood were the essential characteristics of the psychotherapist. In a book about Ferenczi with the delicious title *The Leaven of Love*, Izette de Forest (1954) expounded upon his position as follows:

> The offering of loving care cannot be given, either by parent or by psychotherapist, on demand or in answer to threat. It must be given freely and spontaneously as a genuinely felt emotional expression. And it must provide an environment of trust and confidence and hope, so that the neurotic sufferer can gradually unburden himself of his conscious and unconscious anxieties; of his shame and guilt; of his hostility and plans of vengeance; of his rejected longing to love; of all his deeply hidden secrets. . . . It must provide the environment (no matter how absurd it may objectively appear) which is essential to growth, to the unfolding of individuality. In other words, the therapist must give to the patient a replica of the birthright of love which has denied him, as an infant or a growing child, but which, if granted, would have assured him full stature as an individual in his own right. (pp. 16–17)

Love, one of the most powerful emotions, fits better into contemporary, relational psychoanalysis, a two-person psychology wherein intersubjectivity is both the goal and the medium for transformation. For example, Hirsch and Kessel (1988) reviewed the influence of existential humanists on interpersonalist proponents of love, including Fromm, Searles, Wolstein, and Ehrenberg. Shaw traced early proponents of love within the perspectives of Ferenczi, Suttie, Balint, Fairbairn, Loewald, and Kohut and concluded that "our clinical theories call for and make use of the analyst's emotional responsiveness—in particular, the analyst's capacity to love authentically and use his love therapeutically (2003, p. 257).

Within the field of interpersonal neurobiology, Schore's work highlights dysregulated emotion at the heart of psychopathology, privileging the role of emotion over thought during corrective interactive regulation, while highlighting the role of implicit, embodied processes over explicit, verbal ones within psychotherapy. Marks-Tarlow (2012, 2014) also underscores the importance of implicit processes and emotionally informed perception to the centrality of clinical intuition during psychotherapy, which dovetails with maternal intuition. Only through intuition can clinicians attune to the uniqueness of the individual, the moment, and the "chemistry" of the specific therapist-patient dyad. Furthermore, we suggest that deep and ongoing psychotherapy that goes beyond symptom removal and trauma resolution into full transformative growth is likewise modulated by both forms of Winnicott's quiet and excited love within the psychotherapist-patient dyad.

These experiences set the stage for emotional transferential-countertransferential exchanges between therapists and patients that mirror early life, right brain-to-right brain exchanges necessary for secure attachment. Because "love is the leaven" of early development, we suggest that love is also the leaven for deep healing and post-traumatic growth during long-term, open-ended psychotherapy. Whether or not the strongly emotional experience of love is ever explicitly acknowledged, when therapists and patients internally and nonverbally express their love for one another, this serves to widen perceptual doors, expand tolerance of negative and positive emotions, permit more vulnerability to explore novelty and engage in playful interactions, and mutually amplify safety and trust on both sides of the therapeutic alliance.

We assert that the essential importance of this emotion—"one of the strongest of which the mind is capable" and the "most powerful motivation for human action"—within psychotherapy is that not only does mutual love provide an ideal holding environment for empathic resonance and deep, other-directed understanding, but also love may be the ideal growth-facilitating environment for unleashing creative self-expression throughout life. We end this chapter with a metaphor for the power of love put forth by another psychoanalytic psychiatrist, Henry Krystal (1988), in his classic text *Integration & Self-Healing*:

Just as white light contains all the colors of the spectrum, so love encompasses all the feelings reflecting our living process. When we get a chance to observe it, as in self-healing or in promoting the expansion of the conscious recognition of our selfness, we are especially prone to equate it with life forces, or the full enjoyment of our identity and unity. Love is the affective state that is favorable to the achievement of the most comprehensive self-representation. (p. 78)

CHAPTER 6

Moving Forward: New Findings on the Right Brain and Their Implications for Psychoanalysis

*Keynote Address to the American Psychological Association
Division of Psychoanalysis 2017 Conference*

I'D LIKE TO THANK the American Psychological Association Division of Psychoanalysis for their invitation to present this keynote address. Over the years I've had a number of opportunities to present my ideas here, but this is a special opportunity to offer some thoughts about the future of the field. Indeed in April 1995 in my first contact with Division 39, I introduced my recently developed ideas on neuropsychoanalysis and interpersonal neurobiology on the occasion of the 100th anniversary of Freud's *Project for a Scientific Psychology* (1895). Soon after I published "A Century after Freud's *Project*: Is a Rapprochement between Psychoanalysis and Neurobiology at Hand?" in the *Journal of the American Psychoanalytic Association*. Referring to Freud's early career in neurology, the *Project* represented his attempt "to furnish . . . a psychology which shall be a natural science" (Schore, 1997, p. 295), and toward that end he introduced the concepts that to this day serve as the theoretical foundation and scaffolding of psychoanalysis: primary and secondary processes; principles of pleasure-unpleasure, constancy, and reality testing; cathexis and identification; wish-fulfillment theory of dreams; psychical regression and hallucination; systems of perception, memory, unconscious and preconscious psychic activity; and the concept of regulation. Freud also offered his earliest thoughts about two problems he struggled with for the rest of his career: affect and motivation. He later repudiated the *Project*, and over the rest of the 20th century connections between psychoanalysis and science were weakened and strained. Due to the loss of its moorings to the rest of science, it became an easy target to criticism that it was untestable, and that therefore it was not a proper science (Grunbaum, 1984; Popper, 1962). Yet in 1913, Freud asserted that in the future, "we shall have to find a contact point with biology; and we may rightly feel glad if that contact is already assured at one important point or another" (1913, pp. 181–182).

In 1994, in *Affect Regulation and the Origin of the Self*, I asserted that right brain socioemotional and regulatory structures and functions represented such a contact point, and that the time was right for a rapprochement between psychoanalysis and neuroscience. Over the ensuing three decades, I continued to elaborate the interpersonal neurobiological perspective of regulation theory to describe how beneath levels of conscious awareness, brains align and synchronize their neural activities with other brains, especially in emotional interactions. The theory also describes how the development of the right brain-mind is shaped continually by social experiences, especially those involving emotional relationships, including therapeutic relationships. Indeed over the past three decades, I have built upon Freud's *Project* in order to elaborate modern neuropsychoanalysis, the study of the brain systems that process information at a nonconscious level, specifically suggesting that the right brain represents the psychobiological substrate of human unconscious. This rapidly expanding research on the right brain acts as a source of the essential origins, adaptive functions, rapid dynamics, and pathogenesis of the human unconscious. These experimental, theoretical, and clinical studies can elucidate the deeper mechanism of the invisible, omnipresent unconscious in everyday life.

Furthermore, recent discoveries on neuroscience of the right brain and neuropsychoanalysis of the unconscious mind can act as an integrating force in psychoanalytic theory and clinical practice. Neuropsychoanalytic structure, located in the right brain, integrates various psychoanalytic theories of different functions of the mind, all of which are centered in the fundamental construct of psychoanalysis, the unconscious, the central organizing principle of the field. The construct of the unconscious has thus shifted from an intangible, immaterial, metapsychological abstraction of the mind to a psychoneurobiological heuristic function of a tangible brain that has material form. Thus, we now have a rejoinder to previous critics of psychoanalysis: Scientifically informed psychoanalytic theory can generate hypotheses that can be experimentally tested and is able to formulate more complex clinical approaches. Brain research thus offers valuable data to psychoanalysis, "the science of unconscious processes" (Brenner, 1980). On both fronts, the theory is now genuinely "heuristic," defined by the *Oxford English Dictionary* as "serving to find out or discover something."

Referring to the conference title, I will begin with changes within the consulting room and reformulations of theoretical psychoanalysis, and then advances and new directions in clinical psychoanalysis and psychoanalytic psychotherapy. I'll then use regulation theory to discuss changes beyond the consulting room, and how 21st-century psychoanalysis can offer deeper understandings of human problems in the outside social and physical world. Finally, I will conclude with thoughts on what the conference organizers specifically asked me in their invitation, how the "interface of neuroscience and psychoanalysis will challenge us to think about how our field needs to change as we move forward?" Everything that follows is an expansion of regulation theory, a theory of the development, psychopathogenesis, and treatment of the right brain unconscious subjective self. What I continue to offer is a broad-ranging theory, a systematic exposition of the general principles of a science. The internal consistency, coherence, scope, pragmatic usefulness, and power of the theory is expressed in its ability to formulate testable hypotheses and generate research, as well as to generate both clinical interventions and cultural applications.

RIGHT BRAIN, LATERALITY RESEARCH, AND CHANGES WITHIN THE CONSULTING ROOM: PSYCHOANALYTIC THEORY

Brain laterality (hemispheric asymmetry), originally discovered in the 19th century, is now experiencing a resurgence in neuroscience. This rapidly expanding research is describing the functional and structural differences between the left and right brains, and thereby between a conscious "left mind" and an unconscious "right mind." Many studies are converging to support the idea of a left brain surface, verbal, conscious, analytical explicit self versus a right brain deeper, nonverbal, nonconscious, holistic, emotional, corporeal, subjective implicit self. The right brain is thus the psychobiological source of the rapid spontaneous information processing of the psychoanalytic unconscious mind.

Although until recently lateralization was thought to occur only in humans, it is now clear that the specializations of left and right hemispheres occur in all vertebrates. According to Rogers (2014), the left hemisphere is dominant for routine, established patterns of behavior in familiar circumstances, sequential processing, focused attention to specific targets or cues, and top-down processes guided by learned instructions. In contrast, the right predominates in attention to unexpected, novel stimuli; notices small differences between stimuli; attends to global/geometric cues, face recognition, and social cognition; expresses intense emotion (especially aggression and fear), and is dominant in bottom-up processes that are stimulus driven. Overviewing specifically human studies, Iain McGilchrist concluded, "The right hemisphere . . . has the most sophisticated and extensive, and quite possibly most lately evolved, representation in the prefrontal cortex, the most highly evolved part of the brain" (2009, p. 437). In more recent work, McGilchrist offered characterizations that bear directly upon clinical psychoanalysis: "The right hemisphere both grounds our experience of the world at the bottom end, so to speak, and makes sense of it, at the top end" (2015, p. 100); that this hemisphere is more in touch with both affect and the body; and that "neurological evidence supports what is called the primacy of affect and the primacy of unconscious over conscious will" (2015, p. 100).

Further support for the construct of a right brain unconscious mind comes from neuropsychoanalysis. According to Tucker and Moller, "The right hemisphere's specialization for emotional communication through nonverbal channels seems to suggest a domain of the mind that is close to the motivationally charged psychoanalytic unconscious" (2007, p. 91). Writing in the journal *Neuropsychoanalysis*, Guido Gainotti (2005) asserted,

> The right hemisphere subserves the lower "schematic" level (where emotions are automatically generated and experienced as "true emotions") whereas the left hemisphere the higher "conceptual" level (where emotions are consciously analyzed and submitted to intentional control). (p. 71)

In more recent writings, Gainotti (2012) cited neurological data indicating that the unconscious processing of emotional information is subsumed by a right-hemispheric subcortical route. These data confirm Freud's hierarchical structural theory. They are also consonant with my own model of hemispheric asymmetry, first articulated in 1994, that the right brain is centrally involved in not only the *intrapsychic* implicit processing and self-regulation of emotions and social information, but also in the interpersonal communication and interactive regulation of emotion by a right brain *relational* unconscious, via right brain-to-right brain communications, of face, voice, and gesture. Current neurobiological models of Freud's unconscious are now shifting from focusing on unconscious mental contents to adaptive, essential, unconscious psychobiological processes.

   Indeed, psychoanalysis is currently undergoing significant changes in its central construct, the dynamic unconscious, which for its first century was defined as conscious material that has been repressed by an active force that removes certain elements unacceptable to censorship from consciousness. Yet by 1915, Freud stated, "the repressed does not cover everything that is unconscious. The unconscious has the wider compass: the repressed is a part of the unconscious" (1915, p. 166). Indeed, this reformulation is the central theme of a recent book, *Unrepressed Unconscious, Implicit Memory, and Clinical Work* by Craparo and Mucci (2017). Within the chapters of this volume, a number of authors link *implicit* right brain functions with the *"unrepressed unconscious"*; that is, other essential functional contents of the wider domain of the unconscious. This equivalence of the constructs of implicit and unconscious has been stressed by, for example, Mancia's (2006) work on implicit memory and early unrepressed unconscious, and myself ("The Right Brain Implicit Self Lies at the Core of Psychoanalysis"; Schore, 2011). In the latter, I concluded that the unconscious contains much more than what is repressed by the conscious mind, highlighting the essential role of not only implicit cognition but also implicit affect, communication, and regulation in current relational psychoanalytic models. I then discussed recent developmental and neurobiological studies of implicit processes in early development and psychopathogenesis of the implicit subjective self, as well as implicit affective processes in psychotherapeutic change processes.

Earlier, in 2002, the neuroscientist Joseph LeDoux linked the implicit with psychoanalytic theory in the journal *Science*: "That explicit and implicit aspects of the self exist is not a particularly novel idea. It is closely related to Freud's partition of the mind into conscious, preconscious (accessible but not currently accessed), and unconscious (inaccessible) levels" (2002, p. 28). Echoing this, authors are concluding that "the right hemisphere has been linked to implicit information processing, as opposed to the more explicit and more conscious processing tied to the left hemisphere" (Happaney, Zelazo, & Stuss, 2004, p. 7). More recently, writing in the psychological literature on the functional abilities of the human unconscious, Hassin (2013) cited studies indicating,

> The function of extracting patterns from our environment, also known as implicit learning, has been repeatedly demonstrated; maintaining evidence from past experience, also known as memory, can happen outside of conscious awareness; people can extract information about emotion and gender from subliminally presented facial expressions; comparing oneself with others, a central social function, occurs nonconsciously and even with subliminally presented others; and physical sensations affect perception and social perception. . . . A review of the literature through functional glasses quickly reveals that *many functions that were historically associated with conscious awareness can occur nonconsciously.* (p. 200, italics added)

In my own work, I continue to offer a large body of research implicating right brain structural systems in implicit, rapid, and spontaneous anticipation, recognition, expression, communication, and regulation of bodily-based emotional states beneath levels of awareness (see Schore,

2012). In fact, very recent neuroscience authors are reporting studies on "Right Hemisphere Dominance in Nonconscious Processing" (Chen & Hsiao, 2014), concluding that the right hemisphere has an advantage in shaping behavior with implicit information, whereas the left hemisphere plays a greater role in expressing explicit knowledge. Another on "the unconscious guidance of attention" documents that the right hemisphere temporo-parietal junction plays an essential role in implicit attentional functions that operate outside conscious awareness (Chelazzi, Bisley, & Bartolomeo, 2018). In terms of voice and face processing, Schepman, Rodway, & Pritchard (2015) offered a study titled "Right-Lateralized Unconscious, but Not Conscious, Processing of Affective Environmental Sounds," and Crouzet, Kirchner, & Thorpe (2010) another on "Fast Saccades toward Faces: Face Detection in Just 100 ms," documenting efficient "ultrarapid" processing of unconscious information. This evidence-based research on the right brain unconscious counters Grunbaum's and Popper's critique that psychoanalysis is not testable or falsifiable.

Furthermore, psychoanalysis is now being transformed from a theory of the unconscious mind into a theory of mind/brain/body: Unconscious systems operating beneath levels of conscious awareness are inextricably linked into the body. Spontaneous processes of "bottom-up" bodily-based autonomic and hormonal systems (the release of stress steroids, sex steroids, neuroendocrines) are also part of the right brain domain of the unconscious. In a recent chapter, Russell Meares (2017) stated, "Autonomic activity occurs at an unconscious level." Stephen Porges (2011), perhaps the leading expert on the autonomic nervous system, documented how the hypothalamic-pituitary-adrenal (HPA) axis of organismic homeostasis is asymmetrical, with structures on the right side exhibiting greater control of physiological responses associated with emotion ("top-down"). He also cited studies suggesting that stimuli that are processed primarily by the right hemisphere produce greater cardiovascular response than stimuli processed by the left hemisphere, and that damage to the right hemisphere blunts facial expression, vocal intonation, and autonomic reactivity. In my own studies, I have proposed that "early psychological damage" of the unconscious system is equated with the enduring impact of "relational trauma" (abuse/neglect) on the developing right brain (Schore, 2003a), and that these deficits may be accessed in psychotherapy (Schore, 2003b). That said, more work needs to be done on the enduring impacts of early neglect ("dead mother") in the therapeutic context (see Mucci, in press).

Another major change in the field's organizing principle of the unconscious is reflected in a shift from left brain repression to right brain dissociation, especially in preoedipal psychopathologies. In 2003, I cited extant neurobiological research suggesting that repression is a developmentally more advanced left brain defense against affects that are represented at the cortical level of the right brain, while the earlier appearing and more primitive dissociation is a right brain defense against traumatic affects such as terror, rage, and shame that are stored subcortically in the right brain (Schore, 2003b). In *Awakening the Dreamer*, Bromberg (2006) asserted that repression defines a process that is designed to avoid disavowed content that may lead to *unpleasant* intrapsychic conflict, whereas dissociation blots out *unbearable* experience from consciousness. The right brain unconscious system thus contains not just repressed but also dissociated ("not me") states of self.

Moreover, neuropsychoanalysis reveals essential information about the deeper levels of the topography of the mind, Freud's iceberg model of conscious, preconscious, and unconscious. Recall, only 10% of Freud's iceberg is visible (conscious), whereas the other 90% lies beneath water (preconscious and unconscious). Within the subconscious mind, the preconscious is allotted 10% to 15%, while the unconscious is allotted an overwhelming 75% to 80%. Recall Jung's (1963) dictum, "Man's task . . . is to become conscious of the contents that process upward from the unconscious." In my own work, I have offered a modern neuropsychoanalytic update of Freud's topographic model of stratified conscious, preconscious, and unconscious systems (Schore, 2003b; see Figure 3.2). In line with developmental neurobiological research, the brain matures in a caudal to rostral progression, with subcortical areas maturing before cortical areas. Similarly, the "lower" core of the unconscious develops before higher levels of the preconscious, which in turn evolve before the highest levels of the conscious mind. This progression also mirrors the fact that the right hemisphere matures before the left (Schore, 1994, 2017a). Thus I have proposed that the limbic and emotion-processing areas of the right brain unconscious represent a hierarchical system with an outer, later developing cortical, orbitofrontal-limbic regulated core; an inner, earlier developing cingulate-limbic regulating core; and an earliest evolving subcortical amygdala-limbic regulated core that lies deepest within, like nested Russian dolls.

The three levels of organization of the right brain represent, respectively, three levels of the system unconscious: preconscious, unconscious, and deep unconscious. The unconscious systems of the hierarchical three-tiered cortical-subcortical limbic core thus reflect the early developmental history of the subjective self (Schore, 2013a). A body of research indicates involvement of the right orbitofrontal system in preconscious functions of implicit perception and affect regulation, and in controlling allocation of attention to possible contents of consciousness (Schore, 2003b, 2012). Recall, Freud's (1940) definition of preconscious as "capable of entering consciousness." Epstein (1983) described the salience of "the preconscious level of awareness" in not only "emotions and moods" but also cognitively structuring experience. "It is here that the implicit beliefs and values reside, which automatically organize and direct our everyday experience and behavior" (1983, p. 235). This active involvement of the preconscious in everyday human experience confirms Freud's essential contribution to science, the fundamental role of the unconscious in everyday life.

In light of the concept of a relational unconscious, we may also describe a relational preconscious. Indeed, Kantrowitz referred to "preconscious resonance between patient and analyst," asserting that "It is in the realm of preconscious communication that the interwoveness of intrapsychic and interpersonal phenomena becomes apparent" (1999, p. 72). Psychoanalytic theoreticians and clinicians should reexplore the relational development of preconscious functions (especially in the second year of life), its alterations in psychopathology, and its growth in psychotherapy. The right-lateralized preconscious acts as a regulator of affect consciousness—which affects and at what intensities negative and positive affects enter into conscious awareness.

If the orbitofrontal cortex can be equated with the preconscious functions of what Stern (1985) termed "the subjective self" (Schore, 2003b), the earliest developing "deep unconscious" is equated with Stern's (1985) "core self" and Damasio's (1994) "protoself." The deep unconscious of the earliest corporeal self is connected into the body, specifically via its reciprocal connections with the autonomic nervous system, which has been termed "the physiological bottom of the mind" (Jackson, 1931), a clear description of the deep unconscious. New information suggests maternal-fetal placental transactions occurring in the last trimester *in utero* may shape the primordial emergence of the deep unconscious (Schore, 2013a, 2017b). Neuroscience now demonstrates that throughout all later stages of development, "the right amygdala may subserve a high-speed detection role for unconscious stimuli" (Costafreda et al., 2008, p. 66) and for processing "unconscious emotional learning" (Morris, Ohman, & Dolan, 1998).

The deep unconscious implicit functions of the early maturing amygdala are directly relevant to not only topographic but also clinical models. Markowitsch and Staniloiu characterize the amygdala as "a hub of a network" that "via its multitudinous connections with cortical and subcortical areas forges the integration of emotion, perception, cognition and behavior and might contribute to *a sense of unitary self*" (2011, p. 728, italics added). Dyck et al. (2011) offer an fMRI study documenting "a left-lateralized cognitive and intentional control of mood and a right-sided more automatic induction of emotions that relies less on explicit reflection processes" (p. 2503). With implications for treatments of all early forming self-pathologies, Vrticka, Sander, & Vuilleumier concluded that the amygdala encodes patterns of both social positive or negative images, and that *"this encoding pattern is not influenced by cognitive or behavioral emotion regulation mechanisms, and displays a hemispheric lateralization with more pronounced effects on the right side"* (2013, italics in original).

Todd and Anderson (2009) offered a significant update of the essential adaptive functions of the amygdala system:

> Traditionally, the amygdala has gotten a lot of "bad" press. Popular wisdom has portrayed the human amygdala as the center of an ancient animal id that drives us to rapid impulsive action before our more reasoned judgments can kick in. For a long time, it was considered to be a fear center or threat detector that is instrumental

in allocating processing resources to potentially harmful events. . . .
More recent studies in humans suggest that it is responsive to positive and arousing rather than to strictly negative events, as well as
to ambiguous events. . . . The connectivity of the amygdala places
it *at the center of the brain,* a physical hub linking numerous distant
regions, and it is positioned to allow emotions to influence how the
rest of the brain works, from the first stages of stimulus encoding to
regulating social behavior. (p. 1217, italics added)

Neuroscience thus suggests a reformulation of the deep unconscious—it
is not just a cauldron of chaotic stressors and dense painful negative affects
but also a source generator of intense positive affects. Todd and Anderson
further describe "the amygdala's role in regulating interpersonal distance.
People automatically regulate the distance between themselves and others
on the basis of feelings of personal comfort" and refer to "invisible social
force fields that regulate close physical proximity, suggesting that the amygdala is crucial for the sense of interpersonal space . . . the amygdala should
be more active at close interpersonal distances" (2009, p. 1217). Interpersonal neurobiology may thus elucidate mechanisms of deep unconscious
"uncanny" communications within a co-created intersubjective field.

Right brain interpersonal neurobiology continues to be directly relevant
to the relational trend in psychodynamic models. Recall a central principle
of interpersonal neurobiology dictates that brains align and synchronize
their neural activities with other brains within socioemotional interactions.
This construct lies at the heart of right brain-to-right brain communications. Although I used extant neurobiology to elaborate this principle of
regulation theory in 1994, very recent technologies are just now capable of
measuring two brains in interaction with each other. In my 2012 volume, I
cited Dumas, who was calling for a "move from a classical one-brain neuroscience toward a novel two-body approach" (2011, p. 349). Note the similarity of this to the psychoanalytic psychological move from a one-person
to a two-person psychology (Schore, 2003b).

In the past 5 years, *hyperscanning* methodologies utilizing *simultaneous*
electroencephalography (EEG), functional magnetic resonance imaging

(fMRI), near-infrared spectroscopy (NIRS), and magnetoencephalography (MEG) measurements have been created. This technological advance now allows the study of two brains during real-time social interactions with each other, including during emotional communications. Thus the brain activities of each member of a dyad are simultaneously measured during communication, where "both participants are continuously active, each modifying their own actions in response to the continuously changing actions of their partner" (Dumas et al., 2010). Inspired by studies of *nonverbal* communication and coordination between a mother and her infant and by research on *spontaneous* imitation in preverbal infants, these authors offer a dual EEG study of interbrain synchronization during a social interaction, specifically an adult spontaneous, reciprocal communication with turn taking. In this social interaction of nonverbal imitation, a central foundation of socialization and communication, both share attention and compare cues of self and other's actions. These authors document an *interbrain synchronization* of the right centroparietal regions on a milliseconds timescale in both interacting partners. In addition, the right temporoparietal cortex in one partner is also synchronized with the right temporoparietal cortex of the other (see Figure 1.1 in Chapter 1). This right-lateralized brain system is activated in social interactions and is centrally involved in attentional processes, perceptual awareness, and empathic understanding (Decety & Lamm, 2007). The right temporoparietal junction integrates input from visual, auditory, somesthetic, and limbic areas, and is thus a pivotal neural locus for self-functions involved in multisensory body-related information processing. This right-lateralized interactional synchrony represents what I have called an implicit intersubjective "right brain-to-right brain" interaction between one subjective self and another.

In another hyperscanning study, Stolk and colleagues (2013) used MEG to record two brains sharing novel symbols during live communicative interactions. These authors reported that novel communicative problems up-regulated activity in the *right ventrolateral temporal lobe and ventromedial (orbitofrontal) cortex* in both members of the dyad, and that the overlapping neural right-lateralized up-regulation was present *before* the occurrence of a specific communicative problem and well before the observation of communicative actions (Stolk et al., 2013). In a subsequent work, "Cerebral Coherence between Communicators Marks the Emergence of *Meaning,*" this lab offered simultaneous fMRI brain images on both participants showing that establishing mutual understanding of *novel* signals synchronizes cerebral dynamics across both communicators' right temporal lobes. Interpersonal synchronization occurred only in *pairs with shared communicative history,* in which the partners mutually learned to adjust to each other (Stolk et al., 2014, italics added). Note the similarity of this to the ongoing right brain-to-right brain psychotherapeutic clinician-patient relational context, and that in this nonverbal communication context, meaning is generated in their right (and not left) hemispheres (see Schore, 2012). This disconfirms the idea that the left conscious mind in the verbal hemisphere alone generates *meaning,* a construct of therapeutic action important to psychoanalytic clinicians.

It is tempting to speculate that the interpersonal neurobiological mechanism of right-hemispheric neurodynamic interbrain synchronization may underlie the co-creation of a psychodynamic intersubjective field, one in which the crescendos and decrescendos of the empathic clinician's psychobiological state is in resonance with similar crescendos and decrescendos of the patient's state (see Schore, 2012). This involves more than a synchronization of two interacting right cortical hemispheres, but two right lateralized cortical-subcortical circuitries. Future hyperscanning research should now focus on simultaneous recordings of both the patient's right brain and the clinician's right brain during real-time spontaneous emotional interactions within the evolving therapeutic relationship, and on how these emotional communications induce interbrain synchronization in both the empathic therapist's and the patient's right-lateralized cortical-subcortical regulatory limbic circuits. Furthermore, psychoanalytic theoretical conceptualizations of an intersubjective field may benefit from current applications of physics to interpersonal attraction and bonding that are modeling the electrodynamics of a dyadic state of consciousness generated in a "momentary state of 'limbic resonance'" (Schore 1994) that involves a "subconscious emotional synchronization" within a context of "charged social space-time" (Haas, 2015).

RIGHT BRAIN, LATERALITY RESEARCH, AND CHANGES WITHIN
THE CONSULTING ROOM: PSYCHOTHERAPY

These data fit well with my interpersonal neurobiological model of right brain-to-right brain unconscious communication and regulation across a co-created intersubjective field; that is, an interbrain synchronization of two right hemispheres in an emotion-transacting psychotherapeutic context. In a recent contribution in the Division 29 journal *Psychotherapy*, I offered neurobiological and clinical data to argue that "The right brain is dominant in psychotherapy" (Schore, 2014a). Right brain-to-right brain unconscious affective communications "beneath the words" are expressed in the therapist-patient transference-countertransference relationship. This mechanism is essential to working in preverbal-onset developmental disorders, whereby the optimal clinical approach is to "follow the Ariadne's thread of transference affects" (Brierley, 1937).

In therapy, this right-lateralized system is used to access deeper unconscious systems beneath the surface of the left hemisphere conscious mind. Commenting on current advances in neuroscience and psychoanalysis, Lehtonen and colleagues (2006) concluded,

> The classical approach in psychoanalysis, while centering on metaphoric and symbolic work within fully developed psychoanalytic object relations, has not traditionally included in this work the meaning of the body and the earliest layers of the personality, due to their preverbal and unconscious nature. This view has recently changed. . . . Increasing understanding of the nature of the psychophysiological organization of the basic mental layer is clinically important. . . . It has implications for developmental and treatment issues as well as technical problems of *how to listen, conceptualize and to respond to these early layers of the human personality in the clinical setting.* (p. 1349, italics added)

Indeed, clinicians across various therapeutic domains are now accessing the right brain-to-right brain communication system in order to decipher and utilize intersubjective, affective, bodily-based, implicit-procedural non-verbal communications from the patient's early developing (Gupta et al., 2005; Sun et al., 2005) right hemisphere, which is dominant in human infancy (Chiron et al., 1997; Schore, 1994).

In his most recent psychoanalytic writings, Philip Bromberg (2017) asserted,

> The foundational perspective that shapes my thinking is enriched by, and, in an ever-expanding way, intertwined with Allan Schore's groundbreaking contributions to the fields of both psychotherapy and neuroscience . . . in addition to the key importance of affect regulation and dysregulation, both Allan and I place special emphasis on the phenomenon and concept of *"state-sharing"* (Schore, 2003b, 2011, 2012)—that is, the right-brain to *right-brain communication process through which each person's states of mind are known to the other implicitly.* (p. 7, italics added)

Bromberg stated that this organized dialogue of dynamically fluctuating moment-to-moment state sharing underlies "a good psychoanalytic match."

In my own work, I arrive at a similar conclusion. Within the session, moment-to-moment right brain-to-right brain "state sharing" represents an organized dialogue occurring within milliseconds. In this interactive matrix, both partners match states and simultaneously adjust their social attention, stimulation, and accelerating arousal in response to their partner's signals. From an interpersonal neurobiological perspective, this match reflects mutually synchronized patterns of right brain state matching and state switches within both the patient's and the therapist's right-lateralized emotional brains, as documented by current hyperscanning research.

In applying neurophysiology to psychotherapy, Geller and Porges (2014) proposed,

> [The] bidirectional influence between our brain and visceral organs explains how the therapist's social and emotional responses to the client can potentially, by influencing the physiological state of the client, mediate either an expansion or restriction of the client's range

and valence of socioemotional responding. . . . Bidirectional communication between areas in the right hemisphere promote adaptive interpersonal functioning between therapist and client (Allison & Rossouw, 2013; Schore, 2012; Siegel, 2012). (p. 183)

Furthermore, this communication system is a central mechanism of therapeutic presence, which "involves therapists using their whole self to *be both fully* engaged and receptively attuned in the moment *with and for the client* to promote effective therapy" (p. 178, italics added).

Echoing these ideas in psychiatric writings, Meares referred to "a form of therapeutic conversation that can be conceived . . . as a dynamic interplay between two right hemispheres" (2012, p. 315). In his words,

An interplay between two right brains provides a structure for the therapeutic engagement . . . right hemispheric language . . . is abbreviated, with the utterance often incomplete, and lacking formal syntactical structure. In particular, the subject of a sentence tends to be left out, including pronouns. . . . Furthermore, the language is emotionally expressive. As a consequence, the phonology is salient, the toning and inflections of the voice have a powerful communicative effect that is combined with facial expressions and the movements of the body. This kind of language creates the feeling of *"being with"* in a way that is greater than a logical, completely syntactical left-hemisphere utterance, which sets up a different kind of relatedness. (pp. 312–313, italics added)

More recently, Meares (2017) pointed out,

Although a therapist can foster beneficial change by means of natural talent, this propensity must be trained, honed, and enhanced. It involves a kind of responsiveness that is consistently engaged, in interchange after interchange, in a disciplined way. Change is seen to occur as a result of this continuing relational milieu, rather than as an outcome of intermittent contributions to the therapeutic conversations, such as "interpretations." (p. 145)

Similarly, in the clinical psychology literature, Greenberg (2014) noted, "implicit affect regulation that results from a good therapeutic relationship occurs through right hemispheric processes, is not verbally mediated, is highly relational, and is most directly affected by such things as emotional communication, facial expression, vocal quality, and eye contact (Schore, 2003)" (p. 351). These communications underlie the clinician's state of "therapeutic presence," which involves:

> (a) being in contact with one's integrated and healthy self, while (b) being open and receptive, to what is poignant in the moment and immersed in it, (c) with a larger sense of spaciousness and expansion of awareness and perception. This grounded, immersed, and expanded awareness occurs with the intention of *being with and for the client*, in service of his or her healing process. (p. 353, italics added)

Note a common theme in these descriptions: at the most essential level, the intersubjective work of psychotherapy is not defined by what the therapist does for the patient or says to the patient (left brain focus). Rather, the key mechanism is *how to be with the patient*, especially during affectively stressful moments (right brain focus) (Schore, 2012). The therapist's regulated receptive state allows for participation in the intersubjective communication and interactive regulation of the patient's conscious and unconscious emotional states via an interbrain synchronization between two right hemispheres. In this manner, interpersonal resonance allows for a "specifically fitted interaction" (see Schore, 2012).

In this right brain-to-right brain context, the creative therapist in turn enhances the patient's "integrative self." In the social and personality psychology literature, Kuhl, Quirin, and Koole (2015) offered an article, "Being Someone: The Integrated Self as a Neuropsychological System," in which they distinguish a right hemisphere unconscious "integrative self" from a left hemisphere conscious "conceptual self." The functions of this right-lateralized self include unconscious processing, emotional connectedness, broad vigilance, utilization of felt feedback, extended trust, resilience, and integration of negative experiences. Relevant to the change process of therapeutic action they proposed,

> Human beings developed extended capacities to store their life experiences in long-term memory. This autobiographical memory base allows people to access their prior experiences in relevant situations. The memory base grows each time that people encounter new (unexpected or undesired) experiences that are incorporated into the memory base. It is this extended memory system that forms the basis for the integrated self. (p. 118)

This description applies to the expansion of a right-hemispheric internal working model in a "now moment" (see Schore, 2012).

There is currently agreement on the critical role of "integration" as a goal of psychotherapy. Research now clearly demonstrates that integration is not a function of the left brain conscious mind, but of the right brain unconscious subjective self. Indeed, I have argued that that the integration of past, present, and future occurs in psychoanalytic psychotherapy, a relational regulatory context that facilitates changes in a patient's right brain unconscious systems (Schore, 2012). According to Alvarez, "Schore points out . . . it is not a question of making the unconscious conscious: rather it is a question of restructuring the unconscious itself" (2006, p. 171). This change in the right brain unconscious integrated self in successful psychotherapy is beyond left brain cognitive insight. Relational, affectively focused treatment promotes *changes in the patient's right brain* interpersonal competence, social intelligence, and affiliation motivational systems.

In recent neurobiological research using diffusion tensor imaging scanning, De Pisapia and her colleagues (2014) demonstrated that a number of right brain circuits are functionally activated for "interpersonal competence," the capacity to interact and communicate with others, share personal views, understand the emotions and opinions of others, and cooperate with others or resolve conflict should it occur. In an overview of the literature, Hecht (2014) concluded that the right hemisphere has an advantage over the left hemisphere in mediating social intelligence, identifying social stimuli, understanding the intentions of other people, awareness of the dynamics in social relationships, and successful handling of social interactions.

That said, psychotherapy effects dual motivational systems. Hecht (2014) pointed out that affiliation promotes feelings of togetherness and closeness, while power is expressed in self-sufficiency and distance. He cites extensive neuroscience research that the right hemisphere mediates affiliation motivation, in contrast to the left's power motivation. He states,

> Psychological theories on motivation postulate that human beings have an intrinsic need for affiliation—being connected with and accepted by other people. This fundamental need motivates people to seek warm, stable and intimate interpersonal relationships, form friendships, and affiliate with specific groups. . . . On the other hand humans also have an innate need to maintain their individuality and independence. This need motivates people to acquire power in order to achieve autonomy and freedom that will enable them to master and influence their environments and social relationships, instead of being influenced by them. Ideally, these two coexisting needs—for affiliation and power—would complement and balance each other. Nevertheless, oftentimes they are in conflict and lead to opposite directions. (p. 1)

In line with the fact that the right hemisphere enters into a growth spurt before the left, these neuroscience data support psychoanalytic early right-hemispheric preoedipal deficit and later left-hemispheric oedipal conflict models. As I've recently written, psychotherapy can alter more than the left-lateralized conscious mind. It also can influence the growth and development of the patient's unconscious "right mind" (Schore, 2014a). It is undoubtedly true that both brain hemispheres contribute to effective therapeutic treatment, but in light of the current relational trend that emphasizes "the primacy of affect," the right brain, the "social," "emotional" brain is dominant in all forms of psychotherapy.

Within the perspective of the relational interpersonal neurobiological context of psychotherapy, *changes also occur in the therapist's right brain.*

Discussing the right brain neuroplasticity of clinical expertise, I have suggested that the professional growth of the clinician reflects progressions
in right brain relational processes that underlie clinical skills, including
affective empathy, the ability to tolerate and interactively regulate a broader
array of negative and positive affective self-states, implicit openness to experience, clinical intuition, and creativity (Schore, 2014a). I am now exploring
the right brain origins of creativity, including interpersonal creativity in the
therapeutic context.

Indeed, psychoanalysis has long been interested in the problem of creativity, especially in the earliest stages of the process, which occur beneath
levels of conscious awareness. In 1953, Ernst Kris proposed that "regression
in the service of the ego" acts as a source of creativity, and that all manifestations of creative imagination are expressed in subjective experience.
Three characteristics of this experience are outstanding. First, the individual is aware of the limitation of conscious effort. Second, there is awareness
of a specific feeling, and frequently a very high, emotional charge. Third,
even if excitement rises, the mind tends to work with high precision, and
problems are easily solved. A further common element involves the reaction
of others to the creator. Note the link between creativity and emotion, and
the impact on the creator's mind on the other, via what he termed "creative
communication."

At the same time, another psychoanalytic pioneer in the study of creativity, Theodor Reik (1948), suggested that creative individuals are more
capable of shifting between secondary and primary modes of thinking,
and thereby to "regress" to primary process cognition, which is necessary
for producing novel, original ideas. Reik argued that if the clinician "surrenders" to the regression required to access an uncanny insight, a conscious intuition into the patient's dynamics emerges. If insight originates in
the unconscious, then the only way to reach it is through some degree of
regression to the primary process. He observed, "As rational consciousness
gives way to the primary process, it may feel as if 'the ground' is threatening 'to slip away'" (Reik, 1956, p. 492). Thus it is important that transient
regressions are tolerated, as a rigidly rational consciousness will stifle nonrational hunches. Accordingly, "you have to mistrust sweet reason and to
abandon yourself to the promptings and suggestions emerging from the

unconscious" (Reik, 1956, p. 481). Indeed, he warned that in therapy, creative insight can be displaced by technical machinations.

This proposal is supported by current neuroscience. In groundbreaking studies on split-brain patients, J. E. Bogen and G. M. Bogen (1969) proposed that the right hemisphere is the seat of creativity and that the major obstacle to high creativity is left-hemispheric inhibition of right-hemispheric functions. Huang and colleagues (2013) offered data showing that the left frontal lobe is negatively related to creativity, and that the right hemisphere's predominance in creative thinking may be inhibited by the left part of the brain in normal people. Shamay-Tsoory et al. (2011) observed that the right medial prefrontal cortex mediates creativity, while the left hemisphere language areas may compete or interfere with creative cognition. A release of right prefrontal cortex from this competition facilitates the expression of an original creative response. Note the similarity of this disinhibition to "surrender." In more recent work, Mayseless and Shamay-Tsoory (2015) showed that in enhancing verbal creativity, altering the balance between the right and the left frontal lobes can be used to modulate creative production. Reducing left frontal activity and enhancing right frontal activity reduces cognitive control, thus allowing for more creative idea production. McGilchrist (2009) observed that in order to allow for a left to right hemisphere shift, "We must inhibit one in order to inhabit the other."

Adaptive creative regression thus represents a left to right callosal shift in dominance, a temporary uncoupling of hemispheres, and a disinhibition of Freud's secondary to primary process cognition. "Regression" is defined by the *Oxford English Dictionary* as, "The process of returning or a tendency to return to an earlier stage of development" and "the act of going back; a return to the place of origin." Synchronized "mutual regressions" represent a shift of dominance in both members of the therapeutic dyad from the later maturing left-hemispheric to the earlier developing, foundational right-hemispheric "origin of the self" (Schore, 1994), allowing for new learning and developmental advances in the unconscious system. A modern neuropsychoanalytic perspective suggests two types of adaptive regressions: interhemispheric (topographical, conscious left cortical to unconscious right cortical), and intrahemispheric (structural, downward cortical to subcortical deeper unconscious in lower levels of right brain). These mutually synchronized regressions are prominent in dyadic (re-) enactments, expressions of complex, though largely unconscious self-states and early relational patterns. Adaptive regulated mutual regressions can increase interpersonal creativity, new ways of being with others, in both the patient and therapist.

During treatment, increased access to right brain interpersonal creativity allows for an expanded ability to flexibly cope with the successive social and emotional challenges to the right brain integrated self over different life stages, within changing cultural and social environments. This therapeutic advance represents a fundamental interpersonal neurobiological mechanism that facilitates the growth and development of the right brain subjective self, the psychobiological substrate of the human unconscious, throughout life. Right brain functions, operating beneath awareness, can thus evolve to more complexity over the stages of human development. Neuroscience is now describing progressions in not only "lower" right brain survival functions of the deep unconscious, but also in the high right brain, the source of the most complex human functions, beyond language. A large body of studies now demonstrates that the "emotional," "social" right brain is centrally involved in not only affects and stress regulation but also empathy, intuition, creativity, imagery, symbolic thought, insight, play, humor, music, compassion, morality, and love (Schore, 2012). Indeed, psychoanalysis, like psychology, has overvalued the functions of the surface left-hemispheric conscious mind. These higher functions of the unconscious mind allow for a reformulation and expansion of the essential role of the unconscious in everyday life.

RIGHT BRAIN, LATERALITY RESEARCH, AND CHANGES
BEYOND THE CONSULTING ROOM

Application of regulation theory to ongoing changes in the social environment. Practical applications of right brain psychoanalytic models of early human emotional and social development also generate more complex models of the effects of the *social environment* on the early origins of the unconscious mind. The field has had a long tradition of developmental psychoanalysts such as Sigmund and Anna Freud, Spitz, Klein, Winnicott, Mahler, and Stern. Currently, Beebe, Tronick, Lyons-Ruth, and the Steeles are, like myself, both researchers and clinicians. Along with developmental neuroscience, this research can act as a foundation of evidence-based developmental psychoanalytic science.

Over the past three decades, my ongoing work on modern attachment theory (Schore, 2017a) has described the social and emotional development of the infant's right brain; that is, how early object relational transactions impact the development of psychic structure. Integrating research and clinical models, regulation theory describes the interpersonal neurobiological mechanisms by which the mother's right brain rapidly anticipates, receives, and regulates emotional responses to her infant's emotional communications. The mother's right orbital prefrontal cortex, the locus of attachment control, reads and regulates her infant's amygdala-driven affective states. During a critical period of imprinting of limbic-autonomic circuits in the infant's early developing right hemisphere, the mother-infant attachment relationship is shaped by right brain-to-right brain emotional communications. This model highlights the *enduring impact of interpersonal interbrain synchronization over a right brain critical period.*

Indeed, in 1994 I proposed that during attachment transactions, the child is matching the rhythmic structures of the mother's regulated and dysregulated states, and this synchronization is registered in the firing patterns of the stress-sensitive cortical and limbic regions of the infant's brain, especially in the right brain, which is in a critical period of growth. In this right brain-to-right brain interpersonal synchronization, the infant's early maturing right hemisphere—which is dominant for the child's processing of visual emotional information, the infant's recognition of the mother's face, and the perception of arousal-inducing maternal facial expressions—is psychobiologically attuned to the output of the mother's right hemisphere, which is involved in the expression and processing of emotional information and in nonverbal communication. Recent studies support this model. Nishitani and colleagues documented that "the right prefrontal cortex is involved in human maternal behavior concerning infant facial emotion discrimination" (2011, p. 183). Killeen and Teti reported "greater relative right frontal activation in response to seeing one's own infant is related to maternal negative affect matching during times of infant distress, and greater perceived intensity of infant joy during times of joy" (2012, p. 18).

Furthermore, Meaney and his colleagues offered neuroimaging research of neonates at the *beginning of the first year* and concluded, "In early life the right cerebral hemisphere could be better able to process . . . emotion (Schore, 2000; Wada & Davis, 1977). These neural substrates function as hubs in the right hemisphere for emotion processes and mother and child interaction" (Ratnarajah et al., 2013, p. 193). Research from Tronick's lab on infants in the *middle of the first year* demonstrated that under relational stress, 6-month-old infants use left-sided gestures generated by the right hemisphere. They interpret these data as being "consistent with Schore's (2005) hypotheses of hemispheric right-sided activation of emotions and their regulation during infant–mother interactions" (Montirosso et al., 2012, p. 826). Using near-infrared spectroscopy, Minagawa-Kawai and her colleagues' fMRI study of infant mother attachment at the *end of the first year* observed, "Our results are in agreement with that of Schore (2000) who addressed the importance of the right hemisphere in the attachment system" (2009, p. 289).

Very recent studies are now moving even earlier, into the fetal brain (see Schore, 2014b, 2015, 2017b). In a publication on early right brain regulation and the relational origins of emotional well-being, appearing in the policy journal *Children Australia* (Schore, 2015), I cite an editorial in the *Journal of Child Psychology and Psychiatry* by Leckman and March (2011). Overviewing the field, they asserted, "It has . . . become abundantly clear that . . . the *in utero* and immediate postnatal environments and the dyadic relations between child and caregivers within the first years of life can have direct and enduring effects on the child's brain development and behavior" (2011, p. 334). Directly alluding to the long-term effects of the events at the very beginning of life, they boldly state, "our *in utero* and our early postnatal interpersonal worlds shape and mold the individuals (infants, children, adolescents, adults and caregivers) we are to become" (2011, p. 333). Note the allusion to psychoanalytic developmental models in the phrase "interpersonal worlds."

Further applications of modern attachment theory are offered "The Development of the Right Brain across the Life Span: What's Love Got to Do with It?," a chapter to appear in the companion volume to this, *The Development of the Unconscious Mind*. In that work, I offer evidence that the early bond of mutual love, which generates high levels of strong emotion, intense positive affect between mother and infant, not only shapes the developing emotional right brain but also acts as a relational matrix for the emergence of a capacity to contribute to and share a relationship of mutual love at later stages of life. In another just published chapter, I and my coauthor, Terry Marks-Tarlow, explore "How Love Opens Creativity, Play, and the Arts through the Early Right Brain Development." The early origin of the relational capacity to engage in mutual love and the early origin of creativity are both generated in the early developing right brain (Schore & Marks-Tarlow, 2017). This right brain model is supported in very recent hyperscanning research that simultaneously recorded functional near-infrared spectroscopy (fNIRS) activities during a cooperative, extremely pleasant interactive exchange in lovers. In lover (but not friend or stranger) dyads, both partners demonstrated increased interpersonal brain synchronization in the right superior frontal cortex (Pan et al., 2017). This right-lateralized area has been implicated in the implicit understanding of others' actions and self-awareness, both of which are activated in each lover's right brain. That said, what is needed are hyperscanning studies of the right brain emotional transactions between psychotherapeutic dyads. These studies may bear upon what Bromberg (2011) termed the emergence of "the nearness of you," mutual love in the therapeutic relationship.

Applications to psychopathogenesis. In two recent articles (Schore, 2013a, 2014b), I presented ideas on an early interpersonal neurobiological assessment of attachment and autistic spectrum disorders. Research documents significant alterations of the early developing right brain in autistic infants and toddlers, as well as profound attachment failures and intersubjective deficits in autistic infant-mother dyads. I then apply the model to the assessment of early stages of autism, in the first year. The interpersonal neurobiological functions of the right brain may not only bridge attachment and autism worlds but also facilitate more effective models of early intervention.

Implications for family law, cultural and political systems, and human capital formation. The Australian attachment researcher Jennifer McIntosh and I published "Family Law and the Neuroscience of Attachment, Part l" in *Family Court Review* in 2011 (Schore & McIntosh, 2011). We suggested that current neuroscience can be used to facilitate better legal decisions in family law matters, especially in infancy. Two years later I co-edited a volume, *Evolution, Early Experience and Human Development: From Research to Practice and Policy* (Narvaez, Panksepp, Schore, & Gleason, 2013). In a chapter titled "Bowlby's Environment of Evolutionary Adaptedness: Recent Studies on the Interpersonal Neurobiology of Attachment and Emotional Development," I offered a critique of an aspect of current U.S. culture: early day care. In the United States, most women return to work at 6 weeks, a critical period of early right brain development. Thus I proposed, based on the developmental neurobiological data, that the United States legislate and implement the strategies now operating in other industrialized nations: maternal leave of 6 months and paternal leave of 2 months (Schore, 2013b).

In 2015, I acted as an independent reviewer of *Transforming the Workforce for Children. Birth Through 8: A Unifying Foundation,* published by the Institute of Medicine. In my analysis of this volume on the relevance of advances in developmental sciences for the training of day-care workers and early childhood education, I suggested that it was too cognitively focused, and that relational-emotional development was still being overlooked. That same year I also wrote "Early Right Brain Regulation and the Relational Origins of Emotional Wellbeing" for the policy journal *Children Australia* (Schore, 2015) where I cited Silver and Singer (2014). These authors described the wider economic implications of early brain research for the development of not only the individual, but also the culture:

> Recent advances in neuroscience indicate the importance of healthy brain development in the early years to human capital formation. . . . Investing in child development is the foundation for improved health, economic, and social outcomes. Not getting the early years "right" is linked to violent behavior, depression, higher rates of non-communicable disease, and lower wages, and it negatively affects a nation's gross domestic product. (p. 120)

In Schore (2017b) I cited a study, "What Predicts a Successful Life? A Life-Course Model of Well-Being" by Layard and his colleagues (2014) at the London School of Economics. These authors concluded, "The most important childhood predictor of adult life-satisfaction is the child's emotional health, followed by the child's conduct. The least powerful predictor is the child's intellectual development" (2014, p. F720).

Application of regulation theory to ongoing changes in the physical environment: anthropogenic climate change. In 2017, I published "All Our Sons: The Developmental Neurobiology and Neuroendocrinology of Boys at Risk" in the *Infant Mental Health Journal.* In order to address the problem of why the male gender is at risk for externalizing psychopathologies, I cited a large body of research documenting significant gender differences between male and female social and emotional functions in the earliest stages of development and argued that these result from not only differences in sex hormones and social experiences but also differences in rates of male and female brain maturation, specifically in the early developing right brain. A body of evidence indicates that the emotion-processing limbic system and stress-regulating circuits of the male brain mature more slowly than those of the female in the prenatal, perinatal, and postnatal critical periods. This differential structural maturation is reflected in normal gender differences in right brain attachment functions. Due to this maturational delay, developing males also are more vulnerable over a longer period of time to stressors in the social environment (attachment trauma) and man-made toxins in the physical environment (endocrine disruptors) that negatively impact right brain development (Schore, 2017b).

In terms of the origins of gender-related psychopathology, I described early developmental neuroendocrinological and neurobiological mechanisms that are involved in the increased vulnerability of males to autism, early onset schizophrenia, attention deficit hyperactivity disorder, and conduct disorders as well as the epigenetic mechanisms that can account for the recent widespread increase of these disorders in U.S. culture. Neurobiologically informed psychoanalysis may offer practical models of the deeper origins of human violence.

In that work, I also offered thoughts about the early psychopathogenesis of a variety of male-associated disorders. Anthropogenic climate change is expressed in increased levels of endocrine disruptors in the physical environment, and these ubiquitous neurotoxins are known to alter fetal and postnatal right brain development. Responding to this alarming problem, an international group of researchers declare in the *International Journal of Gynecology and Obstetrics,*

> Exposure to toxic environmental chemicals during pregnancy and breastfeeding is ubiquitous and is a threat to healthy human reproduction. . . . Exposure to toxic environmental chemicals and related health outcomes are inequitably distributed within and between countries; universally, the consequences of exposure are disproportionately borne by people with low incomes. (Di Renzo et al., 2015, p. 219)

Applications to ecology. In 2001, I cited Freud's (1940) initial observations of trauma in early development, and then offered models of the enduring effects of attachment trauma on the right brain and of the origins of the dissociative defense. In 2005, I applied this interpersonal neurobiological model of human infancy to human-induced attachment trauma in wild animals. That year, Gay Bradshaw and I, along with the foremost elephant biologists, published "Elephant Breakdown. Application of Human Attachment Trauma to Animal PTSD" in the journal *Nature* (Bradshaw et al., 2005). In that work, we established for the first time that a human psychiatric disorder exists in another mammal. In a subsequent collaboration in 2007 with Bradshaw in the journal *Ethology* (Bradshaw & Schore, 2007), we continued to argue that anthropogenic stressors are operating in the biosphere, directly negatively impacting the trajectory of evolutionary mechanisms of other species. In this specific case, human culling, especially of matriarchs, interferes with the elephant attachment mechanism and is later expressed in adult males as hyperaggressivity and in adult females as poor mothering functions.

More recently, I have written the foreword for Bradshaw's latest book, *Carnivore Minds: Who These Fearsome Animals Really Are* (2017). Here, Bradshaw called for not only a deeper understanding of the minds of carnivores and wildlife in general, but also a new paradigm that demands a change in how the world is perceived and a change in how we ourselves are viewed. To my mind, this change entails more than coming to a deeper understanding of the consciousness of carnivores. It also requires investigating various states of consciousness of humans, the apex carnivore of the planet and the disrupter of free-ranging populations of carnivores. This kind of expanded self-inquiry must include both the reflected objective awareness of the human conscious mind located in the left brain and the reflective socioemotional awareness of the unconscious mind located in the right brain.

But what if political leadership does not have access to such awareness? Indeed, the existence of this form of anthropogenic climate change in the biosphere (and of anthropogenic environmental toxins) is denied by those at the apex of power. Such personalities devalue and dismiss the unconscious mind in themselves and others and may be driven by hyper-masculine left-hemispheric narcissistic power dynamics and poor right-hemispheric awareness. In a landmark paper, Hecht (2014) offered a large body of neuroscience research documenting that dysregulated power dynamics, mediated by left-hemispheric processes, is expressed in a sense of being socially powerful, dominance, control of others, hostility, Machiavellianism, gloating, and moral judgments based on outcome. In contrast, right-hemispheric affiliation is expressed in empathy, trust, gratitude, fairness, social intelligence, and moral reasoning based on an agent's intentions. McGilchrist (2009) argued that the left hemisphere is continuing to take precedence over the right hemisphere in the current state of world affairs, with potentially disastrous consequences. At this moment in time, the present current leadership reflects this imbalance, reflecting increased left hemisphere power motivation at the expense of or disregard for right-hemispheric communal welfare. The right-hemispheric unconscious mind of a leader at the apex of power deeply influences the culture's collective unconscious and may be an important source of current political, cultural, and psychological insecurity.

Reinvoking the challenging voice of Bob Dylan, the conference title refers to the rapid political changes we're now facing, once again. It also refers to the rapid advances in knowledge we have made in this same period. Over the past three decades, there has been an explosion of knowledge across disciplines as well as an expansion of an integrative perspective within and across fields. All disciplines must move beyond their intrinsic isolation and forge deeper clinical theoretical and research connections into disciplines with which they intersect. Psychoanalysis needs to make an active commitment to this integration and connection. This is especially so in the current political environment that is anti-mental health, anti-science, anti-psychotherapy, and pro-big pharma.

Returning to the beginning of this talk, in my article on the 100th anniversary of Freud's *Project*, I asked is the time right for a "psychology which shall be a natural science?" At the time I speculated,

> The response of psychoanalysis will have to involve a reintegration of its own internal theoretical divisions, a reassessment of its educational priorities, a reevaluation of its current predominant emphasis on cognition, especially verbal mechanisms, as well as a reworking of its Cartesian mind-body dichotomies. This redefinition involves the identity of psychoanalysis itself, in terms of both its self-reference and its relations with the other sciences. In principle, whether or not a rapprochement takes place between two parties depends not only on the information they share in common, but on their individual willingness to enter into a communicative system. (Schore, 1997, p. 833)

Exactly 20 years on, the field has moved toward these goals. But psychoanalysis, "the science of unconscious processes," needs to significantly increase its efforts to continue to incorporate advances in science in order to fuel its growth and relevance. Ernest Jones called the *Project* "something vital in Freud that was soon to become his scientific imagination" (1953, p. 384). We need a return of scientific imagination in 21st-century psychoanalysis.

The unique knowledge psychoanalysis contributes to science and the humanities is its century of studies of the fundamental role of the unconscious in the human experience, the deeper realms of the human psyche. The field must update its self-definition from the frozen image of Freud's 1920s couch in order to increase its standing and status in the eyes of other fields. Psychoanalysis also needs to shift from its too narrow focus on the cognitive unconscious mind to an unconscious right brain/mind/body system.

Annual meetings like this need more inclusion of science from within and outside the field and more commitment to heuristic psychoanalytic research on therapy processes and underlying mechanisms. Division 39 must make deeper connections into fields not only within but beyond psychology. As opposed to a denial of the unconscious at the end of the past century, many disciplines are now studying "implicit" processes beneath levels of awareness. Yet many fields are still centered in a model of a left-hemispheric mind, including clinical and developmental psychology. These connections need to be strengthened into not only science and psychiatry but also different fields of medicine. This could allow for a deeper understanding of the relationships between physical and mental disease and more complex models of psychosomatic disorders. In order to do this, psychoanalytic authors should publish in journals outside of the field.

Changes in education and training. There is a timely need for a critical reevaluation of Freud's theoretical and clinical models, of what to retain, what to leave behind. Courses in developmental and affective neuroscience and interpersonal neurobiology need to be included in academic curricula. An example is the upcoming volume *Core Competencies of Relational Psychoanalysis* (edited by Roy Barsness and published by Routledge). This information should also be integrated into internship training programs. Importantly, Division 39 needs to establish and expand alliances with not only other psychoanalytic organizations but also the much larger population of psychodynamic psychotherapists.

Changes in clinical psychoanalysis. Right brain neuroscience can act as a generator of "evidence-based" clinical models. The field needs to continue its shift in emphasis from solely classical psychoanalysis to face-to-face psychoanalytic psychotherapy. A distinction needs to be made between short-term, symptom reduction/remission and long-term, growth-promoting treatment. More writings are needed on reducing infant, child, adolescent, and adult patients' distressing, affect-dysregulating symptomatology and reestablishing interpersonal functioning in a broad range of disorders, including depression and anxiety disorders, personality disorders, bipolar disorders, schizophrenia, and autistic spectrum disorders. Indeed, neurobiologically informed psychodynamic models need to be incorporated into short-term psychotherapeutic interventions in such disorders.

In fact, there is now a growing body of data on the efficacy of psychodynamic psychotherapy. Compared to cognitive behavior therapy and dialectical behavior therapy, its effects are longer lasting and increase with time. According to Shedler, in contrast to cognitive therapies "psychodynamic therapy sets in motion psychological processes that lead to ongoing change, even after therapy has ended" (2010, p. 101). Shedler concluded that beyond symptom remission, "psychodynamic therapy may foster inner resources and capacities that allow richer, freer, and more fulfilling lives" (2010, p. 107).

Neurobiologically informed psychodynamic treatment uniquely focuses on the patient's dysregulated unconscious emotional functions. As an example, Yang and colleagues (2011) demonstrated that emotional processing operates on a conscious level and in an unconscious (implicit and automatic) mode, with both being associated with different neurobiological pathways. They noted,

> A large body of literature has focused on the conscious aspect of emotion processing as for instance in studies on emotional-cognitive regulation and its abnormalities. In contrast, the unconscious aspect has been considered as the perception and the earlier processing of the emotion that precedes their cognitive regulation. (p. 1)

These researchers show disturbed negative emotional unconscious processing in depressed patients. This is expressed in a deficit of automatically and unconsciously orienting attention to negative social information, specifically sad faces. They concluded,

> Our result may also be clinically relevant in that unconscious negative emotional processing may provide a novel and more viable target for future psychotherapeutic . . . intervention than conscious

emotion regulation strategies. More specifically, it means that we have to target unconscious processing rather than conscious processing as targeted in Cognitive Behavioral Therapy. (p. 6)

In all disorders, psychoanalysis brings an expertise in unconscious, implicit right brain relational communicating and affect-regulating systems within the therapeutic alliance and focuses on the bodily-based internal world of the patient.

Further changes in clinical psychoanalysis. I urge a call for a commitment to early intervention, in order for the field to make a larger impact not only on the individual, but also on cultural, emotional, and physical health, and thereby a broader improvement of the human condition. Though first forged in maternal-fetal and attachment interactions, right brain evolutionary mechanisms continue to evolve over the life span. This trajectory of right brain development can be altered by attachment trauma. Neurobiologically informed psychodynamic models of early intervention during critical periods of the human brain growth spurt (what pediatricians call "the first thousand days") can alter the intergenerational transmission and prevention of psychopathologies.

Changes in theoretical psychoanalysis. Variations in the organization of right brain circuits implicitly processing emotion and stress are relevant to individual, personality, gender, ethnic group, and socioeconomic differences. Yet the invariant properties of right-lateralized limbic-autonomic circuits represent the common expressions of humanness, of fundamentally what it means to be human. As discussed, advances in knowledge of the right brain may act as an integrative and energizing force that can catalyze movement of the field out of the consulting room into the larger social and political culture. As this talk demonstrates, this change involves replacing metapsychological abstractions with right brain neurobiological data. Neuropsychoanalysis needs to be integrated into the central constructs of its theory of the unconscious, *the foundation of psychoanalysis.*

In light of the uncertainties of the current social and political context, there is a sense of urgency to this change—Dylan's lyric "you better start swimmin' or you'll sink like a stone." The lyrics from another Dylan song,

"Forever Young," apply during the present moment of rapid cultural and political change:

> *May your hands always be busy*
> *May your feet always be swift*
> *May you have a strong foundation*
> *When the winds of changes shift*

1. Forever Young
Copyright © 1973 by Ram's Horn Music; renewed 2001 by Ram's Horn Music. All rights reserved. International copyright secured. Reprinted by permission.
"May your hands always be busy May your feet always be swift May you have a strong foundation When the winds of changes shift"

2. The Times They Are a-Changin'
Copyright © 1963, 1964 by Warner Bros. Inc.; renewed 1991, 1992 by Special Rider Music. All rights reserved. International copyright secured. Reprinted by permission.
" . . . you better start swimmin' or you'll sink like a stone"

CHAPTER 7

On the Same Wavelength: How Our Emotional Brain Is Shaped by Human Relationships

Interview with Daniela F. Sieff

INTRODUCTION

Our earliest relationships structure our emotional brain in ways that have long-lasting consequences for our emotional well-being. If we are nurtured by our caregivers, our emotional brain develops in such a way as to allow us to become comfortable with our own emotions and to respond to our social environment healthily. We can make the most of times of joy, and we implicitly trust that we can cope with tough times. Knowing this is at the root of feeling secure. However, if we grow up in an environment that does not nurture our emotional selves, then the development of the emotional brain is compromised. As a consequence, we cannot learn how to regulate our emotions healthily and are easily overwhelmed by them. Because it is impossible to tolerate being emotionally overloaded for long periods of time, our only way to cope is to dissociate; that is, to cut ourselves off from our emotions and prevent them from reaching consciousness. If we have to revert to dissociation often enough, what began as a defense becomes ingrained in our neurological circuits and part of our character. We are trapped in a rigid way of being. We cannot open to the emotions that will make us feel alive. We cannot cope with emotional stress. We cannot grow emotionally. We cannot attain emotional security.

To find our way to an emotionally healthy and secure life once we've suffered early relational trauma is not a question of making the unconscious conscious; rather, it depends on restructuring the unconscious itself. That depends on changing the physical substrate of the emotional brain. The most effective way to achieve such change is through relationally based, emotionally focused psychotherapy with an empathic and attuned therapist who is willing and able to be an active participant in the process.

Daniela Sieff: You emphasize the importance of feeling emotionally secure—why?

Allan Schore: Societies spend a huge amount on defense and on medical research in the hope that we will feel secure in our daily lives, but a feeling of security is a psychological state. All too often our emotional wounds, and the subsequent defenses that we developed, prevent us from feeling secure. An internal sense of safety cannot be imposed upon a passive individual. To feel secure we need to know, at both a bodily and a psychological level, that we have the internal resources to cope with the stressors that accompany human existence. To that end, my work has focused on three questions:

> How do some children develop emotional security?
>
> What prevents other children from developing emotional security, and what are the consequences of that?
>
> What is required of therapy if it is to help those who failed to develop emotional security as children to develop it later in life?

I don't just look at these questions psychologically. A fundamental principle of my work is that no theory of emotional development can be restricted to only a description of psychological processes; it must also be consonant with what we now know about the biological structure of the brain. Moreover, by integrating what we know about the brain into our understanding, we gain hugely important insights into the dynamics of emotional trauma and what therapists need to do to work with it.

Daniela: Can you expand on what we need to be able to do if we are to feel emotionally secure?

Allan: We need to trust that we can appraise what is happening in our social environment and that we can respond adaptively.

Emotions are the medium through which information about interpersonal relationships is transmitted, received, and appraised. At the crudest level, feeling good tells us we are in a propitious situation; feeling bad warns us of possible trouble and prepares us to deal with it. But human relationships are complex, nuanced, and layered, so we need to develop several bodily-based skills if our appraisals of our social world are to be valid:

> *We need to become sensitive to subtly differentiated emotions.*
> When we are born, our emotions are relatively crude—we are happy or we are upset. As we develop, our emotions become increasingly differentiated, shaded, and refined, *yet also integrated.* We learn to create blends of different emotions simultaneously. Things are no longer wholly good or wholly bad. We can feel angry with and compassion for somebody simultaneously. This greater differentiation of our emotional repertoire enables us to respond to interpersonal situations more appropriately.
>
> *We need to learn to tolerate intense emotions.* Every person has what can be envisioned as a window of tolerance with regard to each of our emotions. Within this window we can respond healthily to what we are feeling; beyond it we lose that ability. We begin life with a very a small window of tolerance for intense emotions, but during healthy development the window expands and we become increasingly tolerant of intense positive and negative emotions.
>
> *We need to acquire the ability to differentiate what is happening outside us from what is happening inside.* As children we can't do this, but we need to learn what is mine and what is coming from another person.

Collecting and appraising relational information happens unconsciously. When we implicitly know that we can tolerate intense emotions, accurately perceive what is happening in the external and internal worlds, and respond in a nuanced and appropriate way, we feel fundamentally safe. But when we are cut off from some of our emotions, when we cannot tolerate intense emotions, or when past events color current emotional responses, then our unconscious appraisals will be distorted and our ability to respond adaptively compromised.

Daniela: What shapes the unconscious processing and regulation of emotion?

Allan: We don't come into the world with these unconscious processes in place; rather, they develop through attuned and nurturing early relationships. Our emotions, which include both the subjective experience of our feelings and what is happening in our body, are initially regulated by our caregivers. If our caregivers do a reasonable job, then as our brain develops, we internalize that experience and begin to do it for ourselves. Moreover, upon finding ourselves distressed, we can either turn to somebody else to help us recover from stress or we can rely on ourselves depending on the particulars of the situation.

In contrast, if our earliest years are emotionally impoverished, then our emotional development is compromised and we are left at the mercy of a simplified, unadaptive, rigid, and restricted set of emotional responses. We may overreact to stress, and our response may endure long after the danger has passed. Or we may struggle to regulate any of the intense emotions including shame, rage, disgust, panic, terror, hopelessness, despair, excitement, and elation. Moreover, because our early years weren't nurturing, we don't trust others enough to turn to them for help in achieving that modulation. Then our only option may be to dissociate from those emotions or to use drugs or to self-harm in an attempt to regulate them. When we intuitively sense that we cannot regulate our emotions healthily, that a feeling of emotional security is beyond our reach.

Daniela: What features of the brain are most relevant to understanding emotional regulation?

Allan: It's crucial that we understand the differences between the right hemisphere of the brain and the left. There has been a paradigm shift—instead of thinking of right and left halves of one brain, we now understand that we effectively have two brains, each of which processes information in different ways, and each of which matures in a different rhythm.

Broadly speaking, the left brain is the thinking brain. It is highly verbal and analytical. It operates a conscious emotional regulation system that can modulate low to medium arousal. It is the domain of cognitive strategies. It processes "highly verbal" emotions such as guilt and worrisome anxiety. It constructs linear explanations. It provides us with a close-up and narrow view of details. The left brain does not begin its first period of concentrated development and growth until the second year of life, and so it plays little part in the early relationships that shape our capacity to regulate our emotions and to feel emotionally secure.

In contrast, the right hemisphere is the emotional brain. It processes all of our intense emotions, regardless of whether they are negative such as rage, fear, terror, disgust, shame, and hopeless despair or positive such as excitement, joy, and love. When our level of emotional arousal becomes intense, the left hemisphere goes offline and the right hemisphere dominates. Our window of tolerance for intense emotions depends on the functioning of the right brain.

Our right brain enables us to read the subjective states of others through its appraisal of subtle facial (visual and auditory) expressions and other forms of nonverbal communication. The right brain makes these appraisals so quickly that our body and mental state is altered before we become conscious of what we are feeling.

Because of its ability to read the subjective states of others, the right brain is the seat of emotional empathy—it depends on us feeling what another person is feeling in an embodied way. In contrast, the left brain is the seat of cognitive empathy—it depends on us "working out" what the other is feeling in a less embodied, detached, and colder way.

The autonomic nervous system is the part of the nervous system that functions largely below the level of consciousness to control visceral functions such as heart rate, respiratory rate, digestion, pupil dilation, and so on. It has two branches: the sympathetic branch, which mediates energized arousal and approach, and the parasympathetic branch, which mediates withdrawal, rest, relaxation, and repair. The right brain mediates the balance between these two branches of the autonomic nervous system, and through that determines the somatic aspects of emotion as well as the subjective ones. Connections between the right brain and the hormonal system are another channel through which the somatic aspects of emotion are mediated.

The right brain mediates our emotional and bodily-based response to danger, environmental challenges, pain, and stress. It mediates fight, flight, and freeze through its connections with the autonomic nervous system and hormonal system. Emotionality is the right brain's "red phone," compelling the mind to handle urgent matters without delay.

The right hemisphere has some limited capacity for language. Highly emotive words such as swear words or our own names are processed by the right hemisphere, as are metaphors.

The right hemisphere is more holistic than the left, holding many different possibilities simultaneously. It captures the gist of the situation and the big picture. Dreams, music, poetry, art, metaphor, and other creative processes originate in the right hemisphere. Importantly, and with direct relevance to psychotherapy, the right hemisphere specializes in processing new information.

The first critical period of development for the right brain begins during the third trimester of pregnancy, and this growth spurt continues into the second year of life. It is primarily the right brain that is shaped by our early relational environment and which is crucial to the development of emotional security.

Daniela: Can you talk about the trajectory of early right brain development, in terms of the development of emotional regulation?

Allan: Brains are modular; different areas specialize in different functions, but not all are operative at birth because the axons of many cortical neurons are not yet myelinated and therefore cannot efficiently transmit the electrical signals that constitute brain activity. Also, many of the interconnections that link different brain areas are not yet formed. The three key "regulatory hubs" of the emotional brain (also known as limbic brain), are (1) the right amygdala, (2) the right anterior cingulate (also known as medial frontal cortex), and (3) the right orbital prefrontal (shortened to orbitofrontal) cortex. These regions come online sequentially.

The amygdala begins a critical period of growth during the last trimester of pregnancy, so it is essentially functional at birth. The right amygdala is the brain's alarm center, mediating the fight and flight responses. It is also the first port of call for processing both the nonverbal facial expressions of others and our own internal bodily states. The amygdala is relatively primitive; information from the external environment is imprinted with a positive or negative charge depending on whether the situation is deemed to be nurturing or threatening. This occurs very rapidly and below the level of consciousness. The resulting actions appear as autonomic, innate reflexes. Such speedy responses are crucial for survival, but they are crude.

Around 2 months after birth, the right anterior cingulate begins to come online. It allows for more complex processing of socioemotional information than the amygdala does. It is responsible for developing attachment behavior.

Starting from about 10 months after birth, the highest level of the emotional brain, the right orbitofrontal cortex, becomes active. It continues developing for the next 20 years and remains exceptionally plastic throughout our entire life span. The right orbitofrontal cortex gives rise to conscious emotions and is capable of much finer-grained (albeit slower) information processing than is the earlier developing parts of the emotional brain. It is also the area of the brain that enables us to maintain a sense of continuity and to create an integrated and stable sense of who we are, which in turn forms the platform for self-reflection.

During the second year of life, the right orbitofrontal cortex establishes strong, bidirectional connections with the rest of the limbic system. Once these connections are established, it then monitors, refines, and regulates amygdala-driven responses. We can begin to correct overreaction or underreaction, allowing our emotional responses to be more appropriate to the circumstances. It is the healthy development of the right orbitofrontal cortex and its links to the amygdala that enables us to have a wide window of tolerance for intense emotions and to implicitly respond flexibly and adaptively to our interpersonal world.

Daniela: How does the relationship between an infant and its caregiver shape the development of the emotional right brain?

Allan: Genes code for when the various components of the emotional brain come online, but how each area develops depends on the infant's epigenetically shaped emotional experiences with his primary caregiver. Those experiences, as John Bowlby first described, are circumscribed by the infant's innate drive to become attached (emotionally bonded) to his or her primary caregiver.

The attachment drive evolved partly because infants needed to remain close to their mothers for protection from predators and partly because infants cannot regulate either their bodily functions or their emotional states and need a caregiver to do this for them. The role of regulation is so important that I now see attachment theory primarily as a theory of emotional and bodily regulation. Typically, an attuned caregiver will minimize her infant's discomfort, fear, and pain, and, as importantly, create opportunities for the child to feel joy and excitement. She will also mediate the transitions between these emotional states.

The infant's experiences with his caregiver are then internalized through changes in his brain. Experience activates specific neural circuits, and the more frequently a circuit fires, the more established it becomes, whereupon it is more easily activated in the future. Over time, the infant's emotional core becomes biased toward certain emotional responses, thus creating a particular type of personality organization. In short, brains develop as self-organizing systems, but their self-organization occurs not in isolation, but in the context of another self, another brain.

Daniela: Can you give us a feel for the types of interactions that typically occur between an attuned mother and her infant?

Allan: An infant who is between 3 and 6 months old mainly uses sight to gauge his mother's emotional responses. He'll track his mother's face, and if she is attuned enough to meet his emotional state with an appropriate response, then when eye contact is established both mother and infant implicitly know that the feedback loop between them is closed. The mother's face reflects her infant's reality and aliveness back to him, and he learns to be with whatever it is that he is feeling.

Sometimes, mirroring by an attuned mother amplifies her infant's emotional state. In physics, when two systems match, it creates what is called "resonance," whereby the amplitude of each system is increased. Face-to-face play between an infant and an attuned mother creates emotional resonance and amplifies joy. Together, infant and mother move from low arousal to high positive arousal, which helps the infant to expand his window of tolerance for intense positive emotions, a key developmental task.

Other times, the emotional intensity becomes more than the infant can tolerate, then he will avert his gaze. When this happens, an attuned mother backs off and reduces her stimulation. She then waits for her baby to signal his readiness to reengage. The more the mother tunes her activity level to the infant during periods of engagement, the more she allows him to recover quietly in periods of disengagement; and the more she responds to his signals for reengagement, the more synchronized their interactions. At times, emotional mirroring between mother and infant can be synchronized within milliseconds. *"On the same wavelength"* becomes more than a metaphor, as the subjective internal state of both mother and infant converge, and his emotional reality is both validated and held safely through his mother's ability to be with his feelings.

During this process, a mother inevitably makes mistakes, then the interaction becomes asynchronous. However, when asynchrony arises, a good-enough mother is quick to shift her state so that she can then help to re-regulate her infant, who is likely to be stressed and upset by their mismatch. Rupture and repair allows the child to tolerate negative affect.

Eventually, the face of an attuned mother will be written into her infant's right orbitofrontal cortex. This then acts as an emotionally containing and comforting neurobiological guidance system when she is not physically present.

Daniela: Could you talk about the internal models that are created as a result of interactions between a mother and her infant?

Allan: In response to their caregivers, infants create unconscious working models of what to expect, and these models are then generalized and applied not only to "mother" but also to other people. For example, if the caregiver is mostly attuned, then the infant creates an expectation of being matched by, and being able to match, another human. The child is likely to develop what is known as "secure attachment."

Similarly, moments of misattunement, if repaired in a sensitive and timely manner, lead to the infant believing that others will help calm him when he is upset. Additionally, experiencing his mother's nurturing response to his distress, the infant begins to develop a sense that others will attend to him and that his own activity can influence the effect that his environment has on him. This is the first step toward developing a sense of agency. The timely repair of misattunement also teaches an infant that instances of discord and negative emotions are tolerable. From such learning, an infant develops emotional resilience, defined as the capacity to transition from positive emotions to negative emotions and back to positive emotions. Emotional resilience is key to creating an inner feeling of security and trust.

However, if caregivers are not attuned, an infant will create an internal model that says that other people aren't trustworthy, that he can't really connect to them, and that he is unworthy of being loved. This way of seeing the world is typical of "insecure attachment," and these unconscious emotional biases will guide lifelong behavior, especially when under relational stress.

What is more, the infant of a misattuned mother will frequently be presented with an aggressive expression on his mother's face, implying he is a threat, or with an expression of fear-terror, implying that he is a source of alarm. Images of his mother's aggressive or fearful face, and the resultant chaotic alterations in his bodily state, are internalized. They are imprinted on his developing right brain limbic circuits as an implicit memory, and although they lie below consciousness, they will haunt him for his entire life unless he finds a way to work with them.

Early interactions also create the internal models that affect how the developing infant (and later on the adult) approaches novelty. Between 10 and 12 months, infants start to walk. The toddler can now separate from his caregiver, begin to explore his physical environment, and so learn new things. This ability is fundamental to development, but it can be dangerous, so an exploring toddler needs direction and support from his caregiver. He gets that from referring to his mother's facial expressions, which either encourage or discourage his exploration. However, the infant doesn't only learn how he should feel about the specific objects in his social and physical environment that he is encountering through his mother's reactions; he also learns how to feel about novelty *per se*. The internal working models formed as a result of this learning will shape the way that he approaches the world for the duration of his life, either facilitating a capacity to grow from new socioemotional experiences or inhibiting it.

Daniela: What is happening neurobiologically during attuned, early mother-infant interactions?

Allan: The caregiver's more mature nervous system is regulating the infant's neurochemistry. This, in turn, has a profound influence on the structural organization of the developing brain. For example, the hormone oxytocin is an antidote to stress and promotes bonding and trust. Its release is triggered by sensory stimuli such as a warm tone of voice and touch, and friendly facial expressions. If this system is primed by early attachment experiences, the infant grows into a person capable of trust and of establishing social bonds.

Similarly, the face of an attuned mother triggers the production of high levels of neuropeptides such as endorphins in the infant's growing brain, whereupon the infant's developing neural system learns to associate social interactions with feeling good. Also, when an infant's brain experiences relatively high levels of neuromodulators such as dopamine, serotonin, and noradrenaline, it responds by building more receptors for these bioamines. Conversely, low levels of neuropeptides and neuromodulators result in fewer receptors being created. This difference in the number of receptors is retained in adulthood, and a deficit can increase the risk of psychiatric disorders, such as depression or PTSD.

Critical to postnatal brain development is the formation of connections between nerve cells. A single neuron will have between 10,000 and 100,000 branches, each of which connects to another neuron through a structure called a synapse. In the first year of life, it is estimated that 40,000 new synapses are created every second. This takes an enormous amount of energy. The brain accounts for only 2% of our body mass, but it uses 20% of the calories that an adult consumes and 50% of the calories that a young child consumes. However, a brain doesn't only need calories to build synapses; it also needs to be in an excited and activated state. Think of a car—it is not enough that there is fuel in the tank, the engine needs to be fired-up and running before it will move. It is the positive arousal created by the resonant interactions between an attuned mother and an infant that fires up the infant's brain and creates the conditions necessary for building neural connections.

At the same time, the mother-infant relationship is responsible for the selective death of neurons and for pruning synaptic connections. This is a natural part of development: There is a genetically programmed overproduction of neurons and synapses early in development, and those that are activated by the environment become established, whereas those that are not used atrophy and die. Maternal behavior is the environment in which some neurons and synapses are selected as relevant to the infant's life, whereas others are discarded as surplus to needs. This shapes the trajectory of the infant's emerging self. For example, if a mother doesn't mirror her infant in a way to generate positive arousal, the positive arousal circuits are at risk of atrophy, making it harder in later life for that person to feel joy and excitement. On the other hand, if a mother is attuned and does create positive arousal in her infant, the neurons that are pre-programmed to respond to positive arousal will be fortified.

Daniela: How robust is the developmental process that leads to a healthy self-regulating emotional system?

Allan: The development of a healthy emotional system depends on growing up in a "good-enough" emotional environment. Once the critical growth period for a particular brain area has passed, the structure of that area is more-or-less set, and subsequent development is built on top of that platform. Thus, early adverse environmental factors such as nutritional deficits or dysregulating attachment relationships can have a profound growth-inhibiting effect upon the right brain and prohibit the development of a healthy self-regulating emotional system. The effects can last a lifetime.

Daniela: What happens to the developing brain in an adverse environment?

Allan: There are two ways that the developing brain can be compromised by an inadequate early environment.

Unused brain cells die naturally during the process of development, but early trauma can lead to excessive cell death.

The building of new synapses is reduced, and existing synapses that could be useful are destroyed. The ability to create functional and integrated brain circuits is compromised.

Daniela: Does the timing of relational trauma affect what impact it has?

Allan: Yes! Emotional trauma will negatively impact the parts of the brain that are developing at the time of the trauma. For example, if high levels of stress hormones are circulating in a pregnant mother, it upregulates the fetus's developing stress response—the hypothalamic-pituitary-adrenal (HPA) axis—making the child, and then the adult, hypersensitive to stress. In contrast, relational trauma that occurs around the time of birth has a negative impact on both the developing micro-architecture of the amygdala itself and on how the amygdala connects to the HPA axis, and other parts of the limbic system. Such damage has a profoundly harmful effect on the ability to form social bonds and on temperament. Suffering unrepaired and frequent emotional stress after about 10 months interferes with experience-dependent maturation of the highest-level regulatory systems in the right orbitofrontal cortex. This opens the door to an impaired emotional regulation system, a limited facility for empathy, and problems in distinguishing present realty from irrelevant memories. In the long term, there is an increased risk of developing psychopathologies.

Cell death and overpruning is equally damaging when it interferes with the connectivity between different brain regions. Relational trauma that occurs in the second year is likely to jeopardize not only the development of the right orbitofrontal cortex itself but also its connection to the right amygdala, whereupon it becomes much harder to modify the amygdala's crude responses in accordance with reality. Overreaction becomes the norm, leading to severe problems with intimacy and affection, as well as problems with the control of fear and aggression.

Daniela: What kind of parenting causes damage?

Allan: There are obvious forms of abuse such as physical and sexual abuse, but emotional abuse can be equally damaging. Emotional abuse can result from inconsistent, erratic, and contradictory interactions, from overpowering and overarousing interactions, or from neglect. In any of these circumstances, the infant will suffer long bouts of unregulated stressful negative affects and, too frequently, no interactive repair.

Neglect, which is proving to be the most severe threat to the development of the emotional brain, and "benign" neglect generally, leads to what is called "avoidant attachment." The mother may be averse to physical contact and block her child's attempts to get close to her. She may be ambivalent about being a mother. She may be depressed. The neglect need not be overt—profound psychological harm can occur with a mother who is emotionally unavailable when her infant is distressed, even if she remains in physical contact with her child. Such an infant will learn to recoil from contact in an attempt to avoid the painful emotions roused in him by his rejecting mother. Over time, withdrawal becomes entrenched. For the rest of his life, when under stress he will tend to convey an unconscious, nonverbal message that says, *"Stay away . . . I don't need you . . . don't connect."*

Neurobiologically, the lack of positive mirroring that characterizes neglect means that not enough energy is generated for an infant's brain to grow all its interconnections. Moreover, because there is limited positive arousal, the growth of these brain areas is especially compromised. Such infants develop a bias toward a withdrawn state mediated by the parasympathetic branch of the autonomic nervous system. This is physiologically characterized by a low heart rate and low heart-rate variability.* Temperamentally, these infants tend to grow up feeling helpless, and they have an increased risk of suffering from depression. They often have minimal emotional expression and a limited capacity to experience and to regulate intense emotional states, be they positive or negative. They are susceptible to overcontrolled, overregulated, internalizing pathologies.

Not only is a neglected child denied the interpersonal matrix upon which brain development depends, but also without access to interactive repair, intense affect dysregulation endures as long-lasting stress states. These are psychobiologically toxic. Early maternal neglect significantly increases the process of programmed cell death in the cortex compared to that in healthy development.

Unpredictable and intrusive mothering often leads to what is called ambivalent-anxious attachment. Infants can only cope with a certain intensity of emotional arousal before they move beyond their window of tolerance into a state of stressful emotional dysregulation. To avoid this, an infant will signal his need to temporarily disengage by looking away. However, if the caregiver suffered early relational trauma herself, she may feel abandoned by her infant's move to disengage, and in order to annul her own anxiety, she may redouble her efforts to get her infant to reengage with her. This exacerbates the infant's hyperarousal: Excitatory neurotransmitters and stress hormones flood the brain. Such children appear to have a difficult temperament. Their autonomic nervous system tends to be biased toward the sympathetic nervous system. They express emotions in an excessive way and suffer intense negative moods. They are overly

---

* When our nervous system has developed in a healthy way, our heart rate varies on a moment-by-moment basis. In contrast, if the development of our nervous system has been compromised, then heart variability is low, and low variability is a marker of high risk for both cancer and cardiac disease later in life.

dependent on their attachment figure (presumably to make her feel more secure), but also angry with her and rejecting of her.

The most severe forms of both abuse and neglect create what is called "disorganized attachment." It occurs when an infant has no strategy that will help him to cope with his caregiver, and so he ends up profoundly confused. An infant typically seeks his parents when alarmed, so when a parent actually causes alarm, the infant is in an impossible situation. There is simultaneous and uncoupled hyper-activation of the sympathetic and the parasympathetic circuits. This is subjectively experienced as a sudden transition into emotional chaos. If chronic, it represents a highly neurotoxic state that leads to death of neurons and the destruction of synaptic connections within both circuits.

Daniela: What might cause a mother to behave in such a harmful way?

Allan: Typically, women who can't mother their children in an attuned way are suffering from the consequences of unresolved early emotional trauma themselves. The experience of a female infant with her mother influences how she will mother her own infants. Thus, if early childhood trauma remains unresolved and uncon-scious, it will inevitably be passed down the generations. To put it bluntly, a mother's untreated early relational trauma is burned into the developing right hemisphere of her infant's brain, leaving behind neurological scars.

Daniela: What role does the father play in a child's emotional development?

Allan: Subsequent to a child's relationship to the mother during its first year, the child forms a second attachment relationship to the father in the second year. The quality of a toddler's attachment to his father is independent to that of his mother. At 18 months, there are two separate attachment dynamics in operation. Those who experience being protected, cared for, and loved by their father will internalize that relationship as a lifelong sense of safety. It also seems that the father is critically involved in the development of a toddler's regulation of aggression. This is true of both sexes, but particularly of boys, who are born with a greater aggressive endowment than that of girls.

Daniela: You highlight the damaging effects of long bouts of unregulated shame—what is shame, and why is it so damaging?

Allan: Shame is the emotion elicited during a rapid transition from an excited positive state to a deflated negative one, typically when an interpersonal bond is broken through misattunement. When shame hits, usually unexpectedly, we feel that a spotlight is focused on us, revealing all that is wrong with who we are. We want to bury our head and disappear from view. We feel as if we could die. Shame is always associated with the subjective experience of inner collapse.

Shame becomes part of the emotional palette around the beginning of the second year. When an infant is 10 months old, 90% of maternal behavior consists of affection, play, and caregiving, but between the ages of 13 and 17 months this changes—a mother will express a prohibition once every 9 minutes! That is because she needs to let her toddler know when his exploration is unsafe. Also, around this time a mother starts to become an agent of socialization and must persuade the toddler to inhibit socially unacceptable behaviors. Shame, which has been described as the primary social emotion, is the means through which this is achieved.

Shame is not caused by the child's movement away from the mother or even by the mother's movement away from the child, but by the active blockage of the child's return to and emotional reconnection with the mother. By this age, the securely attached toddler of an attuned mother will have an internalized expectation of being matched by her, so when he returns to his mother full of joy and she fails to match his emotional state, he will experience shock-induced deflation. In such a moment, it is as though his mother becomes a stranger. The toddler's emotionally fragile, nascent self rapidly implodes and collapses. Shame is experienced as spiraling downward—a leakage in the middle of one's being.

Shame induces an intense emotional state that lies beyond the infant's window of tolerance, so the mother needs to instigate inter- active repair. How speedily she does this is crucially important. A brief descent into shame is a necessary part of development, teach- ing the infant to avoid what is socially unacceptable or physically dangerous. However, long periods of unrepaired shame are phys- iologically toxic to the developing brain. They also have negative long-term consequences for the personality, resulting in chronic difficulties with self-esteem.

Daniela: What is the difference between shame and guilt?

Allan: The two emotions, though often confused, are separate and have distinct neurobiological pathways. Shame appears between the ages of 12 and 18 months. At 12 months, the average toddler has three words and at 18 months about twenty words. Shame is therefore intrinsically nonverbal and a product of the early develop- ing right hemisphere. It is experienced implicitly as, what Kaufman described as, *"a total experience that forbids communication with words."* In contrast, guilt develops between 3 and 6 years—a 3-year- old child has an average vocabulary of 900 words and uses three- to five-word sentences. Guilt, the overuse of power, is a product of the later developing verbal, left hemisphere.

The verbal nature of guilt makes it easier to recognize and articulate than preverbal shame, so psychotherapy tends to focus on guilt rather than shame. However, excessive unregulated shame creates far greater emotional damage than guilt does, and we do need to learn to recognize it, bring it to consciousness, regulate it, and heal it.

Daniela: How do infants respond to being left with dysregulated emotions?

Allan: Infants respond through two separate and sequential processes: (1) hyperarousal and (2) hypoarousal.

Hyperarousal occurs when a perceived threat—either imagined or real—is detected by the amygdala, which then activates both the HPA axis and the sympathetic branch of the autonomic nervous system. The activation of the HPA axis culminates in the release of cortisol. The activation of the sympathetic nervous system releases adrenaline. Both cortisol and adrenaline play key roles in mobilizing bodily resources into the service of immediate survival by preparing us for fight or flight. Energy that was being used for nonemergency processes such as digestion or fighting disease is redirected toward survival. The level of glucose in our blood is raised to increase fuel availability. Oxygen intake is increased as the surface of our lungs expands and our breathing quickens. Our heart beats faster and more powerfully in order to speed up the circulation of blood, which is carrying oxygen and glucose to our muscles. Pupils dilate, sweating increases, mental activity speeds up. In children, hyperarousal is accompanied by crying and then screaming—calls for help.

Hyperarousal can save our life, but it is chronic, it becomes a toxic state. So when a caregiver can't help the infant return to a calmer state, or worse when the caregiver escalates the infant's distress, the infant has no choice but to get away from this state of hyperarousal by the only means possible; that is, inwards, through collapse, hypoarousal. Energy leaves the system, and the individual shuts off input from the external world and from his own dysregulated and hyperaroused emotions. This is dissociation. In a connected emotional system, messages about the body's state move up from the body, through the lower levels of the limbic brain and into the right orbitofrontal cortex, where they are experienced as a conscious emotion. With dissociation, this chain is broken. In a state of hypoaroused dissociation, all pain is stilled; a soothing (but deadening) numbness ensues. The numbness is due to the massive elevation of endogenous opioids, which instantly trigger pain-reducing analgesia and immobility, and which inhibit cries for help.

Dissociation, which appears in the first 2 months of life, is a last-resort survival strategy. It represents detachment from an unbearable situation. It is the escape when there is no escape. The infant withdraws into an inner world, avoids eye contact, and stares into space. Dissociation caused by a hypoaroused state brings a constricted state of consciousness, a void of subjectivity.

This state of passive rather than active withdrawal is rooted in our animal heritage. Predators are attracted by movement, so if the potential prey can't outrun the predator, it tries to reduce its chance of being detected by lying absolutely still. Additionally, predators don't like eating animals that they haven't killed themselves, because the animal could have been dead for some time, and its rotting flesh may be carrying disease. The immobility of dissociation mimics death.

Daniela: The Jungian analyst, Marion Woodman, described the collapsed state of dissociation as "possum psychology," what is happening neurobiologically?

Allan: Dissociation is achieved when the parasympathetic branch of the autonomic nervous system comes in over the top of the sympathetic system. This is akin to driving a car with one foot flat on the gas (sympathetic) and the other flat on the brakes (parasympathetic). In the developing brain the simultaneous yet uncoupled activation of the sympathetic and parasympathetic nervous systems is highly toxic and exaggerates the normal processes of cell death and synaptic pruning. That, in turn, means that the capacity for healthy emotional regulation recedes ever-further into the distance.

Within the parasympathetic nervous system, dissociation is mediated by the dorsal, or reptilian, branch of the vagus nerve. The work of Stephen Porges tells us that the vagus nerve has two branches, each originating in a different area of the brain stem. The branch that originates in the dorsal part of the brain stem evolved with the reptiles, and in humans it comes online early during development, even prenatally. In contrast, the branch that originates in the ventral brain stem evolved with mammals, and it comes online later during postnatal development. Activation of the ventral (or "mammalian") vagus facilitates communication via facial expressions, vocalizations, and gestures. It alters heart rate in a finely tuned, flexible, beat-by-beat manner and allows for the subtle shifts of engagement and disengagement required by social relationships. In contrast, when the dorsal (or "reptilian") vagus is activated, dissociation follows. The metabolism is speedily shut down, the heart rate drops rapidly, hiding behavior and passive withdrawal are initiated, and a hypoaroused physical collapse may be triggered.

Daniela: Once an infant starts to turn to dissociation as a defense, how does the dynamic develop?

Allan: As the child learns that his caregiver is unable to help him to regulate either a specific emotion or intense emotions in general, or worse that she exacerbates the dysregulation, he will start to go into a state of hypoaroused dissociation as soon as the threat of dysregulation arises. Neurons that fire together wire together, so each time an infant has to revert to dissociation, the right hemisphere circuitry that instigates dissociation is strengthened, meaning that next time it is triggered even more easily. This is useful for a child who is living with chronic trauma, but those who initially use dissociation to cope with highly traumatic events subsequently dissociate to defend against both daily stressors and the stress caused when implicitly held memories of trauma are triggered.

In the developing brain, repeated neurological states become traits, so dissociative defenses are embedded into the core structure of the evolving personality and become a part of who a person is rather than what a person does.

Daniela: How does dissociation impact our relationship with our emotions and with ourselves?

Allan: Emotions are processed hierarchically in the right brain; first reaching the subcortical amygdala and cingulate, and then the orbitofrontal cortex. It is the orbitofrontal cortex that enables us to become conscious of what we are feeling and to modify the responses of the amygdala. Pathological dissociation severs the connections between the right orbitofrontal cortex and the subcortical limbic brain. We are left at the mercy of the amygdala's crude, rigid, survival-orientated, black-and-white emotional repertory. The finesse and flexibility required to respond to novel socioemotional experiences is missing. As a consequence, we avoid anything new, especially in intimate contexts that may release attachment needs. Emotional learning stagnates, and the ongoing experience-dependent growth of the right brain is truncated.

At the same time, because the right orbitofrontal cortex is responsible for bringing our emotions into consciousness, we never really know what we are feeling. Then we lose the capacity for genuine self-reflection because although our left brain will be telling us what we think, knowing what we think is not enough if we are to engage in meaningful self-reflection. What is more, being cut off from our emotions, we have dead spots in our consciousness so our experience of ourselves becomes riddled with discontinuities. We feel fragmented.

Being cut off from our emotions impacts our sense of who we are more generally; our subjective sense of self derives from our unconscious experiences of bodily-based emotions and is constructed in the right brain. If we cannot connect to our bodily emotions, then our sense of self is built on fragile foundations. At times, we may even lose our sense of physical presence. Many who suffered early relational trauma have a distorted sense of their bodies and of what is happening within them.

Daniela: How does the reliance on dissociative defenses affect our relationships with others?

Allan: Throughout our evolutionary history, the ability to maintain personally meaningful bonds has been vital for our survival, so when danger rather than safety emanates from the early attachment relationship, there are significant consequences for the relational unconscious. For example, we learn to isolate the deeper parts of ourselves in order to protect them from others who are seen primarily as sources of pain rather than comfort. Similarly, having developed a working model of dysregulated-self-in-interaction-with-a-misattuned other, when we are in trouble, we turn away from others instead of approaching them for help.

Another right brain function, affective empathy, our ability to feel what another person is feeling, depends on us connecting to our body's response to that other person. This is compromised when dissociation becomes characterological. Individuals with early relational trauma struggle to feel the empathy that is so vital in meaningful human relationships.

Daniela: What are the implications of characterological dissociation for the way that we interact with our environment and our ability to feel emotionally secure?

Allan: Feeling secure depends on the implicit knowledge that our emotional responses to our social and physical environment are appropriate. While dissociated we are cut off from at least some aspects of our environment, so we are unable to respond appropriately.

Daniela: What does hypoaroused dissociation do to our experience of pain?

Allan: Dissociation, the escape when there is no escape, is a response to overwhelming stress and intolerable pain, and it triggers the release of a massive amount of endogenous opioids—our natural painkillers. But chronically high levels of opioids during the neonatal period influence the wiring of the pain circuits, and the infant grows into an individual who appears not to experience pain as acutely as others. However, this higher pain threshold does not derive from a capacity to tolerate pain—quite the reverse—it derives from the fact that as soon as emotional pain is experienced, dissociation blocks awareness of it. Thus, the pain that is still lived by the body and limbic system doesn't come to consciousness, it is never truly experienced, and its messages go unheeded.

In time, such methods of pain relief may come to be experienced as an inability to feel anything—a loss of aliveness. Then we look for ways to escape this deadness. For example, self-cutting, which is associated with early relational trauma, may represent an attempt to get out of the numbed and lifeless state associated with a chronic elevation of endogenous opioids.

Daniela: You argue that the early development of dissociative defenses may increase the risk of aggression, rage, and violence.

Allan: Violence is aggression that has extreme harm as its goal, and when somebody commits a violent act, it means that his or her developmental trajectory has gone astray. Despite overall decreases in violent crimes in the United States, juvenile homicide rates have increased and now surpass those of adults, so we have to look at early childhood for the causes. We already know that early relational trauma leads to the dysregulation of emotions such as fear and pain. I suggest that rage and aggression can also become dysregulated by early relational trauma. Under relational stress, a developmentally impaired, right orbitofrontal cortex can't regulate the amygdala's response to threatening stimuli, thus it is easy to overreact with unmediated rage or violence to what is perceived to be a threatening and humiliating stance in another. All of this is processed very rapidly, beneath levels of consciousness awareness.

Daniela: Could a dysregulated aggression system, coupled with internalized shame, lead to self-harm?

Allan: Definitely—people can suffer from either externalizing psychopathologies where aggression is directed outward or internalizing psychopathologies where aggression is turned in onto oneself, as it is with self-harm. Donald Kalsched's work on the self-care system is a powerful description of how violence can be internalized and directed from one part of the self to another part.

At the most extreme level, internalized violence, accompanied by a collapse in the right hemisphere, seems to increase the risk of suicide. I'm impressed by the work of Weinberg.* He says when a right hemisphere, which has been compromised by early relational trauma, suffers extreme pain, it may collapse, whereupon it is unable to regulate negative emotions such as loneliness, self-contempt, and murderous rage.

A collapsed right hemisphere also leaves the left hemisphere in control. The left hemisphere is intolerant of ambiguity, thinks in terms of either/or, remains within the box, works with what is already known, and is oriented to simple, linear solutions. Thus it is nearly impossible to find a creative way out of pain. As a consequence, suicide would feel (to the left brain) like the obvious, logical, and only solution.

Weinberg also suggests that the extreme dissociation caused by right hemisphere collapse opens the door to suicide because our sense of who we are is completely cut off from our body, and this would appease our fear of death.

Daniela: If we have suffered early relational trauma, can we do anything?

Allan: Yes! Although early relationships shape the developing brain, the human brain remains plastic and capable of learning throughout

---

* I. Weinberg (2000). The prisoners of despair: Right hemisphere deficiency and suicide. *Neuroscience and Biobehavioral Reviews, 24,* 799–815.

the entire life span, and with the right therapeutic help we can move beyond dissociation as our primary defense mechanism and begin to regulate our emotions more appropriately.

Daniela: What kind of psychotherapy does it take to heal early relational trauma?

Allan: It takes painstaking, relational, embodied, long-term psychotherapy. Emotional regulation, attachment patterns, and dissociative defensives are mediated by the right brain, so healing requires the kind of therapy that can work with the right brain. Because what is held by the right brain isn't immediately available to consciousness, and because what is defensively dissociated is doubly difficult to access, it is a slow process.

Moreover, right brain change depends on corrective emotional *experience*. In early life, the human brain develops within the context of an emotion-regulating relationship with another human being—typically the mother. If we missed out on this as a child, then the therapist-patient relationship needs to facilitate the resumption of the blocked developmental processes. The relationship between therapist and client is called the "therapeutic alliance," and unless it is strong enough, it will not be able to provide a growth-facilitating environment for the patient's underdeveloped right brain.

Daniela: What creates a "strong-enough" therapeutic alliance?

Allan: The patient has to trust that the therapist is benevolent and that the therapist understands him in a deep way that incorporates both mind and body. That means the patient's right brain needs to feel that it is seen, so although a therapist's left brain must listen to the words created by the patient's left brain in order to form an objective assessment of the patient's problem, the therapist must be sensitive enough to pick up, and empathize with, what is going on implicitly within the client's right brain and within his body. All therapeutic techniques sit on top of the therapist's ability to access the implicit realm via the right brain and body. A strong therapeutic alliance depends on the therapist knowing the patient from the inside-out rather than from the top-down.

Another way to express this is to say that the therapist must develop her "intuition." Intuition is defined as "the ability to understand or know something immediately without conscious reasoning." Intuition is implicit knowledge gained through embodied, right brain learning. Intuition takes time to develop, but it lies at the core of clinical expertise. A therapist's bodily-based intuition picks up what is held by the patient's unconscious mind and body, and it is this psychobiological connection that forms the foundation of the therapeutic alliance and which facilitates growth. Shotter has asserted that implicit knowledge relates to how *"people are able to influence each other in their being, rather than just in their intellects; that is, to actually 'move' them rather than just 'giving them ideas.'"* A patient's emotional growth depends on the therapist's ability to move, and to be moved by, those that come to him for help.

Daniela: What are the processes by which the therapeutic relationship helps a patient to resume the blocked development of his or her emotional system?

Allan: The therapist needs to help her patient to reexperience the trauma in affectively tolerable doses. Equally important is that the therapist helps her patient to learn how to regulate the feelings associated with that trauma so that the patient can integrate them into his emotional life rather than having to dissociate when they arise. That requires the therapist's right brain to become the external regulator for the patient's right brain—helping it to tolerate what was once intolerable. In time, the patient internalizes the regulatory capacity of the therapist, learning to do this for himself.

Paradoxically, the greatest opportunity for such learning arises when something in the therapeutic relationship triggers the implicit working models that were formed during the patient's emotionally traumatic childhood, and he automatically begins to activate his old defenses. A fleeting change in the therapist's tone of voice, a momentary facial expression, a subtle gesture, or a single word may set unconscious alarm bells ringing and activate the patient's implicit working model of dysregulated-self-with-a-dysregulating-other. In these moments, past history becomes present reality. The patient is catapulted out of his window of tolerance, becomes emotionally dysregulated, and turns toward his old, unhealthy ways of regulating his emotions. He is at risk of either exploding into a dysregulated state of hyperarousal or of imploding into a dysregulated state of hypoaroused dissociation.

When a patient is catapulted into a hyperaroused state and subjectively experiences the therapist through the lens of the old dysregulated internal working models, it's called, "negative transference." Projective identification occurs when the emotions and unconscious memories associated with early attachment trauma are intolerable. The patient unconsciously communicates his traumatic experiences to the therapist via nonverbal right brain channels but immediately dissociates so that he is no longer overtly expressing or subjectively experiencing them. At that point, it seems that only the therapist is experiencing the emotion. In neurobiological terms, the patient's right orbitofrontal cortex shuts down, and the negative emotion is instantly driven beneath conscious awareness into the right amygdala. The patient's dysregulated hyperarousal still exists, but it is buried beneath conscious awareness.

For a patient who is in the midst of either negative transference or projective identification, there is rupture of the therapeutic alliance. However, if the therapist can maintain an attuned connection to her client, then the door opens to the possibility of working with what got laid down early in the patient's life. Hence, the importance of "rupture and repair."

I'll begin by describing what happens if the therapist can stay connected to a patient who is in the midst of negative transference and then talk about working with projective identification.

When the patient is in a state of negative transference, the therapist's empathic right brain will implicitly pick up the old fears and pain and dysregulation that have come alive in the patient and will struggle to tolerate the resultant negative emotions flowing through her own body, whereupon her patient's right brain will unconsciously pick up on the therapist's distress. However, if the therapist has done her own work, then she will be able to metabolize those negative emotions, whereupon her voice will become calmer and her facial expressions less tense. This, in turn, will be unconsciously picked up by the patient's right brain. At this point, three types of learning that are intrinsic to healing occur:

1. The patient's right brain, noticing the process that the therapist has been through, will observe that dysregulating emotions can be tolerated, metabolized, and integrated after all.
2. The regulation occurring in the therapist's right brain will be actually mirrored by the patient's right brain, thus the therapist acts as an external emotional regulator for the patient. This dynamic happens under the radar of explicit awareness, but it is crucial because it gives the patient a living experience of what was missing during development.
3. The patient can begin to create new working models about the intersubjective world. The unconscious working model of a person who suffered early relational trauma predicts that in times of emotional stress, others will exacerbate stress rather than help to regulate it. Concurrently, the patient will have deduced that when he is emotionally dysregulated, he is unworthy of help. If the therapist remains emotionally connected with the patient when he becomes dysregulated, the expectations of these unconscious, insecure working models are challenged. The patient begins to learn, again from lived experience, that there is nothing defective in him for feeling as he does, and that he is indeed worthy of help when in an emotionally dysregulated state.

In time, as new neural circuits are built, the patient can achieve what's called "earned security." Some of these new circuits connect the right amygdala to the right orbitofrontal cortex, allowing for a greater tolerance and regulation of intense emotions. Other circuits are responsible for the creation of new unconscious working models that embody a healthier way of seeing other people and oneself. The result is a growing sense of well-being and characterological change.

This process is considerably more difficult if the patient is in the midst of projective identification, because the emotions, working models, and memories are dissociated, so they need to be retrieved before they can be regulated and integrated. However, the therapeutic skills needed to work with projective identification are similar to those required to work with negative transference, in that it again requires that the therapist remain linked to the patient when the patient has left the relational field. This allows the patient's right brain unconscious to perceive, in real time, enough of a sense of safety to begin to lift the dissociative defenses. The therapist who waits patiently in the presence of the not yet speakable, being receptive to the not yet formed, sends out a lived message that the dissociated emotion is neither unacceptable nor intolerable. The therapist's resonance with the patient's dissociated emotion also acts as an amplifying mirror, and in a genuine right brain-to-right brain nonverbal dialogue with the therapist, the patient gradually raises to awareness what he needs to be able to consciously feel and articulate, but which, until now, he has had to dissociate from. In doing so, links between the right amygdala and the right orbitofrontal cortex are forged.

Daniela: What is the importance of raising dissociated emotions to a place where they can become conscious and verbalized?

Allan: We experience and cope with life both explicitly through words and conscious thoughts and implicitly through our nonconscious, visceral, bodily-based emotions. When these two domains come together, it allows for a new and more complex sense of our emotional self. Consciously experiencing and naming an emotional experience while living it enables our emotions to develop from their crude early forms, when they are experienced only as bodily sensations, into finely differentiated states.

Becoming conscious of our emotions also allows for emergence of a "reflective self" that is capable of "in-sight," a metaphor that speaks to our awareness of both our hidden thoughts and, as importantly, the rhythm of our inner emotional states.

Daniela: What happens if the therapist cannot contain the negative emotions created in negative transference and projective identification?

Allan: When a patient's traumatic emotions and memories are communicated through negative transference or projective identification, they may hit a therapist's sore spots created by her own attachment history. If the therapist can't regulate the resultant negative emotions, she will try to escape through a verbal interpretation, too hasty an intervention, or by labeling the patient's behavior as something negative such as "resistance." When this happens, the therapist becomes a co-participant in re-creating her patient's trauma, and the patient will be catapulted further into a dysregulated state of fear, shame, and dissociation. The patient's old trauma-derived neural circuitry and defensive working models will be reinforced and strengthened.

There is an old adage in therapy that no patient can achieve a greater level of healing than his therapist has achieved. With modern scientific knowledge we can be more specific: The patient's unconscious right brain can develop only as far as the therapist's right brain can take the patient. Thus the central questions are: When a therapist's wounds are hit, can she regulate her own bodily-based emotions and shame dynamics well enough to be able to stay connected to her patient? Can the therapist tolerate what is happening in her own body when it mirrors her patient's terror, rage, and physiological hyperarousal? Herein lies the art of psychotherapy. It takes many years of experience for a therapist to stay with a dissociating patient who is projecting his trauma onto her. More important, the therapist needs to have worked deeply with her own trauma, and has to keep working with it. A successful therapeutic relationship precipitates emotional growth not only in the patient but also in the therapist.

That said, every therapist will have times when she is unable to contain her own negative emotions and when both patient and therapist are triggered: The term that is used is "enactment." I explore the dynamics of enactment at length in my past book, *The Science of the Art of Psychotherapy*, but there isn't space to go into it here. Suffice to say that periods of mutual misattunement will not cause damage so long as (1) they are temporary, (2) the therapist honestly owns her role in creating the enactment, and (3) the therapist is able to instigate repair. In fact, cycles of misattunement and re-attunement provide opportunities for corrective emotional experiences in that they show the patient that not every instance of misattunement is a precursor to abandonment or neglect, and that even when there is a stressful rupture of the bond, the interactive regulation of a caring other is available for genuine repair.

Daniela: It seems that a certain amount of emotional dysregulation is necessary to effective therapy. Is that right?

Allan: Yes! The therapist must strive to prevent the patient from being catapulted too far beyond his window of tolerance, because this will simply lead to the repetition of old patterns and to the strengthening of old trauma-derived neural circuits. But if it is to be effective, therapy must help to increase a person's tolerance to emotional stress, and if therapy is too safe, this won't happen. You have to be *in* an emotion to learn how to regulate it in a new way—talking about it isn't enough.

The simplest way to describe this is through the diagram shown in Figure 7.1, which is adapted from a diagram by my colleague Pat Ogden. Within the central band of green (see insert for color), we are working with what we can already tolerate, and so there is no emotional growth. Once we get into the more saturated red areas—

the danger areas—we are in such a dysregulated state of either hyperarousal or hypoarousal that we can learn nothing new. It is only by working in the area covered by the turquoise lines, which moves back and forth across the edges of what we can tolerate, that we can grow. Working along these safe-but-not-too-safe edges is how we learn to be with intense emotions and how to regulate them. That learning is embodied through forging neural connections between the right amygdala and the right orbitofrontal cortex.

Working at these edges is not easy! Chaos theory tells us that it is here that the system becomes unstable. However, chaos theory also tells us that it is this instability that creates the potential for

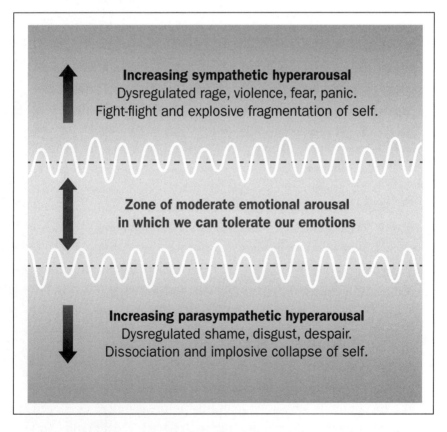

FIGURE 7.1 Adapted by Daniela Sieff. Source: On the same wave-length: How our emotional brain is shaped by human relationships. Interview by Daniela Sieff. Understanding and Healing Emotional Trauma: Conversations with Pioneering Clinicians and Researchers, 2015. Routledge, UK. See insert for color.

the system to head in a totally new direction. In therapy, there are two possible responses to the instability. If the therapeutic alliance is not strong enough, then the patient may fall back onto his long-established dissociative path. However, if the therapist can remain attuned, contain the chaos, and provide a model of a different way to respond, then the patient has an opportunity to open up new neural pathways—ones that are at a more complex and adaptive level of organization and which enable the different parts of the emotional right brain to become more integrated.

Daniela: Short-term cognitive behavioral therapy is currently very popular—can it help with healing relational trauma?

Allan: In the academic discipline of psychology, the cognitive paradigm (which came to dominate the 1980s and 1990s) envisioned human brains as thinking machines, and its research focused on cognitive processes such as explicit memory, rational thought, language, and consciousness. Cognitively based therapy came out of this paradigm; its basic assumption is that we can change how we feel by consciously changing how we think and what we believe. That means that cognitive therapy focuses on language and thought, both of which are located in the left brain. That is rarely effective for patients who struggle with the consequences of early relational trauma, because such trauma impacts the development of the emotional system of the right brain.

In fact, cognitive therapy—when applied to the emotional realm—uses linguistic, rational thought–based strategies to help the left brain gain more control over the right brain and its emotions. In other words, rather than fostering the growth of the right brain, cognitive therapy helps to shore up dissociation and keep our emotions out of mind.

Similarly, people who have trouble regulating their emotions not uncommonly have a left brain that is already more developed than their right brain, and they may well have learned to use rational thinking and words to obscure the deeper emotional experiences and to keep them dissociated. Again, cognitive therapy risks strengthening the very strategies that keep the dissociation in place.

Even if the left brain becomes better able to control the emotions of the right brain, it can only dampen down emotional arousal that is of low or moderate intensity. Regardless of our childhoods, when emotional arousal reaches a certain level of intensity, the left brain goes off-line, and the right brain becomes dominant. Changes made in the cognitive strategies of the left brain are unavailable when this happens. At these times, the only thing that helps is to have created the neural connections between the right amygdala and the right orbitofrontal cortex, which allow us to tolerate and regulate intense emotions. Cognitive therapy, because it works with the left brain, simply can't do this.

Another problem with cognitive therapy is that it often misses the real issues. "Anger management" is a well-known cognitive treatment, but underlying a person's anger may be dissociated fear and shame, and these cannot be accessed through the verbal language of the left brain. Cognitive therapy has no way to work with deeply embodied, underlying dissociated affects. Although it can reduce symptomatology, it can't alter character structure and promote emotional growth.

The final problem of cognitive therapy is that it is generally a short-term treatment, so it is unable to build a strong-enough therapeutic alliance to allow the patient to experience the corrective emotional experiences. Change does not happen when a patient is consciously reflecting on an emotion; it happens when a patient is *in* the emotion and when a resonating and actively involved therapist shows the patient a different way to be with what he is feeling. There is no room for that to happen with cognitive therapy.

In short, relational trauma cannot be addressed through the development of left brain cognitive strategies; rather, its healing depends on working directly with the right brain to build an expanded, more tolerant, more interconnected, and better regulated right brain. Psychotherapy that makes the right brain the focus requires much, much more from both therapist and patient, but it is the only route to genuine growth. We know that not only through the lived experience of therapists and patients but also through all that we've learned about the brain in the past two decades. In fact, I argue that we are in the middle of a paradigm shift in terms of how we understand ourselves. We are moving away from the cognitive paradigm that gave primacy to left brain conscious thinking, interpretations, and verbal language to one that gives primacy to right brain affect, bodily-based emotions, and what is held implicitly in the relational unconscious.

Daniela: Given that compromised neural circuits cause emotional dysregulation, some people argue that the cure lies in psychotherapeutic drugs. What are your thoughts?

Allan: There is no doubt that with certain psychopathologies, emotional dysregulation can be modified by bioaminergic drugs that directly impact the neurochemistry of subcortical brain circuits, but one of the main problems with psychotherapeutic drugs is that they are not site-specific. You may give somebody a selective serotonin reuptake inhibitor such as Prozac, but there are serotonin receptors throughout the entire brain and body. It's a shotgun approach, so you get side effects.

What is more, a drug will not provide a growth-facilitating environment, and thus the patient will not necessarily develop the more connected and expanded right brain that then allows for more complex and adaptive emotional coping mechanisms. In other words, although levels of arousal will be altered, there may be no lasting improvement in processing social cues, no rewriting of the trauma-created internal working models, and no development of the ability to turn to another for help in regulating emotional stress. The change may be limited to returning the individual to a more stable personality rather than enabling the personality to tolerate more novelty and to structurally change and expand. If only pharmacology is used, the patient is denied the right brain growth and development that emerges from a psychotherapeutic process.

Daniela: What message would you like people to take home from this interview?

Allan: The earliest stages of life are critical because they form the foundation of all that follows. Our early attachment relationships, for better or worse, shape our right brain unconscious system and have lifelong consequences.

An attuned early attachment relationship enables us to grow an interconnected, well-developed right brain and sets us up to become emotionally secure. A traumatic early attachment relationship impairs the development of a healthy right brain and locks us into an emotionally dysregulated, amygdala-driven emotional world. Then our only way to defend against intense unregulated emotions is through dissociation. Over time, dissociation becomes characterological. Faced with relational stress, we cut off from the world, from other people, from our emotions, from our bodies, and from our sense of self. We cannot respond adaptively to what is happening in our environment. We cannot develop or grow emotionally. Instead, we are stuck with a limited, crude, and rigid emotional repertoire, a left brain that is desperately trying to keep control, and a deep-seated feeling of disconnection and insecurity. Too many people live like this. Too many people suffer desperate pain because of the emotional insecurity that results from early relational trauma.

For somebody struggling with this, the way to emotional security, and to a more vital, alive, and fulfilling life, does not come from making the unconscious conscious, which is essentially a left brain process; rather, it arises through physically restructuring, growing, and expanding the emotional unconscious itself. That is, it arises through using growth-promoting relationships to change the physical substrate of the right brain. Eric Kandel, the recent Nobel Prize winner, recently stated, "There is no longer any doubt that psychotherapy can result in detectable changes in the brain." The most effective way to achieve these changes is through relationally based, emotionally focused psychotherapy with an empathic and psychobiologically attuned therapist who is willing and able to be an active participant in the process. It is the attuned interaction between the nonverbal right hemisphere of the involved therapist and the non-verbal right hemisphere of the patient that enables the patient to tolerate emotions that previously had to be dissociated, to grow as an emotional being, and ultimately to develop the emotional security that was previously beyond reach.

CHAPTER 8

Allan Schore on the Science of the Art of Psychotherapy

Interview with David Bullard

David Bullard (DB): Allan, you are known for integrating psychological and biological models of emotional and social development across the life span. You've done a great deal of research and writing suggesting that the early developing, emotion-processing right brain represents the psychobiological substrate of the human unconscious described by Freud. Your work has been an important catalyst in the ongoing "emotional revolution" now occurring across clinical and scientific disciplines.

I've been watching my own process while getting ready for this interview, with a lot of left brain work: reading, taking copious notes and thinking, and anxiously trying to figure out the structure for this interview. After all, it isn't every day one gets to interview a person called "the American Bowlby," and whom the American Psychoanalytic Association has described as "a monumental figure in psychoanalytic and neuropsychoanalytic studies"! But essentially, this will be a conversation, and I'd like to begin with a quote attributed to Jung, involving a graduate student who went to him, inquiring as to what he could do to become the best therapist possible. Jung said—loosely translated—"Well, go to the library and read and study everything good that's ever been written about the art and science of psychotherapy, and then forget it all before you sit down to peer into the human soul."

It occurs to me, having followed your work for a while—most recently your writing about right brain communication in psychotherapy—that Jung's quote may be partly what you're writing about.

Allan Schore (AS): Absolutely. The title of my past book, *The Science of the Art of Psychotherapy* (2012), attempts to more clearly understand the relationship between the two, because on the one hand, as so much clinically relevant research now shows us, there is a science that underlies the clinical domain. And there is a certain amount of information and knowledge that we as clinicians must have in order to succeed in the particular area of expertise that we're in—psychotherapeutic change processes.

Yet, at the same time it's also an art, something that is extremely subjective and personal. For most of the past century, it was thought that subjectivity was outside the purview of science. But we now understand psychotherapy changes more than overt behavior and language—it also acts on subjectivity and emotion. As you know, the left hemisphere is dominant for language and overt behavior; the right for emotion and subjectivity. This dichotomy fits nicely with left versus right brain functions. The two cerebral hemispheres process information from the outside—and inside—world in different ways: one from an objective stance, the other from a more subjective perspective. The two brains use different ways of perceiving the world and of being in the world.

Neuroscience has legitimized subjectivity in psychology and in therapy. Both science and clinical theory agree that psychotherapy is basically relational and emotional, and so we now think that emotionally and intersubjectively being with the patient is more important than rationally explaining the patient's behavior to himself. The core self-system is relational and emotional, and lateralized to the right hemisphere, and not to the analytical left brain. As we empathically "follow the affect" and facilitate the patient experiencing a "heightened affective moment," we're intuitively inhibiting the dominance of the left and "leaning right."

DB: Can you speak more about how neuroscience is changing our understanding of the art of psychotherapy?

AS: Let me try to give a broad overview. In the critical moments of any session, the patient must sense that we're empathically with them. Research shows a difference between the left brain understanding of cognitive empathy and right brain bodily-based emotional empathy. In other words, we're experiencing and sharing the patient's right brain emotional subjective states, being with the patient rather than doing to the patient. In this therapeutic context, we have to also be in the right brain to make therapeutic contact, and for the patient to make contact with her deeper emotions. Later we may engage our left brains to more cognitively understand the emotional state, but while we're attempting to "listen beneath the words" in order to "reach the affect" and work with the affect, we must, as Reik said, abandon "sweet reason" and "rigidly rational consciousness" and "abandon yourself" to intuitive hunches that emerge from the unconscious.

Intuition and empathy are right brain functions, and both operate at levels beneath conscious awareness. Bion said we must leave conscious expectation behind in order to really hear the whole patient. So getting back to Jung, he also said, "Man's task is to become conscious of the contents that press upward from the unconscious."

These two different brains, the conscious mind and the unconscious mind, must work together. As my colleague Iain McGilchrist has shown, we are currently out of hemispheric balance. I think psychology has placed too great an emphasis on the conscious mind, and we are now challenging the long-held idea that reason must overcome bodily-based emotion. That the conscious mind needs to control and suppress the unconscious mind, that science and art are always in conflict, and that they would never mesh together. As I've written, with the ongoing interdisciplinary paradigm shift our perspective has changed, and not incidentally the gap between the practice and the theory of psychotherapy has really collapsed in the past two decades.

Getting back to your Jung citation, at the very beginning of our clinical education we're learning techniques, and we're learning the psychological science of psychotherapy. But as we learn our craft and gain clinical experience, ultimately the bulk of our learning comes from being with and learning from our patients—about them as well as self-knowledge. As I see it, our growing clinical expertise expands within the psychotherapeutic relationships we share with our patients. It's what our patients are teaching us, if we are open to it. It's not just about them and the deeper psychological realms within them. It's at the same time becoming more familiar with the deeper core of our own self-system. Being psychodynamically focused, this involves the use of both our conscious left and especially the unconscious "right mind."

I believe that we've overvalued the analytic left mind. So lately, I've looked more carefully at the neuroscience for the overt and subtle difference between the left and right brain/mind. This has shifted my clinical focus from the explicit to the implicit, from cognitive mental content to affective psychobiological process. I now see the change mechanism acting beneath the words—in process more than content. We now have a better idea what this process is about, and how relational interactions literally can change that process and thereby change character structure.

My idea about science is that we need to update ourselves about what is objectively known about the brain and what is known about the body, as well as "knowing" more about our own subjectivity. And that's a continual journey. Fundamentally, our psychotherapeutic exploration of somebody else's subjectivity, which is bodily-based subjectivity, is also an exploration of our own subjectivity. So, there are two types of knowledge here that really underlie psychotherapy change processes: the explicit knowledge of the broader biological and psychological scientific theories, and the "implicit relational knowledge of self and other."

DB: Before we go any further, as a psychodynamic therapist, even a "neuropsychoanalytic" one, what might you say about your

work to therapists who are using more directive methods, such as
CBT and EMDR?

AS: The neurobiologically informed psychodynamic perspective
that I use emphasizes a clinical focus on not only explicit conscious but also implicit unconscious processes. All schools of psychotherapy are now interested in these essential functions that take
place beneath awareness. And all are accessing attachment internal
working models, which Bowlby said operate at unconscious levels
and can be changed by therapy. So I'm interested in not only the
patient's overt behavior but also her internal world, what cognitive
scientists call internal schemas.

My work is fundamentally about how to work with affect, and
so clinically I'm exploring with the patient not only conscious but
also unconscious cognition and, importantly, unconscious affect.
The patient may have no awareness of what neuroscience is now
describing as "unconscious negative emotion." Research has now
established that fear isn't necessarily conscious; you can experience
it without being aware that you're experiencing it. So how do we
detect these unconscious affects?

And then there's the matter of the communication of emotions
within the therapeutic alliance that are so rapid that they occur
beneath conscious awareness. The alliance is a central mechanism
in not only psychodynamic therapy but also CBT, EMDR, experiential, body psychotherapy, and so forth. This gets to what used to
be called the common factors that impact all forms of treatment.
I'm interested in the change mechanisms that occur in all psychotherapeutic modalities, but especially in the right brain, which is
dominant for emotional and social functions and stress regulation.

DB: But let me get in a question for the people who may not have
had much exposure to the kind of neuroscience and the neuropsychoanalytic approach that you've written so much about over the
past two decades. At basic levels, you say that right brain develop-

ment is much more rapid in the newborn or in the developing fetus even. Can you address those implications?

AS: Let me just go wide for a second and then we can kind of dive in here, because the truth of it is that the past two decades have been remarkable in terms of the changes in the field of psychology across the board. I'm thinking about the early 1990s when there was a huge split between researchers and clinicians, where there were divisions within the different schools of psychotherapy, and where the focus was very much on verbal content of the session. Although there were breaks away from classical psychoanalytic theory, the focus was still on undoing repression, making the unconscious conscious, and with interpretations being the major vectors of the treatment. Emotion really had not come into the forefront. But that's the key to the change.

Over the 1970s, we had been moving into a behavioral psychology and from that to a behavioral psychotherapy. Then it transitioned into a cognitive psychology where suddenly, we went beyond just overt behavior and into covert cognition, which became a legitimate field of study. Out of that came cognitive behavioral therapy and then in the 1990s the emotional revolution, as it has been called, began, which posited that affect is primary, as well as affect regulation. And that's where my studies really began, in the early 1990s.

THE REEMERGENCE OF PSYCHOANALYSIS

DB: Did you have much contact with psychoanalysts Joe Weiss and Hal Sampson in San Francisco, who founded a psychotherapy research group and developed control mastery theory?

AS: Not contact, but I was well aware of them, and I'm pretty sure they were aware of me.

DB: They were.

AS: Their work has held up, and its impact continues. There's now an intense interest in gaining a deeper understanding of what used to be called the nonspecific mechanisms of change, in all forms of psychotherapy. They were onto that really early. My first book, *Affect Regulation and the Origin of the Self*, tied together the socio-emotional change processes in early development and in psychotherapy. This was in 1994 and, incidentally, the term "self" was not being used that much back then. Psychodynamic people were still more or less using the term "ego" rather than "self." As I'm sure you're well aware, Jung had put his money on "self" and was much closer to describing the core system than Freud's "ego." The early developmental models of the time were dominated by the cognitive models of Piaget. Everyone had been attempting to try to squeeze Piaget into a psychotherapeutic mechanism. It proved to be kind of an awkward fit. Emotion was the key to attachment.

And so the subtitle of my first book was *The Neurobiology of Early Emotional Development*. That same year, Antonio Damasio had come out with his book *Descartes' Error*, and the whole idea of emotion, which had been ignored by science, began to come out of the closet. Twenty years later, it's well established that emotion is primary in early human development, that affect dysregulation lies at the core of psychopathology, and that affective communications are essential in all forms of psychotherapy.

The second area of basic change is the matter of the interpersonal neurobiology of attachment—a shift from the intrapsychic to the interpersonal. Many people had been looking at attachment theory, but even attachment theory was hard to anchor clinical process in. That had to be worked out: Other than the "strange situation" and the Adult Attachment Interview (AAI), how were clinicians going to use Bowlby's attachment theory and information about early development? That has been a remarkable change. Now just about every clinician has some understanding of the centrality of early development and how that interpersonal developmental mechanism plays out in the therapeutic relationship.

Indeed, early development really has come into the fore in all forms of psychotherapy, with all patient populations. Interpersonal neurobiology—how early relationships shape the brain—has transformed attachment theory. This transformation from what I call "classical attachment theory" to "modern attachment theory" focuses on not only regulation but also dysregulation and ideas of psychopathogenesis, which have also been major themes of my work. My efforts have been to generate a more integrated theory of mind and body, of psychology and biology. In essence, I've attempted to synthesize these fields in order to create a coherent psychobiological model of how the self develops, how dysregulation and disorders evolve, and then ultimately how to treat these disorders.

A couple of other things to mention: Another change over the past two decades has been the reemergence of psychodynamic theory and the revitalization of psychoanalysis, the science of unconscious processes. It took a while, because as you know, classical psychoanalysis was seen as apart from science and was cast out of academia for a long period of time.

But this reemergence has paradoxically been fostered by neuroscience and its interest in rapid implicit processes. Neuroimaging research has established that most essential adaptive processes are so rapid that they take place beneath conscious awareness. I've suggested that the self-system is located in the right brain, the biological substrate of the human unconscious. This differs from Freud's dynamic unconscious, which mainly contains repressed material, banished from consciousness. At any rate, there is now great interest in implicit unconscious processes, and I think we're now coming back to a modern expression of psychodynamic theory. Indeed, all forms of therapy are now looking at right brain-to-right brain transference and countertransference communications and how these are expressed in the therapeutic alliance, beneath the words.

One other major change has been the rediscovery of brain lateralization and the appreciation of the different structural organizations of the right and left brain. Each has different critical periods and growth spurts, and ultimately different specialized functions. For me, the terra incognita literally has always been the early developing right brain, the unconscious. More so than the surface conscious mind, my interest has been in deeper, early forming, nonverbal, bodily-based survival processes. I became especially interested in how we could bring these survival processes into the open and how these could be studied. As a clinician-scientist, everything that I've authored has had to be clinically relevant. It has to fit the way that I work with my patients, as well as scientifically grounded. My theories are heuristic and not only open to research but also able to generate experimental hypotheses that can be tested.

HEMISPHERICITY

DB: You've spoken of the left brain being verbal, rational, and logical, but of the right brain actually having verbal aspects also. How would you describe the verbal capacities of the right brain?

AS: The first person to bring up the idea that all language is not only in the left hemisphere, just for the record, was Freud in 1891 in *On Aphasia*, which still is studied by neurologists. But the idea that everything that is verbal has to, by definition, reside in the left brain is still held by many people. Current neuroscience shows this is not the case. The right also has language. The right stores our own names and processes emotional words. Prosody, the emotional tone of the voice, is right lateralized, as are novel metaphors and making of thematic inferences. So when a patient all of a sudden is in an emotional state and is using an emotional word, the right is tracking that also. Right-hemispheric language creates the intimate feeling of "being with."

DB: And humor is known to be more right brain?

AS: Absolutely!

DB: And it kind of "wakes up" our left brain with recognition?

AS: Yes. Because the processing of what is familiar is left and the processing of novelty is right. Essentially, we're looking for, not the bottom-line preexisting truth, but for the ability to process novelty, especially novelty in socioemotional interactions. And for many patients, intimacy is novelty. So, yes, anything that is new pops into the right brain first, and you actually get bursts of noradrenaline in the right hemisphere, the hemisphere that is dominant for attention. In fact, I'm now citing studies that indicate the highest levels of human cognition—the "Aha!" moment of insight, intuition, creativity, indeed love, are all expressions of the right and not left brain.

DB: It's in the right, but we don't know about it until it shows up in the left. The right brain lets us know what's actually going on, especially in the body, and in the deeper core of the self.

AS: Correct. Essentially, the left has the illusion that it has just discovered something new, but the truth of it is the right has discovered it, and now the left is putting into words what the right just found out about the self, especially in relation to other self-systems. My colleague Darcia Narvaez is showing that morality is also a very high right brain process. A body of research indicates that the right is dominant for affiliation, the left for power.

This gets into some of the matters that Jung and others were talking about—these very high symbolic mechanisms are in the right hemisphere. Here's another example of how neuroscience has changed our ideas about the human experience. It used to be thought that all symbolic processes are a product of the verbal left brain, so the goal was to get the patient to use words, and once there was conscious verbalization, then the patient can understand, and then the unconscious becomes conscious and change occurs. We're now saying that's not quite the case. The ultimate expression of the right brain is a conscious emotion. The ultimate expression of the left brain is a conscious thought. Becoming aware of our bodily-based emotions is more essential than becoming aware of our thoughts. The right brain and the unconscious mind are more connected into the visceral body. As you know, the body has been rediscovered in the past couple of decades. And that's been an enormous change for psychology and psychiatry.

TRAUMA AND DEVELOPMENT

DB: Would you say that has been driven through the clinical work, research, and writing on trauma?

AS: Partly that. But also the developmental work on attachment theory and attachment trauma. Clearly, modern trauma theory, which did not really exist until around the late 1990s, has also been one of the important transformations of the past two decades—the idea that "the body keeps the score," as Bessel van der Kolk put it. But even beyond that, I would suggest it's the rediscovery of the autonomic nervous system that is the major player here. It's now an accepted principle that in order to understand the human experience, it's not just about the voluntary behavior of the central nervous system but also the involuntary behavior of the autonomic nervous system—mind and body. And that's why much of my bodily-based attachment model involves the autonomic nervous system. The mother is literally a regulator of crescendos and decrescendos of the baby's developing autonomic nervous system.

These same bodily-based processes are also involved in the therapist's right brain psychobiological attunement to and regulation of the patient's emotional states. So the body has now embedded itself into the core of models of subjectivity—an embodied subjectivity that is not just an abstraction of the left brain, but of right brain processes also. The body is now seen as essential to right brain-to-right brain intersubjectivity. In my own work, I've argued that this conceptual advance has impacted clinical models, such as somatic countertransference—the therapists' own bodily reactions to patients' conscious and especially unconscious communications. Also, there is the idea that a major function of the therapist is to regulate the patient's autonomic arousal, a clinical concept that has challenged the older idea of neutrality and which expands the previous concept of containment. This perspective attends more to right brain unconscious process than to left brain conscious content. Once again, these scientific advances have transformed our clinical models.

DB: Wouldn't another major transformation be what I heard you saying in a recent workshop: that the very disruptions of intensive therapy allow the repressed traumatic developmental relational issues to come to the surface, and if they're dealt with properly, there then is healing?

AS: Absolutely the case. Except not "repressed," but dissociated. There's also been a shift in defenses, from an earlier clinical model that emphasized insight and the undoing of repression, a model of therapeutic action based on bringing to the patient's consciousness repressed unconscious material. Trauma theory emphasizes working with the deadening of affective consciousness by this other bodily-based survival defense, dissociation. Clinicians are learning to differentiate the two and recognize the latter.

But, yes, the idea about disruptions and repairs came out of the developmental data and was incorporated into my modern attachment theory. My writings emphasize that rupture and repair, both in the developmental and psychotherapeutic contexts, involve important opportunities for interactive regulation of dysregulated affective states.

At the most fundamental level, I'm interested in the mechanisms of change, especially in the early developing right brain self-system. To use an earlier language, what I'm exploring is how the object relational sequences between the mother and the infant shape emerging psychic structure. In more modern terms, these are investigations of interpersonal neurobiology. An interpersonal neurobiology of human development enables us to understand that the structure and function of the mind and brain are shaped by experiences, especially those involving emotional relationships, and to understand how brains align their neural activities in social interactions.

The tie-in from my developmental work to my clinical work is that the same right brain-to-right brain socioemotional processes that are setting up between the mother and the infant later play out in the therapeutic alliance. The model links the right brain growth in early development with later changes in the social and emotional context. And as you pointed out, rupture and repair are potential contexts of emotional growth. So I've paid attention to the work of other developmental psychoanalytic researchers such as Beatrice Beebe and Ed Tronick and Karlen Lyons-Ruth, who are also studying ruptures and repairs.

In my most recent writings, I've focused on the essential role of these repairs in reenactments of attachment trauma, which really is at the heart of the therapeutic change mechanism. I'm describing how both patient and therapist co-construct both the rupture and the repair, and that these ruptures are not technical mistakes, but literally . . .

DB: . . . the universal disappointments that are part of human relationships, and the repairs being the paths of healing?

AS: Beautifully put. Enactments represent communications of previous ruptures that triggered negative affects so intense and so painful that they were dissociated and banished from consciousness. As the therapy progresses and the attachment bond in the therapeutic alliance strengthens, there is enough safety for the patient to disassemble the dissociative defenses and let the affects come online more frequently. And then, what has been buried and packed down underneath dissociation surges into bodily awareness in the presence of a regulating other, now offering a possibility of interactive repair. Jung, who studied dissociation, described how the enduring emotional impact of childhood trauma "remains hidden all along from the patient, so that not reaching consciousness, the emotion never wears itself out, it is never used up." He also stated the trauma may suddenly return: "It forces itself tyrannically upon the conscious mind. The explosion of affect is a complete invasion of the individual. It pounces upon him like an enemy or a wild animal."

In my model of "relational trauma," I've suggested that it's not just misattunements that lead to the traumatic predisposition. It's also the lack of the repair, and that repair and interactive regulation requires a very personal, authentic response on the part of the therapist. Attachment trauma was originally relational, and so the healing must be relational, a mutual process. In Sullivan's words, the therapist is not neutral and detached, but a "participant observer."

LOVE, REPAIR, AND DEEPENING LOVE

DB: Okay, can you take what we are talking about and even apply it beyond therapy to other intimate relationships? Could you actually say to a couple that it's in the very upsets that they have that, if they could approach it in the right way, they'll have a window into learning about some of their earlier wounds or traumas and be able to heal them?

AS: Obviously, the original context of attachment trauma was a very intimate context. I mean the relationship between the mother and the infant defined an intimate context. Her ability to down-regulate negative affect in rupture and repair and up-regulate positive affect in mutual play shaped the attachment bond and the infant's developing right brain. In a secure attachment, the intimate context is characterized by mutual love, and over the course of my studies I'm increasingly using the term love to describe the intensity of the emotional bond. This is more than just pleasant affect. This is intense emotion.

And that love, incidentally, between the mother and the infant also is the mother's ability to pick up communications that are not only joy but also distress and to be able to hold and to feel that in herself, and then to regulate that and communicate back to the baby.

The idea about being able to hold the pleasure and the pain really is the key to this. In the cases of other intimate dyads, this also applies. A number of clinicians are now focusing on the same right brain psychobiological mechanisms in work with couples. The couples' therapist who is working with attachment is able to hold the dyad, to regulate each member of the dyad. She's also facilitating and reading nonverbal emotional communications within the dyad and bringing to awareness affective moments in which they are engaging and disengaging, and switching between various emotional states.

The therapeutic action with couples is to allow each member to become more aware of these rapid automatic processes and how each is communicating or blocking transmissions from the other. As always, the clinical principle is to follow the affect, especially authentic affect, whether positive or negative. And again, rupture and repair are important contexts for right brain development and emotional growth. But even beyond couples therapy, interpersonal neurobiology and affective neuroscience are now being incorporated into group psychotherapy. The focus is on what group members are communicating beneath the words, at conscious and unconscious levels, and how right brain emotional communications and regulatory transactions are occurring in the group relational context.

So, although the emotional contact between humans originates in the mother-infant dyad, it ultimately becomes the way in which individual human beings communicate with other human beings. These deeper communications and miscommunications have little to do with left brain language functions. They have more to do with right brain abilities to nonconsciously read the spontaneous facial expression, tone of voice, and gestures of other humans.

SELF-REGULATION, CO-REGULATION, AND BUDDHISM

DB: Are Buddhist ideas of the self/nonself of interest to you? Or do you get all you need from psychoanalytic thought and neuroscience?

AS: Most of my ideas about the self come from neuroscience and psychoanalysis, including Jung and others. But the idea of self/non-self and multiple self-states has been a focus. In current relational psychoanalytic writings, the concept that comes closest to my own is Philip Bromberg's idea about multiplicity of self-states: that we all have a variety of self-states associated with different affects and motivations. Some of these are operating on a conscious level, others of these on unconscious levels. He calls these latter states "not-me" states as opposed to "me" states (a concept he borrowed from Harry Stack Sullivan).

Depending on context, we nonconsciously switch through these states. Each of these self-states is tied into a motivational system (e.g., fear, aggression, shame, depression, joy). In other words, when threatened, the fear motivational system is triggered. My right brain is attending to and tracking the external threat outside. In that self-state, noradrenaline and adrenaline is higher, cortisol is elevated, the physiology and attentional systems are altered. The memory system is also altered. When the threat passes or I've regulated and coped with it, I become relieved and switch into another self-state, say a quiet alert state or a positively valenced exploratory state. So due to self-regulating mechanisms, we switch through these self-states. Resilience and flexibility is the adaptive ability to fluidly switch depending on what is occurring in the context and what is meaningful at that point in time.

On the matter of Buddhism's concept of self—that self-state of consciousness that is associated with meditation, as I understand the concept, aims to control and still the fluctuations of the mind. The self (mind, awareness) identifies itself with fluctuating patterns of consciousness. Yoga, for example, is a form of mastering or eliminating such fluctuations and the attainment of stable concentration of attention and nonattachment to sensory experiences. With practice, a change from evaluative to nonevaluative self-monitoring occurs during meditation. That said, neuroscience studies show that "compassionate meditation" does have more of a right brain, limbic focus.

I've written that self-regulation can take two forms: interactive regulation in affiliative interconnected contexts, and autoregulation in autonomous contexts. In yoga, the meditating self is acting as an autoregulatory system. My interests in development and in psychotherapy are relational, so I've been more interested in interactive regulation that occurs between human beings.

That said, the key is being able to switch between these two modes of self-regulation. Both of these derive from the early interactive regulation of the attachment relationship. Going inward to control emotion is different from reaching outward to others at moments of loss or joy. The inability to emotionally connect with others is at the core of any relational affect-focused psychotherapy. As I look at the significant problems of the larger world, I'm convinced that we need more connection, not separation and autonomy. For me, where we are in this world right now, really what we desperately need, what's being thinned down on a daily basis, is this capacity for interactive regulation.

We also have the problem that the U.S. and Western cultures emphasize the value of autonomous and independent personalities; they are highly valued over interdependent ones. As I mentioned, the left hemisphere is associated with power and competitiveness, the right with affiliation and pro-social motivations. So, again, that's the reason why I've been more interested in the higher right hemisphere, which processes not only emotional states and higher cognitive functions but also spiritual and moral experiences. It is here in the right where the self is transcended, where the self becomes larger and expanded. In these states, the grandiosity of the self literally is collapsed down, and there is some understanding that one is part of a much larger organism, a much larger sense of being alive. This sounds like the Buddhist autoregulatory self-state.

But let me repeat, interactive regulation is the key to the therapeutic alliance. There is now a push into the relational trend in all forms of psychotherapy. Actually, in psychoanalysis the relational emphasis has always been there. I'm thinking of Ferenczi, Jung,

Kohut, and more recently relational intersubjective psychoanalysis. This relational trend now is coming into mainstream psychology and is seen as the central mechanism of psychotherapy.

I point this out because psychologists can be teaching meditative skills but can also be accessing relational expertise in the therapeutic alliance.

DB: But they better also have those mindfulness skills themselves so they can be present to receive all of what's coming in the interaction rather than kind of stereotypically looking through this variety of theories or thinking of what to do next or how to be.

AS: Right. But I suggested that a certain form of mindfulness, including a bodily awareness, must take place in a relational context. The idea being that there are certain parts of the self that cannot be discovered, that cannot come into awareness, unless they are being mirrored by another human being.

DB: Ah! So it's not just that the relational trauma that gets dissociated can be healed through the relational—there's a Yiddish term "fargin" that means, "joining someone's joy." I love that concept.

AS: That's a great cultural metaphor—sharing someone's joy as well as pain.

A THIRD SUBJECTIVITY

DB: So there may be feelings that you are not going to fully experience until you see them mirrored in a reciprocal emotional interaction.

AS: Exactly. One of the central concepts that I've written about is resonance. In physics, a property of resonance is the tendency of one resonance system to enlarge and amplify through matching the resonance frequency pattern of another resonance system. In psychology, a state of resonance exists when one person's subjectivity is empathically attuned to another's inner state, and this resonance then interactively amplifies, in both intensity and duration, the affective state in both members of the dyad. This resonance can occur rapidly at levels beneath conscious awareness, and it generates what has been called "a third subjectivity." For example, in mutual play states, dyadic resonance ultimately permits the inter-coordination of positive affective brain states, shared joy, which increases curiosity and exploration.

DB: What you just described might also be related to what my Zen friends call "one mind." There's a great quote sometimes attributed to E. E. Cummings about this: "We do not believe in ourselves until someone reveals that something deep inside us is valuable, worth listening to, worthy of our trust, sacred to our touch. Once we believe in ourselves we can risk curiosity, wonder, spontaneous delight or any experience that reveals the human spirit."

AS: Yes, again, it's more than mirroring, it's an intensification of positive arousal and thereby an energetic mechanism, which is a form of interactive regulation.

DB: And it's also accounting for my increasing enjoyment of this interview versus a little bit of anticipatory anxiety about talking with you in the very beginning. But it quickly became exceedingly enjoyable. Can you discuss the variability of people in terms of quiet versus very active internal experiences—either auditory and verbal, some other form of thought, or visually active consciousness in contrast to people who have a naturally occurring or developed quiet mind?

AS: Sure. The first thing that comes to mind is what has been termed as "the quiet alert state." This is the flexible state that the mother accesses to pick up her infant's varying emotional expressions. It's associated with a state of autonomic balance between the

energy-expending sympathetic and energy-conserving parasympathetic branches of the autonomic nervous system. Within attachment communications, the caregiver sets the ranges of arousal, the
set points of the infant's resting quiet alert state. It's relationally
tuned and later affects the individual brain's default state. In other
words, regulation is the key to the quiet mind.

But I'm also thinking about right- and left-hemispheric balance
and individual differences in "hemisphericity." For example in a
resting state, right hemisphericity can be assoicated with a quiet
alert state. But it can also be associated with a history of more frequent negative affect, lower self-esteem, and difficulties in affect
regulation. Greater left hemisphericity, on the other hand, is associated with heavy inhibition of the right brain, repression of emotions,
and overregulation of disturbances. Consciousness is dominated by
continual left brain chatter, and thereby an inability to be emotionally present, to be "in the moment." There are individuals for whom
that chatter is always so intense, so continual, and even so loud
they cannot quietly be with themselves. They can't tolerate internal
silence, and so they can't monitor what's coming from the body and
from deeper strata of the unconscious. They're always in a state of
"doing" rather than "being."

DB: And they have difficulty experiencing their bodies and can't
even tell you what they're sensing or maybe even how they're feeling
because it's just pure thought.

AS: Right. When it comes to emotion and emotion dysregulation, for
a long time people were thinking only about underregulation, that
the emotions are so powerful and so strong that they interfere with
the logical and rational capacities of the left hemisphere. But there is
also another problematic state—where it's overregulated. In that case,
the person is habitually packing down emotions, out of awareness,
and whose left hemisphere is so dominant that it's always "in control." Such individuals "live in the left" and use words to move away

from affect. They're talking about rather than experiencing emotion, from the other side of the callosal divide, not actually allowing themselves to disinhibit the right and to feel what is in the body. And yet, "the body keeps the score." In the most extreme cases, they're dissociative and alexithymic. These are patients who use words in order not to feel; they are overinhibited and susceptible to overregulation disturbances. Think about overly rational, insecure, avoidant personalities who overemphasize verbal cognition and dismiss emotion. Returning to our earlier discussions of recent changes in the science of affect, dysregulation can be either underregulation or overregulation, an avoidance strategy versus an anxious strategy.

IMAGERY

DB: Coincidental with that, I've noticed there are people, such as myself, who are minimally or not at all visual in their memory. Aldous Huxley described this about himself in *Doors of Perception*. If I were trying to visualize my living room, I would say it's like 10% clear.

Other people I know are eidetic or photographic in their imagery. People who have that kind of visual memory can also have vivid imagery intrusively interfere in the present, where a person would be walking downtown and, instead of having a thought or worry that a bus might hit a particular woman, he would see the bus hitting her. Or he would visualize a building falling down—all-intruding upon his peace of mind, as you can imagine.

AS: A few things come to mind from your observations. The classical idea of brain laterality is that the right processes visual and spatial images while the left is involved in language.

But when it comes to imagery, the truth is we forget much of the time that imagery can be in any modality. We usually think about the visual image, as in your example of someone having an image of a bus hitting a pedestrian or a building falling. Or a patient will come up with metaphors that are loaded with visual images. Also think of visual images of faces, especially emotionally expressive faces. But imagery can also be auditory—as when our consciousness becomes aware of a song melody or olfactory images, of an emotionally evocative smell or odor.

So, for those of us who are highly auditory, like both of us, we used to think that was verbal. But as you know, there are nonverbal auditory cues. Aside from the verbal content, the voice itself is communicating essential information, even more important in an intimate moment than the verbal. Most psychotherapists are highly auditory and attuned and very sensitive to even slight changes in the prosodic tone of voice of the patient. It's at that point where we will lean in, so to speak. But we also use our voice as a regulatory tool. In a well-timed moment, we intuitively and spontaneously express our calming and soothing voice, or at other times we'll come in with a more energizing voice, or even a limit-setting voice. Or we're expressing an auditory metaphorical image.

So I think that when we talk about imagery, especially emotional imagery, we're usually thinking of visual images. But there also are tactile images. As in an image of what it feels like at this moment, including what it feels like in your body and in my body, because I can pick this up and put that together with another's facial expression.

But also there's a difference between implicit visual recognition and explicit visual recall. I may not be able to have a conscious memory of a visual representation. But if there's a subtle change in an emotional expression on a patient's face, I can pick it up quickly. And let's remember that when it comes to processing the meaning of nonverbal facial and auditory expressions, this is not occurring at conscious awareness. These interpersonal cues that denote changes in affects and subjectivity are detected and tracked by the right amygdala, at levels beneath awareness. Again, we're listening beneath the words, and these signals are triggering unconscious memory systems of various sensory modalities—auditory and tactile, as well as vision.

DB: Hmmm, it just struck me that I often say that I'm not visual. But I must be visual in my right hemisphere because I have these wonderful, clear, visual dreams.

AS: I agree. Remember with the right brain, you're talking about not only long-term visual memory, but also ultra-short working memory, what has been called the visuo-spatial sketchpad. We hold a momentary image in consciousness long enough to see if it matches with our memory of affectively charged, personally meaningful experiences. At a reunion, when you emotionally see your daughter's face, your right brain can immediately detect that there's something wrong or that she's experiencing shame or joy. That right brain function is essential to our ability to be in close relationships. Someone who is mind-blind to facial expressions will have problems with intimacy.

ALONE IN THE PRESENCE OF ANOTHER

DB: I think back to your former student and couples therapist Stan Tatkin, who has made the point that our partner often knows things about us by looking at our face before we're aware of what we are feeling, which brings us back to the reasonableness of trying to grow with affect co-regulation versus only self-soothing and all of that through meditation. But is there a name for something that would be like co-meditating? I know we're talking about co-regulation.

AS: Well now I'm thinking about Winnicott's idea about being alone in the presence of the other. Remember?

DB: No!

AS: Winnicott talked about the child in the second year achieving a complex developmental advance—the adaptive ability to be alone, and the creation of true autonomy. That is, to be separate, to be processing one's own individuality and one's own self-system in the presence of another. The other is a background presence, so it doesn't get swept into the child. But they're literally both individuating in their presence together. And this is a kind of silent being together without having a need to take care of the other or support the other, of literally that kind of comfort.

So, on the one hand there is the joining of joy, which would be more active so to speak. And on the other hand there is this idea about being alone in the presence of the other, which is more passive. The self-system has stability at that point in time. It can shift out of that state if it needs to, but again, I would suggest to you that comes close to what you're talking about. And that gets into the importance of solitude, the importance of privacy, which in this day and age is being completely forgotten. The poet Rilke said so eloquently, "For one human being to love another, that is perhaps the most difficult of all our tasks, the ultimate, the last test and proof, the work for which all other is but preparation. I hold this to be the highest task for a bond between two people: that each protects the solitude of the other."

REPAIR IN RELATIONSHIP, AND RETURNING TO THE MATTER OF LOVE

DB: I wonder if you would agree with a quote from Kierkegaard when he said "perfect love is learning to love the very one that has made you unhappy." Does that resonate with you at all?

AS: Absolutely the case.

DB: Anything that you would modify?

AS: In my recent lectures, I'm describing the interpersonal neurobiological emergence of mutual love between the mother and infant.

Studies on the functional neuroanatomy of maternal love document that the loving mother is capable of empathizing and feeling in her own body what the baby feels in his body, whether it be a joy state as well as a pain state. When the securely attached mother is in the fMRI scanner viewing emotional videos of her infant in a joy state or in a cry state, positive emotions such as love and motherly feeling coexisted with negative ones such as anxious feeling and worry in the mother herself.

Other studies show that insecure dismissive-avoidant mothers cannot hold the distressed baby's painful negative states. The narcissistic mother only stays connected when the baby is mirroring back a positive state, and this mother is unable to tolerate and repair shame states. So this ability to hold onto both positive and negative affect and not engage in splitting is essential. In fact, in developmental studies, Ed Tronick has shown that even the secure mother is only attuned about 30% of the time. The key is not only the misattunement, but the interactive repair. These misattunements are common—my colleague Philip Bromberg describes frequent collisions of subjectivities within an intimate dyad.

Returning to our earlier discussion, it's the ability to interactively repair these collisions that allows for the strengthening of an emotional connection between an intimate couple. Clinically, it's the emerging ability of the therapeutic dyad to co-create and co-regulate ruptures that allows us to tolerate the negative transference and strengthen the positive transference—to move together from positive to negative and back to positive affective states. That really strengthens the bond, and it leads to resilience. For me that's what Kierkegaard's intuition is describing.

DB: Ah.

AS: But while the moments of emotional connection are important, so are the moments of shared solitude, of being alone in the presence of the other, moments of shared silence. It's very limiting to think that everything has to be filled with words or interpretations.

For some therapists, when there's too much silence they'll start to fill it up with words, for their own regulatory needs. The matter that I'm raising here is that attachment is about the capacity for intimacy. Are intimacy and the capacity for mutual love expanded in long-term psychotherapy? Can patients use what they've experienced in therapy to expand the abilities for forming close and personally meaningful bonds with others, as in deep friendships and long-term romantic relationships? Can they use these relationships as a source of more intense brain/mind/body interactive regulation and autoregulation, and therefore have both interdependence and autonomy?

Both clinical theory and interpersonal neurobiology agree that in optimal social emotional environments, the self-system evolves to more and more complexity. Not only the growth of the left brain conscious mind but also the right brain unconscious mind can be enriched and expanded in deep psychotherapy. By emotionally interacting with other right brains, a secure right brain self can continue to grow and develop to more complexity over the later Eriksonian stages of the life span. The secure self is not a static end state but a continually expanding dynamic system that is capable of both stability and change.

Freud said that, in the end, therapy, and indeed life, was about love and work. Today we might think about that in terms of the expression of the development of the affiliative right and agentic left brains. My work has been an exploration of the primacy of the emotional development of the right brain over the life span. In *The Art of Loving*, Eric Fromm described the intense emotional experience of love as "the experience of union with another being" and proposed that "beloved people can be incorporated into the self." Here's an example of self-expansion that occurs within and between two people.

DB: Well, that's all a lovely way to end. I'll respect your own need for solitude by finishing up this conversation, but I would like to close with asking about your current activities. You're still meeting in several cities with students?

AS: Yes. For almost two decades I've continued to meet with study groups here in Los Angeles. I also have ongoing groups in Berkeley-Alameda, as well as Boulder, and in the Northwest.

DB: In Seattle?

AS: Yes, I Skype with clinicians and researchers in Seattle, Vancouver, and Portland. I'm about to start a Skype group in Australia, also.

DB: Well, all of this time with you, at both a personal and professional level has been delightful. So, thank you so much. I'm sure people are going to enjoy what you brought to today's discussion.

AS: Same on my side, and thanks for today, David. I also greatly enjoyed this back-and-forth dialogue. As you said at the beginning, the key was to have a spontaneous conversation.

CHAPTER 9

Looking Back and Looking Forward: Our Professional and Personal Journey

Keynote Address to the 2014 UCLA Conference,
"Affect Regulation and the Healing of the Self"

THE PAST 3 DAYS have been amongst the most special in my life. They've been special because this occasion provides me the extraordinary experience of receiving direct tangible feedback from my colleagues and peers on this stage and across the country, people I highly value, about the impact of my studies on their own. What a unique and wonderful gift. Despite what on the surface looks like different areas of work, all of these presenters share an intention to use rapidly accumulating scientific and clinical knowledge in order to more deeply understand and indeed better the human condition—no small goal. And I admire the dedication and the courage of each of them. But this occasion is also special because it's happening here at UCLA, with an audience of so many colleagues and friends. I've presented here 13 times, since 1998, the end of the past century, and this conference has allowed me to share the continued development of my ideas and get audience feedback even before they were published, a valuable context for the ongoing development of the body of my work.

This weekend also heightens my awareness of the passage of time, along the course of living one's life. Last month, somehow, *without my permission*, I turned 71, which to ease the shock my mind turned into a "dyslexic 17." One of the conscious goals that runs throughout my life is to remain emotionally and intellectually open to the future, what Bob Dylan calls forever young. But I'm now at a stage in which there is even more *looking backward, into the past,* especially in light of the 20th anniversary of a central moment in my life. In that spirit I'd like to share with you some personal thoughts about the creation of *Affect Regulation and the Origin of the Self* in 1994, and the events even before it that set the foundation of the path that has guided everything from that point of origin.

Earlier, in a stage when *looking forward* was intense, in my late thirties, a husband and a father of two young children, I set out to "write something." Even before that something had a specific shape, I intuitively understood, at both a surface and a deeper level, that the time had come to actively begin the venture. And so in 1980 I began what would turn out to be a 10-year period of independent study, 10 years before I would put pen to paper (note the late-20th-century now almost obsolete reference). In the preceding decade, the 1970s, a time when I had the valuable experience of being the patient in a psychotherapeutic process, I dutifully put in my 10,000 hours of clinical work and had developed some expertise and confidence in the professions in which I was trained, clinical psychology and clinical neuropsychology. But in parallel, my up-close therapeutic work with patients fueled a rapidly growing intense curiosity about the relational processes of psychotherapy—which at the time took the form of the question, "How do minds and brains touch and shape other minds and brains." In order to clear out the substantial amounts of time for this continuing education and self-study, I left my clinical position at the Psychiatry Department at Kaiser Permanente and cut back my private practice from 5 to 3 days. All with Judy's support—even more than emotional support, hard-cash financial support. We switched income responsibilities, and for the entire decade of the 1980s my period of independent study was financed by a Judy Schore grant.

Judy has told you something about my visits to the Cal State Northridge library, just a mile from our home. For about three out of four Saturdays for 10 years, I roamed through the stacks, in a state of pleasurable exploration, like a child in a candy store (again pardon the mid-20th-century reference), back and forth between sections of psychological, psychiatric, biological, chemical, and even physical sciences. When Beth and David were old enough, they'd come along, riding their bicycles on the campus while I immersed myself in journal after journal, and doling out huge numbers of quarters into voracious copying machines. What is most important is that I brought the knowledge back to my home, which is where the careful analysis and synthesis of the knowledge took place. Another 10,000 hours, expanding the evolving science of my earlier education, but this time not at a university but in my home.

Meanwhile I continued to see patients, many of them in long-term psychotherapeutic explorations. What I was learning from them (and about myself) was developing in parallel to my second scientific education. The process of extended "self-study" involved not only the independent, solitary processing of large amounts of external knowledge, but also reflecting upon the increasing knowledge about my own internal emotional world. And perhaps an even greater source was my ongoing development as a husband, father, son, and friend. It is no coincidence that my application of science to the understanding of the most personal and deepest aspects of the human condition was created in the intimate context of my home, and not in an academic institution. Everything I have created about development, and attachment, about subjectivity and intersubjectivity, about shame and joy, about brain and mind has occurred in the close quarters of my life. Which is why my work had to explore subjective emotions and close relationships, at both the conscious and unconscious levels.

Led almost entirely by my curiosity (a personal trait that had been nurtured from my early beginnings under the watchful eye of my loving mother, Barbara Schore) and absolutely trusting my intuition in deciding what to read beyond the fields in which I was trained, for 10 years I enjoyed long states of play, out there in the library and back at my home office. I was acting out in daily life my long-held wish to become a scholar. But a particular kind of scholar. And here I looked backward. My father, George Schore, my role model in so many areas of my life, was a chemical engineer, an applied scientist, an international expert in metal finishing and water pollution, and had numerous patents on electroplating copper and gold recovery processes. In 1976, he had received an award from the Environmental Protection Agency "in recognition of having contributed major efforts and demonstrated a significant advancement in our Nation's continuing struggle for environmental pollution abatement." The plaque hangs in my office. His work was always at the cutting edge, and even ahead of its time. His career, like mine, significantly changed at several points in his life. So I was exposed to the mind of a creative scientist who was continually translating advances in basic chemical science into practical applications.

When I was 21 years old, between college graduation and my postgraduate education, I spent about a year working with my father. At that time he was designing and building the first automated metal finishing systems and sold them to, amongst others, General Electric, General Motors, and IBM. I continued to learn from him. But on one particular occasion he taught me something that was to become invaluable. I went with him to Tampa, Florida, where he was giving a sales presentation to build an automation system for Honeywell, the manufacturer of thermostats (yes, temperature *regulators*). I have a strong visual memory of the room, of my father in the center of a long table, facing seven scientists and executives. I watched him effortlessly field questions posed by an electrical engineer, a chemical engineer, a mechanical engineer, a water pollution expert, and vice presidents from three different departments. He was going back and forth answering each of their technical questions, talking about the automation system in terms of its impact on all of these different fields, and then integrating that information into a system specifically tailored to their needs.

In that "Aha!" moment of recognition and insight, I saw my father in the role of a polymath, and I thought, that's the professional mind that I admired and needed to nurture in myself, one that knows the language of and can communicate with a number of different professions. An ability to fluidly move between disciplines would become the prototype for my burgeoning career as a scholar. This synthetic, integrative approach was opposed to the then (and still) dominant role of specialization and an increased narrowing into one's field. This affectively imprinted autobiographical memory later naturally evolved into an interdisciplinary perspective that pervades all my work. And so I would create a theoretical model that could not only describe but integrate various scientific disciplines—that would chart the points of contact between psychology and psychiatry, biology and chemistry. Early development and emotion would turn out to be a common factor.

So in 1980, as I began the independent study, I had a theoretical perspective to process and understand the various literatures I would encounter. But on a practical level, I had to create a structure that self-organized my time and an environment that could support and allow for the growth of my creativity. The routine I came up with was to visit the library on the weekend, return with 30–40 xeroxed articles, and then spend the weekdays taking notes on each in 100-sheet, 8½ by 11 legal pads. Every third or fourth notebook I found myself recording repeating patterns across fields and began to integrate different research literatures, especially developmental biology, developmental neurochemistry, and developmental psychology. And meanwhile, I'm shuttling between my study and consulting room, where I'm focusing more and more on the relational processes that lie at the core of psychotherapy.

The work expanded my skills as a clinician-scientist, a term that best fit the professional identity I was creating. The scientist part was expressed in careful observations about the patient's and my own subjectivities, especially about the emotional interactions between us, including our internal worlds. But the emerging scientist was also extremely careful about the kinds of evidence that I found convincing and would later use to develop an interdisciplinary theoretical model. My focus was on the boundaries between fields, and the commonalities that lie beneath what appear on the surface to be unrelated phenomena. I became especially confident putting my money on certain organizing principles and theoretical concepts that cut across different sciences. And so when I found the construct of regulation to lie at the core of chemistry, physics, and biology, I knew that any overarching developmental or clinical model could be centered in that.

For 10 years, I was frequently and routinely in a positive state of play, of flow, both intellectually and emotionally. I became very adept at transitioning between different scientific and clinical literatures, at moving between brain and mind, and by 5 years in I became absolutely confident that by creating a theoretical model of emotion and human relationships that integrated psychology and biology, I could *alter the course of clinical practice, and indeed science.* That was the phrase that literally came to mind. And even though my self-image is basically to be a modest man, again something I learned from my father, I became comfortable with that explicit sense of conviction and confidence, even certainty in the power of the model my mind was creating.

I should mention that over the decade, I engaged in one other activity, in order to create an environment that could support my creativity and imagination. At the very outset, I chose to return to the piano. When I was a child, I dabbled with the piano for a couple of years. Now in my late thirties, I took lessons, as an adult. I wanted to not just listen to but create music, and thereby bring music into my homemade ivory tower. I was aware that the music would allow me to understand something in my fingers, in my body, and not just in my mind. I was learning that science, and emotions in particular, were not apprehended just through logical understanding. I also wanted to learn how to visualize what I was learning, to think in images as well as thoughts. Later I realized my intent was to involve my self in exercises that tapped specifically into my right brain, the source of creative processing. And along the way, I was able to give a pretty good imitation of a cocktail pianist. Again, exercises for shoring up (probably no pun intended) my right brain.

In order to come up with a fresh solution to the problems I was addressing, I realized that my right brain implicit learning processes played an even larger role than my familiar left brain approaches. From the outset, I decided never to explicitly memorize anything. And then I found that I had to expand my tolerance for the uncertainty of not knowing, to allow my mind to stay open long enough rather than prematurely closing down the exploratory process with what appeared to be a quick solution. In order to foster the creative process, I never deliberately attempted to intentionally solve anything in particular. Rather, I would just take in large amounts of salient information, with an intuitive bodily-based knack for knowing what is meaningful and essential information to the phenomenon I was attempting to understand. Ultimately, my right brain unconscious mind would recognize patterns, which then my left brain conscious mind would describe verbally. Frequently, these solutions took a visual form. More so than just describing data, at the most fundamental level I was attempting to not only understand different fields but to integrate them, and ultimately to describe underlying mechanisms.

By the end of the decade, the hundreds of legal pads stacked well over 6 feet high, and they contained long sections of detailed notes on research common to and overlapping different disciplines. So after 10 years, I made the decision, again intuitively, to end the period of solitary, independent study (as well as the piano). My plan was to write a psychoneurobiological formulation of emotional development, both in early life and in the therapeutic process I was observing in my practice. And now the next set of questions. How was I going to transport the work of science I had created in my garage (family room and study) into the real world? How could I establish my credentials in order to be offered a publishing contract for a book? I decided to write an article. But on what, and where would it appear?

Coincidentally, in the 1980s, Judy returned to academia for her PhD in clinical social work on a relatively unexplored clinical phenomenon, the emotion of shame. Now when it came to emotions, I found that the kind of work that I was doing with my patients, especially early disturbed patients, was all about emotion. Their interpersonal deficits were fundamentally deficits in coping with a wide array of emotions. I became very interested in the early forming nonverbal emotion of shame, which then led me to the early development of emotions *per se*, a then unchartered landscape in both the clinical and scientific literatures. In addition to becoming acquainted with the (meager) literature on bodily-based shame, I was also studying it clinically, in my work with narcissistic patients, and became convinced that working with this affect was essential to the treatment of all developmental disorders.

So Judy and I wrote an article together on shame and gender development. We submitted it to the *Journal of the American Psychoanalytic Association*, and they would have none of it. However, there was another psychoanalytic journal, one related to JAPA, *Psychoanalysis and Contemporary Thought*. With a sense of relief I noticed that on its editorial board were developmental psychoanalysts like Erik Erikson, Bob Emde, and Fred Pine. When I saw their names, I knew immediately that this journal would be a good fit. I wrote "Early Superego Development: The Emergence of Shame and Narcissistic Affect Regulation in the Practicing Period" and submitted it to that journal. The paper ended with neurobiological speculations about the early development of the right hemisphere. It was accepted immediately. As I look back, I view it as my first articulation of developmental neuropsychoanalysis, the study of the early development of the unconscious mind, as well as a regulation model of the neurobiology of attachment, themes that would become central in not only the 1994 book but also all my subsequent writings.

But I wanted more than to publish a paper—I wanted to come into direct contact and dialogue with the minds I admired. As soon as the shame paper came out, I sent reprints to 40 authors cited in it, and along with it a letter introducing my work and carefully tying it into their own. Incidentally, many of these were child and adult psychiatrists trained in psychoanalysis, like Stan Greenspan, Dan Stern, Jim Masterson, Henry Krystal, and especially Jim Grotstein, who helped me get established here in L.A. And later in that summer, this was about 1991, I got back about 35 letters, and I knew that I had connected into a group of peers, clinicians and theoreticians who were also convinced of the centrality of the developmental perspective. The psychoanalytic article succeeded because the reviewers and readers could evaluate evidence that was familiar to them, observations from both psychoanalytic clinicians and researchers about the early developing mind and inner world.

But now I needed to find out how neuroscientists would respond, and what types of "evidence" was meaningful for them. I needed their feedback, and so I decided to submit to a peer-reviewed neuroscience journal an expanded version of how the early mother-infant relationship was affecting the neurobiology of the developing brain. To get this feedback, I submitted an article to *Behavioral and Brain Sciences*. Although three of the reviewers accepted it, the editor-in-chief rejected it. But one reviewer, Carroll Izard, a major developmental psychologist who had worked with Silvan Tomkins, an early pioneer in the study of emotions, told me to focus less on psychoanalysis and more on John Bowlby's attachment theory, which was more palatable to scientists because of its connections to ethology. At the time I wasn't aware of the fact that 3 months before I offered that article, there was a severe critique of psychoanalysis in that journal.

But even the sting of the rejection was a learning experience. The emotional disappointment led me into parts of myself that I would later describe in my work. Instead of rationalizing the pain or avoiding the risk, or even using Judy to help me booster the injury to my self-esteem, I became aware that I just needed to allow myself to deflate and sink deeper into the momentary defeat. That became helpful to me. In other words, I allowed myself to experience not only the accelerating high-arousal play states, but also the decelerating low-arousal painful deflations. And I found that implicit processes other than my conscious mind would operate down there, and when they had run their course I'd come back up and continue forward. These experiences highlighted the fact that the ability to tolerate both positive and negative emotions was a fundamental aspect of emotional growth and development.

And so now at age 50, with a single journal publication under my belt, I sent a book proposal to a psychoanalytic publisher, Analytic Press, who then passed it along to their scientific division, Lawrence Erlbaum. As it went into the mail, I had the clear thought that everything I had accomplished in my life up to then would have little meaning unless this product of my mind would find a home at a publisher. They immediately accepted the book, although they had severe reservations that it would not sell because they felt that the people who were interested in the biology would not be interested in the psychology, the people who were interested in the psychiatry wouldn't care about the neuroscience, and so on. Remember the positive valence of the term "interdisciplinary" was not yet established when the book came out in 1994. Even so, my initial reaction was one of great relief. I felt that the previous decade had paid off, and that I said exactly what I wanted to say in the book. Indeed, not one word was changed by the copy editor in what turned out to be 700 pages, including 105 pages of 2,500 references.

In the spring of 1994, I got my hands on the book, and that summer I again used the feedback-communication device and wrote 60 letters, sending out many copies at my own expense. But this time in addition to psychiatrists and psychoanalysts, I wrote to neuroanatomists, neurochemists, brain researchers, cell biologists, developmental psychologists, et cetera, literally around the world. And again at the end of the summer, I got back about 50 letters, which I still have. I knew even before the book had "hit the streets" that it would get a good reception. The format of the book included citing a quotation from a major figure in each field at the beginning of every chapter. It was these experts I sent letters to, and when they responded so quickly I knew that it was a done deal. So soon after its birth, I remember thinking I could die now and have the satisfaction of knowing that I had accomplished what I set out to do, "to write something." And then the very positive journal reviews started to come in. The *British Journal of Psychiatry* called me "a polymath," something that had special meaning, and described the book as a "superb integrative work" with a depth and breadth that was "staggering." That brightened up my day.

The "Green Book" in essence was an argument for the power of integrating the psychological and the biological, the scientific and the clinical. The opening paragraph was meant at the time to be groundbreaking, if not revolutionary:

> The understanding of early development is one of the fundamental objectives of science. The beginnings of living systems set the stage for every aspect of an organism's internal and external functioning throughout the life span. Events that occur during infancy, especially transactions with the social environment, are indelibly imprinted into the structures that are maturing in the first years of life. The child's first relationship, the one with the mother, acts as a template, as it permanently molds the individual's capacities to enter into all later emotional relationships. These early experiences shape the development of a unique personality, its adaptive capacities as well as its vulnerabilities and resistances against particular forms of future pathologies. Indeed, they profoundly influence the emergent organization of an integrated system that is both stable and adaptable, and thereby the formation of the self.

I remember *knowing* that the book was at least 10 years ahead of the field, some parts 20 years, especially in terms of scientific research. What I didn't know was if other people would find "the first relationship," the maturation of the infant's brain, emotional development, and an affective description of the baby's emerging consciousness to be as fascinating as I did. I was also surprised that the book, which was written in the language of science, appealed to clinicians. This may be a surprise to some of you, but the book was not an easy read.

The year after the book was born, in 1995, I was invited to join a small group, mostly faculty at UCLA, who were studying how neuroscience could be integrated into psychiatry, psychology, psychoanalysis, and linguistics. And so for the next 2 years this group focused intently on just one volume— my Green Book. The other members of this seminal peer group—Dan Siegel, Lou Cozolino, Regina Paley, and John Schumann—were to write their own books on interpersonal neuroscience and neuropsychoanalysis by the end of the decade. In 1996, I joined the clinical faculty at the UCLA Medical School and also began my first in a number of study groups in Los Angeles, Seattle, Berkeley, Portland, Boulder, and Austin. These groups have since become important sources of feedback from experienced clinicians, as well as of new questions that I later addressed in my writings. The groups have also been a context in which I mentored numerous other professionals. Many began their own writing careers, and a number became Norton authors.

But from the beginning, the book brought another instant bonus— invitations from influential journal editors in a number of different fields. These invitations from high-level developmental, psychiatric, psychoanalytic, and neuroscience peer-reviewed journals allowed me to impact a much larger readership than the book itself and gave me a wide exposure across a wide range of disciplines. This single work also brought me invitations to be a reviewer for or on the editorial boards of dozens of journals, which in turn allowed me to influence the direction of both experimental research *and* clinical models. It also was the generator of numerous invitations to lecture nationally and internationally, and thereby an opportunity to offer my ideas to audiences both here and around the world. If the problem of emotion had been ignored by science for most of the past century, by the end of the 1990s the clinical audiences I was addressing became aware of and indeed very interested in how to apply the new information about bodily-based affect and affect regulation into their work with patients.

As "the decade of the brain" progressed, a rapidly expanding interest in the neurobiology of attachment and in early brain development allowed me to present to dozens of conferences, where I could share ideas with a large number of leading neuroscientists and prominent clinical writers. Many of these people later presented at this UCLA Lifespan Conference. Thanks to Marion Solomon, these UCLA conferences have attained an international reputation for cutting-edge themes and for presenting an intellectual context that allows for an ongoing dialogue between leading neuroscientists, prominent clinicians, and an extremely well-informed audience. But perhaps the most unexpected bonus of the work was the creation, at a later stage of life, of deep friendships with so many colleagues of not only like minds, but like hearts (including many people here in the audience).

Over the past 20 years, my daily life has been profoundly changed yet in some important ways remains the same. I continue to set aside large amounts of time every day for reading and poring over new studies over a broad spectrum of disciplines. Sitting at my desk, I have instant access to every University of California library. The fact that the body of my work has been cited in Google Scholar in well over 10,000 publications over a broad range of scientific and clinical disciplines is a source of great pride. I still see patients in my home office because everything I create in science must ring true clinically. This homemade ivory tower has become the context that allows for the collaborative research with colleagues in different disciplines, some of whom have presented this weekend. It also is the locus of my work as editor of the Norton Series, as well as a reviewer of dozens of journals. Through these various activities, my conscious and unconscious minds are continually stimulated, challenged, and surprised by novel and intrinsically interesting information.

What I learned early on about the organic needs of my imagination continue to be expressed. Looking forward, my curiosity is now turning to, amongst other problems, the early assessment of both attachment and infantile autism, the lifelong impact of love on the right brain, the development of the deep unconscious and the survival functions of the right amygdala, the central role of mitochondrial energy systems in brain functioning, and continued studies of the subtle yet fundamental mechanisms that underlie the psychotherapeutic healing of the self.

Along the course of my personal journey, things have dramatically changed yet remain constant. In addition to the work, the greatest constancy comes from my relationship with Judy. The essential nature of the support that she provides continues to sustain my intellectual *and* emotional needs. The Green Book and everything that has naturally evolved from it has taken us to most of the states in this country and around the world many, many times. Our early investment has paid off nicely, in a tremendously exciting "quiet life." In the Acknowledgments of the 1994 book I said of her, "Through her intellectual keenness and emotional honesty, she continues to reflect and reveal to me those reciprocal emotional processes that are, willingly and unwillingly, most clearly exposed in an intimate human relationship." As I look back, I see this as an attempt to describe the loving bond we've created. This weekend has been an extraordinary "wing to wing" experience for Judy and I. We thank you, colleagues and friends, for this special gift.

References

Aberg, K.C., Doell, K.C., & Schwartz, S. (2017). The "creative right brain" revisited: Individual creativity and associative priming in the right hemisphere relate to hemispheric asymmetries in reward brain function. *Cerebral Cortex, 27*, 4946-4959.

Abraham, A. (2013). The promises and perils of the neuroscience of creativity. *Frontiers in Human Neuroscience, 7.* doi:10.3389/fnhum.2013.00246

Ackerman, S. J., Hilsenroth, M. J., & Knowles, E. S. (2005). Ratings of therapist dynamic activities and alliance early and late in psychotherapy. *Psychotherapy: Theory, Research, Training, 42*, 225-231.

Ainsworth, M. D. S. (1967). *Infancy in Uganda: Infant care and the growth of love.* Baltimore, MD: Johns Hopkins University Press.

Allison, K. L., & Rossouw, P. J. (2013). The therapeutic alliance: Exploring the concept of "safety" from a neuropsychotherapeutic perspective. *International Journal of Neuropsychotherapy, 1*, 21–29.

Allman, J. M., Watson, K. K., Tetreault, N. A., & Hakeem, A. Y. (2005). Intuition and autism: A possible role for Von Economo neurons. *Trends in Cognitive Sciences, 9*, 367–373.

Alvarez, A. (2006). Some questions concerning states of fragmentation: Unintegration, under-integration, disintegration, and the nature of early integrations. *Journal of Child Psychotherapy, 32*, 158–180.

Ammaniti, M., & Trentini, C. (2009). How new knowledge about parenting reveals the neurobiological implications of intersubjectivity: A conceptual synthesis of recent research. *Psychoanalytic Dialogues, 19*, 537–555.

Anders, S., Heinzle, J., Weiskopf, N., Ethofer, T., & Haynes, J. D. (2011). Flow of affective information between communicating brains. *NeuroImage, 54*, 439–446.

Anderson, M. C., Ochsner, K. N., Kuhl, B., Cooper, J., Robertson, E., Gabrielli, S. W., Glover, G. H., & Gabrieli, J. D. E. (2004). Neural systems underlying the suppression of unwanted memories. *Science, 303*, 232–235.

Andrade, V. M. (2005). Affect and the therapeutic action in psychoanalysis. *International Journal of Psychoanalysis, 86*, 677–697.

Andreasen, P. J., O'Leary, D. S., Cizadlo, T., Arndt, S., Rezai, K., Watkins, G. L.,

Boles Ponto, L. L., & Hichwa, R. D. (1995). Remembering the past: Two facets of episodic memory explored with positron emission tomography. *American Journal of Psychiatry, 152*, 1576–1585.

APA Presidential Task Force on Evidence-Based Practice. (2006). Evidence-based practice in psychology. *American Psychologist, 61*, 271–285.

Arlow, J. A., & Brenner, C. (1964). *Psychoanalytic concepts and the structural theory.* New York, NY: International Universities Press.

Arnold, K. (2007). The creative unconscious, the unknown self, and the haunting melody: Notes on Reik's theory of inspiration. *Psychoanalytic Review, 94*, 431–445.

Aron, L. (1998). The clinical body and the reflexive mind. In L. Aron & F. Sommer Anderson (Eds.), *Relational perspectives on the body* (pp. 3–37). Hillsdale, NJ: Analytic Press.

Asari, T., Konishi, S., Jimura, K., Chikazoe, J., Nakamura, N., & Miyashita, Y. (2008). Right temporopolar activation associated with unique perception. *NeuroImage, 41*, 145–152.

Aspland, H., Llewelyn, S., Hardy, G. E., Barkham, M., & Stiles, W. (2008). Alliance rupture resolution in cognitive-behavior therapy: A preliminary task analysis. *Psychotherapy Research, 18*, 699–710.

Bach, S. (1985). *Narcissistic states and the therapeutic process.* New York, NY: Jason Aronson.

Bach, S. (2003). A mind of one's own: Some observations on disorders of thinking. In R. Lansky (Ed.), *Symbolization and desymbolization: Essays in honor of Norbert Freedman* (pp. 387-406). New York, NY: Other Press.

Balint, M. (1968). *The basic fault: Therapeutic aspects of aggression.* London, UK: Tavistock.

Balter, L., Lothane, Z., & Spencer, J. R., Jr. (1980). On the analyzing instrument. *Psychoanalytic Quarterly, 49*, 474–504.

Barrett, J., Wonch, K. E., Gonzalez, A., Ali, N., Steiner, M., Hall, G. B., & Fleming, A. S. (2012). Maternal affect and quality of parenting experiences are related to amygdala response to infant faces. *Social Neuroscience, 7*, 252–268.

Barron, F., & Harrington, D. M. (1981). Creativity, intelligence, and personality. *Annual Review of Psychology, 32*, 439–476.

Barsness, R. (Ed.). (2017). *Core competencies of relational psychoanalysis.* New York, NY: Routledge.

Bartels, A., & Zeki, S. (2004). The neural correlates of maternal and romantic love. *NeuroImage, 21*(3), 1155–1166.

Bartz, J. A., & Hollander, E. (2006). The neuroscience of affiliation: Forging links between basic and clinical research on neuropeptides and social behavior. *Hormones and Behavior, 50*, 518–528.

Basch, M. F. (1983). The perception of reality and the disavowal of meaning. *Annual Review of Psychoanalysis, 11*, 125–154.

Beauregard, M., Levesque, J., & Bourgouin, P. (2001). Neural correlates of conscious self regulation of emotion. *Journal of Neuroscience, 21*, R165.

Beebe, B. (1986). Mother-infant mutual influence and precursors of self- and object-representations. In Masling, J. (Ed.). *Empirical studies of psychoanalytic theories* (Vol. 2, pp. 27–48). Hillsdale NJ: Erlbaum.

Beebe, B., Jaffe, J., Feldstein, S., Mays, K., & Alson, D. (1985). Interpersonal timing: The application of an adult dialogue model to mother-infant vocal and kinesic interactions. In Field, T. (Ed.). *Social perception in infants* (pp. 217–247). New York: Ablex.

Beebe, F. & Stern. D. (1977). Engagement-disengagement and early object experiences. In N. Freeman & S. Grand (Eds.), *Communicative structures and psychic structures* (pp. 35–55). New York, NY: Plenum.

Beebe, F., & Lachmann, F. (2014). *The origins of attachment: Infant research and adult treatment.* New York, NY: Routledge.

Beebe, F., Stern, D., & Jaffe, J. (1979). The kinesic rhythm of mother-infant interactions. In A. W. Siegman and S. Feldstein (Eds.), *Of speech and time: Temporal speech patterns in interpersonal contexts* (pp. 23–34). Hillsdale, NJ: Erlbaum.

Benowitz, L. I., Bear, D. M., Rosenthal, R., Mesulam, M.-M., Zaidel, E., & Sperry, R. W. (1983). Hemispheric specialization in nonverbal communication *Cortex, 19,* 5–11.

Bergman, N. J., Linley, L. L., & Fawcus, S. R. (2004). Randomized controlled trial of skin-to-skin contact from birth versus conventional incubator for physiological stabilization in 1200- to 2199-gram newborns. *Acta Paediatrica, 93,* 779–785.

Bhattacharya, J., & Petsche, H. (2005). Drawing on mind's canvas: Differences in cortical integration patterns between artists and non-Artists. *Human Brain Mapping, 26,* 1–14.

Blonder, L. X., Bowers, D., & Heilman, K. M. (1991). The role of the right hemisphere in emotional communication. *Brain, 114,* 1115–1127.

Blonder, L.X., Burns, A. F., Bowers, D., Moore, R. W., & Heilman, K. M. (1995). Spontaneous gestures following right hemisphere infarct. *Neuropsychologia, 33,* 203–213.

Blum, H. P. (2016). Interpretation and contemporary reinterpretation. *Psychoanalytic Inquiry, 36,* 40–51.

Bogen, J. E., & Bogen, G. M. (1969). The other side of the brain III: The corpus callosum and creativity. *Bulletin of the Los Angeles Neurological Society, 34,* 175–195.

Bollas, C. (1987). *The shadow of the object: Psychoanalysis of the unthought known.* New York, NY: Columbia University Press.

Bollas, C. (2013). *Catch them before they fall. The psychoanalysis of breakdown.* New York, NY: Routledge.

Borgogno, F., & Vigna-Taglianti, M. (2008). Role-reversal: A somewhat neglected mirror of heritages of the past. *American Journal of Psychoanalysis, 68,* 313–328.

Bornstein, R. F. (1999). Source amnesia, misattribution, and the power of unconscious perceptions and memories. *Psychoanalytic Psychology, 16,* 155–178.

Bowlby, J. (1953). *Child care and the growth of love.* London, UK: Pelican.

Bowlby, J. (1969). *Attachment and loss, Volume 1: Attachment*. New York, NY: Basic Books.

Bowlby, J. (1988). *A secure base* (2nd ed.). New York, NY: Basic Books.

Boyer, L. B. (1990). Regression in treatment: On early object relations. In P. L. Giovacchini (Ed.), *Tactics and techniques in psychoanalytic therapy. III, The implications of Winnicott's contributions* (pp. 200–225). Northvale, NJ: Aronson.

Bradshaw, G. A. (2017). *Carnivore minds: Who these fearsome animals really are*. New Haven, CT: Yale University Press.

Bradshaw, G. A., & Schore, A. N. (2007). How elephants are opening doors: Developmental neuroethology, attachment and social context. *Ethology, 113*, 426–436.

Brancucci, A., Lucci, G., Mazzatenta, A., & Tommasi, L. (2009). Asymmetries of the human social brain in the visual, auditory and chemical modalities. *Philosophical Transactions of the Royal Society of London. Series B, Biological Sciences, 364*, 895–914.

Brenner, C. (1957). The nature and development of the concept of repression in Freud's writings. *Psychoanalytic Study of the Child, 12*, 19–46.

Brenner, C. (1980). A psychoanalytic theory of affects. In R. Plutchik & H. Kellerman (Eds.), *Emotion: Theory, research, and experience, Vol. 1*. New York, NY: Academic Press.

Brierley, M. (1937). Affects in theory and practice. *International Journal of Psychoanalysis, 18*, 256–274.

Bromberg, P. M. (2006). *Awakening the dreamer: Clinical journeys*. Mahwah, NJ: Analytic Press.

Bromberg, P. M. (2011). *The shadow of the tsunami and the growth of the relational mind*. New York, NY: Routledge.

Bromberg, P. M. (2017). Psychotherapy as the growth of wholeness. The negotiation of individuality and otherness. In M. Solomon & D. S. Siegel (Eds.), *How people change: Relationships and neuroplasticity in psychotherapy* (pp. 1–36). New York, NY: Norton.

Bronowski, J. (1972). *Science and human values*. New York, NY: Harper and Row.

Brothers, L. (1997). *Friday's footprint*. New York, NY: Oxford University Press.

Brown, S., & Dissanayake, E. (2009). The arts are more than aesthetics: Neuroaesthetics as narrow aesthetics. In M. Skov and O. Vartanian (Eds.), *Neuroaesthetics* (pp. 43–57). Amityville, NY: Baywood.

Bruner, J. S. (1962). The conditions of creativity. In H.E. Gruber (Ed.), *Contemporary approaches to creative thinking* (pp. 1–30). New York, NY: Atherton Press.

Bucci, W. (2002). The referential process, consciousness, and the sense of self. *Psychoanalytic Inquiry, 5*, 766–793.

Buklina, S. B. (2005). The corpus callosum, interhemispheric interactions, and the function of the right hemisphere of the brain. *Neuroscience and Behavioral Physiology, 35*, 473–480. Burghardt, G. M. (2005). *The genesis of animal play: Testing the limits*. Cambridge, MA: MIT Press.

Carretie, L., Hinojosa, J. A., Mercado, F., & Tapia, M. (2005). Cortical response to subjectively unconscious danger. *NeuroImage, 24*, 615–623.

Carson, S.H., Peterson, J.B., & Higgins, D.M. (2005). Reliability, validity, and factor structure of the creative achievement questionnaire. *Creativity Research Journal, 17*, 37–50.

Carter, R. (1999). *The human brain book*. London, UK: DK.

Carter, S., Lederhandler, I., & Kirkpatrick, B. (Eds.). (1999). *The integrative neurobiology of affiliation*. Cambridge, MA: MIT Press.

Casement, P. (1985). *Learning from the patient*. New York, NY: Guilford Press.

Castonguay, L. G., Constantno, M. J., & Holtforth, M. G. (2006). The working alliance: Where are we and where should we go? *Psychotherapy, 43*, 271–279.

Cavada, C., Company, T., Tejedor, J., Cruz-Rizzolo, & Reinoso-Suarez-Suarez, F. (2000). The anatomical connections of the macaque monkey orbitofrontal cortex. A review. *Cerebral Cortex, 10*, 220–242.

Cerqueira, J. J., Almeida, O. F. X., & Sousa, N. (2008). The stressed prefrontal cortex. Left? Right! *Brain, Behavior, and Immunity, 22*, 630–638.

Chapman, L. (2014). *Neurobiologically informed trauma therapy with children and adolescents. Understanding mechanisms of change*. New York, NY: Norton.

Chartrand, T. L., & Bargh, J. A. (1999). The chameleon effect: The perception-behavior link and social interaction. *Journal of Personality and Social Psychology, 76*, 893–910.

Chavez-Eakle, R. A., Graff-Guerrero, A., Garcia-Reyna, J. C., Vaugier, V., & Cruz-Fuentes, C. (2007). Cerebral blood flow associated with creative performance: A comparative study. *NeuroImage, 38*, 519–528.

Chen, L., & Hsiao, J. (2014). Right hemisphere dominance in nonconscious processing. *Journal of Vision, 14*, 1313. doi:10.1167/14.10.1313

Chiron, C., Jambaque, I., Nabbout, R., Lounes, R., Syrota, A., & Dulac, O. (1997). The right brain hemisphere is dominant in human infants. *Brain, 120*, 1057–1065.

Chong, S., Werker, J., Russell, J., & Carroll, J. (2003). Three facial expressions mothers direct to their infants. *Infant and Child Development, 12*, 211–232.

Chused, J. F. (2007). Nonverbal communication in psychoanalysis: Commentary on Harrison and Tronick. *Journal of the American Psychoanalytic Association, 55*, 875–882.

Clulow, C. (2017). Before, between, and beyond interpretations: Attachment perspectives on couple psychoanalytic psychotherapy. *Psychoanalytic Inquiry, 37*, 343–354.

Costafreda, S. G., Brammer, M. J., David, A. S., & Fu, C. H. Y. (2008). Predictors of amygdala activation during the processing of emotional stimuli: A meta-analysis of 385 PET and fMRI studies. *Brain Research Reviews, 58*, 57–70.

Courtney, S. M., Petit, L., Haxby, J. V., & Ungerleider, L. G. (1998). The role of the prefrontal cortex in working memory: Examining the contents of consciousness.

Philosophical Transactions of the Royal Society of London. Series B, Biological Sciences, 353, 1819–1828.

Cozolino, L. (2002). *The neuroscience of psychotherapy.* New York, NY: Norton.

Craparo, G., & Mucci, C. (2017). *Unrepressed unconscious, implicit memory, and clinical work.* London, UK: Karnac.

Crouzet, S. M., Kirchner, H., & Thorpe, S. J. (2010). Fast saccades toward faces: Face detection in just 100 ms. *Journal of Vision, 10,* 16. doi:10.1167/10.4.16

Damasio, A. R. (1994). *Descartes' error.* New York, NY: Grosset/Putnam.

Darwin, C. (1872/1965). *The expression of the emotions in man and animals.* Chicago, IL: University of Chicago Press.

Davies, J. M. (2004). Whose bad objects are we anyway? Repetition and our elusive love affair with evil. *Psychoanalytic Dialogues, 14,* 711–732.

Davis, P. J. (1987). Repression and the inaccessibility of affective memories. *Journal of Personality and Social Psychology, 53,* 585–593.

de Forest, I. (1954). *The leaven of love: A development of the psychanalytic theory and technique of Sándor Ferenczi.* New York, NY: Harper Brothers.

De Pisapia, N., Serra, M., Rigo, P., Jager, J., Papinutto, N., Esposito, G., Venuti, P., & Bornstein, M. H. (2014). Interpersonal competence in young adulthood and right laterality in white matter. *Journal of Cognitive Neuroscience, 26,* 1257–1265.

Decety, J., & Chaminade, T. (2003). When the self represents the other: A new cognitive neuroscience view on psychological identification. *Consciousness and Cognition, 12,* 577–596.

Decety, J., & Lamm, C. (2007). The role of the right temporoparietal junction in social interaction: How low-level computational processes contribute to metacognition. *Neuroscientist, 13,* 580–593.

Dehaene, S., & Naccache, L. (2001). Towards a cognitive science of consciousness: Basic evidence and a workspace framework. *Cognition, 79,* 1–37.

Dehaene, S., Changeux, J.-P., Naccache, L., Sackur, J., & Sergent, C. (2006). Conscious, preconscious, and subliminal processing: A testable taxonomy. *Trends in Cognitive Sciences, 10,* 204–211.

Derryberry, D., & Tucker, D. M. (1994). Motivating the focus of attention. In P. M. Niedenthal & S. Kiyayama (Eds.), *The heart's eye: Emotional influences in perception and attention* (pp. 167–196). San Diego, CA: Academic Press.

Devinsky, O. (2000). Right cerebral hemispheric dominance for a sense of corporeal and emotional self. *Epilepsy & Behavior, 1,* 60–73.

DeYoung, C. G., Grazioplene, R. G., & Peterson, J. B. (2012). From madness to genius: The Openness/Intellect trait domain as a paradoxical simplex. *Journal of Research in Personality, 46,* 63–78.

DeYoung, P. A. (2015). *Understanding and treating chronic shame. A relational/neurobiological approach.* New York, NY: Routledge.

Di Renzo, G. C., Conry, J. A., Blake, J., DeFrancesco, M. K., DeNicola, N., Martin, J.N., Jr., . . . Giudice, L. C. (2015). International Federation of Gynecology and Obstetrics opinion on reproductive health impacts of exposure to toxic environmental chemicals. *International Journal of Gynecology and Obstetrics, 131,* 219–225.

Diseth, T. H. (2005). Dissociation in children and adolescents as reaction to trauma—An overview of conceptual issues and neurobiological factors. *Nordic Journal of Psychiatry, 59,* 79–91.

Dissanayake, E. (2001). Becoming *Homo Aestheticus*: Sources of aesthetic imagination in mother-infant interactions. *SubStance, Issue 94/95,* 85–103.

Dissanayake, E. (2008). If music is the food of love, what about survival and reproductive success? [Special issue on narrative in interaction] *Musicæ Scientiæ,* 169–195.

Dissanayake, E. (2017). Ethology and interpersonal neurobiology together with play provide insights into the evolutionary origin of the arts. *American Journal of Play, 9,* 143-168.

Dorahy, M. J. (2017). Shame as a compromise for humiliation and rage in the internal representations of abuse by loved ones: Processes, motivations, and the role of dissociation. *Journal of Trauma and Dissociation, 18,* 383–396.

Dorahy, M. J., McKendry, H., Scott, A., Yogeeswaran, K., Martens, A., & Donncha, H. (2017). Reactive dissociative experiences in response to acute increases in shame feelings. *Behaviour Research and Therapy, 89,* 75–85.

Dorpat, T. L. (2001). Primary process communication. *Psychoanalytic Inquiry, 3,* 448–463.

Downey, T. W. (2001). Early object relations into new objects. *Psychoanalytic Study of the Child, 56,* 39–75.

Drago, V., Foster, P. S., Okun, M. S., Haq, I., Sudhyadhom, F. M., & Heilman, K. M. (2009). Artistic creativity and DBS: A case report. *Journal of Neurological Sciences, 276,* 138–142.

Dumas, G. (2011). Towards a two-body neuroscience. *Communicative and Integrative Biology, 4,* 349–352.

Dumas, G., Nadel, J., Soussignan, R., Martinerie, J., & Garnero, L. (2010). Interbrain synchronization during social interaction. *PLOS ONE, 5,* e12166.

Dyck, M., Loughead, J., Kellermann, T., Boers, F., Gur, R.C., & Mathiak, K. (2011). Cognitive versus automatic mechanisms of mood induction differentially activate left and right amygdala. *NeuroImage, 54,* 2503–2513.

Edelman, G. (1989). *The remembered present: A biological theory of consciousness.* New York, NY: Basic Books.

Elzinga, B. M., Ardon, A. M., Heijnis, M. K., De Ruiter, M. B., Van Dyck, R., & Veltman, D. J. (2007). Neural correlates of enhanced working-memory performance in dissociative disorder: A functional MRI study. *Psychological Medicine, 37,* 235–245.

Engels, A. S., Heller, W., Mohanty, A., Herrington, J. D., Banich, M. T., Webb, A. G., & Miller, G. A. (2007). Specificity of brain activity in anxiety types during emotion processing. *Psychophysiology, 44,* 352–363.

Enriquez, P., & Bernabeu, E. (2008). Hemispheric laterality and dissociative tendencies: Differences in emotional processing in a dichotic listening task. *Consciousness and Cognition, 17,* 267–275.

Epstein, S. (1983). The unconscious, the preconscious, and the self concept. In J. Suls & A. G. Greenwald (Eds.), *Psychological perspectives on the self, Volume 2* (pp. 219–247). Mahwah, NJ: Erlbaum.

Estrada, C. A., Young, M., & Isen, A. M. (1994). Positive affect influences creative problems solving and reported source of practice satisfaction in physicians. *Motivation & Emotion, 18,* 285–299.

Etkin, A., Pittenger, C., Polan, H. J., & Kandel, E. R. (2005). Toward a neurobiology of psychotherapy: Basic science and clinical applications. *Journal of Neuropsychiatry and Clinical Neuroscience, 17,* 145–158.

Ezhov, S. N., & Krivoschekov, S. G. (2004). Features of psychomotor responses and interhemispheric relationships at various stages of adaptation to a new time zone. *Human Physiology, 30,* 172–175.

Fairbairn, W. R. D. (1943). The repression and return of bad objects (with special reference to the "war neuroses"). In W. R. D. Fairbairn, *Psychoanalytic studies of the personality* (pp. 59–81). London, UK: Routledge & Kegan Paul.

Fairbairn, W. R. D. (1952). *Psychoanalytic studies of the personality.* London, UK: Tavistock.

Falk, D. (2004). Prelinguistic evolution in early hominins: Whence motherese? *Behavioral and Brain Sciences, 27*(4), 491–541.

Feinberg, T. E., & Keenan, J. P. (2005). Where in the brain is the self? *Consciousness and Cognition, 14,* 661–678.

Ferenczi, S. (1926/1980). *Further contributions to the theory and technique of psychoanalysis,* ed. J. Rickman, trans. E. Mosbacher. New York, NY: Brunner-Mazel.

Finkelstein, Y., Vardi, J., & Hod, I. (1991). Impulsive artistic creativity as a presentation of transient cognitive alterations. *Behavioral Medicine, 17,* 91–94.

Finn, S. E. (2011). Use of the Adult Attachment Projective Picture System (AAP) in the middle of long-term psychotherapy. *Journal of Personality Assessment, 95,* 427–433.

Finn, S. E. (2012). 2011 Bruno Klopfer Distinguished Contribution Award. Implications of recent research in neurobiology for psychological assessment. *Journal of Personality Assessment, 5,* 440–449.

Fitzgerald, E. T. (1966). Measurement of openness to experience: A study of regression in the service of the ego. *Journal of Personality and Social Psychology, 4,* 655–663.

Flinn, M., & Ward, C. (2005). Evolution and the social child. In B. D. Ellis and D. F. Bjorklund (Eds.), *Origins of the social mind: Evolutionary psychology and child development* (pp. 19–44). London, UK: Guilford Press.

Fordham, M. (1993). The Jung-Klein hybrid. *Free Associations, 28,* 631–641.

Frederickson, B. (2001). The role of positive emotions in positive psychology: The broaden-and-build theory of positive emotions. *American Psychologist, 56*(3), 218–256.

Freud, A. (1963). Repression as a principle of mental development. *Bulletin of the Menninger Clinic, 27,* 126–139.

Freud, S. (1891). *Zur auffassung der aphasien, eine kritische studie.* [*On aphasia*]. Leipzig, Germany: F. Deuticke.

Freud, S. (1895/1966). *Project for a scientific psychology.* In J. Strachey (Ed. & Trans.), *The standard edition of the complete psychological works of Sigmund Freud* (Vol. 1, pp. 281–392). London: Hogarth Press.

Freud, S. (1900/1953). The interpretation of dreams. In J. Strachey (Ed. & Trans.), *The standard edition of the complete psychological works of Sigmund Freud* (Vols. 4 & 5, pp. 1–627). London, UK: Hogarth Press.

Freud, S. (1912/1958). Recommendations to physicians practicing psycho-analysis. In J. Strachey (Ed. & Trans.), *The standard edition of the complete psychological works of Sigmund Freud:* 14 (pp. 111-120). London: Hogarth Press.

Freud, S. (1913). The claims of psycho-analysis to scientific interest. In J. Strachey (Ed. and Trans.), *The standard edition of the complete psychological works of Sigmund Freud* (Vol. 13, 165–199). London, UK: Hogarth Press.

Freud, S. (1913/1958). On beginning the treatment. In J. Strachey (Ed. & Trans.), *The standard edition of the complete psychological works of Sigmund Freud* (Vol. 12, pp. 23–144). London, UK: Hogarth Press.

Freud, S. (1914/1958). Remembering, repeating, and working through. In J. Strachey (Ed. & Trans.), *The standard edition of the complete psychological works of Sigmund Freud* (Vol. 12, pp. 145–157). London, UK: Hogarth Press.

Freud, S. (1915/1957). The unconscious. In J. Strachey (Ed. and Trans.), *The standard edition of the complete psychological works of Sigmund Freud:* 14 (pp. 159-215). London: Hogarth Press,

Freud, S. (1915a/1957). Thoughts for the times of war and death. In J. Strachey (Ed. & Trans.), *The standard edition of the complete psychological works of Sigmund Freud* (Vol. 14, pp. 273–302). London, UK: Hogarth Press.

Freud, S. (1915b/1957). Repression. In J. Strachey (Ed. & Trans.), *The standard edition of the complete psychological works of Sigmund Freud* (Vol. 14, pp. 141–158). London, UK: Hogarth Press.

Freud, S. (1915c/1957). The unconscious. In J. Strachey (Ed. & Trans.), *The standard edition of the complete psychological works of Sigmund Freud* (Vol. 14, pp. 159–215). London, UK: Hogarth Press.

Freud, S. (1923/1961). The ego and the id. In J. Strachey (Ed. & Trans.), *The standard edition of the complete psychological works of Sigmund Freud* (Vol. 19, pp. 3–68). London, UK: Hogarth Press.

Freud, S. (1940/1964). In J. Strachey (Ed. & Trans.), An outline of psychoanalysis. *The standard edition of the complete psychological works of Sigmund Freud* (Vol. 23, pp. 144–207). London: Hogarth Press.

Fromm, E. (1956). *The art of loving.* New York, NY: Harper and Row.

Fromm, E. (1958). Love in psychotherapy. *Merrill-Palmer Quarterly (1954–1958), 4*(3), 125–136.

Gainotti, G. (2005). Emotions, unconscious processes, and the right hemisphere. *Neuropsychoanalysis, 7,* 71–81.

Gainotti, G. (2006). Unconscious emotional memories and the right hemisphere. In M. Mancia (Ed.), *Psychoanalysis and neuroscience* (pp. 151–173). Milan, Italy: Springer Milan.

Gainotti, G. (2012). Unconscious processing of emotions and the right hemisphere. *Neuropsychologia, 50,* 205–218.

Gant, S. P., & Badenoch, B. (2013). *The interpersonal neurobiology of group psychotherapy and group process.* London, UK: Karnac.

Gebauer, L., Witek, M., Hansen, N. C., Thomas, J., Konvalinka, I., & Vuust, P. (2014). The influence of oxytocin on interpersonal rhythmic synchronization and social bonding. Poster presented at *The Neurosciences and Music—V,* Dijon, France.

Geller, J. D. (2003). Self-disclosure in psychoanalytic-existential therapy. *Clinical Psychology/In Session, 59,* 541–554.

Geller, S. M., & Porges, S. W. (2014). Therapeutic presence: Neurophysiological mechanisms mediating feeling safe in therapeutic relationships. *Journal of Psychotherapy Integration, 24,* 178–192.

George, M. S., Parekh, P. I., Rosinsky, N., Ketter, T. A., Kimbrell, T. A., Heilman, K. M., Herscovitch, P., & Post, R. M. (1996). Understanding emotional prosody activates right hemispheric regions. *Archives of Neurology, 53,* 665–670.

Gill, M. M., & Brenman, M. (1959). *Hypnosis and related states.* New York, NY: International Universities Press.

Ginot, E. (2007). Intersubjectivity and neuroscience: Understanding enactments and their therapeutic significance within emerging paradigms. The empathic power of enactments. The link between neuropsychological processes and an expanded definition of empathy. *Psychoanalytic Psychology, 24,* 31–332.

Ginot, E. (2009). The empathic power of enactments. The link between neuropsychological processes and an expanded definition of empathy. *Psychoanalytic Psychology, 26,* 290–309.

Giovacchini, P. L. (1990). Regression, reconstruction, and resolution: Containment and holding. In P. L. Giovacchini (Ed.), *Tactics and techniques in psychoanalytic therapy. III: The implications of Winnicott's contributions* (pp. 226–264). Northvale, NJ: Jason Aronson.

Giovacchini, P. L. (1991). The creative person as maverick. *Journal of the American Academy of Psychoanalysis, 19,* 174–188.

Glass, R. M. (2008). Psychodynamic psychotherapy and research evidence. Bambi survives Godzilla? *Journal of the American Medical Association, 300,* 1587–1589.

Godfrey, H. K., & Grimshaw, G. M. (2016). Emotional language is all right: Emotional prosody reduces hemispheric asymmetry for linguistic processing. *Laterality: Asymmetries of Body, Brain, and Cognition, 21,* 568–584.

Goel, V., Tierney, M., Sheesley, L., Bartolo, A., Vartanian, O., & Grafman, J. (2007). Hemispheric specialization in human prefrontal cortex for resolving certain and uncertain inferences. *Cerebral Cortex, 17,* 2245–2250. Goldin, P. R., McRae, K., Ramel, W., & Gross, J. J. (2008). The neural bases of emotion regulation: Reappraisal and suppression of negative emotion. *Biological Psychiatry, 63,* 577–586.

Goleman, D. (1995). *Emotional intelligence.* New York, NY: Bantam Books.

Gorney, J. E. (1979). The negative therapeutic reaction. *Contemporary Psychoanalysis, 15,* 288–337.

Greenberg, J. R. (1986). Theoretical models and the analyst's neutrality. *Contemporary Psychoanalysis, 22,* 87–106.

Greenberg, J. R., & Mitchell, S. A. (1983). *Object relations in psychoanalytic theory.* Cambridge, MA: Harvard University Press.

Greenberg, L. S. (2007). Emotion coming of age. *Clinical Psychology Science and Practice, 14,* 414–421.

Greenberg, L. (2014). The therapeutic relationship in emotion-focused therapy. *Psychotherapy, 51,* 350–357.

Grunbaum, A. (1984). *The foundations of psychoanalysis: A philosophical critique.* Berkeley: University of California Press.

Guedeney, A., Guedeney, N., Tereno, S., Dugravier, R., Greacen, T., Welniarz, B., Saias, T., . . . the CADEP Study Group. (2011). Infant rhythms versus parental time: Prompting parent-infant synchrony. *Journal of Physiology, Paris, 105,* 195–200.

Guilford, J. P. (1957). Creative ability in the arts. *Psychological Review, 64,* 110–118.

Guntrip, H. (1969). *Schizoid phenomena, object relations and the self.* New York, NY: International Universities Press.

Gupta, R. K., Hasan, K. M., Trivedi, R., Pradhan, M., Das, V., Parikh, N. A., & Narayana, P. A. (2005). Diffusion tensor imaging of the developing human cerebrum. *Journal of Neuroscience Research, 81,* 172–178.

Haas, A. S. (2015). Modeling and measurement of interpersonal attraction and coordination in charged social space-time. *NeuroQuantology, 13,* 1–9.

Hadamard, J. (1945). *The mathematician's mind: The psychology of invention in the mathematical field.* Princeton, NJ: Princeton University Press.

Hamilton, V. (1996). *The analyst's preconscious.* Hillsdale, NJ: Analytic Press.

Hammer, E. (1990). *Reaching the affect: Style in the psychodynamic therapies.* Northvale, NJ: Jason Aronson.

Happaney, K., Zelazo, P. D., & Stuss, D. T. (2004). Development of orbitofrontal function: Current themes and future directions. *Brain and Cognition, 55,* 1–10.

Hartikainen, K. M., Ogawa, K. H., Soltani, M., & Knight, R. T. (2007). Emotionally arousing stimuli compete for attention with left hemispace. *NeuroReport, 18,* 1929–1933. Hartmann, H. (1958). *Ego psychology and the problem of adaptation.* New York, NY: International Universities Press.

Hassin, R. R. (2013). Yes it can: On the functional abilities of the human unconscious. *Perspectives in Psychological Science, 8,* 195–207.

Hayes, A. M., Laurenceau, J.-P., Feldman, G., Strauss, J. L., & Cardaciotto, L.

(2007). Change is not always linear: The study of nonlinear and discontinuous patterns of change in psychotherapy. *Clinical Psychology Review, 27,* 715–723.

Hecht, D. (2014). Cerebral lateralization of pro- and anti-social tendencies. *Experimental Neurobiology, 23,* 1–27.

Heilman, K. M., Nadeau, S. E., & Beversdorf, D. O. (2003). Creative innovation: Possible brain mechanisms. *Neurocase, 9,* 369–379.

Helton, W. S., Dorahy, M. J., & Russell, P. N. (2011). Dissociative tendencies and right-hemisphere processing load: Effects on vigilance performance. *Consciousness and Cognition, 20,* 696–702.

Henry, J. P. (1993). Psychological and physiological responses to stress: The right hemisphere and the hypothalamo-pituitary-adrenal axis, an inquiry into problems of human bonding. *Integrative Physiological and Behavioral Science, 28,* 369–387.

Herman, J. L. (1992). *Trauma and recovery.* New York, NY: Basic Books.

Hess, E. H. (1975). The role of pupil size in communication. *Scientific American, 233,* 110–119.

Hill, D. (2015). *Affect regulation theory: A clinical model.* New York, NY: Norton.

Hiraishi, H., Haida, M., Matsumoto, M., Hayakawa, N., Inomata, S., & Matsumoto, H. (2012). Differences of prefrontal cortex activity between picture-based personality tests: A near-infrared spectroscopy study. *Journal of Personality Assessment, 94,* 366–371.

Hirata, M., Ikeda, T., Kikuchi, M., Kimura, T., Hiraishi, H., Yoshimura, Y., & Asada, M. (2014). Hyperscanning MEG for understanding mother-child cerebral interactions. *Frontiers in Human Neuroscience, 8,* 118. doi:10.3389/fnhum.2014.00118

Hirsch, I., & Kessel, P. (1988). Reflections on mature love and countertransference. *Free Associations, 12,* 60–83.

Hong, S.B., Zalesky, A., Cocchi, L., Fornito, A., Choi, E.-J., Kim, H.H., et al. (2013). Decreased functional brain connectivity in adolescents with internet addiction. *PLOS ONE* 8:e57831. doi: 10.1371/journal.pone.0057831

Horner, A. J. (2006). The unconscious and the creative process. *Journal of the American Academy of Psychoanalysis and Dynamic Psychiatry, 34,* 461–469.

Horvath, A. O., & Symonds, B. D. (1991). Relation between working alliance and outcome of psychotherapy: A meta-analysis. *Journal of Counseling Psychology, 38,* 139–149.

Huang, P., Qui, L., Shen, L., Zhang, Y., Song, Z., Qi, Z., Gong, Q., & Xie, P. (2013). Evidence for a left-over-right inhibitory mechanism during figural creative thinking in healthy nonartists. *Human Brain Mapping, 34,* 2724–2732.

Hugdahl, K. (1995). Classical conditioning and implicit learning: The right hemisphere hypothesis. In R.J. Davidson & K. Hugdahl (Eds.), *Brain asymmetry.* Cambridge, MA: MIT Press.

Hutterer, J., & Liss, M. (2006). Cognitive development, memory, trauma, treatment: An integration of psychoanalytic and behavioral concepts in light of current neuroscience research. *Journal of the American Academy of Psychoanalysis and Dynamic Psychiatry, 34,* 287–302.

Jackson, J. H. (1931). *Selected writings of John Hughlings Jackson, Vols. I and II.* London, UK: Hodder and Stoughton.

Jacobs, T. J. (1994). Nonverbal communications: Some reflections on their role in the psychoanalytic process and psychoanalytic education. *Journal of the American Psychoanalytic Association, 42,* 741–762.

Jasmin, K. M., McGettigan, C. M. Agnew, Z. K., Lavan, N., Josephs, O., Cummins, F, & Scott, S. K. (2016). Cohesion and joint speech: Right hemisphere contributions to synchronized vocal production. *Journal of Neuroscience, 36,* 4669–4680.

Jaynes, J. (1976/1999). *The origin of consciousness in the breakdown of the bicameral mind.* Boston, MA: Houghton Mifflin.

Johnsen, E. L., Tranel, D., Lutgendorf, S., & Adolphs, R. (2009). A neuroanatomical dissociation for emotion induced by music. *International Journal of Psychophysiology, 72,* 24–33.

Jones, B. P. (1993). Repression: The evolution of a psychoanalytic concept from the 1890's to the 1990's. *Journal of the American Psychoanalytic Association, 41,* 63–93.

Jones, E. (1953). *The life and work of Sigmund Freud: Volume I. The formative years and great discoveries, 1856–1900.* New York, NY: Basic Books.

Jordan, J. V. (2000). The role of mutual empathy in relational/cultural therapy. *Journal of Clinical Psychology/In Session: Psychotherapy in Practice, 56,* 1005–1016.

Joseph, R. (1982). The neuropsychology of development: Hemispheric laterality, limbic language, and the origin of thought. *Journal of Clinical Psychology, 38,* 4–33.

Joseph, R. (1992). *The right brain and the unconscious: Discovering the stranger within.* New York, NY: Plenum.

Joseph, R. (1996). *Neuropsychiatry, neuropsychology, and clinical neuroscience* (2nd ed.). Baltimore, MD: Williams & Wilkins.

Jung-Beeman, M., Bowden, E. M., Haberman, J., Frymiare, J. L., Arambel-Liu, S., Greenblatt, R., Reber, P. J., & Kounios, J. (2004). Neural activity when people solve verbal problems with insight. *PLOS Biology, 2,* 500–510.

Jung, C. (1912). *Symbols of transformation. Collected works 5.* Princeton, NJ: Princeton University Press.

Jung, C. (1961). *Memories, dreams, reflections.* New York, NY: Random House.

Kalsched, D. (2005). Hope versus hopelessness in the psychoanalytic situation and Dante's *Divine Comedy. Spring, 72,* 167–187.

Kalsched, D. (2015). Revisioning Fordham's "Defences of the self" in light of modern relational theory and contemporary neuroscience. *Journal of Analytic Psychology, 60,* 477–496.

Kane, J. (2004). Poetry as right hemispheric language. *Journal of Consciousness Studies, 11,* 21–59.

Kantrowitz, J. (1999). The role of the preconscious in psychoanalysis. *Journal of the American Psychoanalytic Association, 47,* 65–89.

Kaplan-Solms, K., & Solms, M. (1996). Psychoanalytic observations on a case of frontal limbic disease. *Journal of Clinical Psychoanalysis, 5*, 405–438.

Kaufman, G. (1992). *Shame: The power of caring.* Boston, MA: Schenkman.

Keenan, J. P., Rubio, J., Racioppi, C., Johnson, A., & Barnacz, A. (2005). The right hemisphere and the dark side of consciousness. *Cortex, 41*, 695–704.

Kernberg, O. (1976). *Object relations and clinical psychoanalysis.* New York: Jason Aronson.

Khan, M. (1972). Dread of surrender to resourceless dependence in the analytic situation. In *The privacy of the self* (pp. 270–279). New York, NY: International Universities Press.

Killeen, L. A., & Teti, D. M. (2012). Mothers' frontal EEG asymmetry in response to infant emotional states and mother-infant emotional availability, emotional experience, and internalizing symptoms. *Development and Psychopathology, 24*, 9–21.

King, L. A., McKee Walker, L., & Broyles, S. J. (1996). Creativity and the five-factor model. *Journal of Research in Personality, 30*, 189–203.

Knafo, D. (2002). Revisiting Ernst Kris' concept of *Regression in the Service of the Ego* in art. *Psychoanalytic Psychology, 19*, 24–49.

Kohut, H. (1971). *The analysis of the self.* New York, NY: International Universities Press.

Koole, S. L., & Jostmann, N. B. (2004). Getting a grip on your feelings: Effects of action orientation and external demands on intuitive affect regulation. *Journal of Personality and Social Psychology, 87*, 974–990.

Kowatari, Y., Hee Lee, S., Yamamura, H., Nagamori, Y., Levy, P., Yamane, S., & Yamamoto, M. (2009). Neural networks involved in artistic creativity. *Human Brain Mapping, 30*, 1678–1690.

Kris, E. (1952). *Psychoanalytic explorations in art.* New York, NY: International Universities Press.

Kris, E. (1953). Psychoanalysis and the study of creative imagination. *Bulletin of the New York Academy of Medicine, 29*, 334–351.

Krystal, H. (1988). *Integration & self-healing: Affect, trauma, alexithymia.* Hillsdale, NJ: Analytic Press.

Krystal, H. (2002). What cannot be remembered or forgotten. In J. Kauffman (Ed.), *Loss of the assumptive world: A theory of traumatic loss* (pp. 213–219). New York, NY: Psychology Press.

Kubie, L. S. (1958). *Neurotic distortion of the creative process.* Lawrence: University of Kansas Press.

Kubovy, M. (1999). On the pleasures of the mind. In D. Kahneman, M. Kubovy, D. Kahneman, E. Diener, & N. Schwarz (Eds.), *Well-being: The foundations of hedonic psychology* (pp. 134–154). New York, NY: Russell Sage Foundation.

Kuchinke, L., Jacobs, A. M., Vo, M. L. H., Conrad, M., Grubich, C., & Herrmann, M. (2006). Modulation of prefrontal cortex activation by emotional words in recognition memory. *NeuroReport, 17*, 1037–1041.

Kuhl, J., & Kazen, M. (2008). Motivation, affect, and hemispheric asymmetry: Power versus affiliation. *Journal of Personality and Social Psychology, 95*, 456–469.

Kuhl, J., Quirin, M, & Koole, S. L. (2015). Being someone: The integrated self as a neuropsychological system. *Social and Personality Psychology Compass, 9*, 115–132.

Lane, R. D. (2008). Neural substrates of implicit and explicit emotional processes: A unifying framework for psychosomatic medicine. *Psychosomatic Medicine, 70*, 214–231.

Lane, R. D., Ahern, G. L., Schwartz, G. E., & Kaszniak, A. W. (1997). Is alexithymia the emotional equivalent of blindsight? *Biological Psychiatry, 42*, 834–844.

Layard, R., Clark, A. E., Cornaglia, F., Powdthavae, N., & Vernoit, J. (2014). What predicts a successful life? A life-course model of well-being. *Economic Journal, 124*, F720–F738. doi:10.1111/ecoj.12170

Leakey, R. (1994). *The origin of humankind.* New York, NY: Basic Books.

Leckman, J. F., & March, J. S. (2011). Editorial: Developmental neuroscience comes of age. *Journal of Child Psychology and Psychiatry, 52*, 333–338.

LeDoux, J. (2002). *Synaptic self: How our brains become who we are.* New York, NY: Viking.

Lehtonen, J., Partanen, J., Purhonen, M., Valkonen-Korhonen, M., Kononen, M., Saarikoski, & Launiala, K. (2006). Nascent body ego. Metapsychological and neurophysiological aspects. *International Journal of Psychoanalysis, 87*, 1335–1353.

Lenzi, D., Trentini, C., Pantano, P., Macaluso, E., Iacaboni, M., Lenzi, G. I., & Ammaniti, M. (2009). Neural basis of maternal communication and emotional expression processing during infant preverbal stage. *Cerebral Cortex, 19*, 1124–1133.

Levenson, E. A. (1974). Changing concepts of intimacy. *Contemporary Psychoanalysis, 10*, 359–369.

Levenson, R. W., & Gottman, J. M. (1983). Marital interaction: Physiological linkage and affective exchange. *Journal of Personality and Social Psychology, 45*, 587–597.

Levin, F. M. (1991). *Mapping the mind.* Hillsdale, NJ: Analytic Press.

Levine, P. A. (2010). *In an unspoken voice: How the body releases trauma and restores goodness.* Berkeley, CA: North Atlantic Books.

Lichtenberg, J. (2001). Motivational systems and model scenes with special reference to bodily experience. *Psychoanalytic Inquiry, 21*, 430–447.

Lindell, A. K. (2010). Time to turn the other cheek? The influence of left and right poses on perceptions of academic specialisation. *Laterality, 15*, 639–650.

Lindell, A. K. (2011). Lateral thinkers are not so laterally minded: Hemispheric asymmetry, interaction, and creativity. *Laterality, 16*, 479–498.

Loewald, H. (1949). The ego and reality. In *Papers on psychoanalysis* (pp. 3–20). New Haven, CT: Yale University Press.

Loewald, H. (1960). On the therapeutic action of psychoanalysis. *International Journal of Psychoanalysis, 12*, 16–33.

Loewald, H. (1986). Transference–countertransference. *Journal of the American Psychoanalytic Association, 34,* 275–285. Lyons-Ruth, K. (1999). The two-person unconscious: Intersubjective dialogue, enactive relational representation, and the emergence of new forms of relational organization. *Psychoanalytic Inquiry, 19,* 576–617.

Lyons-Ruth, K. (1999). The two-person unconscious: Intersubjective dialogue, enactive relational representation, and the emergence of new forms of relational organization. *Psychoanalytic Inquiry, 19,* 576–617.

Lyons-Ruth, K. (2000). "I sense that you sense that I sense . . .": Sander's recognition process and the specificity of relational moves in the psychotherapeutic setting. *Infant Mental Health Journal, 21,* 85–98.

MacLean, P. (1985). Brain evolution relating to family play, and the separation call. *Archives of General Psychiatry, 42,* 405–417.

Mancia, M. (2006). Implicit memory and early unrepressed unconscious: Their role in the therapeutic process (How the neurosciences can contribute to psychoanalysis). *International Journal of Psychoanalysis, 87,* 83–103.

Manini, B., Cardone, D., Ebisch, S. J. H., Bafunno, D., Aureli, T., & Meria, A. (2013). Mom feels what her child feels: Thermal signatures of vicarious autonomic response while watching children in a stressful situation. *Frontiers in Human Neuroscience, 7,* 1–10. doi:10.3389/fnhum.2013.00299

Markowitsch, H. J., & Stanilou, A. (2011). Amygdala in action: Relaying biological and social significance to autobiographical memory. *Neuropsychologia, 49,* 718–733.

Markowitsch, H. J., Reinkemeier, A., Kessler, J., Koyuncu, A., & Heiss, W. D. (2000). Right amygdalar and temporofrontal activation during autobiographical, but not fictitious memory retrieval. *Behavioral Neurology, 12,* 181–190.

Marks-Tarlow, T. (2010). Fractal self at play. *American Journal of Play, 3*(1), 31–62.

Marks-Tarlow, T. (2012). *Clinical intuition in psychotherapy: The neurobiology of embodied response.* New York, NY: Norton.

Marks-Tarlow, T. (2014). Awakening clinical intuition: An experiential workbook for psychotherapists. New York, NY: Norton.

Maroda, K. (2010). *Psychodynamic techniques. Working with emotion in the therapeutic relationship.* New York, NY: Guilford Press. Maroda, K. J. (2005). Show some emotion: Completing the cycle of affective communication. In L. Aron & A. Harris (Eds.), *Revolutionary connections. Relational psychoanalysis. Vol. II. Innovation and expansion* (pp. 121–142). Hillsdale, NJ: Analytic Press.

Martin, D. J., Garske, J. P., & Davis, M. K. (2000). Relation of the therapeutic alliance with outcome and other variables: A meta-analytic review. *Journal of Consulting and Clinical Psychology, 68,* 438–450.

Martindale, C., Hines, D., Mitchell, L., & Covello, E. (1984). EEG alpha asymmetry and creativity. *Personality and Individual Differences, 5,* 77–86.

Mashal, N., Faust, M., Hendler, T., & Jung-Beeman, M. (2007). An fMRI investigation of the neural correlates underlying the processing of novel metaphoric expressions. *Brain and Language, 100,* 115–126.

Maslow, A. H. (1973). Creativity in self-actualizing people. In A. Rotenberg & C. R. Hausman (Eds.), *The creative question* (pp. 86–92). Durham, NC: Duke University Press.

Masterson, J. F. (1985). *The real self. A developmental, self, and object relations approach*. New York, NY: Brunner/Mazel.

May, R. (1976). *The courage to create*. New York, NY: Bantam.

Mayer, E. L. (2007). *Extraordinary knowing: Science, skepticism, and the inexplicable powers of the human mind*. New York, NY: Bantam Books.

Mayseless, N., & Shamay-Tsoory, S. G. (2015). Enhancing verbal creativity: Modulating creativity by altering the balance between right and left inferior frontal gyrus with tDCS. *Neuroscience, 291*, 167–176.

McCrae, R. R., & Costa, P. T., Jr. (1997). Conceptions and correlates of Openness to Experience. In R. Hogan, J. A. Johnson, & S. R. Briggs (Eds.), *Handbook of personality psychology* (pp. 825–847). Orlando, FL: Academic Press.

McGilchrist, I. (2009). *The master and his emissary: The divided brain and the making of the Western world*. New Haven, CT: Yale University Press.

McGilchrist, I. (2015). Divine understanding and the divided brain. In J. Clausen & N. Levy (Eds.), *Handbook of neuroethics*. Dordrecht, Netherlands: Springer Science. doi:10.1007/978-94-007-4707-4_99

McGilchrist, I. (2016). 'Selving' and union. *Journal of Consciousness Studies. 23*, 196–213.

McWilliams, N. (2018). Core competency two: Therapeutic stance/attitude. In R. E. Barsness (Ed.), *Core competencies in relational psychoanalysis. A guide to practice, study, and research* (pp. 87–103). New York, NY: Routledge.

Meares, R. (2005). *The metaphor of play: Origin and breakdown of personal being* (3rd ed.). London, UK: Routledge.

Meares, R. (2012). *A dissociation model of borderline personality disorder*. New York, NY: Norton.

Meares, R. (2017). The disintegrative core of relational trauma and a way toward unity. In M. Solomon & D. J. Siegel (Eds.), *How people change: Relationships and neuroplasticity in psychotherapy* (pp. 135–150). New York, NY: Norton.

Mendelsohn, E. (2002). The analyst's bad-enough participation. *Psychoanalytic Dialogues, 12*, 331–358.

Menenti, L., Pickering, M. J., & Garrod, S. C. (2012). Toward a neural basis of interactive alignment in conversation. *Frontiers in Human Neuroscience, 6*, 185. doi:10.3389/fnhum.2012.00185

Meyer-Lindenberg, A. (2008). Impact of prosocial neuropeptides on human brain function. *Progress in Brain Research, 170*, 463–470.

Miall, D., & Dissanayake, E. (2003). The poetics of baby talk. *Human Nature, 14*, 337–354.

Mihov, K. M., Denzler, M., & Forster, J. (2010). Hemispheric specialization and creative thinking: A meta-analytic review of lateralization of creativity. *Brain & Cognition, 72*, 442–448.

Miller, G.F., & Tal, I.R. (2007). Schizotopy versus openness and intelligence as predictors of creativity. *Schizophrenia Research, 93*, 317–324.

Miller, S. (1985). *The shame experience.* Hillsdale, NJ: Analytic Press.

Miller, W., & Rodgers, J. L. (2001). *The ontogeny of human bonding systems: Evolutionary origins, neural bases, and psychological manifestations.* Boston, MA: Kluwer Academic.

Minagawa-Kawai, Y., Matsuoka, S., Dan, I., Naoi, N., Nakamura, K., & Kojima, S. (2009). Prefrontal activation associated with social attachment: Facial-emotion recognition in mothers and infants. *Cerebral Cortex, 19*, 284–292.

Mitchell, S. A. (1988). *Relational concepts in psychoanalysis.* Cambridge, MA: Harvard University Press.

Mlot, C. (1998). Probing the biology of emotion. *Science, 280*, 1005–1007.

Mohaupt, H., Holgersen, H., Binder, P.-E., & Nielsen, G. H. (2006). Affect consciousness or mentalization? A comparison of two concepts with regard to affect development and affect regulation. *Scandinavian Journal of Psychology, 47*, 237–244.

Mohr, C., Rowe, A. C., & Crawford, M. T. (2007). Hemispheric differences in the processing of attachment words. *Journal of Clinical and Experimental Neuropsychology, 1*, 1–10.

Montello, L. (2002). *Essential musical intelligence. Using music as your path to healing, creativity, and radiant wellness.* Wheaton, IL: Quest Books.

Montgomery, A. (2013). *Neurobiology essentials for clinicians: What every therapist needs to know.* New York, NY: Norton.

Montirosso, R., Cozzi, P., Tronick, E., & Borgatti, R. (2012). Differential distribution and lateralization of infant gestures and their relation to maternal gestures in the face-to-face still-face paradigm. *Infant Behavior and Development, 35*, 819–828.

Morris, J. S., Ohman, A., & Dolan, R. J. (1998). Conscious and unconscious emotional learning in the human amygdala. *Nature, 393*, 467–470.

Mucci, C. (in press). Borderline bodies. New York, NY: Norton.

Murray, L., & Trevarthen, C. (1985). Emotional regulation of interaction between two-month-olds and their mothers. In T. Field and N. Fox (Eds.), *Social perception in infants* (pp. 177–197). Norwood, NJ: Ablex.

Nadel, J., Carchon, I., Kervella, C., Marcelli, D., & Réserbet-Plantey, D. (1999). Expectancies for social contingency in two-month-olds. *Developmental Science, 2*, 164–173.

Narvaez, D., Panksepp, J., Schore, A. N., & Gleason, T. R. (2013). *Evolution, early experience and human development: From research to practice and policy.* New York, NY: Oxford University Press.

Nemiah, J. C. (1989). Janet redivivus: The centenary of l'automatisme psychologique. *American Journal of Psychiatry, 146*, 1527–1529.

Nicholson, K.G., Baum, S., Kilgour, A., Koh, C. K., Munhall, K. G., & Cuddy, L. L. (2003). Impaired processing of prosodic and musical patterns after right hemisphere damage. *Brain and Cognition, 52*, 382–389.

Nijenhuis, E. R. S., Vanderlinden, J., & Spinhoven, P. (1998). Animal defensive reactions as a model for trauma-induced dissociative reactions. *Journal of Traumatic Stress, 11*, 242–260.

Nishitani, S., Doi, H., Koyama, A., & Shinohara, K. (2011). Differential prefrontal response to infant facial emotions in mothers compared with non-mothers. *Neuroscience Research, 70*, 183–188.

Nolte, T., Hudac, C., Mayes, L. C., Fonagy, P., Blatt, S. J., & Pelphrey, K. (2010). The effect of attachment-related stress on the capacity to mentalize: An fMRI investigation of the biobehavioral switch model. *Journal of the American Psychoanalytic Association, 58*, 566–573.

Noordzij, M. L., Newman-Norlund, S. E., de Ruiter, J. P., Hagoort, P., Levinson, S. C., & Toni, I. (2009). Brain mechanisms underlying human communication. *Frontiers in Human Neuroscience, 3*, 14. doi:10.3389/neuro.09.014.2009

Noriuchi, M., Kikuchi, Y., & Senoo, A. (2008). The functional neuroanatomy of maternal love: Mother's response to infant's attachment behaviors. *Biological Psychiatry, 63*, 415–423.

Northoff, G., Bermpohl, F., Scheneich, F., & Boeker, H. (2007). How does our brain constitute defense mechanisms? First-person neuroscience and psychoanalysis. *Psychotherapy and Psychosomatics, 76*, 141–153.

Nummenmaa, L., Glerean, E., Viinikainen, M., Jaaskelainen, I. P., Hari, R., & Sams, M. (2012). Emotions promote social interaction by synchronizing brain activity across individuals. *Proceedings of the National Academy of Sciences USA, 109*, 9599–9604.

Ogden, P., Pain, C., Minton, K., & Fisher, J. (2005). Including the body in mainstream psychotherapy for traumatized individuals. *Psychologist-Psychoanalyst, 25*, 19–24.

Ogden, T. H. (1994). The concept of internal object relations. *International Journal of Psychoanalysis, 64*, 227–241.

Orlinsky, D. E., & Howard, K. I. (1986). Process and outcome in psychotherapy. In S. L. Garfield & A. E. Bergin (Eds.), *Handbook of psychotherapy and behavior change* (3rd ed.). New York, NY: Wiley.

Ornstein, R. O. (1997). *The right mind. Making sense of the hemispheres.* New York, NY: Harcourt Brace.

Ovtscharoff, W., & Braun, K. (2001). Maternal separation and social isolation modulate the postnatal development of synaptic composition in the infralimbic cortex of octodon degus. *Neuroscience, 104*, 33–40.

Pan, Y., Cheng, X., Zhang, Z., Li, X., & Hu, Y. (2017). Cooperation in lovers: An fNIRS-based hyperscanning study. *Human Brain Mapping, 38*, 831–841.

Panksepp, J. (1998). *Affective neuroscience: The foundations of human and animal emotions.* Oxford, UK: Oxford University Press.

Perani, D., Saccuman, M. C., Scifo, P., Spada, D., Andreolli, G., Rovelli, R., Baldoli, C., & Koelsch, S. (2010). Functional specializations for music processing in the human newborn brain. *Proceedings of the National Academy of Sciences USA, 107,* 4758–4763.

Perez-Cruz, C., Simon, M., Czeh, B., Flugge, G., & Fuchs, E. (2009). Hemispheric differences in basilar dendrites and spines of pyramidal neurons in the rat prelimbic cortex: Activity- and stress-induced changes. *European Journal of Neuroscience, 29,* 738–747.

Phillips-Silver, J., & Keller, P. E. (2012). Searching for roots of entrainment and joint action in early musical interactions. *Frontiers in Human Neuroscience, 6*(26), 1–11.

Pincus, D., Freeman, W., & Modell, A. (2007). A neurobiological model of perception: Considerations for transference. *Psychoanalytic Psychology, 24,* 623–640.

Platt, C. B. (2007). Presence, poetry and the collaborative right hemisphere. *Journal of Consciousness Studies, 14,* 36–53.

Podell, K., Lovell, M., & Goldberg, E. (2001). Lateralization of frontal lobe functions. In S. P. Salloway, P. F. Malloy, & J. D. Duffy (Eds.), *The frontal lobes and neuropsychiatric illness* (pp. 83–89). Washington, DC: American Psychiatric Publishing.

Popper, K. R. (1962). *Conjectures and refutations: The growth of scientific knowledge.* New York, NY: Basic Books.

Popper, K. (1968). *Logic of scientific discovery.* New York, NY: Harper and Row.

Porges, S. W. (2011). *The polyvagal theory. Neurophysiological foundations of emotions, attachment, communication, and self-Regulation.* New York, NY: Norton.

Posner, M. (1994). Attention: The mechanisms of consciousness. *Proceedings of the National Academy of Sciences USA, 91,* 7398–7404.

Quirin, M., Dusing, R., & Kuhl, J. (2013). Implicit affiliation motive predicts correct intuitive judgment. *Journal of Individual Differences, 34,* 24-31.

Quirin, M., Kazen, M., Rohrmann, S., & Kuhl, J. (2009). Implicit but not explicit affectivity predicts circadian and reactive cortisol: Using the implicit positive and negative affect test. *Journal of Personality, 77,* 401–425.

Racker, H. (1968). *Transference and countertransference.* New York, NY: International Universities Press.

Rass, E. (2018). *The Allan Schore reader. Setting to course of development.* New York, NY: Routledge.

Ratnarajah, N., Rifkin-Graboi, A., Fortier, M. V., Chong, Y. S., Kwek, K., Saw, S.-M., . . . Qui, A. (2013). Structural connectivity in the neonatal brain. *NeuroImage, 75,* 187–194.

Ray, D., Roy, D., Sindhu, B., Sharan, P., & Banerjee, A. (2017). Neural substrate of group mental health: Insights from multi-brain reference frame in functional neuroimaging. *Frontiers in Psychology, 8,* 1627. doi:10.3389/fpsyg.2017.01627

Redcay, E., Dodell-Feder, D., Pearrow, M. J., Manros, P. L., Kleiner, M., Gasbrielli, J. D. E., & Saxe, R. (2010). Live face-to-face interaction during fMRI: A new tool for social cognitive neuroscience. *NeuroImage, 50,* 1639–1647.

Reed, S. F., Ohel, G., David, R., & Porges, S. W. (1999). A neural explanation of fetal heart rate patterns: A test of the polyvagal theory. *Developmental Psychobiology, 35,* 108–118.

Reik, T. (1948). *Listening with the third ear: The inner experience of a psychoanalyst.* New York, NY: Grove Press.

Reik, T. (1949). *Fragments of a great confession: A psychoanalytic autobiography.* New York, NY: Farrar, Straus.

Reik, T. (1953). *The haunting melody: Psychoanalytic experiences in life and music.* New York, NY: Farrar, Straus, & Young.

Reik, T. (1956). Adventures in psychoanalytic discovery. In M. Sherman (Ed.), *The search within* (pp. 473–626). New York, NY: Aronson.

Rodman, F. R. (2003). *Winnicott. Life and work.* Cambridge MA: Perseus Books.

Rogers, C. T. (1954). Toward a theory of creativity. A *Review of General Semantics, 11,* 249–260.

Rogers, C. T. (1957). The necessary and sufficient conditions of therapeutic personality change. *Journal of Consulting Psychology, 21,* 95–103.

Rogers, C. T. (1958). The characteristics of a helping relationship. In C. T. Rogers, *On becoming a person* (pp. 39–58). Boston, MA: Houghton Mifflin.

Rogers, C. T. (1961). *On becoming a person.* Boston, MA: Houghton Mifflin.

Rogers, C. T. (1989). A client-centered/person-centered approach to therapy. In H. Kirschenbaum & V. Land Henderson (Eds.), *The Carl Rogers reader* (pp. 135–152). Boston, MA: Houghton Mifflin.

Rogers, L. (2014). Asymmetry of brain and behavior in animals: Its development, function, and human relevance. *Genesis, 52,* 555–571.

Rosen, A., & Reiner, M. (2017). Right frontal gamma and beta band enhancement while solving a spatial puzzle with insight. *International Journal of Psychophysiology, 122,* 50–55.

Rosenberg, K. (1992). The evolution of modern human childbirth. *Yearbook of Physical Anthropology, 35,* 89–134.

Ross, E. D., & Monnot, M. (2008). Neurology of affective prosody and its functional-anatomic organization in right hemisphere. *Brain and Language, 104,* 51–74.

Rotenberg, V. S. (1993). Richness against freedom: Two hemisphere functions and the problem of creativity. *European Journal of High Ability, 4,* 11–19.

Rotenberg, V. S. (1994). An integrative psychophysiological approach to brain hemisphere functions in schizophrenia. *Neuroscience and Biobehavioral Reviews, 18,* 487–495.

Russell, P. (1998). The role of paradox in the repetition compulsion. In J. G. Teicholz & D. Kriegman (Eds.), *Trauma, repetition, and affect regulation: The work of Paul Russell* (pp. 1–22). New York, NY: Other Press. Rycroft, C. (1985). *Psychoanalysis and beyond.* London, UK: Chato & Windus.

Sabbagh, M. A. (1999). Communicative intentions and language: Evidence from right-hemispheric damage and autism. *Brain and Language, 70,* 29–69.

Sachar, E. J., Mackenzie, J. M., Binstock, W. A., & Mack, J. E. (1968). Corticosteroid responses to the psychotherapy of reactive depressions. II. Further clinical and physiological implications. *Psychosomatic Medicine, 30,* 23–44.

Sacks, O. (2008). *Musicophilia: Tales of music and the brain* (Rev. ed.). London, UK: Picador.

Sander, L. W. (1975). Infant and caretaking environment. In E. J. Anthony (Ed.), *Explorations in child psychiatry* (pp. 129–166). New York, NY: Plenum Press.

Sander, L. W. (1992). Letter to the editor. *International Journal of Psychoanalysis, 73,* 582–584.

Sandler, J., & Sandler, A.-M. (1986). On the development of object relations and affects. In P. Buckley (Ed.), *Essential papers on object relations* (pp. 272–291). New York, NY: New York University Press.

Sato, W., & Aoki, S. (2006). Right hemisphere dominance in processing unconscious emotion. *Brain and Cognition, 62,* 261–266.

Satoh, M., Nakase, T., Nagata, K., & Tomimoto, H. (2011). Musical anhedonia: Selective loss of emotional experience in listening to music. *Neurocase, 17,* 410–417.

Saxe, R., & Wexler, A. (2005). Making sense of another mind: The role of the right temporo-parietal junction. *Neuropsychologia, 43,* 1391–1399.

Scaer, R. (2005). *The trauma spectrum: Hidden wounds and human resiliency.* New York, NY: Norton.

Schafer, R. (1958). Regression in the service of the ego: The relevance of a psychoanalytic concept for personality assessment, In G. Lindzey (Ed.), *Assessment of human motives.* New York, NY: Grove Press.

Schepman, A., Rodway, P., & Pritchard, H. (2016). Right-lateralized unconscious, but not conscious, processing of affective environmental sounds. *Laterality: Asymmetries of Body, Brain and Cognition, 21,* 606–632. doi:10.1080/13576 50X.2015.1105245

Schooler, J. W., Ohlsson, S., & Brooks, K. (1993). Thoughts beyond words: When language overshadows insight. *Journal of Experimental Psychology: General, 122,* 166–183.

Schore, A. N. (1991). Early superego development: The emergence of shame and narcissistic affect regulation in the practicing period. Psychoanalysis and Contemporary Thought, 14, 187–250.

Schore, A. N. (1994). *Affect regulation and the origin of the self: The neurobiology of emotional development.* Mahwah, NJ: Erlbaum.

Schore, A. N. (1996). The experience-dependent maturation of a regulatory system in the orbital prefrontal cortex and the origin of developmental psychopathology. *Development and Psychopathology, 8,* 59–87.

Schore, A. N. (1997). A century after Freud's Project: Is a rapprochement between psychoanalysis and neurobiology at hand? *Journal of the American Psychoanalytic Association, 45,* 807–840.

Schore, A. N. (1997). Interdisciplinary developmental research as a source of clinical models. In M. Moskowitz, C. Monk, C. Kaye, & S. Ellman (Eds.), *The neurobiological and developmental basis for psychotherapeutic intervention* (pp. 1–71). Northvale, NJ: Aronson.

Schore, A. N. (1997b). Early organization of the nonlinear right brain and development of a predisposition to psychiatric disorders. *Development and Psychopathology, 9,* 595–631.

Schore, A. N. (2000). Attachment and the regulation of the right brain. *Attachment and Human Development, 2,* 23–47.

Schore, A. N. (2001). The effects of relational trauma on right brain development, affect regulation, and infant mental health. *Infant Mental Health Journal, 22,* 201–269.

Schore, A. N. (2001). The Seventh Annual John Bowlby Memorial Lecture. Minds in the making: Attachment, the self-organizing brain, and developmentally-oriented psychoanalytic psychotherapy. *British Journal of Psychotherapy, 17,* 299–328.

Schore, A. N. (2001a). The effects of a secure attachment relationship on right brain development, affect regulation, and infant mental health. *Infant Mental Health Journal, 22,* 7–66.

Schore, A. N. (2001b). The effects of relational trauma on right brain development, affect regulation, and infant mental health. *Infant Mental Health Journal, 22,* 201–269.

Schore, A. N. (2002a). The right brain as the neurobiological substratum of Freud's dynamic unconscious. In D. Scharff (Ed.), *The psychoanalytic century: Freud's legacy for the future* (pp. 61–88). New York, NY: Other Press.

Schore, A. N. (2002b). Dysregulation of the right brain: A fundamental mechanism of traumatic attachment and the psychopathogenesis of posttraumatic stress disorder. *Australian and New Zealand Journal of Psychiatry, 36,* 9–30.

Schore, A. N. (2003a). *Affect dysregulation and disorders of the self.* New York, NY: Norton

Schore, A. N. (2003b). *Affect regulation and the repair of the self.* New York, NY: Norton.

Schore, A. N. (2005). Attachment, affect regulation, and the developing right brain: Linking developmental neuroscience to pediatrics. *Pediatrics in Review, 26,* 204–212.

Schore, A.N. (2005). A neuropsychoanalytic viewpoint. Commentary on paper by Steven H. Knoblauch. *Psychoanalytic Dialogues, 15,* 829–854.

Schore, A. N. (2009a, August 8). The paradigm shift: The right brain and the relational unconscious. Invited plenary address to the American Psychological Association 2009 Convention, Toronto, Canada. Retrieved from http://www.allanschore.com/pdf/SchoreAPAPlenaryFinal09.pdf

Schore, A. N. (2009b). Relational trauma and the developing right brain. An interface of psychoanalytic self psychology and neuroscience. *Annals of the New York Academy of Sciences, 1159,* 189–203.

Schore, A. N. (2011). The right brain implicit self lies at the core of psychoanalysis. *Psychoanalytic Dialogues, 21,* 75–100.

Schore, A. N. (2012). *The science and art of psychotherapy.* New York, NY: Norton.

Schore, A. N. (2013). Relational trauma, brain development, and dissociation. In J. D. Ford and C. A. Courtois (Eds.), *Treating complex trauma in children and adolescents* (pp. 3–23). New York, NY: Guilford Press.

Schore, A. N. (2013a). Regulation theory and the early assessment of attachment and autistic spectrum disorders: A response to Voran's clinical case. *Journal of Infant, Child, and Adolescent Psychotherapy, 12,* 164–189.

Schore, A. N. (2013b). Bowlby's environment of evolutionary adaptedness: Recent studies on the interpersonal neurobiology of attachment and emotional development. In D. Narvaez, J. Panksepp, A. N. Schore, & T. R. Gleason (Eds.), *Evolution, early experience and human development: From research to practice and policy* (pp. 31–67). New York, NY: Oxford University Press.

Schore, A. N. (2014a). The right brain is dominant in psychotherapy. *Psychotherapy, 51,* 388–397. http://dx.doi.org/10.1037/a0037083

Schore, A. N. (2014b). Early interpersonal neurobiological assessment of attachment and autistic spectrum disorders. *Frontiers in Psychology, 5,* article 1049. doi:10.3389/fpsyg.2014.01049

Schore, A. N. (2015). Plenary address, Australian Childhood Foundation Conference on Childhood Trauma: Understanding the basis for change and recovery. Early right brain regulation and the relational origins of emotional wellbeing. *Children Australia, 40,* 104–113. http://dx.doi.org/10.1017/cha.2015.13

Schore, A. N. (2017a). Modern attachment theory. In S. N. Gold (Ed.), *APA handbook of trauma psychology: Foundations in knowledge* (pp. 389–406). Washington, DC: American Psychological Association.

Schore, A. N. (2017b). All our sons: The developmental neurobiology and neuroendocrinology of boys at risk. *Infant Mental Health Journal, 38,* 15–52.

Schore, A. N. (2017b). The right brain implicit self: A central mechanism of the psychotherapy change process. In G. Craparo & C. Mucci (Eds.), *Unrepressed unconscious, implicit memory, and clinical work* (pp. 73–98). London, UK: Karnac.

Schore, A. N. (2017c). Playing on the right side of the brain. An interview with Allan N. Schore. *American Journal of Play, 9,* 105–142.

Schore, A. N. (In press). *Right brain psychotherapy.* New York, NY: Norton.

Schore, A. N. & Marks-Tarlow, T. (2018). How love opens creativity, play, and the arts through early right brain development. In T. Marks-Tarlow, M. Solomon, & D. J. Siegel (Eds.), *Play and creativity in psychotherapy* (pp. 64–91). New York, NY: Norton.

Schore, A. N., & McIntosh, J. (2011). Family law and the neuroscience of attachment, Part 1. *Family Court Review, 49,* 501–512.

Schore, A.N. (in press). The development of the unconscious mind. New York, NY: Norton.

Schore, J. R., & Schore, A. N. (2014). Regulation theory and affect regulation psychotherapy: A clinical primer. *Smith College Studies in Social Work, 84*, 178–195.

Schore, J., & Schore, A. (2008). Modern attachment theory: The central role of affect regulation in development and treatment. *Clinical Social Work Journal, 36*, 9–20.

Semrud-Clikeman, M., Fine, J. G., & Zhu, D. C. (2011). The role of the right hemisphere for processing of social interactions in normal adults using functional magnetic resonance imaging. *Neuropsychobiology, 64*, 47–51.

Shamay-Tsoory, S. G., Adler, N., Aharon-Peretz, J., Perry, D., & Mayseless, N. (2011). The neural bases of creative thinking and originality. *Neuropsychologia, 49*, 178–185.

Shaw, D. (2003). On the therapeutic action of analytic love. *Contemporary Psychoanalysis, 39*(2), 251–278.

Shedler, J. (2010). The efficacy of psychodynamic psychotherapy. *American Psychologist, 65*, 98–109.

Shuren, J. E., & Grafman, J. (2002). The neurology of reasoning. *Archives of Neurology, 59*, 916–919.

Sieff, D. F. (Ed.). (2015). *Understanding and healing emotional trauma: Conversations with pioneering clinicians and researchers*. London, UK: Routledge.

Siegel, D. J. (1999). *Developing mind: Toward a neurobiology of interpersonal experience*. New York, NY: Norton.

Siegel, D. J. (2012). *The developing mind: How relationships and the brain interact to shape who we are* (2nd ed.). New York, NY: Guilford Press.

Silver, K. L., & Singer, P. A. (2014). Editorial: A focus on child development. *Science, 345*, 120.

Solms, M., & Turnbull, O. (2002). *The brain and inner world*. New York, NY: Other Press.

Sperry, R. W., Zaidel, E., & Zaidel, D. (1979). Self recognition and social awareness in the deconnected minor hemisphere. *Neuropsychologia, 17*, 153–166.

Spezzano, C. (1993). *Affect in psychoanalysis: A clinical synthesis*. Hillsdale, NJ: Analytic Press.

Spiegel, D., & Cardena, E. (1991). Disintegrated experience: The dissociative disorders revisited. *Journal of Abnormal Psychology, 100*, 366–378.

Spiegel, L. A. (1975). The functions of free associations in psychoanalysis: Their relation to technique and therapy. *International Review of Psychoanalysis, 2*, 379–388.

Spitzer, C., Wilert, C., Grabe, H.-J., Rizos, T., & Freyberger, H. J. (2004). Dissociation, hemispheric asymmetry, and dysfunction of hemispheric interaction: A transcranial magnetic approach. *Journal of Neuropsychiatry and Clinical Neurosciences, 16*, 163–169.

Stern, D. (1971). A microanalysis of the mother-infant interaction. *Journal of the American Academy of Child Psychiatry, 10*, 501–507

Stern, D. (1974). Mother and infant at play: The dyadic interaction involving facial, vocal and gaze behaviors. In M. Lewis & L. A. Rosenblum (Eds.), *The effect of the infant on its caregiver* (pp. 187–213). New York, NY: Wiley.

Stern, D. (1977). *The first relationship: Infant and mother.* Cambridge, MA: Harvard University Press.

Stern, D. (1985). *The interpersonal world of the infant.* New York, NY: Basic Books.

Stern, D. (1997). *Unformulated experience: From dissociation to imagination in psychoanalysis.* Hillsdale, NJ: Analytic Press.

Stern, D. N., Bruschweiler-Stern, N., Harrison, A. M., Lyons-Ruth, K., Morgan, A. C., Nahum, J. P., Sander, L. & Tronick, E. Z. (1998). The process of therapeutic change involving implicit knowledge: Some implications of developmental observations for adult psychotherapy. *Infant Mental Health Journal, 19,* 300–308.

Stevens, V. (2005). The art and technique of interpretation reconsidered: The cognitive unconscious and the embodied mind. *Psychologist Psychoanalyst, XXV,* 7-9.

Stevenson, C. W., Halliday, D. M., Marsden, C. A., & Mason, R. (2008). Early life programming of hemispheric lateralization and synchronization in the adult medial prefrontal cortex. *Neuroscience, 155,* 852–863.

Stolk, A., Noordzij, M. L., Verhagen, L., Volman, I., Schloffen, J.-M., Oostenveld, R., Hagoort, P., & Toni, I. (2014). Cerebral coherence between communicators marks the emergence of meaning. *Proceedings of the National Academy of Sciences USA, 111,* 18183–18188.

Stolk, A., Verhagen, L., Schoffelen, J.-M., Osstenveld, R., Blokpoel, M., Hagoort, M. L., van Rooij, I., & Toni, I. (2013). Neural mechanisms of communicative innovation. *Proceedings of the National Academy of Sciences USA, 110,* 14574–14579.

Strachey, J. (Ed.). (1953). *The standard edition of the complete psychological works of Sigmund Freud, Volume VII (1901–1905): A case of hysteria, Three essays on sexuality and other works* (pp. i–vi). London, UK: The Hogarth Press and the Institute of Psychoanalysis.

Sullivan, H. S. (1953). *The interpersonal theory of psychiatry.* New York, NY: Norton.

Sullivan, R. M., & Gratton, A. (2002). Prefrontal cortical regulation of hypothalamic-pituitary-adrenal function in the rat and implications for psychopathology: Side matters. *Psychoneuroendocrinology, 27,* 99–114.

Sun, T., Patoine, C., Abu-Khalil, A., Visader, J., Sum, E., Cherry, T. J., . . . Walsh, C. A. (2005). Early asymmetry of gene transcription in embryonic human left and right cerebral cortex. *Science, 308,* 1794–1798.

Swart, I. (2016). New developments in neuroscience can benefit the learning and performance of music. *Muziki.* doi:10.1080/18125980.2016.1182386

Tangney, J. P., Wagner, P., Fletcher, C., & Gramzow, R. (1992). Shamed into anger? The relation of shame and guilt to anger and self-reported aggression. *Journal of Personality and Social Psychology, 62,* 669–675.

Teasdale, J. D., Howard, R. J., Cox, S. G., Ha, Y., Bramner, M. J., Williams, S. C. R. & Checkley, S. A. (1999). Functional MRI study of the cognitive generation of affect. *American Journal of Psychiatry, 156,* 209–215.

Thatcher, R. W. (1996). Neuroimaging of cyclical cortical reorganization during human development. In R. W. Thatcher, G. Reid Lyon, J. Rumsey, & N. Krasnegor (Eds.), *Developmental neuroimaging. Mapping the development of brain and behavior* (pp. 91–106). San Diego, CA: Academic Press.

Todd, R. M., & Anderson, A. K. (2009). Six degrees of separation: The amygdala regulates social behavior and perception. *Nature Neuroscience, 12,* 1217–1218.

Tomkins, S. (1987). Shame. In D. L. Nathanson (Ed.), *The many faces of shame* (pp. 133–161). New York, NY: Guilford Press.

Trevarthen, C. (1979). Communication and cooperation in early infancy: A description of primary intersubjectivity. In M. Bullova (Ed.), *Before speech: The beginning of interpersonal communication* (pp. 321–347). New York, NY: Cambridge University Press.

Trevarthen, C. (1993). The self born in intersubjectivity: The psychology of an infant communicating. In U. Neisser (Ed.), *The perceived self: Ecological and interpersonal sources of self-knowledge* (pp. 121–173). New York, NY: Cambridge University Press.

Tronick, E., Als, H., & Adamson, L. (1979). The communicative structure of face-to-face interaction. In M. Bullova (Ed.), *Before speech: The beginning of interpersonal communication* (pp. 349–372). New York, NY: Cambridge University Press.

Tronick, E.Z., Bruschweiler-Stern, N., Harrison, A.M., Lyons Ruth, K., Morgan, A.C., Nahum, J.P., Sander, L., & Stern, D.N. (1998). Dyadically expanded states of consciousness and the process of therapeutic change, *Infant Mental Health Journal, 19,* 290–299.

Tschacher, W., Schildt, M., & Sander, K. (2010). Brain connectivity in listening to affective stimuli: A functional magnetic resonance imaging (fMRI) study and implications for psychotherapy. *Psychotherapy Research, 20,* 576–588.

Tucker, D. M., & Moller, L. (2007). The metamorphosis. Individuation of the adolescent brain. In D. Romer & E. F. Walker (Eds.), *Adolescent psychopathology and the developing brain. Integrating brain and prevention science* (pp. 85–102). Oxford, UK: Oxford University Press.

Tutte, J. C. (2004). The concept of psychical trauma: A bridge in interdisciplinary space. *International Journal of Psychoanalysis, 85,* 897–921.

Tuttman, S. (2002). Regression. In Edward Erwin (Ed.), *The Freud encyclopedia: Theory, therapy, and culture.* New York: Routledge.

Ulanov, A. B. (2001). *Finding space. Winnicott, God, and psychic reality.* Louisville, KY: Westminster John Knox Press.

Valentine, L., & Gabbard, G. O. (2014). Can the use of humor in psychotherapy be   taught? *Academic Psychiatry, 38,* 75–81.

Valliant, G. E. (1994). Ego mechanisms of defense and personality psychopathology. *Journal of Abnormal Psychology, 103,* 44–50.

van Lancker Sidtis, D. (2006). The right hemisphere processes a holistic mode for nonliteral expressions and a compositional mode for novel language. *Metaphor and Symbol, 21,* 213–244.

van Lancker, D., & Cummings, J. L. (1999). Expletives: Neurolinguistic and neuro-behavioral perspectives on swearing. *Brain Research Reviews, 31,* 83–104.

Vrticka, P., Sander, D., & Vuilleumier, P. (2013). Lateralized interactive social content and valence processing within the human amygdala. *Frontiers in Human Neuroscience.* doi:10.3389/fnhum.2012.00358

Wada, J. A., & Davis, A. E. (1977). Fundamental nature of human infant's brain asymmetry. *Canadian Journal of Neurological Sciences, 4,* 203–207.

Wallerstein, R. S. (1998). The new American psychoanalysis: A commentary. *Journal of the American Psychoanalytic Association, 46,* 1021–1043.

Wan, X., Cruts, B., & Jensen, H. J. (2014). The causal inference of cortical neural networks during music improvisations. *PLOS ONE 9*(12), e112776. doi:10.1371/journal.pone.0112776

Wang, J., Rao, H., Wetmore, G. S., Furlan, P. M., Korczykowski, M., Dinges, D. F., & Detre, J. A. (2005). Perfusion functional MRI reveals cerebral blood flow pattern under psychological stress. *Proceedings of the National Academy of Sciences USA, 102,* 17804–17809.

Ward, H. P. (1972). Shame—A necessity for growth in therapy. *American Journal of Psychotherapy, 26,* 232–243.

Watt, D. F. (2003). Psychotherapy in an age of neuroscience: Bridges to affective neuroscience. In J. Corrigal & H. Wilkinson (Eds.), *Revolutionary connections: Psychotherapy and neuroscience* (pp. 79–115). London, UK: Karnac.

Weinberg, I. (2000). The prisoners of despair: Right hemisphere deficiency and suicide. *Neuroscience and Biobehavioral Reviews, 24,* 799–815.

Welling, H. (2005). The intuitive process: The case of psychotherapy. *Journal of Psychotherapy Integration, 15,* 19–47.

Welpton, D. F. (1973). Confrontation in the therapeutic process. In G. Adler & P. G. Myerson (Eds.), *Confrontation in psychotherapy* (pp. 249–269). New York, NY: Science House.

Wexler, B. E., Warrenburg, S., Schwartz, G. E. & Janer, L. D. (1992). EEG and EMG responses to emotion-evoking stimuli processed without conscious awareness. *Neuropsychologia, 30,* 1065–1079.

Whitehead, C. C. (2006). Neo-psychoanalysis: A paradigm for the 21st century. *Journal of the Academy of Psychoanalysis and Dynamic Psychiatry, 34,* 603–627.

Winnicott, D. W. (1949). Hate in the countertransference. *International Journal of Psychoanalysis, 30,* 69–74.

Winnicott, D. W. (1955). Metapsychological and clinical aspects of regression within the psycho-analytical set-up. *International Journal of Psychoanalysis, 36,* 16–26.

Winnicott, D. W. (1958a). Withdrawal and regression. In *Collected papers.* New York, NY: Basic Books.

Winnicott, D. W. (1958b). *Through pediatrics to psychoanalysis.* London, UK: Tavistock Publications.

Winnicott, D. W. (1960). Ego distortion in terms of true and false self. In *Matura-*

tional processes and the facilitating environment (pp. 140–152). New York, NY: International Universities Press.

Winnicott, D. W. (1963). The development of the capacity for concern. *Bulletin of the Menninger Clinic, 27*(4), 167.

Winnicott, D. W. (1971). *Playing and reality.* New York, NY: Routledge.

Winnicott, D. W. (1974). Fear of breakdown. *International Review of Psychoanalysis, 1,* 103–107.

Winnicott, D. W. (1975). *The child, the family, and the outside world.* Harmondsworth, Middlesex, UK: Penguin.

Wittling, W., & Roschmann, R. (1993). Emotion-related hemisphere asymmetry: Subjective emotional responses to laterally presented films. *Cortex, 29,* 431–448.

Wolberg, L. R. (1977). *The technique of psychotherapy.* Australia: Grune & Stratton.

Wolfe, B. E., & Goldfried, M. R. (1988). Research on psychotherapy integration: Recommendations and conclusions from an NIMH workshop. *Journal of Consulting and Clinical Psychology, 56,* 448–451.

Wolfradt, U., & Pretz, J.E. (2001). Individual differences in creativity: Personality, story writing, and hobbies. *European Journal of Personality, 15,* 297–310.

Wolitzky, D. L., & Eagle, M. N. (1999). Psychoanalytic theories of psychotherapy. In P. L. Wachtel & S. B. Messer (Eds.), *Theories of psychotherapy. Origins and evolution* (pp. 39–96). Washington, DC: American Psychological Association.

Yanagisawa, K., Kashima, E. S., Moriya, H., Masui, K., Furutani, K., Nomura, M. et al. (2013). Non-conscious neural regulation against mortality concerns. Neuroscience Letters, 552, 35–39.

Yang, Z., Zhao, J., Jiang, Y., Li, C., Wang, J., Weng, X., & Northoff, G. (2011). Altered negative unconscious processing in major depressive disorder: An exploratory neuropsychological study. *PLOS ONE* 6(7): e21881. doi:10.1371/journal.pone.0021881.

Index

Note: Italicized page locators refer to figures or photographs.

ALSO AVAILABLE FROM

THE NORTON SERIES ON INTERPERSONAL NEUROBIOLOGY

The Birth of Intersubjectivity: Psychodynamics, Neurobiology, and the Self
Massimo Ammaniti, Vittorio Gallese

Neurobiology for Clinical Social Work: Theory and Practice (Second Edition)
Jeffrey S. Applegate, Janet R. Shapiro

Mind–Brain–Gene
John B. Arden

The Heart of Trauma: Healing the Embodied Brain in the Context of Relationships
Bonnie Badenoch

Being a Brain-Wise Therapist: A Practical Guide to Interpersonal Neurobiology
Bonnie Badenoch

The Brain-Savvy Therapist's Workbook
Bonnie Badenoch

The Neurobiology of Attachment-Focused Therapy
Jonathan Baylin, Daniel A. Hughes

*Coping with Trauma-Related Dissociation: Skills Training for
Patients and Therapists*
Suzette Boon, Kathy Steele, and Onno van der Hart

*Neurobiologically Informed Trauma Therapy with Children and
Adolescents: Understanding Mechanisms of Change*
Linda Chapman

*Intensive Psychotherapy for Persistent Dissociative Processes:
The Fear of Feeling Real*
Richard A. Chefetz

Timeless: Nature's Formula for Health and Longevity
Louis Cozolino

*The Neuroscience of Human Relationships: Attachment and
the Developing Social Brain (Second Edition)*
Louis Cozolino

The Neuroscience of Psychotherapy: Healing the Social Brain (Second Edition)
Louis Cozolino

The Pocket Guide to Polyvagal Theory: The Transformative Power of Feeling Safe
Stephen W. Porges

Foundational Concepts in Neuroscience: A Brain-Mind Odyssey
David E. Presti

Right Brain Psychotherapy
Allan N. Schore

The Development of the Unconscious Mind
Allan N. Schore

Affect Dysregulation and Disorders of the Self
Allan N. Schore

Affect Regulation and the Repair of the Self
Allan N. Schore

The Science of the Art of Psychotherapy
Allan N. Schore

Mind: A Journey to the Heart of Being Human
Daniel J. Siegel

The Mindful Brain: Reflection and Attunement in the Cultivation of Well-Being
Daniel J. Siegel

The Mindful Therapist: A Clinician's Guide to Mindsight and Neural Integration
Daniel J. Siegel

*Pocket Guide to Interpersonal Neurobiology:
An Integrative Handbook of the Mind*
Daniel J. Siegel

Healing Moments in Psychotherapy
Daniel J. Siegel, Marion Solomon

Healing Trauma: Attachment, Mind, Body and Brain
Daniel J. Siegel, Marion Solomon

*Love and War in Intimate Relationships: Connection, Disconnection,
and Mutual Regulation in Couple Therapy*
Marion Solomon, Stan Tatkin

How People Change: Relationships and Neuroplasticity in Psychotherapy
Marion Solomon and Daniel J. Siegel

For all the latest books in the series, book details (including sample chapters), and to order online, please visit the Series webpage at wwnorton.com/Psych/IPNB Series